CROSSROADS TO ISRAEL

CROSSROADS TO ISRAEL

CHRISTOPHER SYKES

THE WORLD PUBLISHING COMPANY

CLEVELAND AND NEW YORK

CONTENTS

CONTENTS

ILLUSTRATIONS

following page 244

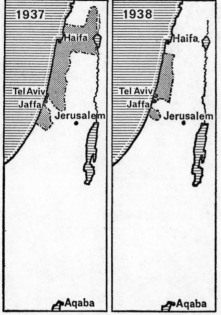

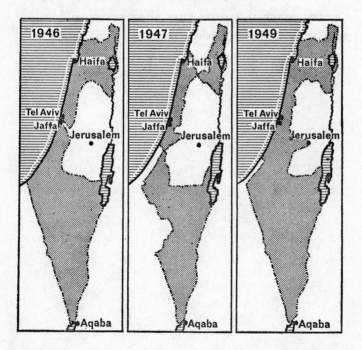

Rough outline maps
showing the proposed,
and the actual, partition
of Palestine, as follows:

I. Peel Commission, 1937
II. Woodhead Commission,
   1938
III. Jewish Agency Proposal,
   1946
IV. UNO Proposal, 1947
V. Armistice lines, 1949,
   and present frontiers

INDEPENDENCE IS A PRIZE THAT MUST BE SEIZED.
IT CANNOT BE HANDED DOWN AS A GIFT FROM ONE
PEOPLE TO ANOTHER.

—JA'AFAR EL ASKARI

PREFACE

Books describing the growth of the Zionist party into the State of Israel can be counted in hundreds. I have read a great number of them, but by no means all. I do not think I have missed any that must be read.

My excuse for adding to their number is twofold: younger generations than my own have reached maturity since these things happened, and among them I have often noticed a complete ignorance of this major event in the life of the Jews and in the history of our country, in spite of the fact that it dominates to a great extent the shape of affairs in the Eastern world. A definitive history cannot be written until we remember our liberal past and repeal the "fifty-year rule." (Happily that rule is only partly effective so long as we belong to an international society, or else nothing of any seriousness could be written on modern historical themes; as it is the rule has unwittingly formed an atmosphere in which propaganda, usually anti-British, thrives with little challenge against it.)

My purpose in these circumstances has been to give not a definitive history but an outline of the event, as simply as this complicated subject allows, concentrating on those points that can be described as crossroads: moments of choice when different action might have changed the character of what followed. My second purpose has been to emulate if possible what few have achieved: to give an account free of bias, as free as the masterly study by Mr. J. C. Hurewitz.

This second and simple aim is remarkably difficult to reach and will, I think, remain so, even when British archives are opened. The whole subject of mandate Palestine, from whichever side it is viewed, appeals strongly to the emotions. It cannot, and in my opinion should not, be otherwise, for if there is an approach decidedly more dislikable and much more of a hindrance to an understanding of these movements and their consequences which tore the heart of men, it is that which tries to reject emotion in favor of a fraudulent god's-eye view. I have tried to avoid that nose-in-air foolery without falling into the opposite fault of spokesmanship. Most people who have written about Palestine have done so because they were drawn to the subject by the emotional attraction. I have experienced the same, and I hope the fact can be discerned in what I have written, but I may have some small advantage in the attempt at impartiality by having first gone to Palestine in 1931, more or less by accident.

I owe a large debt of gratitude to the librarians of the Zionist and Israel State Archives in Jerusalem, and to the librarians and library staffs of the Colonial Office and the Foreign Office. I have indicated more personal debts in the footnotes, but I would like to mention how much I owe to Dr. Yahuda Bauer, Mr. Gavriel Cohen, Mr. Eli Kedourie, Miss Elizabeth Monroe and those I met through her at St. Antony's College, Oxford. In expressing my thanks I may however cause these authorities embarrassment, not only of the bashful kind. Let me say that any historical merit this book may have is largely due to them, and its demerits, to not having consulted them more.

As on other occasions, I must acknowledge a debt to Mrs. Dorothy Baker for much valuable literary advice, and to Mrs. E. H. Harris for producing typescripts.

Christopher Sykes

PART

I

PART

I

1 REASONS, THEORIES, AND SOME CONSEQUENCES

The Balfour Declaration was issued in the form of a letter written by the British Secretary of State for Foreign Affairs to Lord Rothschild. The date was the 2nd of November, 1917. The letter ran as follows:

Dear Lord Rothschild,

I have much pleasure in conveying to you, on behalf of His Majesty's Government, the following declaration of sympathy with Jewish Zionist aspirations which has been submitted to, and approved by, the Cabinet:

"His Majesty's Government view with favour the establishment in Palestine of a national home for the Jewish people, and will use their best endeavours to facilitate the achievement of this object, it being clearly understood that nothing shall be done which may prejudice the civil and religious rights of the existing non-Jewish communities in Palestine, or the rights and political status enjoyed by Jews in any other country."

I should be grateful if you would bring this declaration to the knowledge of the Zionist Federation.

Your sincerely,
Arthur Balfour

The brief and famous letter was to complicate British policy in the East from that time to our own, and perhaps for many years to come. Later it was to have the same effect on American and Russian policy, and to some extent on that of every state with interests in the Moslem Arabic-speaking world. From that day to the present, the Balfour Declaration has been both acclaimed as an act of magnanimity such as is rare in the history of governments, and deplored as the most heinous blunder in the long record of the British Eastern connection. Most of those who praise the deed tend also to blame the doers, believing that their magnanimity, being short-lived, gave way to betrayal and hyprocrisy; those who condemn usually assert that but for the pro-Zionist policy led by Arthur Balfour, Great Britain and the British Commonwealth would have enjoyed happy relations with the Arab States which emerged from the ruin of the Ottoman Empire. There is much evidence for both views, and both can be shown to be largely fallacious.

Nobody knows why the Balfour Declaration was made. Mr. Leonard Stein devoted years to a study of its origins,[1] but at the end of his long and masterly book, his reader cannot say for certain precisely why the coalition government of Lloyd George authorized Balfour to write to Lord Rothschild as he did. Many reasons have been deduced, too many to allow belief in any single clear one.

Strangely enough, the enigmatic Arthur Balfour's own reasons, in spite of the myths that have accumulated about them, are not in much doubt. Both the myths and the reasons are worth looking at in a little detail. The main myth is that this refined, detached and philosophical gentleman walked into the fierce world of Asiatic politics in beautiful ignorance of the dangers in his path. In fact, refined and philosophical as Balfour may have been, he was at the same time a hard and ruthless politician. If Balfour incurs blame it is not because of culpable ignorance but rather on the grounds that he acted with full knowledge of the moral enormity of his deed. In August, 1919, less than two years after the Declaration, he wrote a memorandum on Syria, Palestine, and Mesopotamia (modern Iraq), in which he stressed with all his accustomed lucidity the contradictions in the various pledges given in the course of the war. He referred to

[1] Leonard Stein, *The Balfour Declaration*. London 1961.

the Anglo-French declaration of November, 1918, in which the Allies assured the peoples of the three countries that the purpose of Allied policy was "the setting up of national governments and administrations that shall derive their authority from the free exercise of the initiative and choice of the indigenous population." Having pointed out that in Syria the population had no choice in 1918 other than a French-controlled administration, Balfour continued his memorandum as follows:

The contradiction between the letter of the Covenant and the policy of the Allies is even more flagrant in the case of the independent nation of Palestine than in that of the independent nation of Syria. For in Palestine we do not propose even to go through the form of consulting the wishes of the present inhabitants of the country, though the American Commission[2] has been going through the form of asking what they are. The four great powers are committed to Zionism and Zionism, be it right or wrong, good or bad, is rooted in age-long tradition, in present needs, in future hopes, of far profounder import than the desires and prejudices of the 700,000 Arabs who now inhabit that ancient land.

In my opinion that is right. What I have never been able to understand is how it can be harmonised with the [Anglo-French] declaration, the Covenant, or the instructions to the Commission of Enquiry.

After referring to the fact that the Palestine Mandate would not readily promote national independence, he added:

In fact, so far as Palestine is concerned, the powers have made no statement of fact that is not admittedly wrong, and no declaration of policy which, at least in the letter, they have not always intended to violate.[3]

Not much beautiful ignorance there.

He gave frequent expression to his positive reasons for encourageing a Zionist policy. He was prompted by a simple and deep conviction. In public speeches, in private conversation, and in minutes written within the

[2] This refers to the American King-Crane Commission. On March 15, 1919, the Peace Conference decided to send an Allied Commission of Inquiry to the Near and Middle East. For diplomatic reasons the British, French, and Italian governments withdrew, but President Wilson persisted and sent the American delegates Henry C. King and Charles R. Crane. Their mission lasted from the 16th of June to early August, 1919. They reported to the U.S. delegation to the Conference in an anti-British, anti-French, and anti-Zionist sense.

[3] Documents on Foreign Policy, 1st series. Vol. IV.

walls of the Foreign Office, he described himself as "an ardent Zionist," but this did not mean that he was a natural Judeophil; on the contrary, in common with many Zionists of the time, both Jew and Gentile, he accepted many of the allegations made against the Jews by anti-Semites. At the same time he believed that the Jews were the most gifted race to appear on earth since the ancient Greeks, but that lacking a territorial center, a "National Home," they lacked self-respect and dignity, and too often tended as a result to use their gifts for mischievous ends. This to his mind was the consequence of a gigantic historical injustice which it was a duty of civilization to set right. He expressed his reasons most clearly in his maiden speech in the House of Lords. The date was the 21st of June 1922. He was replying to a motion by Lord Islington that "The Mandate for Palestine in its present form is unacceptable."

I hold [he said] that from a purely material point of view, the policy that we initiated is likely to prove a successful policy. But we have never pretended—certainly I have never pretended—that it was purely from these materialistic considerations that the Declaration of November, 1917 originally sprung. I regard this not as a solution, but as a partial solution of the great and abiding Jewish problems.

My noble friend told us, and I believe him absolutely, that he has no prejudice against the Jews. I think I may say that I have no prejudice in their favour. But their position and their history, their connection with world religion and with world politics is absolutely unique. There is no parallel to it, there is nothing approaching a parallel to it in any other branch of human history. Here you have a small race, originally inhabiting a small country, I think about the size of Wales or Belgium, at any rate of comparable size to those two, at no time in its history wielding anything that can be described as material power, sometimes crushed between great Oriental monarchies, its inhabitants deported, then scattered, then driven out of the country altogether into every part of the world, and yet maintaining continuity of religion and racial tradition of which we have no parallel elsewhere. That in itself is sufficiently remarkable, but consider, it is not a pleasant consideration but it is one that we cannot forget, how they have been treated during long centuries which in some parts of the world extend to the hour and the minute in which I am speaking. Consider how they have been subjected to tyranny and persecution, consider whether the whole culture of Europe, our whole religious organisation of Europe has not from time to time proved itself guilty of great crimes against this race. I quite understand that some members of this race may have given, doubtless did give, occasion for much ill-will and I do not know how it could be otherwise, treated as they were, but if you are going to lay stress on that, do not forget what part they have played in the intellectual, the artistic, the philosophic and the scientific development of the world . . .

Our policy may fail. I do not deny that this is an adventure. Are we never to have adventures? Are we never to try new experiments? I hope that your lordships will never sink to that unimaginative depth, and that experiment and adventure will be justified if there is any case or cause for this justification. Surely it is in order that we may send a message to every land where the Jewish race has been scattered, a message that will tell them that Christendom is not oblivious of their faith, is not unmindful of the service they have rendered to the great religions of the world, and most of all to the religion that the majority of your lordships' House profess, and that we desire to the best of our ability to give them that opportunity of developing, in peace and quietness under British rule, those great gifts which hitherto they have been compelled to bring to fruition in countries that know not their language and belong not to their race? That is the ideal which I desire to see accomplished, that is the aim which lay at the root of the policy I am trying to defend; and though it be defensible indeed on every ground, that is the ground which chiefly moves me.

One of the material benefits which Balfour probably had in mind, in the opening passage of the above extract, was the possible strategical value of Palestine as a British base. Many people consider this to have been the principal reason why the Declaration was made. Was it?

The first paper on Zionism addressed to the British Cabinet in the course of the First World War was written in November, 1914 by Herbert Samuel, at the time president of the local government board. He was only the second practicing Jew to hold ministerial office in England. This paper laid considerable stress on the political and strategical advantage to be gained from a predominantly Jewish Palestine in special relations with Great Britain.

Later in 1915 Herbert Sidebotham, the leading political journalist of his time, gave expression to similar ideas, first in an article, and then in a "Memorandum on British Policy." Under the leadership of Sidebotham and C. P. Scott, the famous editor of the *Manchester Guardian,* there grew up what might be called a Manchester school of Zionism. It was of great importance since many of the moving spirits of the Zionist party, for example Harry Sacher and Dr. Weizmann himself, were Manchester men who exchanged views with and were influenced by these powerful Midland Gentile supporters. It was through Scott that Dr. Weizmann first met Lloyd George. The British strategical interests of the Manchester school occupied a large place in Zionist thinking, Zionist diplomacy, and Zionist propaganda at that time.

Here at the very outset there is remarkable irony in the story of what happened in the years from the Balfour Declaration to the establishment of the State of Israel. Strategical considerations were always repugnant, in the Zionist context, to the mind of Balfour, who opposed the mandate for Palestine's being awarded to Great Britain, and persisted, so long as there was the smallest hope of success, in trying to persuade the United States to undertake the responsibility. But to many people in undersecretarial and lesser but influential ranks of state service in England, Zionism in Palestine seemed a marvelous opportunity for countering any sort of French establishment in Syria. Ridiculous as it seems today, many British political and military thinkers at the time of the First World War and after considered that an increase of French authority in Syria, especially in the form of a protectorate or a similar system, would gravely imperil the communications with India, and in all seriousness many policy planners put forward the proposition that Great Britain should supply advisers to governments and obtain maximum concessions, should, in effect if not in name, establish British protectorates over the whole Arabic-speaking world, as a safeguard against the rapacity of France! It was logical for such people to welcome the idea of a Jewish National Home which would need a British garrison to protect it in Palestine, all the more so as the British position in Egypt (on the other side of the canal) was threatened internally. But these strategical Zionists obtained little following at first among ministers and the military hierarchy. In a short time the sense of the army was against Zionism and against the whole conception of maintaining a garrison in Palestine as part of a Zionist policy. The temporary military administration which was the first to rule Palestine after the Turkish defeat became notorious for anti-Zionist bias. Among men in power in Britain strategical considerations were only a minor influence toward the Balfour Declaration.

But belief can give strength to demonstrably false ideas, and there was plentiful belief in the postwar world that the Balfour Declaration was in essence part of a British strategical ruse. To the Arabs and the ancient Jewish community of Palestine, British strategical considerations supplied the obvious and only possible answer to the riddle. Government by conspiracy was familiar to them, and to transplant one population in order to overawe another was a maneuver to which they and their fathers had grown sadly accustomed as the subjects of the Sublime Porte. It was no use telling Arabs anywhere in the world the sort of things that Balfour so impressively told the House of Lords in June, 1922, and it is unlikely that at any time from 1917 to the present day, a single Arab has believed that altruism, idealism, or a regard for justice played any part at all in a British policy favoring a Jewish National Home. The people of the Middle East preferred to seek an explanation in a myth and a truth; in the myth of innate British cunning encircling the globe (in this case with Jewish aid) in order to pursue dark and gigantic ambitions, and the reality of British preoccupation with the nearby Suez Canal.

The British administrators and garrison in Palestine came to accept the second part of this explanation, and in the gradual course of time the idea that the British interest here was and always had been strategic came to be accepted as axiomatic. Such an idea suited the British temperament. There was no general widely shared emotion behind British administration in the Holy Land comparable to the French emotion for Syria. That English, Scots, Irish, and Welsh were the guarantors of peace in the city of three faiths, that in their hands they held in solemn trust the unique scene of the life of Jesus Christ on earth, these things meant nothing to the Philistine British mind. Efforts to stress the point were apt to arouse merriment or irritation. Lord Balfour's speech, if delivered to British troops on the Mount of Olives, would have been met with derision. The British were readier to accept more everyday explanations: that the British services "had a job to do" and were there "to watch the Canal."

The irony is that the strategically minded school, repudiated by the foremost British champion of Zionism, and unpopular with the army directorate, led the policy in the end. In a sense they were justified. There can be no doubt at all that in 1939 the fact of Palestine's having become a large garrison area was of very great advantage in the organization of the British Middle East Command. But this success of strategic Zionism had to be paid for in ruinous coin. The initial belief hardened into a conviction that a British stronghold in Palestine was absolutely indispensable to the stability and even the survival of the British Commonwealth of Nations, and this led British governments into blind mistakes whose consequences may never be righted. None of this could be guessed at the time. What must be remembered now is that within a few years of 1917 a perhaps inevitable though wholly fallacious assumption was made by all parties in Palestine that strategic considerations had alone prompted Balfour's letter to Lord Rothschild.

So far this is to consider British reasons for this British act of state; but what reasons prompted the beneficiaries to organize influence on Lloyd George's government? What were the Jews trying to do? Amid many

uncertainties here is a simple question with a simple answer. The Zionists
wanted a Jewish State. There was no secret about it for anyone who
troubled to find out. They had said that a State was their object over and
over again. The foundation document of modern Zionism was Theodor
Herzl's book published in 1896, and its title was *Der Judenstaat*, literally
"The State of Jews," and he made it perfectly clear that by this he meant a
State in the ordinary sense. In the age of nationalism there was nothing
else that he could mean.

During his lifetime Herzl was involved in much party dispute within
Zionism, and he came into considerable conflict with Chaim Weizmann,
at that time a young and irreverent deputy to the Zionist congresses, but
after his death in early middle age in the year 1904, Herzl was revered
throughout the Jewish world. Even opponents of Zionism honored him as
the instigator of a great and noble ideal, and Zionists saw in him a supreme founding father of modern times. To this day the lightest criticism
of Herzl by Jew or Gentile is apt to be resented by Zionists anywhere in
the world. Though he altered many of his ideas in accordance with a
flexible and versatile mind, Herzl never altered his central idea, namely
that the Jews should have a State, and that only by enjoying this common
human right could they have the respect of the world and inner peace.
This was the idea, enthusiastically shared by Balfour, which inspired Zionism. Any Zionist leadership which departed radically from this idea was
bound to fail.

But in spite of this openly expressed desire for a State, Zionism incurs
grave accusations of double-dealing on this very matter. Anti-Zionists
have no difficulty in quoting numerous contradictory Zionist utterances
made in the years of the first phase of Zionist establishment, encouraging
at one moment and denying at another the idea that the Jewish National
Home meant a Jewish National State.[4] The evolution of the term "National Home" before this period adds weight to the charge that Zionism
was from the beginning a movement of questionable straightness. The
term was invented by the once well-known and somewhat fantastic
thinker and man of letters, Max Nordau, one of Herzl's earliest associates.
He related how, on his advice, this term, rather than that of *Judenstaat*,
was adopted as a description of the Zionist goal at the first Zionist Congress held at Basle in August, 1897. He gave this account: "I did my best
to persuade the claimants of the Jewish state in Palestine that we might
find a circumlocution that would express all we meant, but would say it in

[4] This is fully discussed in *Nisi Dominus, A Survey of the Palestine Controversy* by
Nevill Barbour. London, 1946.

a way so as to avoid provoking the Turkish rulers of the coveted land. I suggested 'Heimstätte' as a synonym for 'State' . . . This is the history of the much commented expression. It was equivocal, but we all understood what it meant. To us it signified 'Judenstaat' then and it signifies the same now."

Surely this is most damning evidence. "Circumlocution . . . the coveted land . . . equivocal, but we all understood . . ." Does not this read like one of the milder passages from "The Protocols of the Elders of Zion," republished, it is pertinent to remark, in 1917 with an introduction definitely associating the Elders with Herzl and his party? Was this not proof of a duplicity that peculiarly and sinisterly marked a Jewish search for power? In the light of Nordau's revelation, what is one to make of Nahum Sokolov, Weizmann's closest collaborator, writing in 1918: "It has been said and is still being obstinately repeated by anti-Zionists again and again, that Zionism aims at the creation of an independent 'Jewish State.' But this is wholly fallacious. The 'Jewish State' was never a part of the Zionist programme?" Sokolov had, a year before writing this, given similar assurances to a representative meeting of anti-Zionist Jews in Paris and to Cardinal Gasparri in Rome, and Sokolov was not the only Zionist leader to give such disavowals. Influenced by such statements, the Cabinet of 1917 was officially advised by Sir Mark Sykes that in asking for a National Home the Zionists were not seeking a Jewish republic. That they were in fact seeking just that, is clear today.

The unpleasant truth must be faced that the Zionists in London in 1917 were undoubtedly guilty of double-dealing. For every utterance of a Sokolov or a Leon Simon that the Zionists had no ambitions for a State, there were contrary assertions, usually addressed to Jews. The aim seems to have been to allay fears and maintain party fervor simultaneously by means of contradictory announcements of policy, an unscrupulous practice of which every political party is guilty at some time. But apart from party tactics, there was another and stronger reason for the extraordinary contradictions in Zionist statement. It was that they were engaged in a venture without precedent in recorded history, and in consequence neither they nor their friends could have any idea at all what immediate (as opposed to ultimate) goal they were making for.

Two things are necessary to a state: a territory and a population. The first the Jews had on terms which were precarious; they had not received a precise pledge, as they had hoped, for "the establishment of Palestine as the National Home of the Jewish people," but for "the establishment *in* Palestine of *a* national home for the Jewish people," a hazy definition.

Population they had hardly at all. Estimates of Jewish numbers in Palestine under Turkish rule are unreliable and vary, but the Jewish minority seems to have totaled around 80,000 in 1914, and to have sunk to somewhere around 65,000 by 1917. The total population in that year was somewhat below 700,000. The Jews of Palestine comprised less than ten percent of the whole population, and—a most important detail—only a minority of this minority were Zionists. The National Home depended from the beginning on immigration from abroad, and no one then had or could have the least idea how large an immigration would be attracted to Zion by the Balfour Declaration. Jews might arrive by the millions or only by the hundreds, and there was no reason for Jewish optimism in this respect. There had been no Jewish mass migration to Palestine in modern times. Nearly all the migrations from Russia in the nineteenth century had been to central Europe and the United States, and the doors of America were still wide open. For the Zionist leaders to have demanded a Jewish State, or for a British government to have sponsored one, might have been to invite ridicule and instant disaster on the whole venture. Yet the intention of a Jewish State could not be forgotten or the leaders would be repudiated.

Chaim Weizmann, that most astute and realistic of negotiators, understood this and said so. He retrieved Jewish honor to some extent because he had no recourse to Sokolov's dubious evasions. By speaking plain he exasperated, as he was to continue to exasperate for many years, many of the enthusiasts among his followers. The best recorded exposition of the Zionist situation in its first days of responsibility was made by him at a London conference of Jewish delegates in May, 1917, five months before the Declaration. He said: "One reads constantly in the Press, and one hears from friends, both Jewish and non-Jewish, that it is the endeavour of the Zionist movement immediately to create a Jewish State in Palestine. Our American friends have gone further, and they have even determined the form of this State, by advocating a Jewish Republic. While heartily welcoming all these demonstrations as a genuine manifestation of the Jewish national will, we cannot consider them as safe statesmanship . . . States must be built up slowly, gradually, systematically and patiently."

There was no suggestion here that the State must not be built at all. Such a suggestion was "not to be named" among the Zionist leaders or among the British politicians who were primarily responsible for the pledge. The belief that Weizmann and his associates deceived Balfour and Lloyd George in this matter can be shown to be wholly untrue, even when account is taken of the wish-fulfilling deception of Sir Mark Sykes. Without any doubt the Gentile and Jewish leaders shared the hope that a National Home would grow into a Jewish State at some future time which they did not try to particularize. To that extent the charge of double-dealing can be modified.

Nevertheless the inconsistencies of Zionist statement, which the leaders left for the most part as they were, did great harm to their cause. Excusable as they are in the low light of political morality, they left a lasting blemish on the political conduct of Zionism. In later years it became a Zionist habit to speak not only in two but in several voices, to run several lines of persuasion at the same time. A result was to debauch the movement with propaganda to an extraordinary extent so that Zionists, preoccupied with higher truth at the expense of the yet more essential lower truth, got a not undeserved reputation in the world for chronic mendacity. But this lay in the future.

At the time of the Declaration British ministers were not disturbed by Zionist contradictions. In all probability this was because they shared with the Jews not only the hope for a Jewish State but in varying degrees an astonishing optimism that the transformation of Palestine from a Moslem Arabic-speaking land into a Jewish Hebrew-speaking land could be accomplished peacefully. This was not so absurd a mistake as appears today. Palestine was not a country then but a hotchpotch of "sanjaks" or sub-provinces, ruled from both Damascus and Constantinople: an administrative muddle confused further by the presence of several large religious minorities, some of which enjoyed extraterritorial privileges. The force of Asiatic nationalism was underrated everywhere by Europeans, and it was assumed that in Palestine (a name lost to local tradition) it could never be of importance. One reason why the authors of the Declaration went ahead with their policy was that they believed, on informed and logical grounds, that Palestine was one of the only places in the world where it could safely be put into operation. From this, probably, sprang the legend that Balfour thought that after the expulsion of the Turks the country would be empty.

Apart from the reasons, theories, and influences mentioned already, there were others that were transitory, that dominated the argument for the Declaration for a short time, and that to some minds account singly and satisfactorily for the outcome. There is the famous story of how Lloyd George was won to Zionism by his gratitude to Dr. Weizmann for his wartime services in chemistry, but though Lloyd George gave the story in great detail, so that it cannot be disregarded, there is no reason to suppose that this indicates a primary motive.

At one period, in late 1916 and early 1917, a belief that a pro-Zionist declaration would swing American Jewish opinion toward the Allies, and so influence American opinion in general, was a considerable, even a major, incentive to British politicians, but little if anything is heard of this belief in the final stage of negotiation. It seems to have been forgotten. At another period it was greatly feared that the Germans were about to forestall the Allies with their own promise of a Jewish National Home. In the last phase before November, 1917, it was believed that open British support of Zionism would detach Russian Jews from the Bolshevik party and so ensure that the Revolution would remain not only moderate but the belligerent ally of France and Britain. This last belief, though even less realistic than fears of German Zionism, certainly accelerated the issue of the Declaration. All these transitory impulses certainly influenced the event, but none of them can wholly account for it, and it remains impossible to say with precision what degree of influence any of them exerted. All of them, except the Lloyd George chemistry theory, were based on extremely exaggerated ideas of the extent of Jewish influnce in the world. Such ideas were entertained both by Jews and Gentiles, and most of all by the anti-Semites who had invented them in the first place. It was an error typical of a great age of finance in which Jews had enjoyed remarkable success, and in which the power of finance itself was immensely overrated.

There were probably other "imponderable" reasons which were never documented and so remain unevidenced. It has been said that Arthur Balfour had an uneasy conscience at the illiberal terms of the Aliens Act of 1905, passed when he was Prime Minister, and that he sought a contrary deed in the Declaration. Other even less definable impulses may be deduced with some confidence: escapism, that bitter need of men in time of war, the desire to take part in a peaceful and constructive act at a time when the destruction of battle was laying Europe waste as at no time since the Thirty Years War; secret fears about Jews and a desire to ship them away; shame at the persecution of the Jews by Britain's Russian ally. These things can only be guessed at, but it is possible that they had a great part in the most surprising act of state in the history of modern England.

It is also possible that a number of responsible people looked on the Declaration, with its imprecise language, merely as a morale-raiser for Jews, which they and everyone else would forget at a later stage:[5] for all

---

[5] See *Orientations* by Ronald Storrs. London, 1937. He was working in Whitehall in November, 1917, and he records that the importance of the Declaration did not impress itself on him.

its solemnity the pledge, it could be supposed, would go into the limbo of general forgetfulness, as other solemn pledges of the First World War did, and as the Atlantic Charter has done in our own time. If some people thought along these lines, and it is difficult to believe that no one did so in the cynical atmosphere of political life, then they were the most deluded of all.

2   INTERREGNUM WITH CHAOS

A few weeks before the end of the First World War Balfour asked the
Foreign Office for a comprehensive memorandum on the various British
pledges given since 1914 to leaders of the Arabic-speaking world. It seems
that he sought to be assured, if possible, that our undertakings were not so
contradictory that they could not be reconciled. He was informed that the
pledges, for all their variety, might be reconciled in the mind of a lawyer,
but not in the minds of the Arabs to whom the pledges had been made.[1]
To these unfortunates it merely seemed that they had been promised a
glorious career of national independence, but in the event had been subjected to colonial rule. Only in the peninsula were Arabs nationally free,
as they usually had been (in practice if not in theory) for hundreds of
years.

Arabs blamed the French more than the British. Rightly so. The British

[1] Zeine N. Zeine, *The Struggle for Arab Independence*. Beirut, 1960.

tried to be accommodating sometimes, the French never. It soon came about that differing policies and sophisticated interpretation of Anglo-French and Anglo-Arab pledges led the British and French not only into bitter mutual controversy, but into violent conflict with the peoples whom they claimed to have freed. In the two and a half years immediately succeeding the First World War they were faced by Arab accusations of treachery and deceit, and by patriotic rebellions which they put down with bloodshed. The pleasant dreams passionately entertained in the war by British orientalists (but not by French ones) of an Arab nation rescued from the degrading tyranny of "The Unspeakable Turk" and, with gratitude in every heart, progressing under high-minded European tutelage toward a future as resplendent as their long-vanished past; these noble visions faded when the leaders of the same Arab nations began to equate Arab nationalism with anti-Europeanism. Immediate British action, of the kind ultimately taken, might conceivably have prevented this situation, but in the event it was not till the March of 1921 that a belated but imaginative attempt was made by the British Colonial Secretary, Winston Churchill, to achieve a final and harmonious settlement.

By that time Palestine had passed through many vicissitudes since November of 1917. As in Syria, Egypt, Mesopotamia, and Persia, its basic problem was nationalism. Since everything in the story turned on the growth of this political factor in Asia it is worth looking at it again.

In spite of the Arab revolt and the glamor given to it by the fame of T. E. Lawrence and the Emir Feisal, Arab nationalism was not taken very seriously in the West. It was believed for good reasons that though nationalism was certainly a force in Asia it was a minor one, as it had been in Europe in the remote past. It was noted that the movements which had affected the modern Ottoman world were markedly different, and in some ways much superior to the nationalisms which had shaken Europe at the same time. These movements were more wide-sweeping and ideological: Pan-Islam and Pan-Turkism had been reminiscent of militant Catholicism and militant Protestantism, not of the Risorgimento. The Arab revolt seemed another such movement, in this case Pan-Arabism, and, as with that other fallacy that Oriental nationalism was comparable, say, to German nationalism in the early seventeenth century, this misreading was seductive because it contained a large measure of truth. The revolt really was Pan-Arab in part. King Hussein and his family were foreigners in Syria, and yet the planned climax of the revolt was that Feisal ibn Hussein should enter Damascus as an Arab liberating Arabs. T. E. Lawrence's propaganda to the men of the Hejaz was always Pan-Arab in character and this did not lessen its force. Syrian nationalists did in fact acclaim Feisal as their king less than two years after their liberation. The Syrian throne, of which Feisal was soon deprived by the French, was one of the shakiest on record, but it was an acknowledged throne, and it appeared much more solid than it really was to people in love with the pleasing error that Arabs sought to revive Omayyad and Abbasid glories in far-stretching unions.

The error was of the kind only open to learned men, and in this dangerous pass in human affairs, at this Asiatic crossroads where history really was at least half bunk, the more learned the man, the more heinous sometimes his errors. Among the large number of Englishmen who found themselves at the end of the war occupying positions of authority in the liberated Arab world, the most widely read in orientalist studies was Arnold Wilson, acting Chief Civil Commissioner in Mesopotamia from March, 1918. This brilliant and scholarly man was convinced that the very notion of Arab nationalism was a contradiction in terms, and thus in the regime which he instituted in Baghdad he took so little account of it as even to arouse the anxiety of the illiberal Lord Curzon. His regime most notably aroused something more: a bloody insurrection against the British regime in May, 1920.

For this Wilson must not be blamed too much. Error leads to error, and if the wisdom of the wise is of no help, to whom else should the ignorant turn? The belief that Asiatic nationalism, if not to be ignored, was at least amenable to discipline, led to another intelligent misapprehension: that men living in lands desolated by cynical misrule would prefer sound administration as the reward of victory, to the prestige of national independence, a blessing which, certainly in early stages, can confer nothing much more on the desperately needy people concerned than the privilege of looking at a new flag and listening to the banging of indigenous military bands. Why should educated men have foreseen that such a privilege often means far more than security and justice?

With the remarkable exception, in spite of his Pan-Arabism, of T. E. Lawrence, British statesmen, administrators, and orientalists all tended toward this underrating of nationalism outside Europe, outside the Christendom which nationalism had helped to destroy. But while the whole matter remained unproved and even untested, these people understood and misunderstood it in different contexts. Often we find the same man seizing the question at one moment and blind to it the next. This often makes the conduct of individuals puzzling. During the war years the most indefatigable champion in London of Eastern nationalism was Sir Mark Sykes, but he saw nothing inconsistent in simultaneous proposals for independent Arab and Armenian states and for the mandate scheme. Sir Reginald Wingate, a former Governor General of the Sudan, understood better than any other administrator of his rank the importance of nationalism in Egypt, and as a result of his recommendations for a British policy combining with Egyptian nationalism, he was ruined by the imperially minded Curzon. Yet it was Curzon, as noted already, who took alarm at the Indian Empire character of Wilson's regime in Mesopotamia, and it was Sir Percy Cox, the most enlightened of all Arabists and the palladin of the liberal cause in imperial affairs, who defended Wilson to Curzon. Eighteen months before this, Sir Percy Cox, appalled by the chaotic misgovernment and consequent destitution of Persia, had suggested to the Foreign Office that some form of British protectorate should be extended to that country, and his proposal had been emphatically disapproved, not in liberal-minded London but in Delhi and by the government of India from whom Wilson had learned his ideas.[2] None of the British principals, certainly not Lawrence when it came to Palestine, wholly escaped inconsistency, or the fallacious belief in a general preference for sound rule over independence. Again the reason is that the fallacy embodied so much truth. It continued to do so as long as nationalism remained a much weaker force in Asia than in Europe, and in the years after 1918 it was still much weaker. Until very recent times the proportion of Eastern nationals who were prepared to act the "collaborator" with an outside power capable of civilized rule was, compared with a European population, much larger and included much more respectable people.

But during the 1920's an extraordinary drama emphasized the force of nationalism as it had perhaps never been emphasized before. Dispossessed Turkey herself, under Mustafa Kemal (Ataturk), rejected the emotional delights of Pan-Islamic or Pan-Turkish imperialism for those of European homeland-patriotism. Then the lesson of the Balkans was there for everyone to read: that the withdrawal of empire is always followed by particularist nationalism, even in the very center of the former empire. Something like this had happened with the Dual Monarchy, but even after the example of Turkey the lesson was not learned quickly.

From the time of Allenby's advance into Palestine until June, 1920, the country was ruled by a military administration as occupied enemy terri-

[2] The government of India turned down Cox's proposal not chiefly on the grounds of excessive responsibilities but on the more moral grounds that Great Britain would thereby incur a charge of bad faith from Persian nationalists.

lives in peacefulness. Both kinds of Zionists were to be found throughout
the period of the mandate and after. Both claimed to be the authentic
voice of Israel. The point to notice here is that both were demanding a
revolution such as has never been accomplished by peaceful means in any
populated country, except (as was impossible in this case) by a long unconscious process. Both were driven forward by a deep determination to
free the Jews from the strain of living as a "problem," and both knew the
embitterment and exasperation of centuries of homelessness and deferred
hope. It was wisely said by an enemy of the Jews that "for anyone whose
heart is set on a particular home or shrine, to be locked out is to be locked
in. The narrowest possible prison is the whole world." [5] The door of that
prison had been opened; escape was before the eyes of the prisoners; but
now the men who had opened the door offered them instead of revolutionary encouragement and the freedom of the Promised Land, this intolerable fairness. It was described as "equality of obligation," meaning equal
obligations to Arabs and Jews. From within a few months of the Balfour
Declaration there were Jews in Palestine who began to look on the British
as jailers.

The new ruling British power, even if it had been staffed exclusively by
Zionists, would have found it difficult to be on easy terms with Zionism
since whatever the Jews did toward even the most modest realization of a
National Home was bound to complicate administration, but relations
were forced into mutual exasperation by the action of the British government in April, 1918. They sent a Zionist Commission to Palestine headed
by Dr. Weizmann and containing British, French, and Italian members.[6]
Their arrival marked the beginning of Anglo-Jewish discord on the official level in Palestine. This was not the fault of the Commission or of the
British authorities who unwillingly received it, but of the manner in
which it was sent. No close definition was given either to the Commission
or to the ruling authorities as to what the terms of the Balfour Declaration
meant, and this vagueness, as appears later, seems to have been no accident. As remarked earlier, it was impossible to know what a Jewish National Home meant before it was clear how many Jews wanted to go
home, so, in these circumstances, a policy seems to have been adopted
by the British government of calculated inaction and vagueness. The initiative for this policy probably lay with Balfour. The result was inevitable.

[5] G. K. Chesterton, *The New Jerusalem*. London, 1920. The chapter on Zionism is
one of the most deplorable and ridiculous things Chesterton wrote at any time,
and like everything he wrote it contains flashes of genius.
[6] For details see *Trial and Error* by Chaim Weizmann. London, 1949.

As the first historian of the mandate has put it: "The Zionists were encouraged to be dynamic and invited to be unreasonable. The Administration were compelled to give the appearance of anti-Zionists reluctantly pursuing a pro-Zionist policy." [7] The author adds that the majority of the administration really were anti-Zionist, and really were pursuing the official policy with reluctance, but that the purposely negative direction under which they operated forced this role on them, whether they welcomed it or not.

As early as August, 1919, the abolition of the Zionist Commission was being urged [8] on Military GHQ Cairo by the Chief Political Officer of O.E.T.A. (Occupied Enemy Territory Administration), as the Palestine regime was called. The Administration had two main grounds of complaint: that the Zionist Commission looked on itself as the government, and that with their distrust went an inveterate habit of intrigue.

From the first the Commission had taken on itself the right to define the shape and needs of future Palestine. In December, 1918, they had called a conference in Jaffa where they had formulated an "Outline for the Provisional Government of Palestine." The country was to be acknowledged, they declared, as "The Jewish Homeland in whose affairs the Jewish people as a whole shall have the determining voice." The Jewish flag was to be the national emblem and the name Palestine suppressed in favor of "Eretz Israel": the Land of Israel. This conference set the tone for a long career of power-seeking, and the airing of grievances. The Commission never made it easy, and usually made it impossible for the O.E.T.A. to cooperate with them. For example they complained that the administration showed prejudice in not expanding existing Jewish battalions into a Palestine garrison, yet when one of these battalions was ordered to Cyprus, a regimental soviet proclaimed a strike against their leaving the national homeland, and it does not seem to have occurred to them that such action increased O.E.T.A.'s reluctance to raise further Jewish units. While the influential American Zionist Louis D. Brandeis was visiting Palestine in 1919, he took it on himself to act as the Commission's spokesman and proposed to the chief administrator that every implementation of policy must receive the prior agreement of the Zionist Commission. From early days the Commission had come to consider that it was not their place to consult O.E.T.A. regarding their plans, but the other way round. To O.E.T.A. they were prepared to render the respect due from ministers to an extremely constitutional sovereign, a respect which could

[7] John Marlowe, *The Seat of Pilate*. London, 1959.
[8] Israel State Archives.

turn to furious republicanism at the smallest sign of absolutism. O.E.T.A. was of necessity an absolute power.

The second ground of complaint, namely against the Commission's habit of intrigue, had appeared with the departure of Dr. Weizmann as their effective head. Their use of President Wilson's friend Brandeis provided a typical example, although this was an exceptional occasion. In the ordinary way of business, the administration mournfully noted, when the Commission could not get what they wanted from O.E.T.A. they would refer the matter direct to the London headquarters of the Zionist organization who would represent the matter direct to the Foreign Office who would refer it once more to the Palestine administration. This complicated procedure was part of that intense suspicion of all authority which the dominant Slav group (very suspicious of their Western brethren) had brought with them from their miserable life in the house of Russian bondage. The Zionist leaders who knew that life best had once fallen in love with the idea of British colonialism; in the discussions before the Balfour Declaration they had often referred to the Colonial Office in terms more suggestive of an affair of the heart than a political negotiation, and they had either not known or preferred not to know that all administration, good and bad, shares a certain grim humdrum element of oppression. When they found that the rule of their fancied angels had something in common with the rule of the Czarist police, they did not stop to ask whether it shared inevitable and essentially innocuous things but gave way to a mass impulse of disillusion and embitterment and hate. The angels became devils in their eyes. They saw themselves as the victims of a conspiracy, and as always happens to people prone to persecution-mania, their behavior drew some people on to persecute them in reality.

O.E.T.A. was staffed by no carefully trained service, but had to rely on a mixed company who had drifted to Palestine on the tides of war.[9] Inevitably they included some unsuitable persons, and, as must happen where plenary powers come suddenly and unlooked-for to the inexperienced, there were officials who grew arrogant and contemptuous, and looked down on the people in their care as a tiresome gaggle of "yids" and "wogs." But by a most curious shift in affairs the full and somewhat abnormal Zionist capacity for protest was not directed at people of this kind, but at a man of scrupulous manners and long experience, who had a genu-

[9] Ronald Storrs wrote that apart from a few professional soldiers O.E.T.A. personnel "included a cashier from a bank in Rangoon, an actor-manager, two assistants from Thos. Cook, a picture-dealer, an army coach, a clown, a land-valuer, a bo'sun from the Niger, a Glasgow distiller, an organist, an Alexandria cotton-broker, a taxi-driver, two schoolmasters, and a missionary."

ine desire to do well by the Zionist movement. This was Ronald Storrs, the military governor of Jerusalem and its neighborhood. He became the central subject of the anti-British propaganda campaign of the Zionists. A legend of wickedness and anti-Semitic conspiracy grew round him and is believed to this day in Israel.

It is not difficult to see why the protest and the legend should have fixed on him. He was a first-class orientalist in a great British age of Oriental studies; he was known to almost every Arab notable in Asia, and moreover he had been at the center of the then little recorded and tortuous political moves which had resulted in the Arab Revolt against Turkey. Why should such a man be a friend of Zionism against Arabs? Why rather should not such a man, as the friend of Arabs, be a bitter enemy of Zionism? These were crude and obvious reasons for prejudice against him. There were subtler ones as well which may have been more powerful.

Ronald Storrs was no narrow specialist: he was an excellent amateur of music, an accomplished pianist, widely read in Greek, Latin, French, and English literature, and being a decidedly vain man he carried his learning lightly but ostentatiously. The Jews of Palestine were by far the most cultured society in the Near Eastern world, and in Ronald Storrs they found, as they did not often find with Englishmen, a man who shared treasured interests with them. He was such a being as their leaders had dreamed of when they had passionately insisted that the British Colonial Office, and no other authority, was alone fit to rule such holy soil. Here was a man who understood their feelings and shared them in a world that was often hostile and usually lacking in sympathy. But this same being also proved to be a conscientious British civil servant. He had nothing to give except this maddening British gift of fairness, and the fact that he gave it with a somewhat extravagant show of diplomatic good manners, instead of with the accustomed British gaucherie and blast of pipe smoke, merely increased the bitterness of disillusion and convinced his former friends that he was a monster of hypocritical intrigue. They could not resist the pleasures of exaggeration, and the fact that Storrs was in so many respects the mental superior of his colleagues gave rise to a belief that this District Commissioner was no obedient government servant but the originator of the British government's Eastern policies. Enormous accusations were made against him. In his diaries and memoirs Richard Meinertzhagen relates that when he himself was Chief Political Officer under Allenby he was informed (and apparently believed) that Storrs encouraged and even to some extent organized the Arab-Jewish disorders of 1920. Such allegations were made against Storrs from 1918 to 1926, the year of his departure. The frequency of the complaints, and the fact that they were supported by Zionist leaders, even on occasion by Dr. Weizmann,[10] meant that he was the subject of frequent investigation by his superiors. Nothing was ever even faintly proved against him beyond the fact that with his anxiety to please he sometimes appeared to give promises which he could not, or as Jews (and Arabs) said, did not fulfill. The story of his unhappy Palestine career is extremely interesting. It adds a curious proof that the task which the British government undertook was beyond accomplishment. A sensitive and intelligent man was at no advantage over a stupid or oafish one—unless he took sides.

The whole notion of "equality of obligation" was nonsensical. Such dichotomy is only possible where there is something like equality of circumstance, and there was none between the Zionist Jews and the indigenous people. In economic standard of life, in ability and enterprise, the great majority of the Jews were hundreds of years in advance of the great majority of the Arabs, and at the same time the title of the Arabs to political mastery in this Arabic-speaking land was infinitely stronger than that of the Jews, judged not only by historical precedent but by the basic policy declared by the Allies of the First World War.

Strangely enough, if the equality of circumstance between the two people had been even less, then the equality of obligation could have been disregarded without inflicting intolerable injustice. But as things were, a policy of equality of obligation, though quite impractical, could not be avoided. There was in Palestine a small educated Arab class which included men who had enjoyed high office under the Turkish sultan, and this class, small as it was, was also much too big to allow of any possibility that Palestine could be politically transformed without danger of strife. Though the Arab population as a whole was "backward," it was not primitive enough for Balfour's purpose. The National Home was established at an unpropitious time. The age of colonial imperialism was passing rapidly, and Zionism, one of the most powerful of all manifestations of the nationalist age which succeeded, found itself closely bound to imperialism. It depended for its foundation and early growth on the success of British imperialism, and in the twentieth century that meant the failure of Arab nationalism.

By the opening months of 1920 the postwar "Eastern Question" demanded some sort of an answer. It had been hoped that a draconian peace treaty with Turkey would have been signed by the Allies long before this, but all calculations had been proved wrong by the astonishing resilience

[10] Israel State Archives.

of the Turks themselves under their new national movement. While uncertainty persisted over this central matter, the "Arab question," in Syria, Palestine, and Iraq naturally remained without any sign of solution, and the cause of increasing exasperation. There had been disorder in all three countries. The outlook was one of increasing bloodshed and a revival of Turkish power. Unless something was done the war in the East would have been fought in vain. Arab nationalism had to be appeased.

To understand what happened next the reader needs to know the main outlines of the British and French undertakings in Arabic-speaking countries, and the modifications of them resulting from other commitments, because this was one of those moments in the history of Zionism when events in Palestine were of acute interest to the Arab Moslem world in general.

The foundation document in the British undertakings was to be found in the correspondence conducted in the autumn of 1915 and the first month of 1916 between Sir Henry MacMahon, High Commissioner in Egypt, and the Sherif Hussein of Mecca. MacMahon officially proposed that as a reward for a rebellion against the sultan and caliph led by this ruler and guardian of the main shrine of Islam, Great Britain would stimulate national independence in the whole Arabic-speaking world. Exception was made of areas in the southeast where the British government was in special treaty relations with local rulers, and of the coastal strip west of Damascus and extending northward to the Anatolian frontier. MacMahon mentioned that within "the proposed frontiers" Great Britain was only free to act "without detriment to the interest of her ally France." He did not indicate the dimensions of those interests for the good reason that he did not know what they were. It was made clear that Arab independence would be realized from within some form of protectorate system to be run exclusively by Great Britain. There was no mention of Palestine anywhere in the ten letters exchanged. MacMahon's proposals were never formally embodied in a treaty, but as he conveyed the proposals as "declarations" of policy "on behalf" of the British government, Arab apologists are on strong ground when they say that they had the force of a treaty. If not, then the Balfour Declaration likewise had no such force. The proposals received added importance from the fact that, though to the last there was some flirting by Hussein's family with the Sublime Porte, when they were accepted in principle by Hussein, his sons proceeded with the famous revolt.[11]

[11] The most interesting and authoritative account of the origin of the MacMahon-Hussein correspondence, of MacMahon's personal view, and of the change in atti-

The MacMahon correspondence was later held to be a monstrous piece of false dealing especially as it took place at the same time as the opening moves toward the conclusion of the Sykes-Picot agreement which divided most of the Ottoman Empire into zones of influence. There is one defense to be found in the fact that MacMahon made no promise or even suggestion of Arab independence without a condition of European tutelage, and a further defense in the aims of the negotiators of the Anglo-French agreement. Both Monsieur Georges-Picot and Sir Mark Sykes were sincere idealists who anticipated with others the school of thinking that resulted in the League of Nations and the mandate system.[12] Unfortunately for them there was a party of extreme reaction in Paris, led by two men, Etienne Flandin and Franklin Bouillon, who dominated French Near East policy. Picot was not strong enough to stand against them and they saw to it that the French mandatory regime in Syria and Lebanon was of classic imperialist vintage, suited more to the age of the French King Charles X than that of the American President Wilson. This triumph of reaction was a disaster for everyone concerned, especially France. MacMahon could not be expected to foresee any of this, but a more respectable government in London would have warned him strongly that the French would unquestionably demand a big say in the Arab future.

MacMahon himself was a decent, honest man. He was of feeble personality and without any remarkable gift of imagination or mental drive. He was without the ability to assert his will against his superiors; he was gentlemanly and kindly in character, tending to believe well of those he met, just the sort of man who at moments of crisis is apt to be kept conveniently misinformed by people who cannot fear him. He was very much the wrong man for the place and time. It is probable that the British government, after being bullied and thwarted in Cairo by Lord Kitchener, seized the chance of appointing a tame man as the Field Marshal's successor. This kind of maneuver usually fails in the long run.

In the winter of 1917-1918, by which time Sir Henry MacMahon had been abruptly dismissed by an irritated government (as usually happens to men in his position), the Sherifian leaders received two grave shocks in the shape of two modifications of the MacMahon pledges as they had interpreted them. One shock was the issue of the Balfour Declaration, the other and much heavier shock was the publication by the Bolshevik gov-

---

tude of British officials in the East toward the transaction, is to be found in "Cairo and Khartoun on The Arab Question 1915–1918" by Elie Kedourie, published in *The Historical Journal*, VII, 2 (1964) pp. 280–97.

[12] The Sledmere (Sykes) papers frequently indicate this especially for 1917.

ernment of the terms of the Sykes-Picot agreement which divided the whole Arab world north of the peninsula into French and British zones, Russian claims having vanished with the czar. It was then that the Allies took action that raised much more telling charges of false dealing than those made against MacMahon's inconsistencies. After much ineffective propaganda to Arab nationalists, the French and British governments in November, 1918, issued the joint declaration referred to in Balfour's 1919 paper. It promised that French and British activity in lands freed from Turkish rule would be confined to the "offer" of "such support and efficacious help as will ensure the smooth working of Governments and Administrations which those populations will have elected of their own free will," together with similarly selfless labor in the fields of economic and educational development. As Balfour pointed out, it was quite impossible to carry out the terms of this declaration in Syria or Palestine.

The feelings of Arab nationalists were never reconciled to the Sykes-Picot agreement, or the Anglo-French arrangements which derived from it. The shock administered by the Balfour Declaration to the same feelings was equally heavy as regards Arab nationalists living in Syria and Palestine, but not as regards the nominal leaders of Arab nationalism to whom the pledges of independence had been made. Considering how much the declaration was to mean in the future, the Sherifians were put at ease on the matter with surprisingly little difficulty. In the course of negotiations with them, three main acts of compromise between the Arab and Jewish causes were sought and in a sense effected. All three were in favor of the Zionists.

The first was in January, 1918, when the head of the Arab Bureau in Allenby's headquarters, the eminent orientalist D. G. Hogarth, went to Jidda to confer with Sherif Hussein, now elevated to kingship. Hogarth's general purpose was to reassure King Hussein as to the pledges conveyed over two years before by Sir Henry MacMahon, and his particular purpose was to set his mind at rest regarding Syria and Palestine. He explained the aims of the Balfour Declaration in an emphatic statement which cannot be said to have left the king in doubt. Here is what he was authorized to say: "Since the Jewish opinion of the world is in favour of a return of the Jews to Palestine, and inasmuch as this opinion must remain a constant factor, and further as His Majesty's Government view with favour the realisation of this aspiration, His Majesty's Government are determined that in so far as is compatible with the freedom of the existing population, both economic and political, no obstacle should be put in the way of the realisation of this ideal." He pointed out that the Moslem-

Christian-Jewish character of Palestine necessitated the establishment of "a special regime . . . approved by the world." Palestine was thus most unequivocally excluded from the original MacMahon pledges to Hussein.

The king seems to have shown some anxiety as to whether the Balfour Declaration implied a Jewish State, but the subject does not seem to have been taken to any conclusion. Hogarth's account is somewhat vague here. "The King" he reported, "would not accept an independent Jewish State in Palestine, nor was I instructed to warn him that such a state was contemplated by Great Britain." It can certainly be said, however, that given the condition that a National Home did *not* mean a Jewish State, King Hussein accepted the Balfour Declaration. He was encouraged in acceptance by being informed that "the friendship of World Jewry to the Arab cause is equivalent to support where Jews have a political influence. The leaders of the movement are determined to bring about the success of Zionism by friendship and co-operation with the Arabs and such an offer is not to be lightly thrown aside." Hogarth in the course of conversation insisted further on the value of this Jewish support throughout the world, and his pleading was successful. King Hussein, he reported, "agreed enthusiastically, saying he welcomed Jews to all Arab lands."

It may well appear that the debate as to the compatibility of the MacMahon pledges with the Balfour Declaration is settled by this crucial interview. After such a candid exchange of information and views there was no cause, provided Zionism remained moderate, for sneers about the twice-promised land. The interview might indeed have settled the case once and for all if King Hussein or the British government had proceeded to publication of these agreements and concessions, but neither did so. It can be assumed that the king feared that publication would gravely weaken his prestige in Islam. It is often forgotten that no matter how great the anti-Turkish feeling supporting him, the position of Hussein, as a high Moslem ecclesiastic who had turned upon his spiritual overlord the caliph at the instigation of uncircumcised infidels, was "delicate." The British government hesitated, probably, for the same reason, since the revolt depended on Sherifian leadership. So, instead, the British and French governments proceeded by gradual stages to the publication in November of the Anglo-French declaration which gave a wholly contrary impression of the state of things.

Hogarth himself, a sardonic man without illusions, did not overrate the value of his services on the occasion of this interview. He had a low opinion of Hussein who had been giving increasing signs of megalomania, with the result that most of his British benefactors had come to regard him as something of a joke. Sir Mark Sykes used to call him "the marmozet." In his concluding paragraph Hogarth wrote as follows: "The King probably knows little or nothing of the actual or possible economy of Palestine and his ready assent to Jewish settlement there is not worth very much. But I think he appreciates the financial advantage of Arab co-operation with the Jews."

Concessions to Zionism were also made by Hussein's son, Emir Feisal. His authority to speak for the Arab interest in general was not officially questioned at the time when he made them.

In June of 1918 Dr. Weizmann had traveled from Palestine to meet Feisal at his headquarters north of Aqaba. The two men impressed each other favorably and the results of the encounter were remarkable from the point of view of reconciling Arab and Zionist claims. The first fruits appeared half a year later.

On the first day of the Peace Conference, in January, 1919, Feisal laid a memorandum before the delegates in which he stated the claims of "the Arabs of Asia." He said this of Palestine: ". . . the enormous majority of the people are Arabs. The Jews are very close to the Arabs in blood, and there is no conflict of character between the two races. In principles we are absolutely at one. Nevertheless, the Arabs cannot risk assuming the responsibility of holding level the scales in the clash of races and religions that have, in this one province, so often involved the world in difficulties. They would wish for the effective super-position [sic] of a great trustee, so long as a representative local administration commanded itself by actively promoting the material prosperity of the country."

Precisely what this meant is difficult to say but the general drift, friendly to Zionism and to the idea of a protectorate, is unmistakable. The meaning was further elucidated by a deposition made by Feisal at a meeting of the Supreme Council in February. He asserted that "Palestine, for its universal character, should be left on one side for the mutual consideration of all parties interested."

But the most important consequence of the temporary Weizmann-Feisal alliance was an agreement drawn up between them in London in the autumn of 1918 and signed shortly after Feisal had submitted his memorandum in Paris. The agreement contained nine articles of which the fourth and seventh are important historically. Here are the texts:

IV. All necessary measures shall be taken to encourage and stimulate immigration of Jews into Palestine on a large scale, and as quickly as possible to settle Jewish immigrants upon the land through closer settlement and intensive cultivation of the soil. In taking such measures the Arab peasant and tenant farmers shall be protected in their rights, and shall be assisted in forwarding their economic development.

VII. The Zionist Organisation proposes to send to Palestine a Commission of experts to make a survey of the economic possibilities of the country, and to report upon the best means for its development. The Zionist Organisation will place the aforementioned Commission at the disposal of the Arab State for the purpose of a survey of the economic possibilities of the Arab State and to report upon the best means for its development. The Zionist Organisation will use its best efforts to assist the Arab State in providing the means for developing the natural resources and economic possibilities thereof.

Feisal added a codicil in his own writing, and this was signed by both parties. It ran as follows:

> Provided the Arabs obtain their independence as demanded . . . I shall concur in the above articles. But if the slightest modification or departure were to be made, I shall not then be bound by a single word of the present Agreement . . .

This was a clever move by Feisal but just too clever to work. His immediate plan was to obtain international sanction for an independent State of Syria which would include Palestine and the modern country of Jordan: this was what was meant by "the Arab State." He was working in this agreement for Jewish help, possibly influenced by Hogarth's insistence to King Hussein (very typical of the time) on the enormous international power of Jewish influence. He evidently overestimated that influence more than most and hoped by thus allying himself with Weizmann and Zionism to force British support of the Greater Syria plan. Feisal was overplaying his hand, probably at the instigation of his chief adviser, T. E. Lawrence. But whatever his mistakes, it must surely be acknowledged that the three initial attempts at Arab-Jewish reconciliation—the Hogarth interview, Feisal's memorandum (elaborated to the Supreme Council), and the Feisal-Weizmann agreement—do effactually dispose of the idea that the Balfour Declaration was utterly unacceptable to the gallant leaders of the Arab revolt, and was a cruel repudiation of a solemn pledge to the family of the Sherif of Mecca.

These three episodes gave the British and Jews strong claims as regards their intentions in Palestine. The claims were not pressed by either of them. Why was that? In the present state of information one can only guess the reasons. So far as the British government were concerned, they could not welcome a Feisal-Weizmann agreement whose obvious purpose (on Feisal's side) was to establish a Greater Syrian Kingdom, because if Feisal were to achieve such a thing, it must bring Great Britain and France into the fiercest mutual antagonism. If the terms of the Sykes-Picot agreement were to be upheld, and the French insisted on this, then a unified Syria would be under the direction of two protecting powers: the French in the north and in the capital of Damascus, and the British in the south. French and British mandatory policies were unlikely to be identical and from that circumstance, even with goodwill of which there was little, there had to emerge a chronic state of Anglo-French enmity. These fears were not extravagant: in the event, the fact that French mandatory policy in modern Syria and Lebanon was unrelated to British mandatory policy in Iraq, Transjordan, and Palestine was a continual cause of friction and suspicion culminating in a British invasion of Syria in 1945. In the earlier time considered here, the idea of war between France and Great Britain over the Eastern question was often in men's minds.

British diplomatic alarm at the implications of the Weizmann-Feisal agreement is easily understandable, but it is difficult to see why the British government never availed itself of the earlier episode, the concession to Zionism given by King Hussein to Hogarth. It has been mentioned that in the first place there may have been good reasons for suppressing the information, but it is hard to see why Hussein's valuable concession continued afterward to be almost completely neglected. An account of the meeting was included in a memorandum prepared by the Foreign Office for the guidance of Arthur Balfour at the Peace Conference,[13] but after that it never seems to have been thought of again until its publication in a White Paper twenty years after, many years too late to be of the least value. The fact that the concession was made orally certainly took away from its importance, but this did not mean it had no importance at all. However, for reasons suggested in the next chapter the advantage was not followed up.

The Jews might appear to have had more to gain by these Sherifian concessions than anyone else, and yet they never pressed them as strongly as they might have done. It is unlikely that they ever heard of Hogarth's interview till years later, but the Zionist leaders were of course fully informed about Weizmann's agreement with Feisal. Later, Zionist publicists made much of it, but at the time it aroused enthusiasm in very few. It was

[13] Israel State Archives.

not what the Jews wanted. They wanted a State and they feared entering into any agreement which did not acknowledge their right to build one. Dr. Weizmann, seeing things as a scientist, knew that no situation is stationary, and his consistent belief (which for reasons of party he often concealed) seems always to have been that, given adequate Jewish immigration and no precisely defined agreement, a "State situation" would gradually and inevitably evolve for the Jews many years hence, long after his own lifetime or that of any other living person. But such sophisticated thinking could never be to the taste of a militant political group. More typical of what the Zionist leaders felt to be an appropriate statement was that made by Dr. Eder (reckoned a moderate) when giving evidence to a commission of inquiry in 1921. The commission reported him thus: "In Dr. Eder's opinion there can be no equality in the partnership between Jew and Arab but a Jewish predominance as soon as the numbers of that race are sufficiently increased . . . There is no sophistry about Dr. Eder. He was quite clear that the Jews should and the Arabs should not have the right to bear arms and he stated his belief that this discrimination would tend to improve Arab-Jewish relations." This point of view was a long way from the spirit of the Paris agreement, and was more widely shared.

The only person, apart from Weizmann, who seems to have been wholeheartedly for the agreement was the other signatory, Emir Feisal, and his enthusiasm only lasted so long as he remained in a state of innocent ignorance. Though a national leader, he also had not learned the nature of modern nationalism, and he overrated his own position. Having been accepted as a spokesman for "the Arabs of Asia," he forgot the awkward fact that the Sherifian leadership which he represented had never been fully or uncritically accepted outside the Hejaz. He forgot or ignored the fact that an important declaration of British policy toward the Arab world made in the summer of 1918[14] had been occasioned by the disgust of Syrian politicians at the prospect of a Sherifian domination of all Arabic-speaking territories. By 1919 the position of Feisal, installed in Damascus as supreme administrator, was no stronger than it had been in the war. He was the leader of all Arabs so long as he said and did what all Arabs wanted him to, or so long as he received agreeable pledges on their behalf, but as soon as he said or did otherwise, or received discouraging modifications of pledges, he was a foreign Bedouin chief. The position is a familiar

[14] The Declaration to the Seven, a British pledge to work for Arab independence conveyed on June 16th, 1918, to seven Syrian notables in Amman in answer to a memorial submitted by them to the Foreign Office.

one all over the world. If an American President, speaking as a leader of the English-speaking world, declares that Great Britain deserves to be accorded the highest respect among the nations, an Englishman feels something like allegiance to him, but if the same President, speaking in the same role, warns Great Britain that she should abandon an overseas possession, the Englishman discerns a gross and interfering foreigner. If Feisal had been a Palestinian Arab of Jerusalem his treaty with Zionism might have had some feeble hope of acceptance, but since he was who he was, it had none at all. He soon found out for himself that his power was very limited and stopped a long way short of enforcing agreements with Dr. Weizmann.

Poor Feisal was one of those men who are hoisted by circumstances into lofty and dangerous positions such as might only be maintained with difficulty by a Napoleon. This grave, handsome, ill-educated, well-meaning, and weak man could only have survived as the lord of Greater Syria and the leader of Arabian Asia if he had been supported either by a France whole-heartedly dedicated to the cause of Arab nationalism and independence, or by Syrian politicians remarkably endowed with patience and skill. But of course France was totally opposed to Arab nationalism in Syria, and the politicians who served Feisal were as reckless as they were silly. He had to follow their lead. His fall was rapid and inevitable. Its course need not be traced in detail here, but it should be briefly indicated because it was in small part occasioned by Zionism and had great effect on the fate of Palestine.

When Feisal returned to Damascus in January of 1920 he had been away for four months. Since November, 1918, he had in all spent only five months in Syria, and during his last absence the character of the regime of which he was the head had changed radically. British troops and advisers had been withdrawn in November, 1919, and French troops had entered Lebanon. Had Feisal been there to explain matters to the people, disaster might have been averted, but as things were this vent gave new impetus to extremist agitation which was directed not only against the French but against Europeans in general, and was turning against Feisal himself. He came back to Damascus to face increasing propaganda to the effect that he was a French agent, and he could only live this down by going along with Syrian extremism. He thus lost all his allies.

By a paradoxical maneuver, on the 8th of March, 1920, a "General Syrian Congress" forced Feisal's hand by electing him King of United Syria, which now included Lebanon besides the Transjordan territory of the former vilayet, and Palestine. The unfortunate new king did what little he could to maintain stable rule. The feat was quite beyond him. He incurred renewed French enmity by not signing the draft agreement between himself and the French government, while continuing to suffer a fatal loss of prestige from the knowledge that such an agreement existed. His foolish old father added his rebukes to those of the agitators in the towns of Syria. News had also leaked out of his agreement with Dr. Weizmann and he was accused of being in Jewish pay. To correct this impression he lent his name to anti-Zionist propaganda,[15] and associated himself with anti-Zionist resolutions passed the day before his elevation by the General Syrian Congress. This constituted the most complete possible repudiation of his former friendly attitude, for less than a week before this there had occurred, at the instigation of the Congress, the attack on a Jewish settlement in north Palestine in which Trumpledor had been killed. How could Feisal hope after this to exercise effective rule over the growing Jewish minority of Palestine according to his claim? And Zionism was not the greatest of his minority problems. By co-opting the Christian Lebanese into Greater Syria, the Congress had presented their king with a permanently disloyal segment of the population which alone of the Greater Syrians, wished for French rule as protection against Moslem persecution. It was now that many people in Syria itself compared the disorder of the present with the tranquillity of Ottoman days and looked for deliverance to Mustafa Kemal Pasha of Turkey; efforts were made by one Syrian party to interest that great leader in a campaign for the redemption of their country. At the same time Feisal's closest advisers had differing interests and, despite his protests, pushed the poor man into all possible contradictions of policy. While his Palestinian friends forced him further and further into anti-Zionism, his Iraqi friends contrived a new and colossal act of folly for him.

These were the months when the rebellion in Iraq was preparing and Feisal reluctantly but nevertheless definitely sanctioned aid to the rebels; the first action of the rebellion was led by two of his officers. By his anti-Zionism he was indirectly adopting an anti-British policy; by nominally supporting rebellion in Iraq he was doing so directly; by both actions he was alienating his only champion at the conference table. His ultimate conflict within Syria was with the war party which demanded that he lead them in a victorious campaign against the French army. He did stand up against these people, but now it was too late to save a Sherifian regime. In July, 1920, the king was forced into exile by the French, who extin-

[15] Israel State Archives. Zeine, *op. cit.*

guished the independent State of Syria by direct military action. They did this with a ruthlessness toward those entrusted to their care for which they had to pay dearly in subsequent years.

With the disappearance of Feisal from the Syrian and Palestinian scene went the Feisal-Weizmann agreement as well. Since Feisal had taken up anti-Zionism among the desperate expedients of his reign in Damascus, this was no great loss, but in the redispositions of territory occasioned by his fall, Zionism, as appears in the next chapter, suffered a setback which, though inevitable, placed it at a permanent disadvantage. Before that, however, Zionism was to pass through a critical phase in its fortunes and enjoy its greatest political triumph since November, 1917. To follow what happened it is necessary to look again briefly at the general scene from a different angle.

It was becoming increasingly clear to the politicians of the West that a peace treaty with Turkey was not to be concluded for some time yet, so in April, 1920, the Allies decided that so far as the Arabic-speaking world was concerned they would implement the provisions of such a treaty as they envisaged. Such action was, of course, highly illegal. Arab apologists have execrated it as a piece of ill-disguised imperialism encouraged by Zionists with the object of profiting from injustices done to their fellow-Semites. Though arguments against the conference of San Remo, where the decision was taken, can be made to appear formidable, this irregular conduct was more public-spirited than otherwise. It was the only sensible thing to do, for in spite of the self-interest shown by the powers as a result of this decision (it gave impetus to French aggressiveness in Syria), the only alternative was to keep the Arab world in a state of restive uncertainty. But it is true that alone of the Middle Eastern peoples the Zionists got what they wanted from the conference.

By this time O.E.T.A.'s attempt in Palestine at a policy of caution and equity had developed or degenerated into one of active anti-Zionism, in practice if not in theory. The situation is best described in the memoirs of a moderate Zionist, Horace Samuel. He said that while many accusations leveled against the administration by Jews may be dismissed, what O.E.T.A. "did do . . . was to make every Arab realise that it was absolutely an open question whether a Zionist or an Arab policy was to be eventually adopted, to allow the impression to be broadcast that the administration favoured an Arab policy and that the policy of H.M.G. could be deflected by the requisite amount of vim and determination." [16] An

[16] Horace Samuel, *Unholy Memories of the Holy Land*. London, 1930.

anti-Zionist friend and admirer of Sir Louis Bols singled out this passage as an accurate description of his policy. In April of 1920[17] Bols wrote to London again to urge that the Zionist Commission be abolished. The letter arrived at a critical time. It was forwarded to the Foreign Secretary, Lord Curzon, who was at San Remo attending that fateful conference. The British delegation included Lloyd George and Arthur Balfour, and it is probably not fanciful to believe that Bols's letter incited them to the most uncompromising declaration of policy which circumstances allowed them. At all events they acted in accordance with such a supposition. In the terms of the mandate for Palestine, drafted by the British and endorsed by the conference, the Balfour Declaration was quoted in full. Sir Herbert Samuel agreed to go to Jerusalem in the summer as the first High Commissioner, and to found a civil administration. O.E.T.A. was to cease. This was indeed a great victory for Zionism.

It is convenient to close this chapter by considering the rights and wrongs in the conflict which now drew to an end between the military regime and the Zionist Commission. The debate continues in Israel today, and also among many people with memories of British-ruled Palestine. There can be little doubt that the accusation that the Commission attempted to usurp rule is fully justified, and there can be no denying the assertion made by Ronald Storrs in his book that their refusal to employ to full advantage the services of Sephardic Jews of Egypt and Palestine was one among many indications which showed how little was their desire to come to terms with the Arabs. The same has been said by other Jewish and Gentile authorities. To a freshly established administration such as O.E.T.A., deficient in trained men and struggling to impose order on the ruins left by chaotic predecessors, perpetual nagging interference and obstruction by the Commission must have been utterly maddening. One can be surprised that the relations between the two authorities were not worse than they were.

The usual defense of the Zionist Commission is that they were only acting within their rights, but this is very doubtful in many cases. A much sounder defense is that they were absolutely forced by circumstances and as a condition of survival to establish a maximum and often inadmissible interpretation of what their rights were, because they were in a dangerous situation. Any civilized administration, even the best, tends to be "minimalist" by temperament; only in rare moments of public enthusiasm does

[17] Jeffries, *op. cit.*

it show an opposite tendency. The establishment of Zionism in Palestine, contrary perhaps to the hopes of the authors of the Balfour Declaration and the Zionist leaders, proved to be no such moment. O.E.T.A. asked only one thing of the Zionists as of everyone, that they should cause them the least possible bother.

If the Zionist Commission had done what most people outside the Zionist party wanted them to do; if they had been nice-mannered, accommodating, broad-minded, discreet, friendly to Arab nationalists, they could and almost certainly would have been maneuvered into a position of minor importance, that of a welfare organization for a number of Jewish settlements, and from such a position escape might have been extremely difficult, perhaps impossible. All the evidence suggests that this was the position which the administration would have liked the Jews to occupy, not (except in isolated cases) through ill-will toward them, but, to their credit, through a genuine wish to be fair to both sides, and, less to their credit though not to their blame, through keen regard for the pleasures of a quiet life, especially after the fatigues of a long war. Their conduct of policy became anti-Zionist because they were enemies to enthusiasm and Zionism lived on enthusiasm. In this pass, the Zionists could not rely on the logic of events to save them.

The pressure of Jewish immigration on Palestine was not as great as they had hoped. In 1919, 1,806 entered, in the next four years the annual figures varied between eight and eight and one-half thousand.[18] The reason for this relatively small response to Zionism was in part that the United States was still open to immigrants, and yet more that the greatest number of Jews who wanted to dwell in the National Home were in Russia, and the Soviet government forbade emigration and outlawed Zionism as a cult. It seemed then to those who were in charge of Zionist operations that the building of the New Jerusalem must be very slow of accomplishment, occupying several generations. This was a matter for the most extreme alarm among the Zionist leaders, and even Dr. Weizmann's statesmanlike belief in gradualism did not save him from something like panic here. The ancient history of the Jews had given them, along with an overestimate of their power, an exaggerated idea of their weakness. It is odd to remember today that in the nineteenth century, many Jewish writers, among them the forerunners of Zionism, had been obsessed with a dread that the Jewish people would vanish without trace under the in-

[18] Mark Wischnitzer, *To Dwell in Safety:* A Study of Jewish Emigration from Europe. Philadelphia, 1948.

fluence of tolerance and assimilation, and that their great heritage would pass away forever.[19] If there was one thing that Zionist Jews feared, it was that their movement would end in nothing more than a new Jewish minority being assimilated into another environment. Their weak position in Palestine made them strident in asserting their claims.

This stridency was very much blamed at the time and after, but in retrospect it can be put to the moral credit of Zionism. Here is another irony in the story. During the whole of the interwar period Palestine was full of stories of the wicked, crafty deceptiveness of the incoming Jewish settlers, but in fact the Zionist leadership was throughout guilty of an opposite fault, if fault it was, that of irrepressible indiscretion. The Zionists kept Palestine in a continual state of excitement by proclaiming Jewish rights and Jewish ambitions from the housetops. In the opinion of at least one British administrator of the time this showed the good sense of moral courage. In the early days, in face of the administration's hesitancy to publish the Balfour Declaration (following forlorn hopes that the breeze might blow over), the Jews told the Arabs what the Arabs were sure to find out in the end.[20] Perhaps this policy was foolhardy, but it was honest. More honest than that of O.E.T.A. In the appalling times which lay ahead, and when Jewish desire for a great pressure of immigrants on Palestine was tragically realized, the Zionist leadership in Palestine did at least have the moral advantage that they had declared their intentions from the beginning and had, in Palestine at least, made no secret of their determination to build a State.

[19] A recent speech by Mr. Ben-Gurion attacking the way of life of Jews living outside Israel is one among many pieces of evidence that this fear has not died down.
[20] Sir A. Kirkbride gave this opinion to the author.

3   1921

O.E.T.A. officially died on the first of July, 1920; on this day Sir Herbert Samuel assumed office as the first High Commissioner of the newly mandated territory, and Palestine entered a period of vigorous administration. O.E.T.A. had done valuable preliminary work in all essential departments, especially in communications and health; under the civil administration their work showed substantial returns, and was forwarded. For the first time in centuries Palestine enjoyed prosperity; the death rate fell, the birth rate rose, the population grew from these natural causes and from the immigrations of both Arabs and Jews. Plans were drafted for the establishment of representative institutions. To outward appearances the country began to show a splendid example of reclamation under enlightened European rule.

The appointment of Sir Herbert Samuel, and also of his chief secretary, Mr. Wyndam Deedes, a friend and admirer of Dr. Weizmann's, allayed the misgivings of the Zionists and they anticipated a period of government under which the National Home would be so firmly established that its further growth to statehood would be certain and perhaps more rapid than anyone dared to guess then. Here was a High Commissioner who not only knew Zionists as a fellow-Jew, but had been the first protagonist of Zionism in British politics. He showed early in his new post that he had not departed from this loyalty. Among his first legislative acts were the establishment of Hebrew as an official language and a satisfying agreement with the Zionist Commission on the number of Jewish immigrants who might enter the country yearly as settlers. While Arabs looked on in alarm, the Jews gave this forceful ruler an enthusiastic welcome such as they never gave to another. Remembering the first days of the civil administration, Ronald Storrs has told of the deep emotion that overcame a gathering at Rishon le Zion when Samuel attended the blessing of the first vintage and, as part of the ceremony, read from the law in Hebrew. Israel Cohen records how the congregation in the Grand Synagogue of Jerusalem felt that they were present at the hour of fulfillment when, on the Sabbath following the feast of Ab which commemorates the destruction of the Temple, the High Commissioner read from the Book of Isaiah:

> Comfort ye, comfort ye my people, saith your God.
> Speak ye comfortably to Jerusalem, and cry unto
> her, that her warfare is accomplished.

All this passionate admiration, expectation and gratitude evaporated in a very short time, and the name of Herbert Samuel, the ablest High Commissioner of Palestine appointed by the mandatory, is not especially honored in Israel today.

His trouble was the same as had beset the military administration. He was committed to the same policy of "equality of obligation," and unlike his predecessors he was determined to carry it out vigorously according to the spirit and letter of the law. He believed in it. He wrote as follows to Storrs, then acting Chief Secretary before the arrival of Deedes: "You know my policy with regard to the non-Jewish population—not only to treat them with absolute justice and every consideration for their interests in matters relating to the establishment of the Jewish National Home, but also to adopt active measures to promote their well-being." [1] Once more fairness was the rule in a situation where fairness could be of no avail.

[1] Ronald Storrs, *Orientations.* London, 1937.

Zionists were shocked and saddened when in a dispute over property rights in the distict of Beisan, Samuel adjudicated in favor of the Arabs. This was one incident of many which showed the Jews plainly that Samuel's loyalty to Zionism was to a moderate form of Jewish nationalism, taking no account of statehood in a foreseeable future, and including as a cardinal principle appeasement of Arab hostility.

In March of 1921 Samuel was responsible for a characteristic act of policy when on the death of the Mufti of Jerusalem he obtained the election of his half-brother Haj Amin el Husseini. This young man had fled from Palestine after the disorders of 1920 and had been condemned to fifteen years' imprisonment *in absentia* for his part in arousing the Arab population to anti-Zionist violence. His appointment as Mufti was the most criticized and, as later events were to show, the most criticizable of Samuel's actions as High Commissioner, but those who condemned it forgot that in obtaining this appointment Samuel was acting in conformity with the best, most liberal, and most fruitful traditions of British overseas rule: to avoid splitting territories under British administration into pro-British and anti-British faction, to co-opt the patriotic element into the responsibilities of government. But Zionists could hardly be expected to see the elevation of their avowed enemy in this light, and they began to accuse Samuel of weakness and timidity. Widespread indignation, however, belongs to a later period, for little was then known of Haj Amin, and everyone in Palestine, Jews, Arabs, and British, was more interested at that time in the threatening developments occurring in the eastern part of the British mandated territory. These events were connected with the dethronement of Feisal and his expulsion from Damascus.

Sir Herbert Samuel had been in Jerusalem for less than two weeks when Feisal entered Palestine as a refugee. The High Commissioner accorded the fallen king chivalrous honors in the course of his journey from Haifa to Suez on his way to London. There Feisal pleaded his cause without success but with result.

In the meantime the collapse of United Syria brought into being a fantastic anomaly in the administration of the British mandated territory. The southern half of the former vilayet of Syria, due east across the Jordan from Palestine, had been under Feisal's rule. By the San Remo decisions this territory came under the British Palestine mandate. As one might expect, Feisal's rule over these lands had never been very firm, but it had been rule of a sort. Now, suddenly, the territory was left without any rule at all, and the High Commissioner in Jerusalem had neither the monetary nor manpower resources to undertake reorganization immediately. He acted with bold improvisation. After a meeting of notables convened at Es Salt, Sir Herbert Samuel, after promising to promote self-government in the eastern territory, sent a few Arabic-speaking officers with small detachments of police across the Jordan with general instructions to maintain order. This they had to do in highly peculiar circumstances. Under the wayward rule of Damascus, as indeed under the Ottoman Empire, the people east of Jordan had learned to look after themselves in a crude manner, and on the collapse of Feisal's kingdom they formed themselves into minute independent states. The main task of the British officers was to prevent these states from waging war on one another. The most southern of them had its "capital" at Kerak where the town was then sited entirely within the walls of the ruined Crusader stronghold Crac du Desert. The British adviser was Major Alec Kirkbride, and with a fine sense of history he named its administration, of which he was elected president, "The National Government of Moab."

The mandatory had a long-term policy for these territories. It was hoped that when they had come under efficient economic administration they would serve as a settlement area for Arab proprietors who (it was believed) could be induced, as the Jewish National Home expanded, to migrate to productive Transjordan land in exchange for their home acres in west Palestine. This plan seems not to be documented, at all events in published material, nor to have gone beyond the stage of verbal discussion, but that the plan existed is not in doubt.[2] Events overtook it.

Six months after Sir Herbert Samuel's arrival, and before he had had time to regularize the odd state of things east of the Jordan, unexpected occurrences forced a solution. Feisal's elder brother, the Emir Abdullah ibn Hussein, decided to avenge the family insult of Syria. He assembled an army and went to Ma'an which was then within the Hejaz frontier and the next-door district to the National Government of Moab. From Ma'an the emir announced in January, 1921, that he intended to march with his two thousand men through the Transjordan territories toward Damascus. His declared intention was to make war on the French in order to turn them out of Syria as they had turned out his brother. The president of Moab asked his superiors for instructions: whether to resist the emir (which he could not do with fifty uncertain policemen), or whether to welcome him (which he could). The reply from Jerusalem ran as follows: "It is consid-

[2] Sir Alec Kirkbride, *A Crackle of Thorns*. London, 1956. Also a communication to the writer. There is in existence a letter from Sokolov in which he warns Weizmann, on grounds of political inexpediency, against a plan then afoot to expropriate Arab landlords from Palestine.

ered most unlikely that the Emir Abdullah will advance into territory which is under British control." Kirkbride considered that this left the initiative to him, and when the emir, very shortly after, proceeded with the threatened advance the president of Moab welcomed him. Within a few weeks the National Government of Moab and all its little sister-autonomies vanished as the emir established something resembling a central administration in Amman. He had become prince of these territories by acclamation.

At the time of these happenings great changes, to be called great if judged by their effect on the future, were occurring in London. A result of the conference of San Remo was that British responsibility for the rule of Palestine and other mandated territory was transferred from the Foreign Office to the Colonial Office, an arrangement intended from the beginning and only put off by the delay in making a treaty with Turkey. In terms of personalities this change meant that the territories left the care of Lord Curzon, an emphatic opponent of Zionism but one who had never allowed his prejudice to influence his official actions, and entered the care of the Colonial Secretary, Mr. Winston Churchill, who wished Zion well from his heart.

Mr. Churchill, unlike Lord Curzon, had taken no part in the discussions and negotiations which had led to the Balfour Declaration and to the complicated diplomatic situation governing French and British pledges and claims in the Arab world. He came fresh to the whole business and he determined, in keeping with his character, to act the part of the new broom. His first move was to establish a Middle East Department attached to the Colonial Office, and early in 1921 he decided to call a conference of senior British officials holding positions in the Arabic-speaking world. They were to meet him in Egypt. His two main purposes were to reduce the British expenditure incurred by administrations and garrisons, and (what is of lasting interest) to reach a final settlement in keeping with the undertakings made in the name of the British government during the war.

The conference met in Cairo in the second week of March and lasted a fortnight. The agenda[3] fell into three divisions: Iraq, Palestine (including Transjordan), and British commitments in the Arabian littoral of the Persian Gulf and Aden. Iraq was the main subject and consequently the dominant personality of the conference, after Mr. Churchill, was Sir Percy Cox who arrived from Baghdad with a retinue of twenty persons including his

[3] From a copy of the agenda communicated to Sir Herbert Samuel in February, 1921. Israel State Archives.

Oriental Secretary, Miss Gertrude Bell. Before leaving London Mr. Churchill and his advisers had made up their minds what they wanted the conference to decide, and they do not seem to have been seriously opposed on any main issue. One of these issues was the appointment of Feisal to be the ruler of Iraq. It was planned that there would be a referendum in the summer and that he would be enthroned as King Feisal I later in the year. So it came about. He obtained his second kingship as a result of elections which could be harshly but not inaccurately described as "rigged," and were believed then and later to constitute a grave blot on Britain's reputation in the East. The transaction was never easy to defend, but the subsequent history of Iraq in the next thirty years did, on the whole, justify before history the high-handed action of Mr. Churchill, Sir Percy Cox, and Gertrude Bell. Feisal himself thus vanished for good from the Palestine scene, but the previous events of his life continued to exert influence there.

The decision to elevate him to the throne of Iraq made it impossible for the British government to do other than acknowledge Abdullah as the ruler of the Transjordanian territory where he had established himself. There were pressing family reasons for this. At the time when Feisal was elected King of United Syria in 1920 Abdullah had been elected King of Iraq, and he was reported to be far from pleased at the latest promotion of his younger brother without any reference to his own stronger claims. It followed that for the British government to have denied his present status in Transjordan, or to have limited his sovereignty in a way to humiliate him, would have been completely against the purpose of the conference: to reach a settlement with the leaders of Arab nationalism. So with practical sense Mr. Churchill decided to act the kingmaker to this acclaimed king.

The agenda and presumably the discussion at the conference on Palestine was dominated by this Transjordan question. The line of argument appears to have been that since it was necessary to acknowledge Abdullah as a lawful ruler, it followed that the administrations of Palestine and the country east of the Jordan, though remaining under one High Commissioner, should be entirely separate. Other Palestine matters discussed at the conference were the future relations of Palestine and foreign powers; administrative machinery; the judiciary; finance; the size of the permanent garrison; the withdrawal of those British forces which were in excess of the agreed number, and the relations of the High Commissioner's Advisory Council (a representative but nominated body instituted by Sir Herbert Samuel) with an elected body, "the Legislative Council," which the High Commissioner planned to bring into being in the immediate future. The term *Zionism* does not appear on the original draft of the agenda and that it was discussed is only deducible from two items, "Policy in Palestine under the Mandate" and "Special Subjects." The urgent thing was to settle Feisal and Abdullah.

On the 24th of March, when the conference was concluded, Mr. Churchill went to Palestine. There is a well-authenticated story that at Gaza he and the High Commissioner courteously acknowledged the yells of the people, unaware that the latter were demanding a massacre of the Jews.[4]

Soon after his arrival Mr. Churchill met Abdullah himself, who was conducted from his principality to Jerusalem by T. E. Lawrence. In a brief conference the emir agreed to Mr. Churchill's main conditions for British recognition of him as ruler of Transjordan. They were that he should acknowledge the British mandate in his territory, in return for which he would receive financial aid and a light measure of British guidance, and that he should abandon his project of making war on France, a proposition which suited the unwarlike Abdullah perfectly. Recognition was ratified by the British government later in the year. The small principality and later Kingdom of Transjordan thus formally came into being.

It has been claimed, notably by Sir John Glubb, that the establishment and development of Transjordan under British auspices was a most praiseworthy and statesmanlike act. The claim is without question a very substantial one, but only a very selfless Zionist can be expected to join in the praise without reservation. The moment when this new shift in affairs came was a critical one for the Jews. Since November, 1917, throughout these lands between Africa and Turkey, Zionism had been a subject of angry preoccupation among Arab nationalists, but it had hitherto taken second place to the agitation for a United Syria. With the disintegration, without hope of restoration, of United Syria, the order of preoccupation was reversed, and Arab nationalism began to find fresh impulse in the wrongs of the Palestinian Arabs. In the words of H. V. Temperley: "It may be remarked that had the Sherif's son, the Emir Feisal, not been ejected from Syria by the French, much less might have been heard of his father's claim to Palestine."

In these untoward circumstances the project of resettling Arabs from Palestine on Transjordan land had to be completely put aside. The High Commission had lost much of its freedom of action in acknowledging Abdullah because his sovereign independence had to be maintained, as to

---

[4] *T. E. Lawrence by his Friends,* edited by A. W. Lawrence (Contribution from Capt. Maxwell H. Cook). London, 1937.

appearances at first, and in the course of time more and more as to fact. The emir could not agree to any close collaboration with Zionism without suffering a fatal decline in popularity and prestige, in neither of which, after the first enthusiasm, was he rich. (He had to face a rebellion against himself before the end of 1921.) The British government likewise could not possibly insist on any close connection between pro-Zionist measures in Palestine and Abdullah's internal policy in Transjordan without undoing what most British people concerned regarded as a master stroke. It took a year and a half for this redirection of policy to receive ratification in its final form when, in September, 1922, the Council of the League of Nations accepted a British proposal that Transjordan should be exempted from all clauses in the mandate providing for a special regime in the holy places and the development of the Jewish National Home in Palestine; but the policy had been established in effect from the moment of Mr. Churchill's interview with the emir.

The Zionists had neither attempted nor planned any settlement in Transjordan. The number of Jews living there permanently in 1921 has been reliably estimated at two, or according to some authorities, three persons. There was an unorthodox Zionist dream for extending Jewish colonization to the limits of possible cultivation beyond the river, but there is no sign that anyone was occupied then in giving it reality. For that reason, it can be assumed, the Transjordan settlement of 1921 did not make an immediately unfavorable impression on Zionists. When, a year later, the Zionist organization was invited to express its satisfaction with the shape and political organization of British mandated Palestine and Transjordan, even so fierce an extremist as Vladimir Jabotinsky, the founder and commander of the Jewish Legion in the war, added his signature willingly.[5] In later years Zionist propaganda referred to the transaction as "a serious whittling down of the Balfour Declaration," as the cause of "a rankling sense of disappointment" [6] and as a betrayal. It was sarcastically noted that the British government had been a remarkably long time in discovering that Palestine stopped short at Jordan. It could be said in reply that the Jews had been a remarkably long time in registering a claim which would certainly have been resisted from the beginning. There is little Israelite history to be recalled east of Jordan, and the National Home was a monument to history.

But if the later Zionist propaganda about Transjordan was contrived, the feeling and anxiety which it expressed were real. The chances of a

[5] Chaim Weizmann, *Trial and Error*. London, 1949.
[6] Israel Cohen, *The Zionist Movement*. London, 1945.

permanent Arab-Zionist reconciliation were always extremely slight, but they were inevitably brighter when and if Zionism had some room for maneuver. Gradually it became clear that the separation of Transjordan from Palestine removed this freedom from Zionism and confined it to close limits. Occurring at a time when Arab nationalism was beginning to find a coherent shape in Palestine, the transaction threw Zionism back on itself yet more, making it less and less inclined or able to seek accommodation. As suggested, all this would probably have happened in any case, but the policy of acknowledging the new emirate (a policy to which, it must be remembered, there was no alternative) in the long run increased the probability of strife. This is usually the effect of multiplying frontiers.

Mr. Churchill stayed a week in Jerusalem. He visited the principal cities of Palestine and some of the Jewish agricultural settlements. Arab nationalist propaganda, concentrating more and more on anti-Zionism, was rising to a climax of anger against Great Britain, and when Mr. Churchill visited Jaffa he drove through streets in which houses were shuttered amid other signs of mourning. His reception in the Jewish settlements was by contrast cordial in the extreme. Gossips in Palestine said afterward that this prejudiced him in favor of the Jews and against the Arabs, but there was no particle of truth in this. The final results of the Cairo conference so far as Palestine was concerned, were equally distressing to Arabs and Zionists. The task of reaching a workable, harmonious, and permanent settlement in post-Balfour Palestine proved to be beyond Winston Churchill, as it was beyond the power of every person who attempted it by peaceful means.

One very significant event marked Mr. Churchill's visit. An Arab delegation came to see him in the name of the Moslem-Christian Association which claimed to represent the whole Arabic-speaking community, the vast majority of the inhabitants. The Association had grown out of a "National Congress" of Palestinian Arabs which had first met in 1919. Its leader was Musa Kazim Pasha el Husseini, a relative of the Mufti who had been governor of Jaffa under the Ottoman Empire, and mayor of Jerusalem in the days of O.E.T.A. He had resigned his last appointment as a protest against the adoption of Hebrew as an official language. He was a respected man with a decent record of public service. Like most Arab political leaders in Syria and Palestine, he knew something of administration from Ottoman experience, but had the feeblest understanding of political negotiation. He was implacably anti-Zionist. Musa Kazim and his fellow delegates had a strong hand against the British government, but they played their cards with the greatest ineptitude. Nevertheless here, three and a half years after the Balfour Declaration, was a representative delegation of Palestinian Arabs, and this was something new. The British government were more used to Zionist delegations.

When they waited on Mr. Churchill in Jerusalem, the Moslem-Christian Associates immediately overplayed their hand. They asked him to rescind the Balfour Declaration, to command total cessation of Jewish immigration and to agree to the appointment of a national government answerable to a popularly elected parliament. "You ask me," replied Mr. Churchill, "to repudiate the Balfour Declaration and to stop immigration. This is not in my power, and it is not my wish." He went on to enlarge on the right of the Jews to a national center within their ancient homeland. He then directed the attention of his visitors to the second part of the Balfour Declaration, and there is no more lucid expression of the policy of equal obligation than in what Mr. Churchill said of "the sacredness of Arab civil and religious rights." "I am sorry," he told the delegation "that you regard the second part as valueless. It is vital to you and you should hold and claim it firmly. If one promise stands so does the other. We shall faithfully fulfill both. Examine Mr. Balfour's careful words, Palestine to be 'a national home' not 'the national home,' a great difference in meaning. The establishment of a national home does not mean a Jewish Government to dominate the Arabs."

As regards the plea of the delegation for a Palestinian government and parliament Mr. Churchill spoke his mind openly and, in the opinion of some, with recklessness. "The present form of Government," he said, "will continue for many years. Step by step we shall develop representative institutions leading to full self-government, but our children's children will have passed away before that is accomplished." The prospect of waiting for independence till some time in the middle years of the twenty-first century depressed the delegation and confirmed them in that persistent Arab belief that Zionism was part of a subtle strategem to keep Syria and Palestine permanently enslaved by her new overlords. They planned to go to London and Geneva later in the year and to resist to the uttermost.

A month after Mr. Churchill had sailed home there was another outbreak of violence and communal strife. It was a far more terrible, significant, and bloody occurrence than the Easter riot of the year before. It does not seem to have been premeditated, nor to have had any close connection with the Colonial Secretary's visit, but to have been the sudden outcome of many months of brooding and fear. Two factors had greatly heightened anti-Zionism. First, although the officially agreed figure for Jewish immigration was large, some Zionists had been guilty of organizing illegal immigration, mostly of people with the sort of political records which would have stood them in bad stead with the British authorities. Their numbers were, of course, greatly exaggerated by apprehensive Arabs. Secondly, as the agitation against Zionism grew, the Jews, not unnaturally, began to organize their defense. This involved some arms-smuggling, and again the statistics were wildly exaggerated. Throughout, and regardless of danger, the members of the Zionist Commission persisted in their habitual indiscretion.

The disaster was set off by a quarrel in which Arabs had no part. There was a small and energetic Communist party among the Jewish immigrants, known in Hebrew as *Mitlagat Poalim Sozialistim* and usually referred to as Mopsi. It was believed that Mopsi took orders from Trotsky in the course of personal visits by its leaders to Moscow. The group was passionately resented by the majority of Zionists, and notably by the moderate Socialist party known as *Achduth Avodah* meaning Unity of Work. On the first of May, 1921, the moderates held a traditional May Day procession in Tel Aviv. Mopsi held a rival celebration and the two parties came into collision near the seashore by the outskirts of Jaffa. It is possible that Arabs saw in this all-Jewish riot (in which there were no casualties) the beginning of an attack on themselves. At all events some desperadoes flew to arms, and their first assault on the Jews was the most horrible; they went to a Zionist hostel for immigrants in Jaffa and murdered the unfortunate people living there awaiting settlement, twelve men and a woman.

The rising spread from Jaffa and although troops were hurried to the scene and martial law declared on the 2nd of May, a state of disorder continued for the best part of a week. Settlements were attacked and the defending Jews were grateful for their illicit arms and training. In one or two cases they "anticipated situations" by attack, but throughout the Arabs were the main aggressors. There were 314 casualties, 48 Arabs and 47 Jews killed, with 73 Arabs and 146 Jews wounded. As always, to those living amid the turmoil and the "thousand deaths" of imagination surrounding such horrors, the slaughter and destruction seemed even more ghastly than it was.

By the scale of what was to come when the twentieth century had found its second wind, the disorders of 1921 were not memorable. Their lasting importance lay in what followed from them.

A commission of inquiry was assembled and sat under the chairmanship of Sir Thomas Haycraft, Chief Justice of Palestine, to examine the event and its origins. Before the commission was well into its task Sir

Herbert Samuel took an initiative which cost him much of his former popularity with the Jews. He suspended Jewish immigration, and, to quote a contemporary witness, "The High Commissioner certainly lost the confidence of the Zionists for the time being. The idea was even canvassed of making representations to the Colonial Office to get him recalled there and then." [7] It seemed a most harsh action to penalize in this way the victims of so hideous an outrage as these May riots. But Sir Herbert Samuel was not acting through timidity, as his critics said now, as they had said before, and were to say again, but in accordance with a long-term plan. It seems that both he and the Colonial Secretary believed that they could contain Zionism within moderate limits for long enough for the Arabs to forget their apprehensions, after which the National Home could grow naturally and in peace. They both found themselves in opposition to the ever-indiscreet Zionist Commission. They were following, as they were bound to follow, a policy that was exactly similar in aim to that of the military regime, but they followed it in a very different spirit. Churchill and Samuel were devoted to Zionism; they both had the courage of their convictions, and they were both experienced politicians who would never tolerate such a stratagem of fatuousness as that of O.E.T.A. in attempting to conceal the Balfour Declaration. They acted in the open. A cardinal principle of Sir Herbert Samuel's policy (for he influenced as much as he obeyed the government) was that the natural wrath of the Palestinian Arabs must be appeased. The events of May, 1921, did not weaken but confirmed him in this resolve.

On June 3rd, the king's birthday, and only a month after the disorders, the High Commissioner took the occasion of an official reception to make a definitive statement of policy. He reviewed the state of Palestine and the intentions of the government in some detail. He said as follows about the Zionist interest:

> I am distressed that the harmony between the creeds and races of Palestine, which I have desired most earnestly to promote, has not yet been attained . . . Let me in the first instance refer to the unhappy misunderstanding that has existed with reference to the phrase in the Balfour Declaration "the establishment in Palestine of a National Home for the Jewish people." I hear it said in many quarters, that the Arab people will not agree to their country, their Holy Places, their lands being taken from them and given to strangers; that they will never agree to a Jewish Government being set up to rule the Moslem and Christian majority. People say that they cannot understand how it is that the British Gov-

[7] Horace Samuel, *Unholy Memories of the Holy Land.* London, 1930.

ernment, which is famous throughout the world for its justice, could ever have consented to such a policy. I answer that the British Government, which does indeed care for justice above all things, has never consented and never will consent to such a policy. That is not the meaning of the Balfour Declaration. It may be that the translation of the English words into Arabic does not convey their real sense. They mean that the Jews, a people that are scattered throughout the world but whose hearts are always turned to Palestine, should be enabled to found here their home, and that some among them, within the limits that are fixed by the numbers and interests of the present population, should come to Palestine in order to help by their resources and efforts to develop the country, to the advantage of all the inhabitants. If any measures are needed to convince the Moslem and Christian population that these principles will be observed in practice and that their rights are really safe, such measures will be taken. For the British Government, the trustee under the Mandate for the happiness of the people of Palestine, would never impose upon them a policy which the people had reason to think was contrary to their religion, their political and their economic interests.

He went on to the question of Jewish immigration, and announced what the character of the forthcoming regulations would be. Travelers on a visit of three months or less, people of independent means, members of professions intending to practice in the country, families and dependents of residents, people with a definite prospect of employment, all might enter Palestine, "but," added Sir Herbert, "the conditions of Palestine are such as do not permit anything in the nature of a mass immigration." (When these regulations came into force, they were to be interpreted with much liberality.) From the immigration question Sir Herbert turned to the threat of communism as embodied in Mopsi. A small number of "new arrivals," he said, "are tainted with the pernicious doctrines of Bolshevism which carry with them the economic ruin of all classes in any country that they enter." He promised the suppression of Mopsi. He referred to the Haycraft Commission which had not yet presented its findings, and in a concluding section of his statement he said he hoped that representative government would soon be established in Palestine.

The speech was ill received by Zionists both in Palestine and in the Head Office in London, indeed perhaps worse in London where the Zionists seem to have been going through a phase of indignation exceeding that of their representatives. In the last days of May, Samuel Landman, the secretary of the Zionist organization in London, had been in conflict with his opposite number in Palestine, Dr. Eder, Landman maintaining that the

Zionist Commission had shown weakness in accepting the suspension of Jewish immigration, an accusation which Eder angrily repudiated.[8]

The Zionists had three strong objections to Samuel's statement. The first was that it implied that the blame for the atrocities lay with Mopsi rather than with Arab agitators, and although within Zionism Mopsi was bitterly resented, the Jews felt, with much justice, that in the eyes of Palestinians Samuel's interpretation of events placed unfair blame on Zionism in general. The second objection, though not so described, was to the policy of "equality of obligation" of which the statement was an eloquent expression. In the words of Sir Herbert Samuel, Zionists believed that the assurance given to the Arabs "precludes, or at any rate postpones to an almost indefinite date, the full realisation of their ideals."[9] Their third objection was on very difficult ground. Zionism had from the first been one of the most democratic of political movements, making its appeal to the mass, to the unprivileged, to those who looked for a better way of life, both spiritually and materially. Such a movement, especially when developing under the British auspices it had so eagerly sought, was inevitably committed to parliamentarianism. But in the present state of things in Palestine representative government of any kind was the last thing Zionists wanted, for they saw an elected assembly keeping them in a permanent state of insignificant minority and smothering the growing National Home by means of respectable procedure. It was a realistic objection but one very difficult to make in the open. In the end, however, the Zionists, with exemplary courage, accepted the proposal, and, as appears later, their fears were laid to rest by the imbecility of their opponents.

Sir Herbert Samuel, for all his buoyant optimism, had no delusions about the effect of his speech. In his report to the Colonial Office in the same month he noted that it had aroused the hostility of the most typical and the most influential Zionists, and that only a minority of Orthodox Jews and older settlers grasped that the moderate and gradualist policy of the British government provided the only way to build the National Home on sound foundations. He put his hope in the older generation of Jewish pioneers who were on good terms with the Arabs and who, he said, might yet afford a bridge between the old and new inhabitants leading to a peaceful establishment of Zionism. His words have the ring of facile optimism today, but if the history of Europe in the next twenty-five years had been less repulsive, what he hoped for might have come about.

Sir Herbert Samuel went on to consider the reactions of the Arabs, both

[8] Zionist Archives. Jerusalem.
[9] Sir Herbert Samuel to Mr. Churchill, June 13th, 1921. Israel State Archives.

Christian and Moslem. They still demanded the reversal of the Balfour Declaration, but there was less extreme opinion among them than among the Jews. The moderates had welcomed the statement, though regretting that its terms had not been "more far-reaching and specific." They regarded the concessions to Arab demands as a "first installment" and hoped that the delegation would obtain more in London. Sir Herbert noted the most significant thing to emerge from the May riots, and that was that the mob had developed an "interest in public affairs" and a race consciousness not discernible before. This was the first time that the people of Jaffa had been led in such numbers and to such excesses by agitators and from this he foresaw the probability of much trouble in the future; the ordinary populace were discovering their power to resist.

He made an interesting remark about the Moslem clergy. "There has as yet," he wrote, "been no clear indication of the attitude of the Turbaned class—the Moslem religious leaders—towards the present political agitators." Though they might be content with the role of spectator for the moment, they would not remain in this neutral state for long and "may be relied on to appeal to a quarter where the tongue is the weapon and fanaticism the impulse." Haj Amin was playing a waiting game.

Sir Herbert concluded that no matter what the difficulties the attempt to reconcile Arabs and Zionists must be persisted in. "The only alternative is a policy of coercion which is strong in principle and likely to prove unsuccessful in practice." He regarded the visit of the Moslem-Christian delegation to London as an opportunity for the government to achieve reconciliation, since the members were not extremist. But he also warned as follows: "There is always the danger that this delegation like others may be repudiated by those who sent it, and any result which it may bring with it on its return may be rejected as unacceptable." [10]

In those words Sir Herbert indicated the main and fatal predicament of the territory he administered. Moderation in nationalism is only practiced, and perhaps only can be practiced, by people who have experienced independence for a long time. New nationalism is always extreme. In Palestine the nationalism of the Arabic-speaking inhabitants was so new that many still doubted its existence, but already its ruling force was fanatic.

[10] Sir Herbert Samuel to Mr. Churchill, June 13th, 1921. Israel State Archives.

4 THE HARVEST OF 1921

On the 14th of June, 1921, Mr. Churchill addressed the House of Commons and informed Parliament of the arrangements he had concluded and the intentions of the government in the Middle East. It is a curious fact that this is the only official account of the Cairo conference to have been made public. The reason (apart from the distressing British passion for secrecy) is not, so far as can be seen, that shameful conspiracies were laid in Cairo, but rather that amid the fearful preoccupations of the postwar years the importance of this meeting was not noticed. The British press made no comment of any interest, and those who had taken part in the conference seem, without exception, to have underestimated what they had done. It figures hardly at all in any memoir. It is the occasion for a gap in the letters of both Gertrude Bell and T. E. Lawrence. Sir Winston Churchill has little to say about it in his writings, and he seems to have gone to Cairo in something of a holiday mood. His juniors complained that he would delay briefing himself with important papers while he concentrated on the more congenial task of writing *The World Crisis,* and they criticized him for setting apart so much time for painting Egyptian and Palestinian landscapes. The occasion at one meeting when Lawrence made a facetious remark and was reduced to blushing silence by Gertude Bell's rapping out "You little imp!" is almost the only anecdote from the day-to-day meetings to be remembered. The conference did not skimp its work, nor was it guilty of unthinking decisions. For all their imperfections its achievements were roughly the best that an imperfect situation allowed, and the holiday mood can even suggest that men sometimes do well when they are not conscious of five thousand years of history looking down on them. But it is true nonetheless that this underestimate of Winston Churchill's remarkable initiative, not least by himself, helped on a general and dangerous tendency in government circles to regard the Palestine issue as minor.

In the light of subsequent history Winston Churchill's statement to Parliament was candid and showed full awareness of where difficulty and danger lay. Only his remarks on Palestine need be remembered here. He owned in his introduction that British undertakings were in conflict, and when, after describing the Iraq situation, he turned to this subject again, he said that "the cause of unrest in Palestine, and the only cause, arises from the Zionist movement and from our promises and pledges to it." In a later passage he said: "The difficulty about this promise of a National Home for the Jews in Palestine is that it conflicts with our regular policy of consulting the wishes of the people in the Mandated territories and of giving them representative institutions as soon as they are fitted for them, which institutions, in this case, they would use in order to veto any further Jewish immigration."

He described the tenseness of the political situation in Palestine as being more due to Arab nerves than to any real threat of overwhelming Jewish immigration, and he emphasized in passing that Arab standards of living tended to rise in the vicinity of Jewish settlements. "There really is nothing," he said, "for the Arabs to be frightened about." He then turned to Transjordan affairs, making no comment on the effect of the new settlement on Zionism. "We had recourse," said Mr. Churchill, "to the good offices of the Emir Abdullah . . ."

The debate which followed brought out for the first time clear expression of the supposed strategical value to Britain of a Palestine base. Josiah Wedgwood stressed the injustice of accusing the Jews of involving Britain in expenses which would in any case be incurred by the necessity of maintaining a British garrison there to guard the Suez Canal. In a speech following him Lord Robert Cecil asserted strenuously and in vain that the Balfour Declaration had been issued with no such motives in mind. He was not believed. One of the last and most interesting speeches in the debate was contributed by Commander Kenworthy. He pointed out that Great Britain in the flush of victory was presented with the temptation of excessive power and should resist it. "By garrisoning these nations in Asia," he said, "we run the risk of going the way of the Roman Empire and other Empires which have died by super-Imperialism." But he only applied these remarks to the subject of Iraq. When he came to speak of Palestine he confessed to an ardent admiration for Zionism and applauded, in similar terms to those of Josiah Wedgwood, the strategical value of a British military base for which Zionism opened an opportunity.

The debate showed one thing clearly: that all parties accepted the Balfour Declaration as binding on future British policy. The Declaration had been purposely vague, but now three and one-half years later in 1921, with Winston Churchill as the responsible minister attempting a final definition, there was a chance, not to come again, to issue a second governmental declaration of the same gravity, expressing the promise in precise terms, again with all-party agreement, again accepted as binding on all parties. Such an act of state was not impossible while Lloyd George as Prime Minister still enjoyed the prestige of a victorious national leader and Arthur Balfour still held office. The opportunity was missed for various reasons of which the most important perhaps was that arrogant British mood of carelessness, that overconfident conviction, shown more than most by Balfour in the onset of old age, that Britain and her Empire had nothing much to be alarmed about in a problem involving small populations in a small area.

Dr. Weizmann was in London at this moment and, a month after the debate in June, he had an interview with the Prime Minister, Balfour, and others. He left a record which, even if allowance is made for some unconscious misreporting in his favor, is telling evidence of an extraordinary unseriousness in the approach to this matter of the leading British ministers (Winston Churchill possibly to be excepted). The document was first published in Colonel Richard Meinertzhagen's *Middle East Diary 1917–1956*. As an ingredient of that remarkable book it attracted little attention, as it was but one incredible item among many, not the least extraordinary being an emergent self-portrait of the author as a Zionist extremist who recommended the adoption of anti-Jewish laws in England among other singular discords of will and temperament. Surrounded by the self-revelation of *Middle East Diary* Weizmann's record of his meeting could hardly make the impact that it was entitled to, and reviewers may have suspected the Colonel of touching up the original to harmonize with the rest. But the record as published is perfectly genuine and is to be consulted in the Israel State Archives. Though some of it is beside the immediate point, the document is worth quoting in full:

Notes on conversation at Mr. Balfour's house on July 22nd, 1921.

Present: Mr. Lloyd George, Mr. A. J. Balfour, Mr. Winston Churchill, Sir Maurice Hankey, Mr. Edward Russell, Dr. Weizmann.

Dr. W reported on his visit to America, explained the situation there —Zionist, Jewish and General—and delivered message to British Government entrusted to him by Sir A. Geddes—LG very interested.

Dr. W further explained the fight with the Anglo-Zionist Organisation at the results of which LG expressed great satisfaction and said: "it is very creditable to you."

AJB: "You ought to tell the P.M. the position of Zionism at present."

Dr. W replied that while he was away in America "building up," the whole position became vitiated by the developments of the situation in Palestine, e.g. Samuel's speech which was a negation of the Balfour Declaration.

WC (interrupting): "Why?"

Dr. W produced speech and read it, showing difference between it and the Declaration. The Declaration meant an ultimate Jewish majority— and this speech would never permit such a majority to eventuate.

WC demurred at this interpretation of the speech.

LG and AJB both said that by the Declaration they always meant an eventual Jewish State.

Dr. W continuing on position of Zionism, stoppage of emigration, non-granting of necessary concessions for development, lack of security for Jewish population, apropos of which he said—"We were gun-running and I can't allow it."

WC (interrupting): "We won't mind it, but don't speak of it."

Dr. W: "I would like it sanctioned. Is it agreed?"

They all agreed to this.

WC took official view of the Administration showing the difficult situation that had arisen owing to the B. Declaration which was opposed by the Arabs, nine-tenths of the British officials on the spot, and some of the Jews in Palestine. He said it was a poor country in which destitute emigrants could not be dumped.

Dr. W refuted this and spoke of "representative Government Project."

WC quoted Mesopotamia and Transjordania, to which Dr. W replied: "You will not convince me that self-government has been given to these two lands because you think it right, it has only been done because you must," to which LG, AJB, and WC all agreed.

Dr. W: "If you do the same thing with Palestine it means giving up Palestine—and that is what I want to know."

LG to WC: "You mustn't give representative Government to Palestine."

WC: "I might have to bring it before the Cabinet." Of course questions affecting the National Home would be eliminated from the purview of the representative Government.

Dr. W said this was impossible, and after a general refutation of arguments used, the talk became general for a while.

Then WC spoke of the Arab delegation and felt sure that a *modus operandi* could be worked out with them for the next three years.

Dr. W doubted this, he regarded the Arabs as political blackmailers and could only talk with them when he knew the position of the British Government.

LG: "Frankly speaking, you want to know whether we are going to keep our pledges?"

Dr. W: "Yes." AJB nodded.

LG: "You must do a lot of propaganda. Samuel is rather weak."

Dr. W: "The irony of the situation is that we are charged with being a burden on the British taxpayer which is nonsense," and he pointed out why, to which LG and AJB agreed but not WC.

Dr. W pointed out the absurdity of the charge that we were taking the bread of the Arabs—LG laughed and asked how much money we had spent, and he was impressed by Dr. W's answer. Further, Dr. W explained how difficult it was and how much this money represented for Zionists in present situation and insisted that everything depended on them having confidence.

WC: "Well, what would satisfy you in the way of immigration?"

Dr. W: "I can't formulate it in numbers, but in conditions, e.g. The granting of the large Rutenberg concession"[1]—he agreed to the severance of the Palestinian army from H.Q. in Egypt—he looked upon the formulation of a neutral police as a very good idea.

LG at the end of the conversation said that a part of the money should be set aside for the purpose of bribing the Arabs.

Dr. W said that this was neither moral nor rational and the price is very heavy. It is easy to work with the Arab Nationalist leaders "on your backs, but that we won't do." Now the presence of the British makes it difficult to enter into intimate relations with the Arabs.

[1] See pp. 87 ff.

All felt as the Arab delegation was coming a practical way out must be found.

LG to AJB: "You ought to make a big speech again in the Albert Hall on Zionism."

AJB: "I will do it with pleasure."

WC then left.

AJB accompanied LG to his car talking over affairs and on his return said: "It was a very satisfactory conversation and action will follow. You must write out your desiderata."

Dr. W: "You have the document" to which AJB said he had read it and it seemed all could be accepted and some had already been agreed upon. Then he added "It is all right, the P.M. is very keen on the affair, has a high regard for you, and understands your difficult position." [2]

The Arab delegation arrived in London in August. In September they went to Geneva where after conducting a long siege they succeeded in meeting Arthur Balfour, who spoke to them with graceful and studied vagueness of the "experiment" of Zionism. It was their only meeting with him.[3] They returned to London in the autumn. As at their first encounter with Mr. Churchill in Jerusalem they persisted in demanding that the Balfour Declaration be annulled. This was understandable enough, but unfortunately for them, the delegation, with their feeble understanding of the art of political maneuver, made annulment a condition of any acceptance of any feature of the mandate. They took up their permanent stand on a policy of boycotting. Throughout the negotiations which lasted for a little less than a year they refused to meet Weizmann or any of his party officials on the grounds that as nationals of Palestine they would not appear as suppliants before alien immigrants. The effect of this line of conduct was not at all disadvantageous to the Zionists, for it relieved them of the very awkward predicament into which an official discussion of the second clause of the Balfour Declaration would have placed them: the Jews were not forced into defining to Arabs what they understood by "the civil and religious rights of the existing non-Jewish communities."

In February of 1922 Mr. Churchill set before both parties, Jewish and Arab, official proposals for a legislative council in accordance with the High Commissioner's promise. There had been (as noted) much Zionist objection, shared by British ministers, to any form of representative government in Palestine, and it may be taken as certain that if any attempts were made to go back on the declared promise they were thwarted by Sir

[2] It is to be noted that Transjordan was not mentioned at this meeting.

[3] J. M. N. Jeffries, *Palestine the Reality*. London, 1939.

Herbert Samuel. In spite of Lloyd George's counsel, "You mustn't give representative Government to Palestine," Winston Churchill offered it, and indeed pressed it on both parties. The proposals were for an enlargement and democratization of the existing Advisory Council. The latter contained seven Arab, three Jewish, and ten official members, all appointed by the High Commissioner; the new Legislative Council was to be composed of nine Moslem Arab, three Christian Arab, three Jewish and eleven official members, all, except the officials, being chosen by election. Given the prevalence of anti-Zionism among British officials the composition of this proposed chamber was indeed a matter for Jewish fears. But the Arabs feared more. They only saw danger in this offer because it made provision for Jewish membership. With pathetic obstinacy they clung to their negative policy unaware of its far greater dangers to them. In the course of correspondence with the Colonial Office they declared that they would only cooperate in the working of a constitution which not only revoked the Balfour Declaration but was opposed to alien immigration of any description, and by persisting in this course they wrecked ultimately any hope for some form of Palestine government in which they would have some say.[4] The fault was not entirely theirs. Within the Conservative party an anti-Zionist group was forming, and it has been stated, on the authority of Lord Samuel, that the Arab delegation were encouraged by some members of Parliament to pursue their boycott.[5] Only if they did so, it was argued, would a future Conservative government be enabled to revoke the pledge to Zionism. The Arabs followed the advice.

The Arab case was strong, but bad handling quickly weakened it. After rejecting the proposal for a Legislative Council the delegation asked that their extreme demands should be met "in accordance with the spirit of Article 22 of the Covenant," forgetting that by their refusal of a substantial measure of democracy they had so affronted "the spirit of Article 22" as to remove it appreciably from the discussion. They appealed also to Article 20, which asserted that international arrangements made prior to the Covenant lost validity if they were in contradiction to Covenant undertakings. They claimed that the Balfour Declaration was in this class. Feisal's conduct at the Peace Conference could have been cited by the British government to dispose of this argument but never seems to have been referred to. The political ineptitude of the Arab delegation was infectious.

[4] Command Paper (a British Government publication, hereafter abbreviated as Cmd.) 1700.
[5] Marlowe, *op. cit.*

During the last stage of the negotiation the Arabs moved the argument to the MacMahon correspondence, and here they were undoubtedly on extremely firm ground, or would have been if they had known how to exploit it. As mentioned already, Palestine had not been referred to anywhere in the course of those letters and was noticeably absent from the most important item in the correspondence. This was a letter sent by MacMahon to Sherif Hussein on the 24th of October, 1915, in which he defined the area where, to quote his words, "Great Britain is prepared to recognise and support the independence of the Arabs." The area had evidently been worked out with care, and anyone reading (or writing) MacMahon's definition could not suppose otherwise than that Palestine was part of it. But it was now the endeavor of the Colonial Office to prove that unmentioned Palestine had in fact not been included but definitely excluded from the area in which Arab independence was to be assured. It was quite true that a neighboring area (chiefly represented today by modern Lebanon) had been excluded in this very letter of October 24th. The excluded territory had been described in these words: "The districts (*wilaya*) of Messina and Alexandretta and portions of Syria lying to the West of the districts of Damascus, Homs, Hama and Aleppo." By no stretch of the imagination do "portions of Syria" so described include Palestine which lies not to the west of Damascus but to the south, a matter not open to dispute! Sir Henry MacMahon then and later maintained that when conducting the correspondence Palestine was always excluded in his mind, but "since he omitted to mention the fact" to Sherif Hussein this argument can have no force. It was not used at the time. Instead, in the course of correspondence with the Arab delegation, Mr. Churchill stated: "This promise to recognise the independence of the Arabs was given subject to a reservation made in the same letter, which excluded from its scope the country lying to the West of the Vilayet of Damascus." [6]

Even the incompetent Arab delegation had no difficulty in giving a conclusive reply to this odd statement. They pointed out that the original document made no mention of any vilayet (an Arab word related to *"wilaya"* denoting a province or major administrative division), and further that there was no such thing, and never had been such a thing as a "Vilayet of Damascus." There had been a Turkish vilayet of Syria of which Damascus was the capital, and it was a truly odd notion, and ascribed to Sir Henry MacMahon an improbable degree of ignorance or incapacity to suppose that he endeavored to indicate the vilayet to his correspondent by the term "district (*wilaya*) of Damascus." It would be

[6] Jeffries, *op. cit.* The letter was suppressed in The White Paper.

as sensible to describe the County of Northumberland as the district of Newcastle, or the State of Maryland as the Baltimore countryside.

The Colonial Office courteously accepted the correction and redrafted the passage as follows in the final statement of policy issued in a government White Paper of the 30th of June, 1922:

> It is not the case, as has been represented by the Arab Delegation, that during the War His Majesty's Government gave an undertaking that an independent national government was to be at once established in Palestine. This representation mainly rests upon a letter, dated the 24th of October, 1915, from Sir Henry MacMahon, then His Majesty's High Commissioner in Egypt, to the Shereef of Mecca, now King Hussein of the Hedjaz. That letter is quoted as conveying a promise to the Shereef of Mecca to recognize and support the independence of the Arabs within the territories proposed by him. But this promise was given subject to a reservation made in the same letter, which excluded from its scope, among other territories, the portions of Syria lying to the West of the district of Damascus. This reservation has always been regarded by His Majesty's Government as covering the Vilayet of Beyrout and the independent Sanjak of Jerusalem. The whole of Palestine was thus excluded from Sir Henry MacMahon's pledge.

The MacMahon correspondence was not only unpublished in those days, but its very existence was unknown except to a few in the Foreign and Colonial offices. The Arab delegation did not think (as Zionists would have done in the same situation) of giving the letters to the press for publication. Incomplete quotation gave the general reader a confusing idea of their subject, and the brief controversy over the "Vilayet of Damascus" was artfully complicated by its presentation in the White Paper: only the Arab side of the exchange was fully published with the result that it was difficult for an uninformed person to make out just what the argument was about. All this talk of sanjaks and so on struck the majority of the reading public as obscure and picturesque, as a matter for orientalists; and so an absolutely indefensible interpretation of MacMahon's key letter passed without challenge and became the basis of the British claim to conduct the mandate in a fashion to allow for the growth of Zionism.

Fourteen years later the Peel Commission, the ablest royal commission to inquire into the affairs of Palestine at any time, felt obliged by precedent to treat these sophisms of 1922 as Britain's title to her position. The Jews, as might be expected, seized the unexpected advantage which the Colonial Office gave them by this interpretation, and from that time to the present the passage quoted above from the White Paper of 1922 has been used extensively in Zionist propaganda.[7] Such political action by the Jews was only human, but it was also short-sighted. By accepting the advantage uncritically they accepted a humiliating position: that of people whose station in life was based on a piece of sharp practice. The propaganda which they made out of the fallacious arguments of the White Paper could only be effective with people who were ignorant or already converted to their cause. The people whom they needed to convert and never did in sufficient numbers were the ordinary personnel of the administration in Palestine.

For the British, the Colonial Office's dubious action in 1922 had subtle psychological consequences, so far as Palestine was concerned. With the British right to rule as they saw fit established on such feeble grounds, with British men and women in the country continually surrounded by wailing Arabs complaining that they had been betrayed, and with no convincing argument to put against these complaints, more and more British people found their self-confidence, and with it any sense of dedicated service in this historic land slowly, unconsciously, and unmistakably ebbing away. There was always a minority who felt otherwise but they became a small minority. With the majority there came in the place of confidence a feeling that, as Arabs maintained, Britain had established herself in Palestine by clever swindling, and it may be said with certainty that Arab propaganda, so inept in the outside world, was very effective with Englishmen in Palestine service. Very few believed that they were there for honorable reasons, and the growth of cynicism spread far. The process was slow but little interrupted.

Why the advisers of Winston Churchill led him into this course is unknown. The matter remains very puzzling. When people defend their actions by the falsification of documents (as this amounted to) they usually do so because they are helpless in a desperate situation. But the most extraordinary fact of the attempted and bungled settlement of 1922 is that the British government had all the authority they needed if they wished to show that MacMahon's correspondence with the Sherif was not the last word on the future of Palestine.

It was then that the accord on Zionism with the Arab leadership needed

[7] Even Mr. Leonard Stein forgets his historian's impartiality when writing on this subject: ". . . while, on a minute examination of the language used by MacMahon . . . a case can be made out for the view that Palestine was not unambiguously excluded, it is a purely verbal case, unrelated to the substance of the matter and devoid of merits." *The Balfour Declaration*, London, 1961.

to be made public. There were perhaps acceptable reasons why Feisal's agreements and concessions were best not remembered while he was being provided by the British government with a second empire, but no such argument applied to the concessions conveyed to Hogarth by King Hussein. Recourse to Hogarth's testimony could furnish an invincible case, for if the king's concessions to Zionism were rejected on the grounds that they had been made by one not competent to speak for the people of Palestine, Hussein's original acceptance of pledges from MacMahon could be dismissed as invalid for the same reason. But the advantage was neglected. The explanation may lie in the fact that Winston Churchill took too much advice from T. E. Lawrence who was opinionated and imperfectly informed. Richard Meinertzhagen recorded of this time: "I was much struck by the attitude of Winston towards Lawrence, which almost amounted to hero-worship." Hogarth himself had retired to Oxford and the Ashmolean Museum and seems never to have been consulted or to have asked to be consulted. He had lost interest, and the record of his interview with Hussein appears in no published State papers between 1918 and 1939. It is always possible that that abnormal love of official Britain for secrecy for its own sake, even when (as with the Casement diaries) secrecy costs the good name of the British people, can account for everything here, but the most likely explanation of why the government preferred a fallacious and tortured argument to a piece of direct and useful evidence is that it had simply been forgotten that Hogarth and Hussein had ever had an interview at all.

The White Paper of 1922 was intended as the expression of a definitive Palestine settlement. It gave Zionism much of what it had asked for. Yet it was almost as unwelcome to the Jews as to the Arabs. The crucial passage of the White Paper, so far as Jewish interests were concerned, ran as follows:

> When it is asked what is meant by the development of the Jewish National Home in Palestine, it may be answered that it is not the imposition of a Jewish nationality upon the inhabitants of Palestine as a whole, but the further development of the existing Jewish community with the assistance of Jews in other parts of the world, in order that it may become a centre in which the Jewish people as a whole may take, on grounds of religion and race, an interest and a pride. But in order that this community should have the best prospect of free development and provide a full opportunity for the Jewish people to display its capacities, it is essential

that it should know that it is in Palestine as of right and not on sufferance.

According to the then Attorney General of Palestine, the statement was drafted by Sir Herbert Samuel. Even to this day there are Zionists who regard him as a renegade for having done so, for having conceded so much to Arab nationalism, to the enemy whom they could not acknowledge as one. This was the first time that the Zionists had to face the consequences of their reckless use of propaganda, for there was nothing in this statement which had not been said many times by their own spokesmen. It was not what they wanted and was at the same time extremely difficult to dissent from.

In moments of crisis the complexity of Dr. Weizmann's character became apparent. The detachment of the scientist which enabled him to take far-sighted views of the needs of his people never made him other than an intensely emotional man who was often at the mercy of his feelings. No man loved England more for her inherent and generous liberal spirit, and at moments of dissatisfaction no man said harder things of British double-facedness and perfidy. Without his leadership Zionism might have completely missed its unique opportunity in the First World War, and yet one can think of few leaders who played more dangerously with the often fatal expedient of resignation. To his mind the three-sided negotiations of 1921 and 1922 were disastrous to his cause, and at this time he came to share that state of panic for the future which was a frequent condition with the Zionist leadership. His consistent belief was that Zionism would and only could reach its natural fulfillment (and in the twentieth century that fulfillment could only be statehood) as a natural part of the process and development of events. But once aim and fulfillment were closely defined (as they had not been in his agreements with Feisal), then events were constricted and denied development; under such circumstances Zionism could be condemned to a perpetually minor role. Engulfed in emotion he saw the British aim of a moderate settlement not as an expression of that liberal spirit which he so admired but as a reflection of what he felt to be the High Commissioner's surrender to the anti-Zionism of his subordinates.

Considering his pertinacity in negotiation and the toughness that such pertinacity needs, Weizmann was a surprisingly touchy man. He was an easy prey to despair. Shortly after his meeting with Lloyd George, Balfour, and Winston Churchill he was urged by both Samuel [8] and Wyndham

[8] Israel State Archives.

Deedes, in the course of correspondence, not to come to Palestine while the government was negotiating in London with the Arab delegation. This advice hurt him bitterly. It seems to have convinced him that British policy was now intent on an anti-Zionist course and at this crucial moment in Zionist fortunes he planned to resign the leadership. He was only dissuaded from doing so by a letter from the mother of Wyndham Deedes.[9] It was as well for Zionism that he allowed himself to be influenced by her for the opposition to Zionism within the Conservative party was gathering strength and had obtained valuable support outside.

In June of 1922 it found expression in a motion introduced by the liberal statesman Lord Islington in the House of Lords. It ran:

> The Mandate for Palestine in its present form is unacceptable to this House because it directly violates the pledges made by His Majesty's Government to the people of Palestine in the Declaration of October 1915, and again in the Declaration of November 1918, and is, as at present framed, opposed to the sentiments and wishes of the great majority of the people of Palestine; that therefore its acceptance by the Council of the League of Nations should be postponed until such modifications have therein been effected as will comply with the pledges given by His Majesty's Government.

Lord Islington's speech was the most able performance of the debate. What he said about the injustice of an act of state involving other people, and made with no reference to their feelings and in contradiction to other undertakings, followed a familiar line of argument which need not be repeated here, but it should be noted that he did not strengthen his case with a close analysis of the MacMahon correspondence. As with others, he was only aware of the letter of October, 1915, and not of the correspondence as a whole. The most famous speech of the occasion was made by Arthur Balfour. In it he described his Zionist faith more fully than he did at any other time. It has already been quoted at length in the first chapter of this book. It was his first appearance in the House of Lords and though this speech was one of the most eloquent of Balfour's life it was not successful. It was an appeal to the emotions alone and lacked incisiveness. He produced no evidence and no argument to show that the establishment of Zionism in Palestine was not a violation of pledges made to Arab nationalism, but he took his stand rather on the proposition that to do a great right it was expedient to do a little wrong, though he was careful to put it less crudely. Although Lord Islington was embarrassed by the support of

[9] Zionist Archives, Jerusalem.

Lord Sydenham (who seemed to have recently swallowed the Protocols of the Elders of Zion[10]) he obtained agreement to his motion and the government was defeated in the Upper House by a large majority. The result again threw Dr. Weizmann into a state of the utmost perturbation and he went to seek explanation and advice from Arthur Balfour himself. He found the statesman in his usual state of bland calm. He assured Dr. Weizmann that the event should not be taken seriously. "What does it matter," he said in his languid way, "if a few foolish lords passed such a motion?" [11]

Two weeks later the anti-Zionist Conservatives led by Sir William Joynson Hicks were decisively defeated in the House of Commons. In the meantime the Zionists had made up their minds over the difficult question of whether or not to accept the government's policy in which the most important item was the proposal for a Legislative Council. They recognized that they had in fact no choice and on the 18th of June, 1922, Dr. Weizmann sent a masterly and guarded letter to Mr. Churchill.

> Sir,
>
> With reference to your letter of June 3rd. I have the honour to inform you that the Executive of the Zionist Organisation have considered the statement relative to the policy of His Majesty's Government in Palestine . . . and have passed the following resolution:
> "The Executive of the Zionist Organisation, having taken note of the statement relative to British policy in Palestine, transmitted to them by the Colonial Office under date of June 3rd 1922, assure His Majesty's Government that the activities of the Zionist Organisation will be conducted in conformity with the policy therein set forth."
> The Executive observe with satisfaction that His Majesty's Government, in defining their policy in Palestine, take occasion once more to reaffirm the Declaration of November 2nd 1917, and lay it down as a matter of international concern that the Jewish people should know that it is in Palestine as of right.
> The Executive further observe that His Majesty's Government also acknowledge, as a corollary of this right, that it is necessary that the Jews shall be able to increase their numbers in Palestine by immigration, and understand from the statement of policy that the volume of such immigration is to be determined by the economic capacity of the country from time to time to absorb new arrivals. Whatever arrangements may be made in regard to the regulation of such immigration, the Executive

[10] The Zionist extremists, he said, "seem to have been quite aware that a world war was coming" in 1914.

[11] Weizmann, *Trial and Error*. London, 1949.

confidently trust that both His Majesty's Government and the Administration of Palestine will be guided in this matter by the aforesaid principle.

The Zionist Organisation has at all times been sincerely desirous of
proceeding in harmonious co-operation with all sections of the people of
Palestine. It has repeatedly made it clear both in word and deed that
nothing is further from its purpose than to prejudice in the smallest
degree the civil or religious rights or the material interests of the non-
Jewish population. The Zionist Organisation will continue on its side to
spare no efforts to foster the spirit of goodwill to which His Majesty's
Government have pointed as the only sure foundation for the future
prosperity of Palestine. The Executive earnestly hope that the statement
of policy which His Majesty's Government propose to issue will once and
for all dispel such misapprehensions as may still exist, and that, loyally
accepted by all parties concerned, it may mark the opening of a new era
of peaceful progress.

I have etc.
Chaim Weizmann

On July 6th the White Paper received the approval of Parliament. In
September the Arab delegation returned to Palestine. The Congress which
they represented successfully organized a boycott of the elections to the
Legislative Assembly, and when Sir Herbert Samuel reverted to the nominated Advisory Council the Arabs successfully boycotted that too. As a
last expedient Samuel in 1923 endeavored to establish an Arab Agency as
a counterweight to the Zionist Commission. This proposal was refused by
the Arab leadership with indignation. As a result of their consistently negative policy Palestine till the end of the mandate never obtained representative government even in crude form, and as a natural result could not
avoid the evils of arbitrary rule. The original fault was not with the British or the Jews.

The immediate troubles of the Zionists were not brought to an end by
the approval of the White Paper. They had great dangers before them
still, because the anti-Zionist group in the Conservative party tried to keep
faith with the Arabs whom they had misled. They drew together for a
further attack on the pro-Zionist form of the mandate. They launched it
with care, skill, and sincerity and it is a matter for surprise that they had so
little success.

With the enforced resignation of Lloyd George in October, 1922, with
the disappearance of Winston Churchill from the government, and above
all with the Conservative victory in the general election of that autumn,

the anti-Zionists seemed to be in a strong position. They had obtained a masterful ally in Lord Northcliffe, who had visited Palestine in February, 1922, and was moved by what he saw and heard to take a strong anti-Zionist view; he said that as a result of confused policy "this country runs the risk of becoming a second Ireland." [12] *The Times* and the *Daily Mail*, both under Northcliffe's direction, undertook systematic anti-Zionist propaganda. The most important move in this newspaper campaign was made by Mr. J. M. N. Jeffries, a brilliant correspondent who was sent out to Palestine in the autumn of 1922 in order to gather material for a series of articles in the *Daily Mail*. He served Northcliffe extremely well. He obtained a copy of the Arabic text of the MacMahon correspondence. His articles appeared in the *Daily Mail* during January and February of 1923 and in them he made public a retranslation of the full text of these letters which the government had been at such pains to keep hidden.

Publication came too late for Northcliffe's purpose. If the letters had been made accessible to politicians and the public in the early part of 1922 they would quite certainly have altered the outcome of the Churchill White Paper, probably in an anti-Zionist sense though not necessarily so: by making it impossible for the Middle East Department to indulge in their vilayet fantasies, they might have forced the pro-Zionist argument onto good ground. But whatever might have been the effect of publication then, it was another matter with the long and tedious negotiations at last terminated, the White Paper accepted, and public interest elsewhere. (The French had entered the Ruhr.) The effect was also weakened by the manner in which the letters were presented. Jeffries' articles, for all their brilliance, were too long, too elaborate, and too intemperate, drawing no distinction between the Jewish moderates and extremists, trying to make a bogeyman out of Mr. Norman Bentwick (a hopeless task), and launching into absurd accusations that Winston Churchill had embezzled public money at the Cairo conference. Nevertheless, the publication of the letters was the cause of grave Jewish anxiety, and it heartened the anti-Zionists in the House of Lords to return to the attack.

The occasion was the news of the successful Arab boycott of the endeavor to elect a council in Palestine. On the 27th of March, 1923, Lord Islington introduced a motion in the House of Lords "to ask His Majesty's Government whether in the elections for the Legislative Council just concluded in Palestine it is not a fact that the whole Arab electorate refrained from voting in protest against the new Constitution; whether in view of this protest by so overwhelming a majority of the population of Palestine

[12] Jeffries, *op. cit.*

His Majesty's Government will not now consider the desirability of modifying the Constitution so as to bring it into closer accord with the sentiments of the native population and the Arab Community throughout the East; and to move for papers."

This time he was able to speak to his brief with more force and freedom thanks to Jeffries' articles, and he made excellent fun of the nonexistent vilayet. He did not make the same effect as in the previous debate, in spite of his increased supply of ammunition, because this time Balfour was not there to listen. He moved for papers showing the Palestine budget and for a full report on the election fiasco.

The major speech of the occasion was made by Lord Grey, an early supporter of the first proposals made in the war for a British Zionist policy. He now spoke in a way to distress and disappoint Jewish listeners. "A Zionist home," he said, "undoubtedly means or implies a Zionist Government over the district in which the home is placed, and if ninety-three per cent of the population of Palestine are Arabs I do not see how you can establish other than an Arab Government without prejudice to their civil rights. That one sentence of the Balfour Declaration seems to me to involve, without overstating the case, very great difficulty of fulfilment."

Lord Islington's motion was agreed to but owing to the form of words in which it was expressed, this did not mean that the government suffered another defeat on Palestine. One of the most interesting things in the debate occurred after the motion. Lord Raglan rose to ask whether Palestine was considered by the government as a strategical asset with which Great Britain must not part. He said that Zionist propaganda often insisted that this was the case but that military opinion did not support the idea, and he quoted Sir Henry Wilson as having declared that "the military occupation of Palestine, so far from being beneficial, was most deleterious to the British Empire." In his reply the Colonial Secretary, the Duke of Devonshire, affirmed in the most emphatic manner that Great Britain was in Palestine solely at the instance of the League of Nations, and that no question of strategy was involved.

Lord Raglan had accurately described army opinion. In his reply the Duke of Devonshire was in all probability speaking with perfect sincerity, but the view he expressed was out of date. Service ideas were changing and it was this, perhaps, more than any other single factor, which defeated the Conservative anti-Zionist movement. In the summer of 1923, acting from pressure within the party, the Cabinet appointed a committee to examine the whole question of British policy in Palestine with special reference to the Balfour Declaration. The three services and the Colonial

Office all submitted their views, and these views were in accord, excepting that of the army, the only service, it should be remembered, with experience of rule in the country. The General Staff kept its eyes on Egypt and considered Palestine a military encumbrance and nothing more. But the other authorities agreed that it was essential to maintain British arms in Palestine for the defense of the Canal in case a withdrawal from Egypt became necessary at any time. The conclusion reached by the committee and accepted as policy by the government was that the mandate must continue to be administered by Great Britain, that it could not be administered unless the principle of the Balfour Declaration was maintained, the reason being that any other policy could only be pursued with "a substantial sacrifice of consistency and self-respect, if not of honour." The stategical argument for British support of Zionism was from now on official. It had not been before.

Arthur Balfour played in only one more scene in Jewish history. In March of 1925, at the age of seventy-seven, he paid his first and only visit to Palestine. The occasion was one of high drama into which a spirit of outrageous comedy intruded. The object of his pilgrimage was to declare open the Hebrew University on Mount Scopus, that hill neighboring the Mount of Olives, which overlooks the Holy City. The ceremony itself, at which he appeared robed as the Chancellor of Cambridge University, passed impressively, Balfour speaking briefly, the main speech being made by Sir Herbert Samuel. Balfour was received by the citizens of Tel Aviv, and by Jewish colonists with an enthusiasm that amazed him. The Palestinian Arabs received him with a display of public mourning. It is said that, though he readily agreed not to visit the Mosque of Omar, he was not aware that there was any special intensity of feeling against him. It is certain that his private secretary destroyed the hundreds of telegrams of protest awaiting him at Government House and did not inform him of their existence. He passed through silent streets in the old city of Jerusalem and assumed that friendly salutations addressed to his companion, Ronald Storrs, were addressed to him. At Damascus, where he traveled from Jerusalem and where his life was in danger, it is reliably reported that he had to be persuaded not to appear at a window when he heard the yells of a hostile mob in the street outside his hotel, it being his impression that he was being cheered.[13] A young man in government service in Palestine, George Antonius, was selected to accompany Balfour on this journey, and when Antonius as a Christian Arab tried to explain to him that a nationalist opposition was gathering and increasing against Zionism, he

[13] Sir Walter Smart, then Vice-Consul at Damascus. A communication.

listened with close attention and then remarked that whatever trouble was to be expected and faced as a result of his policy, the "experiment" and also the consequences flowing from it were "extraordinarily interesting." [14] The danger to his life increased during every hour of his visit to Damascus until the French authorities forcibly hurried him out of Syria and confined him for three days to the safety of his boat.

It is impossible to know what his real thoughts and feelings were during this incident. He confided in no one. It has been suggested that under his ostentatious charm he was a total cynic, but this does not agree with the little that is known for certain about his character. It is more likely that in the last twenty years of his life he fell in love with an idea, and that with the obstinacy of old age he was able to close his mind, formidable and luminous as it was, to anything which interfered with the idea.

The Zionists were and still are faithful friends to their supporters but they have always shown themselves merciless to those who changed their minds about Zionism, no matter how sincerely they may have done so, and no matter what services they may have previously rendered the cause. They remained and remain still, and with reason, faithful in affection to the memory of Arthur Balfour.

[14] George Antonius. A communication.

PART

PART

II

5 THE PLUMER STORY

In June of 1925 Sir Herbert Samuel terminated his period of office as High Commissioner in Palestine. The moment was one of more crisis than usual, such as dimly foreshadowed events in the next decade. For the first time since 1917 Jewish immigration pressed heavily on Palestine as a result of faraway events.

The trouble began in Poland where the Jews constituted a far higher proportion of the people than in any other country in the world. They numbered three million, accounting for 10 percent of the whole population, and to their fellow citizens they seemed to be even more numerous. This was because they were mostly found in the middle class where the Poles were scarce, and also because, following traditional Jewish ways, they gathered closely in certain areas. In Pinsk, for example, and in some other provincial towns of east Poland the Jewish population formed as much as 90 percent of the whole. Even in the capital the Jews were estimated as accounting for 30 percent of the inhabitants of Warsaw. In these circumstances it was inevitable that the Polish national revival was accompanied by some anti-Semitism, and as usually happens with all forms of xenophobia, the alien people were identified with any and every sort of enemy: they were accused of being simultaneously pro-German and pro-Russian, always in the sense of treason, and of being at once Communists and shameless profiteers. There were horrible anti-Jewish incidents in the course of the campaigns against Russia during 1918 and 1919, in Lemberg where over seventy Jews were killed in the course of forty-eight hours of plundering, in Pinsk where Jews of both sexes were shot and others publicly flogged. Similar atrocities took place in Lida and Vilna.

Disasters of this kind were not typical of the reviving country, however, and should not be thought of as acts of policy. The Jewish problem in Poland (and Jewish writers themselves allow the expression when dealing with this abnormal concentration in one country) never led Polish governments into a policy of systematic oppression such as imperial Russia practiced with far less provocation. If the government meanly maintained some contemptible discriminatory laws inherited from czarism, it can also be said that Polish administration made genuine efforts to combine the Jews in the new state, but circumstances were such that they were impelled to ask them to accept impossible disadvantages, or rather to forgo advantages which were precious to them and on which their prosperity depended. The Poles wanted to build up a middle and professional class of their own and this could only be done within Poland by imposing restrictions on Jewish middle-class activity, by diminishing the quotas for Jewish university membership and eligibility for state employment of every kind. Naturally the Jews resisted such measures to the utmost, and their sense of grievance, of living in a country dedicated to their destruction, was greatly increased by the fact that at the same time as these sacrifices were demanded of them, taxation fell more heavily on them than on any other component group. This was because Poland with its aristocratic traditions had the aristocratic vice of privileged exemption. Since Jews could not enjoy tax exemptions they, to all appearances, payed taxes which enabled Poles to pay only a fraction. These practices maintained a chronic state of mutual irritation, but it should be remembered again that the moment was also one of high idealism in Poland and that there were many people who were opposed to the inequity of taxation and the anti-Jewish impetus, and worked for a state of things in which the whole nation could live in harmony. Little was heard in Poland of the German nonsense of racialism.

The Jews of Poland did not ease matters by their own behavior. They showed a full measure of the prevailing Slavonic recklessness. They were led by extremists who seem in many cases to have been fools as well. Many of them had been demoralized by years of degrading treatment in the Russian Pale of Settlement and were ill suited to be members of a free self-governing community. Like the Ottomanized Arabs of Palestine they were unthinking oppositionists. They considered that they had a political duty under all circumstances to oppose authority; to obstruct anything, good or bad, kind or cruel, that authority at any time wanted to do. As members of Parliament they soon brought the parliamentary system into danger of total breakdown. When Zionism spread among them it at first increased their tendency to excess.

The doctrines of Jewish nationalism seem to have been expounded to them by ill-qualified missionaries, and as a result the Zionism adopted by the Jews of Poland was very different from that taught elsewhere. It became extremely popular. The Jews of Poland seized with delight on the idea of a National Home, but they did not see that this involved any necessity to uproot themselves and trudge off to a geographical Zion (especially as many rabbis disapproved of the plan), since they had accustomed homes in Poland to which they were attached. A movement began among them for establishing a Jewish National Home within the Polish frontiers; they conceived of a dispensation in which the Jews would not only have their own separate education, but would be liable to their own laws and taxes administered by their own separate Parliament; they aimed to live as a separate nation within the state. Amid the turmoil of the immediate postwar years, the Jews did in fact succeed in establishing something of this kind for a short time in Lithuania, an event which caused much rancor.

This heretical Zionism was mercifully short-lived, and as the Jews of Poland and the Baltic left these fantasies they began to look for salvation in terms of the Eretz Israel of history and geography. In the years when Wladislaw Grabski dominated Polish politics, especially in matters of economy, the Jews began to migrate in increasing numbers to Palestine, a movement sometimes known among them as the "Aliyah Grabski"—or Grabski Exodus.[1] This appellation appears to do injustice to the minister's reputation, since it implies that he initiated anti-Jewish measures; this was

[1] Exodus has a different meaning to "Aliyah" but it expresses its emotional significance. The word is often more prosaically translated as "immigration." The literal meaning is "ascension" in the sense often reflected in the Authorized Version "going up to Jerusalem."

not so, but his was the outstanding political name at a time of great Jewish unhappiness and unrest in the largest of their European communities. In 1925 over seventeen thousand Jews entered Palestine from Poland. This occurred at the same time as a temporary relaxation of the emigration laws in Russia, and as a result Jewish immigration into Palestine in that year reached the unprecedented total of 34,386.

From 1917 to the present time, Zionist spokesmen have tried to persuade the world that the Arabs of Palestine had in reality no hostility to Zionism and welcomed the immigration of other people into their native land. In this hopeless endeavor the propagandists have a huge and obstinate array of facts against them, but they can, without having recourse to evasions or misrepresentations, point to one very striking piece of evidence in their favor. The mass immigration of 1925 had no political repercussions either in Palestine or in the neighboring countries. Neither the national congress of the Arabs nor the Moslem-Christian Association was moved to action. Nothing in the way of protest was heard from Syria, nothing from Abdullah's principality east of the Jordan, and nothing from Feisal's Iraq. Haj Amin continued to bide his time. This very curious absence of reaction does suggest that there was a possibility, faint but real, that with vigorous statesmanship, and the application of a consistent and well-grounded policy by the best political minds and talents of Great Britain, Palestine might have ceased to belong to the weary category of the world's "problems" and "sensitive points." On the other hand it may be that the essential tragedy of Palestine was merely disguised at this time by the fact that the first and second High Commissioners were men of remarkable ability and lofty character who compelled obedience through respect. Certainly there is no more striking evidence that the first High Commissioners were outstanding men than the fact that one retired and the other succeeded, in absolute peacefulness, at a moment of potential danger.

The appointment of Field Marshal Lord Plumer as Sir Herbert Samuel's successor came as a disappointment to the Jews. They seem to have taken it for granted that all High Commissioners would henceforth be chosen from among their own people and Lord Plumer was the kind of man they dreaded: ultra-British, conservative, devoted to the cause of the Commonwealth and Empire. The Jews took it as axiomatic that, like all good Empire-men, this one must be a natural and uncritical friend of Arabs and all things Moslem, and a natural enemy of Zionism (probably an anti-Semite). More than other people the Jews were associated with the intelligentsia and were easily prone to its prejudices and thinking conventions. "The Holy Land," moaned a Zionist newspaper of Palestine when the appointment was announced, "or the Jewish Homeland, whichever you will, are both objects of deep study calling for the highest attributes, intellectual and spiritual, in an official and an administrator. In this respect Lord Plumer is only an average resident [of England], the type of law-abiding, God-fearing, church-going, perfect old gentleman . . . We stressed some time ago the necessity of having an intellectual government." They assumed that with Plumer as High Commissioner the policy of O.E.T.A. would be revived.

Lord Plumer was not an impressive man at first sight. Douglas Duff, who served in the police throughout the Field Marshal's term of office, vividly described how he appeared to him at a first meeting in Jerusalem: "With his receding chin, ruddy complexion, bushy moustache and monocle, he resembled an American cartoon of a British General, and he was by no means tall." If O.E.T.A. was to be revived, then this choleric little military man was precisely what the chief revivalist might be expected to look like.

The Zionists missed the rarely discovered truth that, in the words of Max Beerbohm, "men do not often look like themselves." Plumer was perhaps the best man produced by the British Army in the First World War, and it is significant that while the reputation of every one of his contemporaries in the military hierarchy has been subjected (rightly or wrongly) to damaging criticism, his has remained untouched and even unchallenged, although in prominence and fame he was second only to Lord Haig. He was a man of exact and self-confident mind, precisely aware of his abilities and his limitations, of active imagination, and no prejudice that went beneath the skin. He was a sensitive man of wide sympathy to whom the horrors of the campaigns in France and Flanders were so continual a burden on the mind that he could hardly speak of them and keep control of his feelings.[2] He was the opposite of the unfeeling war-chief of legend. In 1919 Plumer, more than any other single man, had been responsible for the abandonment of those war measures which were causing starvation in Germany; no man was more naturally disposed to sympathize with the revolt against injustice which was at the core of Zionism. But the Zionists, who, through conventional thinking, tended at first to misjudge Plumer, but later changed their minds, were right to distrust him in one respect: no man was more naturally disposed to believe that "equality of obligation" was the right and only principle on

[2] E. Mills, Assistant Chief Secretary to Plumer in Palestine, quoted in Sir Charles Harington's biography *Plumer of Messines*.

which Palestine could be ruled. He looked on fairness as one of the highest ideals.

He arrived at the railway station of Jerusalem on the 25th of August, 1925. Before getting into his car for his official entry he noticed among the waiting entourage two couriers holding silver-topped staves and dressed in all the gold-laced magnificence of Turkish kavasses. He was told that they were supplied by the government to lead his procession. He said that he did not wish them to take part and ordered them instead to convey his baggage to Government House.[3] Throughout his term of office he was strongly averse to any needless official pomp because he found it distasteful in a land where Jesus Christ had lived in poverty. His first official action as High Commissioner was to go with Lady Plumer to the Anglican Cathedral in order to pray. They did this before entering their new home, the hideous Kaiserin Viktoria Augusta hospice on Mount Scopus, then used as Government House.

His dislike of pomp did not mean that he was in the least inclined to dispense with formality in the conduct of his mission; on the contrary he was exacting in this respect, and people who had official business with him were often intimidated by the soldierly strictness with which he assumed the role of the king's representative. He was the most methodical of men. As the High Commissioner on duty he was a commanding officer on parade, and when he was off parade he was not only easy in manner but he demanded that full measure of freedom which he held to be the soldier's inalienable right. Not content with finding practical and less gorgeous employment for his two kavasses, he even objected to having any escort at all when he went for sight-seeing walks by himself, as he much enjoyed doing in his leisure hours. These unaccompanied walks were a cause of anxiety to the police, especially as Lord Plumer, in conformity with the custom of officers stationed in London, was usually dressed on these occasions in a smart blue suit complete with stiff white collar, bowler hat, and a tightly rolled umbrella, all of which made him extraordinarily conspicuous in the thronged medieval alleys of the old walled city.[4] It was as he emerged from Herod's Gate, at the end of one of these private explorations, that Lord Plumer first met Douglas Duff. He took the opportunity to convey his disapproval of the police's setting a secret watch to guard him in the shape of a plain-clothes detective whom he had detected in turn from his clumsy shadowing.

[3] Harington, *Ibid.*
[4] Douglas V. Duff, *A Sword for Hire.* London, 1934.

The politicians of Palestine were quick to try to lure what they took to be a simple-minded soldier into unguarded statements which might be turned to profit later. It is related that at a first official interview a Zionist asked him "What is your policy?" to which he immediately replied that he had not got one. His duty as High Commissioner, he said, was to receive the instructions of His Majesty's Government and carry them out with what exactness he could.

Early in his Palestine career the Arabs thought that they had caught him out in an act of indiscreet favoritism. Not long after his arrival he went with Lady Plumer and his daughter Miss Eleanor Plumer to attend a Jewish sports-meeting in Tel Aviv. They were presented with Zionist badges and his daughter asked him in a whisper what she should do with it. Lord Plumer's large mustache always made it easy for him to speak without being seen to do so. He muttered: "Put it on and take it off outside." At the end of the meeting the band played "God Save the King" during which the Field Marshal and his party stood to attention, but hardly had they relaxed than the band began to play the mournful and stirring melody of Hatikvah, the Zionist anthem, while the whole concourse of Jews remained standing rigid. Lord Plumer immediately removed his hat and signed to his party to stand to attention again. "What are they playing?" whispered his daughter. "I don't know what they're playing," returned Lord Plumer, "we'll find out afterwards."

The wearing of the badges was not discovered by the press, but Lord Plumer's homage to Zionism during the playing of Hatikvah was, and next day the Arab papers were full of wrathful comment. A deputation came to wait on him, confident that they had cornered him. Lord Plumer received them with his usual grave courtesy and listened to their protest. He replied in some such words as these: "I was the guest of these people in Tel Aviv, and to have sat down while their anthem was played would have been to forget the duties of a guest toward his host. Don't you think so?" This appeal to the venerable laws of hospitality on which Arabs pride themselves perplexed the deputation, and while they were searching for an answer Lord Plumer pressed his advantage: "What would you have done, if you had been there?" he asked. The suggestion that these Arab notables might attend Jewish festivities confused them further, and they blusteringly tried to bring the conversation round to straight political discussion, but Plumer stuck to the original point. "Let me put it this way," he said, "suppose I came as a guest to some festivity organised by yourselves, and at the end of it you played your national anthem, and I deliberately sat down, would you not regard my behaviour as most unmannerly?" The deputation was silent. "By the way," asked Lord Plumer, "have you got a national anthem?" In some embarrassment they confessed that they had not. "In that case," said Lord Plumer concluding the interview, "I think you had better get one as soon as possible. If I can help in any way I shall be only too glad to do so." After this the Arab press abandoned their protest. The leaders did not follow up Lord Plumer's musical offer and they remained to the end without an anthem.[5]

The most famous example of Lord Plumer's turning the tables on those who came to him with unreasonable complaints occurred later in his term of office. Again an Arab deputation came to him, this time to request that he forbid a Jewish military parade to be held for the laying up of the regimental colors of the Jewish battalions (Royal Fusiliers) in the Grand Synagogue of Jerusalem. The request was well calculated to offend Plumer, who had a passionate conviction that it was a duty of all civilized men to accord honor to those who had endured the sufferings of a world war. The deputation were on unfavorable ground, in any event, but one of their number was so unwise as to tell Plumer that if he allowed the parade to take place he and his colleagues "could not be responsible for order in the city." In his sternest manner the High Commissioner replied that he did not wish them to be responsible for order as he planned to be responsible himself.

None of these incidents involved serious matters of policy, but they illustrate the formidable character of Lord Plumer and his highly idiosyncratic skill in negotiation. They may suggest some anti-Arab bias in his conduct of affairs. This was not the case at any time, but the Jews were quicker than the Arabs to appreciate the kind of man they had to deal with and so, unlike the Arabs, they avoided situations in which they were liable to be humiliated through putting themselves in the wrong. Nevertheless, they were slow to trust him. It was some time before Dr. Weizmann dropped his suspicion that Plumer was an enemy to Zionism,[6] and in other circumstances a bitter struggle might easily have arisen between Plumer and the Zionists. As things were they resented to the end his strict application of the rule that Jewish immigration must depend on the estimated economic capacity of the country to absorb new citizens, and his insistence without exception that Jews could not enter unless they had adequate private resources or definite prospects of work; but the years of

[5] The Hon. Eleanor Plumer. A communication.
[6] The Hon. Eleanor Plumer.

1926 to 1928 were a period of Zionist weakness in which it would have been the greatest folly on their part to antagonize government. It looked to some people, and not only enemies, as if the Jewish national movement was about to come to an end.

There is a radical difference to be noted between the *Völkerwanderungen* of Zionism in the 1920's and those of the thirties. In the first decade of Zionist enterprise in Palestine there was a far stronger sense of voluntary experiment among Jews than was the case in the bitter, more savage years of the 1930's. In Plumer's time Zionism was still the concern of a small Jewish minority and it was by no means looked on then as an act of disloyalty if a Jew came to Palestine to try the experience of living the national life, and then decided against it in favor of the ease of the Diaspora. Throughout these earlier years the figures of Jewish immigration had to be offset against substantial figures of emigrants. Between 1920 and 1924 nearly 13 percent of the recorded immigrants left the country. In the four years succeeding, Jewish[7] emigrants from Palestine amounted to over 33 percent of those who came in.

Nineteen twenty-five was the fatal year and again the trouble began as before in Poland. The government following that of Grabski attempted a currency reform which failed and the result was a Polish economic collapse similar in effect to the 1921 inflation crisis in Germany and prophetic of the world slump of 1929. The result in Palestine was appalling, especially as this Polish economic disaster occurred at the same time as the introduction of currency restrictions in eastern Europe. Thousands of Jewish immigrants suddenly found themselves penniless. Numerous Jewish businesses broke down. The number of those out of work rose in the course of two years from 400 to 8,500.[8] The dimensions of the case have been vividly described by an eyewitness and eminent Jewish authority, Mr. Robert Weltsch: "Unemployment was a regular feature, workers lived on an appalling minimum, often on the dole, which was a heavy unproductive drain on the Zionist exchequer. There was genuine starvation in the communal settlements and elsewhere. Zionist money-chests were empty, officials and teachers did not get their salaries and were finally paid by some paperbills issued by institutions or even by private persons. Debts accumulated everywhere."[9] During 1926 Jewish immi-

[7] Figures in Israel Cohen, *The Zionist Movement*. London, 1945.
[8] Peel Report. Cohen, *op. cit.*
[9] Meyer Weisgal and Joel Carmichael, eds., *Chaim Weizmann: A Biography by Several Hands*. London, 1962. Referred to hereafter as Weizmann Biography.

gration was maintained at a high figure, the majority still coming from Poland, but in 1927 it dropped from nearly 14,000 in the year before to 3,034.[10] In this year 5,071 Jews left Palestine.

The tide turned in 1928 but not in any way to hearten Jewish nationalists. In this year the surplus of immigrants over emigrants amounted only to ten, and there seemed no reason to foresee high immigration figures again in the near future. Economic disaster had inflicted one great injury on the National Home, and it looked now as though prosperity in the Diaspora was about to inflict another. Marshal Pilsudski's seizure of power in 1926 seemed a happy event for the Jews of Poland. He was the enemy of the reactionary anti-Jewish right wing, and after the illegality of his coup d'état, he needed support within the country and respect outside, especially in the League of Nations. There was something (though not very much) of the genuine liberal about him too. All this led the dictator to repeal the discriminatory laws against Polish Jews and to reach a wide measure of agreement with their leaders. In the 1920's the character of modern dictatorship was only understood by prejudiced victims. Optimists believed that anti-Semitism in Poland, and even in the world, was a thing of the past. Inevitably this state of opinion adversely affected Zionism. With bad news about the plight of their fellow religionists in Palestine Polish Jews began to think afresh; a National Home in an uncomfortable country seemed no longer a pressing need except to dedicated souls. Even when the liberalism of Pilsudski was seen for the fallacious thing it was, there appeared to be no need for such drastic countermeasures as a move to Asia, for next door to Poland was republican Germany, now a wealthy state and morally regenerated (some said) into the bargain. Germany had not only repudiated the last vestige of discriminatory law, but contained the most prosperous Jewish community in Europe, possibly in the world, in which Jews were outstandingly successful in almost every department of the national life. In 1928 only a lunatic could have foreseen with any accuracy the shape of things to come.

If this was a golden age, as many progressive people believed, it could only cast a leaden shadow on Jewish hopes in Palestine, and perhaps one of the finest achievements of Zionism was the way in which the new home-landers not only survived, not only kept the hope alive, but expanded their work of reclamation. On the agricultural side, which then and always came first in Zionist preoccupations, the progress was slow, only about 10,000 acres being added to the Zionist property of approximately

[10] Cohen, *op. cit.* This figure includes illegal immigrants. He gives the number of legal immigrants as 2,320.

238,000 acres, but it never declined as it easily could have done in the circumstances.

On the industrial side the situation was equally precarious, and, among many alarming signs in 1927, the municipality of Tel Aviv was threatened with bankruptcy. It was rescued by an advance of funds from the administration. But in spite of the desperate plight of Zionist trade and commerce in these years, and the danger to its financial backers, Jewish investment in the building of Tel Aviv, and in a variety of industrial enterprises aiming at the modernization of the country, never flagged. The most important of these enterprises was known as the Rutenberg Concession, or the Palestine Electric Corporation, which received its final ratification from Lord Plumer in March, 1926. This enterprise occupies a curious position in Zionist history.

Pinchas Rutenberg was a Jewish exile from Russia. He had been Minister of Police under Kerensky. In the disasters following the Bolshevik seizure of power he had organized the escape of many of his fellow countrymen from Odessa, and himself migrated to England. He immediately set to work, in consultation with Zionist leaders, on a comprehensive scheme for supplying commercial electricity to Palestine by harnessing the waters of the Auja river near Jaffa, and the upper Jordan with its tributary, the Yarmuk. He tried to interest British financiers in the scheme without success, but did succeed in interesting British politicians, notably Mr. Winston Churchill, who, as Colonial Secretary, accepted it in 1921. Subsequent handling of the scheme was criticized with good reason. Misleading statements were made in Parliament with the result that a scheme for water-powered electrification appeared to be open to tender from all quarters, while in fact Rutenberg's scheme had not only been secretly accepted, but Arab and British claimants to special consideration were roughly and even threateningly told to "accommodate themselves" as best they might. All this gave the concession a sinister appearance, although to grant it was a piece of enlightened administration rather than the opposite. As appears clearly now, the operation was difficult to perform in perfect decency within the political climate of Britain in the 1920's, and the result was a clumsy compromise between state socialism and capitalist enterprise.

Rutenberg himself seems to have done nothing in the least dishonest during the whole course of the transaction, but at a time when Russian Jews were supposed to be the origin of the world's misfortunes, and when concession mongers in the Levant had left an evil memory, this Jew (once of the Russian police!) inevitably got all the blame for the improprieties of the deal. For the moment, in the early twenties, the concession did much harm to the reputation of Zionism. The Vatican, which, from a somewhat pro-Zionist attitude in the days of Benedict XV, had returned to one of severe disapproval under Pius XI, voiced a widespread feeling of suspicion. In February, 1922, the British Minister to the Holy See, Count de Salis, was given a gloomy lecture on the subject by Cardinal Gasquet. Zionism, he suggested, meant converting the Holy Land into a happy hunting ground for financiers and concessionaires.[11] This was a view widely shared by members of the Conservative party in England. Money-making not of their own often genuinely shocks such people.

Rutenberg got the worst of both worlds in an unexpected way. Not only was he looked on with all the horror reserved for the bloated capital-ist, but the fact that his proposal was not tempting to financiers in the City of London, who judged that it could not make large profits, also shocked his anti-Zionist critics. They said that this showed that his object was not straightforwardly commercial, but political, and that his real intention was to increase Zionist power. This of course was true. Arabs saw it clearly and fearfully, and their alarm was mixed with hope when they knew that they had many sympathizers in Britain and among the British officials who ruled them.[12]

But the most curious thing about the Rutenberg story is in its later chapters. From 1919 to 1930 it could be described as a strong talking-point against Zionism used by Arab politicians and anti-Zionists of all kinds. The case against it was valid. The whole manner in which it had been granted showed scandalous favoritism, and to add to resentment Pinchas Rutenberg was an active Zionist politician who often took the extreme side.[13] Yet when Arabs in the next decade took to arms and at-tempted anti-Zionist protest on an international scale, when they deployed all the propaganda forces they could command, this Rutenberg business seems to have been quite forgotten. The most brilliant of all Arab propa-gandists, George Antonius, does not even mention Rutenberg's name in his

[11] Israel State Archives. It is possible that Vatican disapproval of the Rutenberg Concession influenced the drafting of the concluding sentence of Article 11 of the mandate: "Any such arrangements [with the Jewish Agency] shall provide that no profits distributed by such agency, directly or indirectly, shall exceed a reason-able rate of interest on the capital, and any further profits shall be utilised by it for the benefit of the country in a manner approved by the Administration."
[12] The granting of the Rutenberg Concession is described in accurate detail, though in a very hostile manner, in *Palestine the Reality* by J. M. N. Jeffries.
[13] Weizmann, *Trial and Error*. London, 1949.

famous book, *The Arab Awakening.* This was in part due to the fact that the initial resentment could not be maintained at fever pitch because the Rutenberg Concession proved a sluggish starter. For four years Rutenberg could not obtain sufficient funds to exploit his opportunity except in a small way. His concern was not able to declare a dividend before 1933. Nevertheless, in the end, the Palestine Electric Corporation did what its promoters hoped. It still exists in part in Israel, and is considered one of the country's most valuable assets. Rutenberg's administration was scrupulously honest, employed labor among Arabs and Jews to an extent that the people valued, and lost in practice all character of being a grievance. It again provides evidence that in a better historical time, Israel could have grown in peace, though it must always be remembered that peaceful national growth is almost unknown.

During his last year of office, from 1927 to 1928, Lord Plumer initiated two measures of reform, one in the civilian and one in the service sphere. The former concerned land tenure.

He appointed a committee under the Attorney General, Mr. Norman Bentwich, to improve the existing legislation devised to protect tenants (especially on agricultural land) from unjust eviction. It was very widely believed that this matter was the most important with which the administration had to deal, and that if it could be rightly resolved then indeed Zionism in Palestine might cease to be a problem. As in nineteenth-century Ireland the wrongs of evicted tenants were at the heart of a burning grievance, but here, in contrast to Ireland, the facts of the matter were of baffling obscurity.

The agitation had first become keen and prominent in 1920 when the Zionist Commission bought one of the largest properties in Palestine. The estate, which was situated in the valley of Jezreel and about 50,000 acres in extent, belonged to a Beirut family called Sursok, absentee landlords who in the course of the sale made little provision for the compensation of their tenants. Then dreadful stories were told of how peasant families had been turned out as beggars from the humble houses where they had dwelt as useful citizens for generations, so that they might make way for rich Jewish newcomers. Arab activists used to organize excursions to the scene of the disaster where they would harangue their audience, drawing special attention to a collection of hovels which the Jews had wisely demolished as a sanitary measure. The agitators spread the idea, which was accepted, that in reality the Jews had torn down these Moslem houses, as they would tear down any Moslem building, including the mosques of Jerusalem, "out of hatred for the Sons of the Faith." [14] This was part of a widespread propaganda effort which was the most effective of any undertaken at any time by the Arab leadership. For all its extravagance this propaganda line pointed to a hardship that in the nature of things could not be wholly imaginary and did not merely concern politics but the immemorial needs of everyday life. The question troubled the consciences of many Jews including those of some Zionist enthusiasts.

Influenced by the outcry following the Sursok sale the administration had, in this same year 1920, passed a Transfer of Land Ordinance which required government agreement to all sales of immovable property, making their intention clear in a section which provided that consent would only be given when and if the Director of Lands was "satisfied that any tenant in occupation will retain sufficient land in the district or elsewhere for the maintenance of himself and his family." The reason that Plumer appointed his committee seven years later was that the apparently definitive 1920 ordinance had never worked.

It is not known for certain why it never worked, nor why the subsequent labors of Bentwich and his successors likewise failed. Lord Plumer's initiative resulted in a new ordinance promulgated after his time in 1929. Its failure, and rising tension in the country, prompted successive administrations to supersede not only this ordinance, but subsequent ones, in 1932, 1933, 1934, and 1940. The 1940 ordinance which was to be one of the great Zionist grievances, restricted Jewish purchase drastically and belongs to another chapter. But the preceding ordinances, which were closely and solely concerned in effect with tenant rights, exasperated most Zionist leaders to an almost equal degree because they appeared to favor Arabs most unfairly: they seemed to make it impossible for Zionists to establish settlements in tenanted country. This was indeed the whole problem of Palestine: it was inhabited. But the Jews need not have worried about the particular aspect of the matter covered by the prewar land ordinances. Although, according to what Arab nationalists said, it was immeasurably more to the interest of Arabs than Jews to claim the protection offered by the various ordinances, the Arabs seem throughout to have preferred to effect sales with little and if possible no recourse to the Director of Lands. Only one official and detailed estimate after inquiry was made at any time, and that was before the promulgation of the 1932 ordinance. It was then found that since 1919, in a period when the Jews had acquired about 115,000 acres, only 664 known Arabs could be classi-

[14] Douglas V. Duff, *Galilee Galloper*. London, 1935.

fied in the sense of existing law as evicted tenants, in the approximate ratio, that is, of one person to every 173 acres. Of these displaced persons only a hundred or so were known to have availed themselves of the opportunity for resettlement offered by the administration: that is, one to every 1,150 acres; extraordinary figures when it is remembered that Palestine was small and relatively closely populated.

The natural conclusion to be drawn from these statistics was that in reality there was no great evicted tenant problem,[15] and the fact that when the Peel Commission raised the matter with Arabs they received evasive replies confirmed the impression. Yet for all the evidence such a conclusion was manifestly false. The full truth of the matter can never be known now, but explanations were put forward in various official Palestine statements from 1921 onward. They were summarized in the report of the Peel Commission, and in postwar years they were given to the general reader by Mr. Albert Hyamson and Sir John Glubb. According to the latter, the trouble started long before Zionism or the mandate, in unsuccessful Ottoman attempts at modernization. Before the late nineteenth century, documents attesting legal titles to property were unknown in the Ottoman Empire, and when the government in Constantinople made such documentation compulsory, the reform was hard to put into execution in this part of the world for two reasons. It was not preceded by a land survey, and it was resisted by the people. If you were an Ottoman subject you hid from the government. You preferred not to disclose your identity to the authorities. If you could write you avoided signing your name.

The result of attempted reform under these conditions was an unusually intricate piece of Oriental confusion. To quote Sir John Glubb:

> Few cultivators registered their lands. The officials of the Lands Department, however, found in the new procedure a fruitful source of personal profit. In return for a bribe, many of them were willing to register any land in the name of anybody who asked for it. A number of enterprising persons "bought" land from the Turkish government in this manner. A few perhaps already had some connection with the district, had lent money to the farmers or had been in business relations with them. Others had no connection whatever with the land . . . In most cases, the original farmers continued to cultivate as in the past, except that now they had to pay rent to a city dweller, whom they had rarely, or perhaps never, seen.[16]

---

[15] Israel Cohen maintains this in *The Zionist Movement*.
[16] Glubb, *Britain and the Arabs*. London, 1959.

While the number of absentee landlords was thus artificially multiplied, the peasant cultivators lost none of their traditional mistrust of the government, and when the hated Ottoman rule gave way to one supposedly intent on a transfer of population, the Arab peasantry found themselves confirmed in their old habits. It did not matter how unselfish administrative action may have been (and in these efforts to protect tenants it is hard to discover any bad motive), the people whom they were designed to benefit preferred to keep away. They did as they had always done and avoided government like the plague.

Interested parties, Jewish and Arab, knew how to take advantage of this situation. The gruesome story of Samuel's 1920 ordinance is best related by Albert Hyamson,[17] a singularly fair and learned Jewish authority.

Under this legislation land could not be transferred unless the interests of the tenant were safeguarded by the retention of sufficient land for himself and his family. The interests of both the vendor and the purchaser were, however, opposed to this. The purchasers were ready to pay high prices, above the hitherto current value, but required vacant land for settlement. The vendors, having no local interests, were, of course, anxious to sell at the highest possible prices. They quickly found at small cost a means of circumventing the legislation. In this they had as allies the money-lenders to whom most of the peasants were heavily indebted. The course taken was to persuade and pay the tenants (before steps were taken for a transfer of the land) to vacate their holdings. When the transfer took place the land was consequently empty, without tenants for whom to provide. And all parties were satisfied—the vendors, the purchasers and presumably the money-lenders, permanently, and the tenants for a short period. The only exception to this general satisfaction was the High Commissioner and his officers. They had never intended that their legislation should have such a consequence. These proceedings continued for eight years, during which many of the larger estates passed out of the hands of the larger owners, for the most part resident abroad, into those of one or other of the subsidiaries of the Zionist Organisation. Under the new owners, with the expenditure of money for development, a far larger population than previously was supported. In 1929 a new Ordinance was enacted, but this provided even less protection for the tenant. This mainly provided for the compensation for disturbance to tenants who lost their holdings and also for any improvements they had made. In fact it merely legalised the practice that had grown up.

[17] *Palestine Under the Mandate*. London, 1950.

In the circumstances of Palestine under the British mandate, the only people who could have safeguarded the interests of the Arab peasantry would have been a patriotic landlord class with public-spirited traditions. The long blight of Ottoman rule had produced a class more like the opposite of this description. They were often vociferous nationalists, sincere in their resentment of the Zionism out of which a certain number of them made their fortunes. True to form, they often laid the blame for any lack of conscience in their behavior on the mandatory powers. It was said, in the case of the Sursok deal, that since "the iniquitous division of the country" these proprietors were put to the harassment of obtaining passports and visas in order to visit their estates, and so they had no alternative but to do what they did.[18] Landlords who fail their people have always been prolific of excuses. This one must be among the feeblest recorded.

As is evident, if the explanation given above of the Palestine tenant problem is true (and it is supported by the best opinion), then by the very nature of the case it is not open to precise documentary proof. Statistics must be largely guess-work. The Sursok deal is known to have involved the eviction of about 8,000 tenants "compensated" at three pounds ten shillings a head, but this was a famous episode. There were many similar though lesser ones of which next to nothing is known. The governing principle is fairly evident, but the details and the preponderance of one element over another remain obscure today and were probably equally obscure then.

Lord Plumer was obviously not to be blamed in any way for the failure of his attempted reform of land tenure. In another direction, however, in which he had specialized knowledge, he undertook reforms whose failure was to some extent his own fault. He decided to reorganize the security forces.

One of the main purposes of the Cairo conference, it will be remembered, was retrenchment in the overseas commitments. It appeared to Lord Plumer that the small territory of Palestine was burdened with disproportionately enormous and expensive forces. These had been established after the bloodshed of 1921 and consisted of a Palestine gendarmerie, semimilitary, semipolice in character; a separate British gendarme force (mainly recruited from the former Royal Irish Constabulary), and a garrison numbering 4,000 in 1921 and reduced in the course of years to one-battalion strength. The above was in addition to the normal civilian po-

[18] Evidence taken before the Peel Commission.

lice. Lord Plumer decided to reduce these forces drastically, because they were no longer needed in such strength.

As his term of office drew to a close he could look with some complacency on the events of his years as High Commissioner. Only in Palestine, among all the countries of the Arabic-speaking world, had peace been consistently maintained without any act of suppression and (even more remarkable) without a sense of precariousness as in Iraq and Egypt. Only one incident of Lord Plumer's administration could be described as a military operation, and then only just so; a small affray in Transjordan between government troops (in this case Arab legionnaires) and nomads who were refusing tax payment.

Zionists were loath to concede that Sir Herbert Samuel's policy of concession to Arab nationalism had indeed brought reconciliation, but appearances strongly suggested that this was the case. There was no sign of a revival of the 1921 troubles and one potent reason for this, so it seemed then, was that during these years Dr. Weizmann showed himself a master of political moderation, in firm opposition to the extremists of his party. In the two years after the crucial year of the Cairo conference and the Jaffa riots he came to look at the Arab situation anew. In America in June, 1923, he spoke as follows to a Jewish gathering in Baltimore:

> For years we have drafted political resolutions that we Jews want to live in peace with the Arabs. We have passed resolutions which have the character of a pledge. But as soon as it comes to taking decisive and effective steps to carry out those resolutions, because the realisation of all these problems is a question of life or death of our work in Palestine, one is attacked from all sides. A clamour is raised that one sells out to the Arabs or to someone else all that is sacred to Zionism. It should be clear to our great politicians that one cannot put off the Arabs with empty talk. For years we have made decisions, and whatever the Jewish National Home will ultimately become, even if it absorbs millions of Jews and if, as I hope, there will be a Jewish majority in Palestine, it will nevertheless remain an island in the Arab sea. We have to come to an understanding with this people which is akin to us and with which we have lived in concord in the past . . . In Eretz Israel there is . . . a people which resists our coming and which holds Palestine encircled from the North and South, East and West, and with it we have to arrange ourselves in a serious way.[19]

[19] Dr. Weizmann's intervening remarks on this occasion are somewhat away from the present subject but may be quoted in a footnote as a fine example of his idosyncratic and vigorous humor. "Naturally," he said, "it would be better if Palestine

Two years later, in 1925, at the Fourteenth Zionist Congress held in Vienna, Weizmann spoke with the same force in the same sense. In the course of an address he said:

> Palestine must be built up without violating the legitimate interests of the Arabs—not a hair of their heads shall be touched. The Zionist Congress must not confine itself to Platonic formulae. It has to learn the truth that Palestine is not Rhodesia and that 600,000 Arabs live there, who before the sense of justice of the world have exactly the same right to their homes as we have to our National Home. As long as this thought has not penetrated into our flesh and blood, you will always have to look for artificial narcotics, but you will see the future in a false perspective.

If utterances such as these (and quotations could be multiplied) had been made only to Gentile or Arab audiences they could have been dismissed as part of a public relations effort, but it was thus that Weizmann spoke to his own people and at risk to his popularity and leadership.

It was all the more easy to interpret such words as a weakening or even as an end of Arab-Jewish hatred and strife because the continuing peace in the territories either side of the river Jordan persisted at a time when to the north, for nearly two years from July, 1925, the nationalists of Syria and the French ruling power were in a state of violent armed conflict causing mutual atrocity and costing thousands of lives. It would have been in the normal pattern of events for this national excitement to have spread south to the Arabs of Palestine, fellow Syrians, and among them to have taken a bellicose anti-Zionist and anti-British form. But under Plumer no calamity of this kind came about.

How much was this due to Plumer?

It has often been asserted that if Plumer had remained for another two years or had been followed by some outstanding personality of the same caliber, then the long peace of the 1920's would probably have continued. A more general opinion, shared by many Zionists, is that the peace was due to the weakening of the whole Zionist effort in Palestine after 1925, and especially the failure of Jewish immigration. Arabs began to believe that Zionism was a short-lived movement of which they had in truth nothing to be afraid. The Peel Report went so far as to say, "It stands to reason

---

and the neighbouring countries were unpopulated. It would be better still if the Nile flowed there instead of the Jordan, better still if Moses had led us to America instead of Palestine, better still if we had to deal with Englishmen and not with Jews. But we have to deal with Jews and in Eretz Israel there is the Jordan, and there is a people, etc."

that the main cause of Arab quiescence was the sharp decline in the fortunes of the National Home."

Lord Plumer himself was the last man to overrate his contribution; indeed with the modesty which was the most winning feature of his singularly attractive character, he gravely underestimated the weight of his personality in Palestinian affairs. All the more easily, in consequence, he allowed himself to believe that the Palestinian problem was capable of early solution. His administration and the British government, encouraged by the peaceful demeanor of the Arabs, took comfort from Dr. Weizmann's generous propaganda for a lasting Jewish-Arab accord, and they looked on the Jewish opposition to it led by Vladimir Jabotinsky and the Revisionist Party as an irrelevant lunatic fringe. Jabotinsky had formed this party in 1925, by which time he had declared himself against any cooperation with Arabs until the Jews were their effective masters in Palestine, and he was pressing for the formation of a Jewish Legion to conquer the Promised Land. Understandably, British politicians and administrators accorded no importance to this fantastic figure and his fantastic party who talked of conquest at a time when the Zionist organization was at its wit's end how to man the agricultural settlements. The mood of government everywhere in the Locarno years was liable to optimism; wherever one looked there were signs (if one wished to see them) of old wounds healing while new unscathed generations entered the scene. It is sometimes forgotten today that in what may be called the world of public imagination the twenties were an extremely sentimental period.

As policy followed optimism, both the Palestine and British gendarmerie were disbanded and only the normal civil police force retained. At the same time the Palestine garrison was reduced to a single squadron of armored cars under R.A.F. command. It is recorded on good authority that on the last occasion when Lord Plumer was in Jerusalem on November 11th, which day, he always insisted, was to be celebrated with the fullest solemnity, it was found that there was no British artillery available to fire the salute to the dead, and the authorities were obliged to ask the guardians of the Mosque of Omar for the loan of the ancient cannon used to announce the fast during Ramadhan. An admirer of Lord Plumer said that his presence was worth a battalion at least, and that a practical government would have sent a battalion at least to Palestine when Plumer left. This was not done, however.

In 1928 Lord Plumer asked to be relieved of his post. He was seventy-one years old but extreme age came on him early, as it did on many men who had endured the war. His health deteriorated and he left at the end of

July. He was the subject of the usual farewell encomium from the usual multiplicity of sources, but in his case there was a rare element of sincerity in the tribute. Two farewell episodes, those with the supreme representatives of the Arab and Jewish communities, were unusual.

In the same summer there was a meeting of the Arab-Moslem-Christian Congress, and now in 1928, six years too late, the Arab leadership recognized that they had made an appalling blunder when they refused the offer by Winston Churchill and the Lloyd George government of a legislative assembly. The Congress unanimously resolved to demand the establishment of parliamentary government in Palestine, and at their farewell audience the Executive of the Congress handed a memorandum to this effect to the High Commissioner. He promised to convey this to the right quarter.

Lord Plumer's farewell audience with the delegation of the Jewish National Council, the Va'ad Leumi, was one of those extraordinary comedies which occasionally lightened the fateful procession of events in the Holy Land. It was an unfortunate comedy from the point of view of the Zionists. The delegates were introduced on July 29th by Weizmann's personal representative in Palestine, an English Jew called Frederick Kisch. With the representatives Kisch brought the two chief rabbis, in order (to follow his account) "to show a united front." He went on to say:

> Unfortunately I had reckoned without the persistence through the ages of the feud between the Pharisees and Sadducees.
>
> "Rabbi Kook acquitted himself quite honourably—if at excessive length—of the task of delivering a farewell benediction, but Rabbi Jacob Meir found it necessary to exploit the occasion for a demonstration against the Chukath-Hakilloth and the Kneseth Israel. He declared that the statutes were contrary to religion, and that speaking in the name of the Sephardim, his community would never accept them. He was personally aggressive and offensive to Lord Plumer in the matter, and when he observed that the official interpreter was tactfully toning down his words, he repeated them in French, adding in conclusion: 'Vous pouvez dire cela, si vous voulez, à Sa Majesté.'
>
> "Poor Lord Plumer, who had prepared himself for an exchange of farewells, could not understand what it was all about, or how he had erred. It was indeed most painful. The incident quite spoiled the ceremony." [20]

Next day Lord Plumer left Palestine and the last official post of his long career. To this day he is remembered by older people both in Israel

[20] From Kisch's published diaries.

and Jordan with affection and as a just man. A little over a month after his departure, in September of 1928, trouble broke out between Arabs and Jews in the old city of Jerusalem. It led to further trouble and the next year the peace broke down.

6 PRELUDE TO TRAGEDY

The incident which reopened violence between Arabs and Jews was sadly typical of life as it has been lived for centuries in Jerusalem. The presence in one land and in one city of three great religions, subdivided in turn into differing religious communities, has from a remote age turned a large part of Palestine experience into something resembling a ceaseless and inconceivably elaborate game of chess; a game played by armed opponents whose every move is informed by passionate faith. Even in the heat of battle the similarity to chess is rarely lost, and the religious rioting which has desecrated the Holy City more often than can be counted has rarely taken the form of a straight fight provoked by grave theological differences; almost invariably the disputants fly to arms because someone has placed a venerable lamp on an unagreed lampstand, or has moved a venerable stone, or has opened a venerable door, or has said his prayers in some venerable place where someone else claimed exclusive rights. Such occurrences in Palestine have so much potential force that in the 1850's they could act as the (admittedly artificial) *casus belli* of a minor world war. Christians have no right to look down on Jews and Moslems because in 1928 Arab-Zionist hostility was reawakened by the putting up of a screen in a street.

Douglas Duff was present at the beginning of the trouble and has left an account.[1] On the eve of the Jewish feast of Yom Kippur, the Day of Atonement, he and the District Commissioner of Jerusalem (Ronald Storr's successor) took a walk round the old city, at the conclusion of which they called on the Mekehmeh es Sheria, the religious court attached to the area of the Mosque of Omar, the Haram es Sharif or "Noble Sanctuary." Their room overlooked the Wailing Wall, that towering rampart of huge-cut stone which is what remains of Herod's temple, the last temple of the Jewish nation. From the final Roman conquest in the second century till 1948 Jews used to repair here in order to lament the fall of this august shrine and kiss its ruin, an office usually performed with liturgical formality but often enough, and especially after the arrival of many young Jews to whom this ancient devotion was new, with passionate outcries and weeping. In whatever style this mourning was expressed, it was always an intensely moving thing to witness.

In the course of his visit to the religious court, the District Commissioner looked out of the window and down on the alley which runs along the base of this most famous of walls, when he was surprised to see an object "made of lath and cloth exactly like an ordinary bedroom screen" standing on the pavement a third of the way along. A more judicious man would have said nothing till later, but it seems that this over-conscientious official, remembering all that he had heard of the disorder that could follow the smallest sacred innovation, and perhaps foreseeing another Crimean war arising out of this paltry beginning, turned to Duff in nervous excitement and asked him if he had ever seen a screen there before. He had, because in fact it had been on view at a religious ceremony to mark the Jewish New Year ten days before. (Its purpose was to segregate men from women at prayers.) Duff gave a guarded reply to the effect that he did not remember. The District Commissioner did not take the hint and exclaimed that this was "an infringement of the status quo ante." His lack of reserve, according to this witness, was most unfortunate. "Some of the religious sheikhs belonging to the Mosque," Duff relates, "had entered the room, and the District Commissioner turned to them and asked them if they had seen the screen. The crafty old gentlemen had not, but, always

[1] Douglas V. Duff, *op. cit.*

willing to make capital at the expense of the Jews, immediately assumed miens of righteous indignation." The fat was now in the fire, and this scruffy little piece of furniture was destined to be the starting point of a long and terrible chapter in the internecine feud of Arab and Jew.

It would be tedious to relate the screen's subsequent history in close detail, especially as this has been done several times already. The story is like an incident from one of Trollope's ecclesiastical novels translated into Hebrew and Arabic and with the author's large-minded humanity subtracted from the telling of it. Both sides took as their ruling motto, "Dogged does it."

The rabbi in charge of the forthcoming ceremonies was ordered to remove the screen, the District Commissioner having been persuaded by the vehement sheikhs of the noble sanctuary that the wall was as sacred to Moslem as to Jews. (Quite untrue.) The rabbi promised to do so in the early morning of Yom Kippur, but being prevented by his congregation obtained an extension of the time-limit till nine o'clock when the police arrived under Duff and duly dismantled the screen. Unknown to the police, nine o'clock unfortunately coincided with a solemn moment in the ceremony. Jewish ladies battered the offending Gentiles with parasols. Arabs invaded the area. The British were accused by Zionists of wantonly injuring the worshipers and of having, through hatred of the Jews, purposely and blasphemously chosen this moment for the interruption of the service. These mad accusations (never since withdrawn in official Zionist publications) seem to have had the unlooked-for effect of putting confidence into the Arab leadership. It opened up new possibilities to their eyes. Suppose these accusations were true, they asked themselves, then, if they were, what were Arabs waiting for? Perhaps the British were their friends after all! The sanctuary officials began to follow up their advantage. They began to build an extension to the Mufti's house above the wall, obtained the services of a muezzin to utter the Moslem call to prayer on a nearby roof, and later undertook road works so as to transform the pavement before the wall from a blind alley into a thoroughfare, a proceeding which the legal advisers of the administration reluctantly declared to be within the rights of these pious clergymen.[2] The circumstances of the dispute caused the Arab leadership to move insensibly into the hands of the Supreme Moslem Council presided over by the Mufti, a fact of significance. He and his colleagues undertook widespread propaganda to the effect that the Jews planned to lay hands on all Moslem holy buildings, in proof of which a forged Zionist picture was distributed showing

[2] Israel Cohen, *The Zionist Movement*. London, 1945.

the Mosque of Omar with the Jewish flag flying from its dome.[3] In full keeping with the time-honored squalor of religious dispute in Jerusalem, the Supreme Council arranged that a rowdy Moslem ceremony known as the Zikr, in which the Name of God is loudly invoked to a drum and cymbal accompaniment, be held sufficiently near the wall to distract Jews effectively from their devotions. The League of Nations was appealed to. The British government reaffirmed the Turkish status quo in a White Paper. But the flames had been lit and this was not the way to put them out. The conflagration sank down in the course of 1929, but remained smoldering. Blood had flowed, but no one so far had been killed.

Lord Plumer's successor had arrived in Palestine during December, 1928. He was Sir John Chancellor whose main experience as a senior official had been in Africa, Trinidad, and as a principal secretary to the Imperial Defence Committee. He and his appointment have been harshly judged. Like many another man who has taken up a task at a critical moment he had to suffer the consequences of his predecessors' mistakes, without enjoying their advantages. He had not, like Sir Herbert Samuel, the prestige of a famous statesman, nor was he a victorious and much beloved military commander like Lord Plumer. The British government has been accused of making a merely routine appointment without regard to the critical character of Palestine, but this is not true at all. The Colonial Secretary in 1928 was Leopold Amery, the last Colonial Secretary to have been involved in the negotiations leading to the Balfour Declaration,[4] whose final text, he claimed, had followed his draft. In his mind Palestine was among the first of preoccupations and when Plumer requested leave to retire Amery picked as the next High Commissioner the most successful Colonial Governor in the service. The misfortune was that Sir John Chancellor arrived in Palestine at a bad moment when the screen nonsense, after a temporary abeyance, was reviving, and having started off on the wrong foot he never got on the right one.

This is, of course, to consider his administration only from the point of view of Arab-Jewish strife. Other things happened in Palestine besides this, and as a general administrator he lived up to the high expectations

[3] Report of the Shaw Commission, Command Paper 3530 of 1930.
[4] In 1917 L. S. Amery and Sir Mark Sykes were each known as "Assistant Secretary to the War Cabinet." In fact they had the authority of junior ministers and were sometimes empowered, as in the Sykes-Picot Agreement, to act as plenipotentiaries for the government. Mr. Amery once explaind to the writer that they adopted the inferior title of "Assistant Secretary" as this enabled them to sit in the House of Commons as private members without having to answer questions there.

with which he had been selected. Under his rule the construction of the harbor at Haifa was inaugurated, the most important of several major undertakings in the economic field. But in common with all High Commissioners after Lord Plumer, he was unable, in spite of valuable services, to emerge from the ordeal of Palestine with an unclouded reputation. One reason for this was that Chancellor not only arrived when Arab-Jewish hatred had suddenly and unexpectedly flared up, but that, during his first year in Palestine, events elsewhere enlarged and intensified the area of the storm. These should be outlined.

During 1928 the Jewish Agency was established in its final form. For the first time the Zionist leadership officially took this title. It may seem strange that it had taken seven years from the issue of the mandate to constitute the Jewish Agency on a permanent and definitive footing. The delay was due partly to the extremely complicated and contentious party rivalry within the Zionist movement, but yet more to Dr. Weizmann's endeavors to transform the Jewish leadership in Palestine from a party headquarters into something far more imposing: into an expression of the will of the whole Jewish people. This policy was not originated by Weizmann but was laid on him by Article 4 of the mandate which, having stated that "an appropriate Jewish agency" would act with the administration in National Home affairs, went on to say in the second paragraph: "The Zionist organisation . . . shall be recognised as such an agency. It shall take steps in consultation with His Britannic Majesty's Government to secure the co-operation of all Jews who are willing to assist in the establishment of the Jewish National Home."

Dr. Weizmann remembered how nearly the Balfour Declaration had been prevented by the opposition of non-Zionist Jews. He knew that among influential Western Jews a large proportion disapproved of Jewish nationalism and preferred that Judaism should count solely among the religions of the world: they had noted that Roman Catholicism had gained immensely by the loss of national involvement in a Papal State. From the non-Zionist Jews of the world, a majority in western Europe and America, came the most insidious and most dangerous threat to the National Home. To counter it Dr. Weizmann set himself the formidable task, one that appealed to his capacity for diplomacy and for thinking big, of turning the propositions of Article 4 into a political reality. He succeeded in getting so large a proportion of leading Jews to cooperate with him, and incidentally thereby to relieve the alarming financial straits of Zionism in Palestine, that it appeared that he had succeeded in the task he had set himself. It was almost as difficult a task as the long negotiations with the Allies whose outcome was the Balfour Declaration. It took him from 1923 to 1929.

In the summer of that year, the Sixteenth Zionist Congress met at Zurich. After a heated debate the delegates endorsed provisions for an extended Jewish Agency. The principal terms were, in brief, that the governing body of the agency was to number 224 and be composed half of Zionists and half of non-Zionists, the same proportions applying to the Administrative Committee of forty and the Executive in Palestine. The protocol was signed at a festive gathering on the 11th of August. A spectacular array of the most eminent Jews of the time figured on the platform. With Dr. Weizmann and his veteran colleague Nahum Sokolov sat Sir Herbert Samuel, Lord Melchett, Sir Osmond d'Avigdor Goldsmid, Louis Marshall and Felix Warburg (representing American Jewry), Sholem Asch the novelist, Léon Blum, and Albert Einstein.

The establishment of the Jewish Agency is one of those Zionist episodes about which it is difficult to make up one's mind. Without any doubt, the achievement was to a large extent illusory. No amount of treaty-making could diminish the fact that the Zionists were far removed in spirit and purpose from those non-Zionist Jews who wished well to the National Home but wished equally well and in most cases better to the Diaspora. Between the two parties was the extreme difference between enthusiasm and rational piety; between those who are absolutely convinced of the absolute truth of an ideal and those who merely admire the ideal; between love and platonic friendship. The agreement was distasteful to the pioneers in the settlements of Palestine who were only just emerging from a bitter crisis and were still struggling for bare survival, and the majority of the Zionist party determined that the accord of Zurich should operate exclusively in the interest of those who were bearing the heat and burden of the day. They succeeded.

From the first it was found difficult to define the term "non-Zionist" in such a way as to exclude anti-Zionists, since the last thing that any of the Jews wanted was to allow the Zurich accord to be used as a Trojan horse by enemies of the National Home. The definition finally agreed was "a person associated with the Agency otherwise than in the capacity of a member and representative of the Zionist Organisation." When the accord was signed in Zurich, Palestine (which still had a considerable non-Zionist Jewish population) was among the countries invited to send non-Zionist representatives. The definition gave the Zionist Executive their chance, and they proceeded to elect as their non-Zionist spokesmen six members of the Jewish national council, the Va'ad Leumi, a Zionist body if ever there was one, but if you chose to interpret the Zurich agreement legalistically, and in no other way, not within the definition. In the party struggle following Zurich, the definition was to prove a formidable weapon in the hands of the uncompromising wing of Zionism, and in the end they used it to defeat entirely the cause of non-Zionist representation. Albert Hyamson sums the matter up lucidly. "There were instances," he relates, "of men and women holding office in one of the Zionist institutions, resigning and appearing a week later as non-Zionist members of the Agency . . . But these breaches of the spirit if not of the letter were, however, not sufficient. The proportion of non-Zionists were gradually reduced until in the end the Executive of the Jewish Agency [in Palestine] consisted of seventeen Zionists and three non-Zionists. Finally there was no election of non-Zionists at all after 1937 and henceforth the Jewish Agency was an undisguised alias for the Zionist Organisation." [5]

This sequence of events might suggest that Dr. Weizmann's protracted labors ended in total failure. As regards his immediate aim, there can be no doubt that he failed, but the subsequent history of Zionism equally suggests that in his ultimate aim, that of bringing to his side the leading Jews of the world, few of whom belonged to his party, he acheived much. There was always a danger, especially among Russian Jews with their long experience of a ghetto life, that Zionism would become parochial in mind. Weizmann had opened many windows and had brought the movement into live relationship with the outside world. The reward of his labors was hardly visible in the years succeeding Zurich, but more than ten years after, and thanks to the line of policy which he inaugurated in 1923, Zionism obtained the advantages of world association. The aim of the British government in helping these endeavors, that of bringing a permanently moderating influence to bear on Zionism, was completely frustrated.

The immediate effect of Zurich on affairs in Palestine was disastrous. The Arab nationalist leaders took careful note of the congress and the accord, misinterpreted much of what they noted, and became panic-stricken. Zionist affairs have always been marked by an extraordinary complexity and the politically inexperienced Arabs very naturally mis-

[5] The negotiations leading to the final and extended establishment of the Jewish Agency are described in some detail in Israel Cohen's *The Zionist Movement, op cit.*, and more fully, and from a personal point of view, in Dr. Weizmann's autobiography. Both writers skate over the "awkwardnesses" which are pungently indicated by Albert Hyamson in his *Palestine Under the Mandate*. London, 1950.

understood the party debate at the Sixteenth Congress and confounded it with the accord, seeing all the proceedings of Zurich as a single event. Like many other enemies of the Jews they thought they detected a huge world-wide clandestine plot informing everything that the Jews did. But the Sixteenth Congress was a very remarkable Zionist event and the Arabs were not wholly to be blamed for their extravagant fears.

The main party dispute at the congress was between the moderate party led by Weizmann and the extremists, of whom Vladimir Jabotinsky was the most commanding personality, though he was too extremist to be a leader of all the groups opposed to Weizmann. The subject of controversy has been ably summarized as "the old dispute between the 'political' Zionists who, dominated by a sense of urgency, wished to subordinate everything to getting as many Jews into Palestine as quickly as possible, and the 'practical' Zionism of Weizmann and his supporters who, apart from realising the practical necessity of accommodating themselves to financial realities and to the best that could be made of British policy, laid great stress on the building up of the idealist content of the National Home by basing it on agricultural settlement and co-operative institutions." [6] It was another struggle between rational policy and enthusiasm. In the end (as usually happens in nationalist affairs), the enthusiasts won, but their victory was still many years off. The Arabs, with the occasional perspicacity that fear gives to people, saw that ultimate victory, but, as happens to men with shut minds, they were blind to everything else. They did not notice a fact of great importance on which abler men might have built a realistic policy, namely that at the congress Weizmann and the moderates heavily defeated the extremists. What they noticed and thought about was the speech delivered by Jabotinsky on the first day.

There can be no doubt that Jabotinsky spoke for many Zionists. In his opening remarks he summed up what he had to say. "What is a National Home?" he began.

> So far as I understand it this word has simply one meaning for the soul of the Jewish people, and that is a National State with a preponderant Jewish majority, and in which the Jewish will must decide the form and the direction that the life of the community must follow. And I believe also that in the consciousness of the Jewish people the expression "an openly and legally assured National Home (*Heimstätte*)" [7] has this one meaning alone. On occasion men may, at the point of the pistol, plead that this word National Home can have other meanings. But once every

[6] John Marlowe, *op. cit.*
[7] A reference to the resolution of the First Zionist Congress.

year it is allowed to the Jews, even as it was to the Marranos,[8] to stand in the presence of the Sanctity of the people, and to declare openly: "Yes, I have acted under compulsion; Yes, I have denied what I believe true, but all the same—our Vow!" [9]

What does the word Palestine mean? Palestine is a territory whose chief geographical feature is this: that the River Jordan does not delineate its frontier but flows through its centre.

What is the meaning of Zionism? Zionism does not mean some kind of endeavour to furnish suffering Jewish people throughout the world with a moral rallying point, a source of consolation, in Palestine. The word Zionism has always meant the practical solution of the political, economic and cultural tragedy of many millions. Scientists may argue as to whether the thing is possible or not, and how long it will take to accomplish. We are not assembled here to take part in such a debate. What I wish to assert is this: that in the soul of our people the word Zionism was never a consolation-stunt (*Trost-spielung*), but has always stood for that endeavour to rescue millions from a tragic situation. And I wish further to assert that a"charter" or a "Mandate" is an obligation laid on the civilised world, an obligation laid on a great nation and signed with its word of honour, not just to "smile nicely at us from over the way" (*günstig gegenuber zu stehen*), not just to "keep friendly with us," (*freundlich zu behandeln*) but, in accordance with a solemn promise, to found a colonisation régime in Palestine, and to organise the necessary administrative machinery to open up territory on either side of the Jordan for the reception of great colonising masses.

In more detailed and practical passages of his speech Jabotinsky called for the repudiation of the 1922 White Paper, and urged that attempts to appease the anxieties of the Arabs should not be persisted in as, until a Jewish majority in Palestine had been achieved, this was a mistaken policy.

It is not altogether surprising that utterances of this kind, followed by a demonstration of the solidarity of all Jews of all parties in favor of the National Home policy, gave Arabs the idea that the Jews of the world were massing for an attack on them.[10]

---

[8] Clandestine Spanish Jews of the sixteenth and seventeenth centuries. The meaning of the nickname is doubtful.

[9] Our Vow—Jabotinsky used the Hebrew words "Kol Nidrel," literally "All vows," the opening words of the opening prayer at the celebration of the Day of Atonement.

[10] The Peel Commission, following its immediate predecessor, considered that the extension of the Jewish Agency was largely responsible for the revival of violent anti-Zionism among Arabs.

The atmosphere in Jerusalem was growing more tense and the goading policy of the Supreme Moslem Council over the Wailing Wall had the desired effect of driving Jews to exasperation. The finding of the law officers that there was no legal objection to the Moslem authorities' turning the pavement of the wall into a thoroughfare if they so wished came as a final and infuriating exacerbation of their feelings, and the general resentment was kept alive by the Zionist Press and professional agitators. In August came the news of the Sixteenth Congress and the Zurich accord, and a little after, on the fifteenth, fell the Fast of Ab. On this day a group of young men and women of Jabotinsky's party, the Revisionists, marched in a body to the government offices in Jerusalem with a protest against British policy. Having submitted their protest they declared their intention of going to the Wailing Wall. The officials hesitated whether to allow this but came to the conclusion that they would put themselves in an invidious position if they forbade Jews to visit this most sacred of shrines on the feast commemorating the destruction of the Temple by the Romans. When the permission was granted, the young Revisionists marched to the wall where, to quote Albert Hyamson, they held "an anti-Arab demonstration, with loud demands for the ownership of the wall and the taking of an oath to defend it at all costs." The next day was a Friday when great numbers of Moslems came into Jerusalem to attend the mosque services. They invaded the wall area but the police were with difficulty able to control the riot,[11] which was quickly forgotten in the horror of what happened next.

It is conceivable that the second Wailing Wall upheaval, like the first, might have had no enormous consequence if a murder had not been committed at this time. A Jewish boy kicked a football into an Arab garden. The Arab saw the hand of Zionism, and there was a brawl in which the innocent youth was stabbed to death by a Moslem. The Zionists seized the occasion of the boy's funeral to make a demonstration. Precisely what happened after that is not known beyond the fact that on the ensuing Thursday and Friday, August 22nd and 23rd, great numbers of Arab peasants came into Jerusalem armed with clubs and knives. A few of them had firearms.

The chief of police in Jerusalem noticed the carrying of clubs and ordered that the incoming crowd should be disarmed. The attempt to do this was discontinued, as he testified later, because the operation proved difficult and provocative.[12] This probably means that he had too few reliable

[11] Marlowe, Cohen, Hyamson, *op. cit.*
[12] Shaw Report.

men. Alarmed at the situation he went to the Mufti and asked why the crowd were carrying clubs. With his habitual and charming air of innocence the Mufti replied that recent events had made them afraid of the Jews. There was no need to worry, he said. The chief of police was convinced of his good faith. Later in the morning the Mufti and one of his colleagues of the Supreme Moslem Council addressed a mass meeting in the noble sanctuary. They said nothing that could be called incitement but at the conclusion of the meeting the mob rushed out into the streets of Jerusalem and attacked every Jew they could see. They murdered several. And now violence broke out on a more terrible scale than had yet been seen in the country.

It was now that the disastrous effects of Lord Plumer's reduction of forces showed. The British police numbered less than three hundred. The Arabs in the police force refused to combat fellow Arabs, and the administration, fearful of an outbreak of civil war, not only refused the request of the Zionist authorities for the arming of a large number of Jewish men for the protection of the settlements, but even the use of Jewish police.[13] This decision has generally been blamed. As a result of it, utterly insufficient forces endeavored to maintain order while awaiting reinforcements from the British garrison in Egypt.

They had to wait three days, while the infection of murder spread so rapidly that it is difficult and even impossible to believe that this sudden outbreak of savagery was unplanned. Several Jewish settlements were quickly and utterly laid waste between Jerusalem and Haifa and in the south. The most ghastly incident was at Hebron. There was a Jewish population there of over 700 people, an ancient community centered on a Talmudical college. Armed bands intent on slaughter reached Hebron on the 24th. The police were Arab and they stood passively by while their fellow Moslems moved into the town and proceeded to deeds which would have been revolting among animals. There was an inn in the town where some Jews had fled for safety. The Arabs killed and dismembered twenty-three of them with daggers and axes in an upper room, so that, according to a witness, blood ran down the stairs and soaked through the ceiling and splashed on to the floor beneath. This was not half of the crime. In all the Moslems killed sixty Jews including children, and wounded nearly as many. Had it not been for one brave man (mentioned later) the massacre might have been even worse than it was.[14]

[13] Cohen, *op. cit.*
[14] Douglas Duff ascribes the violence of the Hebron atrocity to the fact that many Arab peasants in the neighborhood were in debt to Jewish merchants in the town.

Even after the arrival of military reinforcements, but before dispositions were completed, Arab rioters committed a last abomination in the little northern town of Safed. Twenty people, including children, were murdered and over a hundred houses were burned or otherwise destroyed. In the whole course of the rising 133 Jews were killed and 339 wounded, 116 Arabs were killed and 232 wounded. All the Jewish casualties were due to Arab action, and all the Arab ones to police action except for six killed in a Jewish counterattack between Tel Aviv and Jaffa.

While these things were happening the High Commissioner had been on leave. He hurried back and reached Jerusalem on the 29th of August, a day before the Safed atrocity. He was not to be blamed for being on leave at the time of the uprising, in spite of warning rumbles, for if attention had been paid to every threat of violence, then no one in authority in Palestine would ever have taken leave at all after the summer of 1928. Sir John Chancellor does, however, seem to have shown lack of foresight and nerve in the proclamations which he issued on his return. Again he is not to be blamed too rigorously. Today 1929 and 1930 can be recognized as a crossroads moment when mistakes could not be easily undone.

The first proclamation was issued on September first. It condemned the "savage murders perpetrated upon defenceless members of the Jewish population." The mistake occurred in the fifth paragraph where Sir John Chancellor stated as follows: "In accordance with an undertaking which I gave to the Committee of the Arab Executive before I left Palestine in June, I initiated discussions with the Secretary of State when in England on the subject of constitutional changes in Palestine. In view of recent events I will suspend these discussions with His Majesty's Government." Written in the heat of indignation this statement assumed the guilt of the Arab political leadership before any evidence had been heard on the subject. The nationalist leaders and the Mufti could hardly miss so easy a trick, and when they protested Sir John Chancellor was under obligation to express himself anew and in milder terms. In a second proclamation, issued a few days later, he stated that an inquiry into the conduct of both sides would be held as soon as possible. This suggestion that the murderers and their victims were on a level naturally hurt and infuriated the Jews of Palestine and those who were with them in the horrors they had lived through. Douglas Duff accurately described the general impression made by the High Commissioner's action: "The Proclamation . . . in which

---

The fact is not to be set aside when stated on his authority, but is most unlikely to have been more than a small subsidiary cause.

he expressed his horror of the savage atrocities of the Arabs was humbly withdrawn and almost an apology offered to them for the terms that had been used." The inquiry was to be held under the chairmanship of Sir Walter Shaw, a former chief justice of the Straits settlements.

At this dark moment in Zionist history, the movement was without the support of a sympathetic Colonial Secretary in London. The government of Stanley Baldwin had fallen in midsummer of 1929; Leopold Amery had gone, and the new Colonial Secretary under the premiership of Ramsay MacDonald was Sydney Webb, who had been made Lord Passfield for the purpose. In spite of a large Jewish membership, the Labour Party had no views on Zionism. The principal movers in the Balfour Declaration had been Conservatives and Liberals, and the attempt to make it an all-party pronouncement by engaging the interest of George Barnes counted for nothing among Labour politicians twelve years later. The Labour Party of those days was professedly international but in practice had as insular a character as any trades union spokesman; on the subject of Palestine it was uncommitted. The Jews and Arabs of Palestine were faraway people of whom most of the government and its supporters knew and wished to know little. But an exception to this state of mind was to be expected of Passfield and his wife, Beatrice Webb. They represented the intelligentsia, and parochialism was not a likely fault with them. When it is remembered how large a proportion of the Zionists of Palestine were convinced socialists, and that their movement was almost united in a wish to achieve a socialist order, it is indeed strange that Sydney and Beatrice Webb should have been strong anti-Zionists who (with a little more clarity and firmness) might have brought Zionist expansion to a grinding halt. But if their lack of sympathy with the Jewish cause was certainly not due to insularity, it may possibly be ascribed to the opposite. Unlike most of their colleagues they knew international socialism not as a dream but as a reality, and, as their later performance in the Russia of Stalin was to show, they were gullible people. England has been lucky that British anti-Semitism has been almost wholly confined to middle- and upper-class minorities, and has always lacked, from the beginning of the modern racialist form of the movement, a broad popular base. But in France and Germany it was otherwise, and since the late nineteenth century Continental socialism had maintained strong anti-Semitic wings. They confounded hatred of Jews with anticapitalism. It has been noted already how the Rutenberg concession had appeared to associate Zionism with big business, and this fact could easily have influenced the internationally minded Webbs into radical distrust of the movement. To say as much may be to do them a grave injustice, but it is no injustice to say that Lord Passfield (representing as always "our partnership") was the most anti-Zionist Secretary of State with whom Zionists had to deal at any time.

Immediately on receiving the news of the massacres Dr. Weizmann hurried to London from Switzerland where he was holidaying after the congress. He found a chill atmosphere in Westminster, very different from the cordiality with which he had been received in the days of Lloyd George, Arthur Balfour, Winston Churchill, or Leopold Amery. He used to say in the past that Zionists found encouragement in Whitehall and obstruction in Palestine, but now he found more formidable obstruction in Whitehall than he had yet found in Jerusalem. He wanted to meet Passfield but, for the first time since 1917 in his long experience of British government, he found himself treated somewhat as an outsider; the interview was not readily granted and had to be sought for through tiresome intrigue. At length Josiah Wedgwood introduced him—not to Passfield— but to Beatrice Webb. "I can't understand," she snapped, "why the Jews make such a fuss over a few dozen of their people being killed in Palestine. As many are killed every week in London in traffic accidents, and no one pays any attention." When Lord Passfield at length received Dr. Weizmann he made it clear that he was strongly opposed to mass Jewish immigration into the National Home.[15]

In September Sir Walter Shaw began his labors as head of the latest royal commission on Palestine. From the first, Zionists, Jewish and Gentile, were afraid that he would exceed his terms of reference which were to inquire into the immediate causes of the Wailing Wall riots and their sequel, and which excluded considerations of major policy. It seems that Passfield's anti-Zionism was known in the political world, for in spite of previous assurances given by the Prime Minister, a letter asking for a further assurance that the commission would not touch major policy was printed in *The Times* on the 20th of December. The letter was signed by Arthur Balfour, Lloyd George, and General Smuts. The assurance was repeated. This appearance in *The Times* was the last public action of Balfour's life. But in spite of the assurance that Balfour thus asked for and received, Shaw contrived to influence major policy for a short time.

There is no need here to give the details of the commission or its report. They have been given many times already, and in common with most royal commissions on Palestine, this one did not ultimately have any effect on the future. Its findings would have been better if the Zionists had not antagonized the commission by overplaying their hand; for example they

[15] Chaim Weizmann, *Trial and Error*. London, 1949.

laid accusations against the British police which they soon found it necessary to withdraw with the admission that what they had alleged was groundless,[16] and this, with similar extravagances, naturally gave the commissioners the idea that they were not serious people. This can account in part for the fact that Shaw and his colleagues took little notice of strong Zionist evidence that members of the Arab Executive and the Supreme Moslem Council had organized and incited the riots. Such depositions were in any case unwelcome. They went against a fixed British idea that the Mufti was well-intentioned, a man of sense and decency and a persistent influence for moderation.[17] Haj Amin's own later bloodthirsty career, in which he once even outdid Hitler himself in cruelty against the Jews, leaves no doubt that the Zionists were giving valuable information when they denounced him. But Shaw only went so far as to say that the Mufti was to blame for not having done more to stop the riots, and neither he nor his colleagues (with one exception) could accept the idea that the Mufti was a positive factor of unrest, and in character a very crafty, ruthless, dedicated, and evil man. Haj Amin had done well to bide his time for so long.

The Shaw Commission reported, in the face of much contrary evidence, that the attack on the Jews was "unpremeditated." Reacting against Zionist exaggerations, it reported perhaps too indulgently on the conduct of the administration in attempting to maintain order. It may be said that on the events themselves of August, 1929, it gave way to that fashionable twentyish mood of complacency and optimistic interpretation, but on the deeper causes it looked with disquiet. It pointed to the "landless and discontented class" being formed by Zionist expansion as the main origin of trouble and urged that "directions more explicit" (meaning of course "restrictions") should be "given to" (meaning "imposed on") the management of the National Home.

Its main recommendations were that the government should give a precise statement on its obligations to the "non-Jewish communities"; should strengthen its control of Jewish immigration so as to prevent a repetition of the mass movements of the midtwenties; that the eviction of tenants should be rigidly held in check until a thorough land survey had been completed; that the Jewish Agency should be made to understand that it had no share in the government of Palestine; that there should be press laws aimed against inflammatory propaganda; that a separate commission should determine rights around the Wailing Wall, and that the garrison

[16] Hyamson, *op. cit.*
[17] *Cf.* contemporary reports and articles in *The Times.*

and police should be permanently maintained at appropriate strength. It will be noted that except for the last two, all these recommendations have something of a pro-Arab anti-Zionist tendency. The Shaw Commission did not make a distinction between anti-Zionism and regard for the "non-Jewish community." Unlike the British government and administration it recognized that the two were incompatible. The sentence in Shaw's report which most angered Jews was the one he used in discussing the Churchill White Paper of 1922. "There was no clear direction," wrote Shaw, "to assist either party in the fulfilment of their aspirations."

In discussing the development of the National Home, the land question, and suchlike, Sir Walter Shaw was clearly going beyond his assured terms of reference, but he put them forward as matters requiring governmental thought and decision if peace was to be restored. He would, indeed, have been guilty of dereliction of duty if he had not mentioned these things.

The commissioner who differed from his colleagues on the question of the responsibility of the Arab leadership for the massacre was Henry Snell, who represented Labour on this all-party body. He accepted the Zionist evidence on the Mufti (supported by British police evidence), and in this he was without question wiser than his colleagues. He took a Zionist view of the Palestine situation, and for this his name was, and still is, held in honor. But though he said some pertinent things about the riots on this occasion, it is difficult to see much statesmanship in his wider views. His major recommendation was that, to fulfill the primary need of Palestine, it was necessary "to change the Arab's minds." This belongs to a class of large soothing phrases often used by politicians in times of stress, phrases such as "initiate goodwill" or "establish a world authority," which indicate truly enough vast and absolute answers to fearful and agonizing questions, without the smallest suggestion toward what Henry James described as "the dear little deadly question of how to do it."

The Shaw report is the starting point of a certain rhythm to be noticed from then on in the affairs of Palestine under the mandate. A royal commission goes out to the troubled land; its recommendations lead to the sending of a subsidiary commission to make definitive proposals on how to put the recommendations into effect; the proposals conflict with too much of settled conviction and involve too much political risk to be acted on; both commissions prove to have been a waste of talent and time. This frequent sending of abortive commissions to Palestine was part of that belief which continues at the present time, namely that if one can only get a clear statement of any problem, its solution must likewise become clear.

The belief appears to be true of only a few areas of experience and was never to be true of Palestine.

The commission following that of Sir Walter Shaw was headed by Sir John Hope Simpson. He was chosen because his official career had given him experience in the task of transposing and resettling populations; he was at the time of his appointment a member of the League of Nations commission in charge of the exchange of Turks and Greeks following the victory of Mustafa Kemal. As Mr. John Marlowe wittily remarks, "he was thus temporarily transferred from the task of repairing the consequences of one, to the task of attempting to ensure the maintenance of another of Lloyd George's Near Eastern policies."

According to Dr. Weizmann's autobiography, Lord Passfield promised to arrange for Weizmann to meet Hope Simpson before he left on his mission, but the promise was broken.

Since none of Hope Simpson's proposals bore fruit his report, like its predecessor, need not be discussed in this study with any fullness. The value of his work was to some extent vitiated by the fact that on his main subject, the land question, he was misled into using an erroneously low estimate of the amount of cultivatable land within the Palestine borders. The whole tone of his proposals tended toward minimum development. By this time, the summer of 1930, the great economic slump was moving toward climax; unemployment was rising in Europe and America, and it seemed the merest folly to promote new expansionist schemes liable and likely to crash and thereby bring about a return of the destitution from which Jewish Palestine had just escaped. In only one respect did he recommend new large-scale investment, and that was in land on which to settle the landless fellahin whom he reckoned at 30 percent of the rural population. In this connection he advised concurrent expansion of schools, pointing out that a man without the rudiments of learning is not able to benefit from agricultural education. With the miseries of unemployment always in mind, he criticized the labor policy of the Zionists. From the beginning they had followed a natural tendency, in keeping with the "return to the land" idealism of Zionism, to employ Jewish workers in preference to others in the budding colonies, but during the hard times of the midtwenties this had become something of a principle, and, in the view of Sir John Hope Simpson, something of a vice as well. "The principle," he wrote, "of the persistent and deliberate boycott of Arab labour in the colonies is not only contrary to the Mandate, but it is in addition a constant and increasing source of danger to the country."

The feature of Hope Simpson's report which caused most exasperation to Zionists was his recommendations as regards Jewish immigration. He stated his "personal belief" that when development schemes were in full operation there would be room in Palestine for the whole existing population "on a higher standard of life than it at present enjoys" and for 20,000 immigrant families, about 100,000 people; but since he made it clear that he was not only referring to Jewish immigrants, the Zionists could only expect to benefit by a definitive immigration of some 50,000. "If there are suitable Arab workmen unemployed," he said, "it is not right that Jewish workmen from other countries should be imported to fill existing posts." He made, however, a subtle reservation. He stated that since Jewish capital was only imported with the object of employing Jewish labor, a stoppage of the import could not affect Arabs, but on the contrary would in the long run afford them some economic benefit.

The Hope Simpson report was thoroughly to the taste of Lord Passfield, who proceeded to publish a White Paper on government policy in which he incorporated all the commission's recommendations on land, immigration, and employment, omitting the reservations in favor of the import of Zionist capital. The White Paper was a strong statement of the doctrine of "equality of obligation." One paragraph summed the matter up: "Attempts have been made to argue in support of Zionist claims that the principal feature of the Mandate is the passage regarding the Jewish National Home and that the passages designed to safeguard the rights of the non-Jewish community are merely secondary considerations qualifying to some extent what is claimed to be the primary object for which the Mandate has been framed. This is a conception which His Majesty's Government have always regarded as totally erroneous."

Jews were irritated at the patronizing and (as many of them believed) hostile[18] tone of the language used toward them. The government, the paper declared, "has received little assistance from either side in healing the breach between them during the months of tension and unrest which have followed on the disturbances of August 1929, and to the differences created by the mutual suspicions and hostilities of the two races has been added a further grave obstacle, namely an attitude of mistrust towards His Majesty's Government."

Since the Passfield White Paper went the way of the Shaw and Hope Simpson reports, it also need not occupy much space here, especially as it has been ably analyzed and discussed elsewhere.[19] Two details are worth noticing. Following Hope Simpson the paper compares "colonisation under Zionist auspices" with the operations, involving excellent Jewish-Arab relations, of the Palestine Jewish Colonisation Association (the P.I.C.A.). The latter body was the descendant of the philanthropic enterprises of Baron de Hirsch, a Zionist pioneer only in the sense that he worked (most valiantly) to obtain territory, preferably in South America, where Jews, especially the persecuted of imperial Russia, might settle in peace. To some extent he succeeded and he influenced Herzl's first Zionist ideas, but he and his movement, the Jewish Colonisation Association, were remote from the classic nationalist Zionism of the National Home. The P.I.C.A. was mainly occupied in sustaining the old Russian settlements dating from the late nineteenth century, and the similar foundation of Baron Edmond de Rothschild. As a body, incorporated in the Zionist organization, they had no influence in the politics of active Zionism, and to invite Jews to model themselves on this excellent philanthropic society was to misread nationalism again. It was to ask them to return to the mind and habits of a past age.

The second point to be noted is that the offer was renewed of a Legislative council composed of the High Commissioner and twenty-two members (of whom twelve would be elected) with the right of appeal to the League of Nations.

The White Paper was published on the 21st of October, 1930, and it caused a political commotion which quickly scared the Labour government first into modification and then into recantation. All the surviving members of the coalition which had issued the Balfour Declaration were in opposition[20] and as a result the government found themselves threatened by a formidable combination; the outraged feelings of Jews throughout the world, political opponents such as Lord Cecil who were moved to action by what they held with passion and sincerity to be a breach of contract, and by party leaders who saw a marvelous political opportunity. Dr. Weizmann rode the storm with all his old skill and with the help of prominent Jews of Great Britain and America. His formal resignation

---

Cohen and Dr. Weizmann's autobiography are very interesting; Dr. Weizmann's especially so as an eye-witness account, but they are both extravagantly biased even by Zionist standards. John Jeffries gives a very full and able account from an Arab and anti-Zionist point of view, with much curious detail, but he makes a complicated story even more complicated than it was as he wrote under the mistaken impression that Lord Passfield was a Zionist. As a result he unconsciously represents that eminent economist as a mixture of lunatic and contortionist.

[20] Arthur Henderson, Foreign Secretary 1929-31, had resigned from the Coalition Cabinet in August, 1917.

from the presidency of the Zionist organization, and of the Jewish Agency as well, was followed by the resignations of Mr. Felix Warburg from the chairmanship of the Agency's administrative committee and of Lord Melchett from the chairmanship of the Council. On the 18th of November the White Paper was strenuously debated in the House of Commons and it became clear that a sizable section of the Labour Party opposed the anti-Zionism of the attempted policy. At one point Lloyd George accused Ramsay MacDonald of failing the trust he had inherited with office and breaking the word of England. In a rare flash of eloquence the Prime Minister answered him as follows: "It was not a word we inherited. We inherited words, and they are not always consistent."

As soon as the clang of battle filled the air, Lord Passfield decided not to fight. Four days previous to the debate he officially announced that "doubts having been expressed" about "some passages of the White Paper," he had called a conference with representatives of the Jewish Agency. At the meeting of the conference, in which, according to Dr. Weizmann, Lord Passfield "proved to be the head and fount of the opposition to our demands," the Zionists slowly gained their object. Dr. Weizmann converted Ramsay MacDonald to a pro-Zionist point of view. After this things went the way he wanted. The debate ended with a letter from the Prime Minister to Weizmann, which was read by MacDonald in the House of Commons on the 13th of February, 1931. In form the letter was an explanation of the inner meaning of Passfield's White Paper, in effect it was a complete repudiation of his policy. It reaffirmed all the Zionist liberties which Passfield, acting on Hope Simpson's guidance, had threatened. "It was under MacDonald's letter to me," wrote Dr. Weizmann eighteen years later, "that the change came about in the Government's attitude, and in the attitude of the Palestine Administration which enabled us to make the magnificent gains of the ensuing years." [21]

During this 1929-1931 episode the Palestine Arabs made one striking appearance in the last stages. It will be remembered how they requested constitutional government in 1928, and that a Legislative Council was proposed in Passfield's White Paper. This was not mentioned in MacDonald's letter, and it remained a cause of Jewish anxiety. As in the past Jewish refusal or boycotting of a constitution was in too direct opposition to Jewish liberalism to be undertaken without the danger of a radical party-split and of a perhaps fatal loss of sympathy in the world. Zionists were pledged to democracy. As before, the Arabs saved them. In Decem-

[21] *Trial and Error, op. cit.*

ber, 1930, the government, at Dr. Weizmann's suggestion, invited the Arab leaders to meet the Zionists at a round table conference to discuss the constitutional issue. This was to present the Arabs with the old temptation which had half-ruined them already, and again it proved too much for them. They could not resist another opportunity to practice boycott. They refused the invitation. The constitutional issue thereupon lapsed for six more vital years.

It can be put to the credit of the short-lived Labour government which Lord Passfield served that their indeterminate policy did bring a brief period of peace to Palestine. The reasons for this cannot be documented or proved but can be guessed at with some confidence.

Both sides had achieved something beyond expectation. The Arabs had provoked appalling disorders and had ended up with an official affirmation of their national rights, accompanied by unwelcome reservations, it is true, but unmistakably an assurance, and a proof moreover that their cause had powerful friends in the mandatory power. The Zionists had had to face a stern check to their ambitions, an official declaration that Balfour's Zionist policy must be limited and confined to an extremely modest program of national self-expression,[22] yet in less than four months they had achieved a recantation by their opponents, an assurance by letter that the letter of 1917 known as the Balfour Declaration defined an unchangeable principle of British policy. (How foolish were the Zionist delegates at the 1931 Congress who blamed Weizmann[23] for being satisfied with a letter!)

The lull in the Arab-Jewish conflict was, in all probability, largely due also to unexpected economic developments. Palestine had suffered an economic blizzard in the twenties while most of the world was enjoying prosperity and expansion of trade. By a remarkable stroke of poetic justice Palestine in the early thirties felt relatively little of the effects of the great Depression (outside the important field of agriculture) when these were at their height elsewhere. In some respects the country was in advance of others in showing signs of recovery. This was entirely the work of the Jews and can probably be accurately described as being in part the first fruits of Weizmann's policy for an enlarged Agency. In spite of Hope Simpson's and Passfield's discouragement, and in spite of the Depression, there was considerable British and American Jewish investment in Pales-

[22] On p. 5 of the Passfield White Paper (Cmd. 3692) it is suggested that the obligation to Zionism had been discharged by 1930, since under the Mandate the Jewish community already "has in fact its own 'national' characteristics."
[23] *Trial and Error, op. cit.*

tine in these first years of the thirties.[24] Concurrently there was a fresh rise
in Jewish immigration, not so drastic as to provoke fears of Jabotinsky's
"great colonising masses on either side of the Jordan," but at the same
time sufficient to supply needed skill to exploit opportunity, and to bring
in additional wealth. A large part of the population, Jewish and Arab in
equal degrees, felt the stimulation of reviving trade and wide demands for
manual labor; all this at a time when figures for unemployment in Germany stood at over six million.

But the resulting peace was sullen and only escapists believed that it
could endure. Arab-Jewish cooperation might be found here and there but
no thinking person with knowledge of Palestine could delude himself that
such cooperation could be the foundation of a polity; indeed the tendency
of thinking people, especially of those who remembered the hopes of
other years, was to deny that economic health gave any measure of political peace at all.[25] It was sound deduction that the generous beliefs and
aspirations that fitfully illuminated the Palestine of Sir Herbert Samuel and
Lord Plumer had gone, and could never return. Sir John Chancellor had
no delusions. He retired from the High Commission in July, 1931. His
disappointment at not having been able to bring peace and stability to
Palestine remained with him for the rest of his life.

The events which opened with the episode of the screen in the street in
1928 and led to the White Paper of 1930, and then to its repudiation,
formed the last crossroads in the history of mandated Palestine during a
period of relative world peace. There was then no immediate prospect of a
world war; the troubles of the time were social and economic. The years
around 1930 were to prove the last period in which it was possible for
Great Britain to define policy in mandated Palestine without reference to
overpowering pressures from without. It may be apposite here to look at
some of the signs of those times.

Palestine has been described as the land of three faiths, meaning of
three ancient religions. In 1930 it was also the land of three new religions: Arab nationalism, Jewish Zionism, and British belief in British
Empire interests. The third of these requires a longer phrase for description than the other two, and indeed can be described in several different
ways. The reason is that it was vaguer and meant different things to different people. It entirely lacked the simple immediacy, the clear appeal to

[24] Hyamson, op. cit.
[25] Cf. an article in The Observer by Lord Samuel. 8th July, 1934.

loyalty of the other two. It was much the weakest of the three and was inevitably to go down first. At this time, the early thirties, the two stronger were beginning to turn on the weakest, independently of each other, and in no spirit of forgetting their fierce mutual hate.

One of the greatest of epigrams is that of Clemenceau: *"Ce qui donne du courage ce sont les idées."* The history of Palestine under the mandate allows one to test this saying with almost mathematical precision.

The ideas informing Zionism were powerful ones, proved by time, expressed in the greatest prose and poetry which have survived from the ancient world. Those British who ten years before thought that Zionism was an innocuous plaything at which they could safely "smile nicely from over the way" were probably overinfluenced by the fact that Zionism had been a very slow starter. Herzl's predecessors made little impact on Jews or Gentiles, and the Zionism of Herzl himself never rallied more than a Jewish party in his time. Weizmann's efforts to draw a Jewish majority into that party had met with as much failure as success, and his enlargement of the Jewish Agency was only the result of a long uphill struggle. All this suggested that Zionism was essentially a minority movement and therefore a small-scale and easily contained force. But the slow start disguised the fact that old and enduring ideas were adapting themselves to modern forms, a necessarily gradual process, and that since 1917 this process showed no recession. It disguised the fact that one day the movement would be so powerful that no one would be able to contain it, from within or without.

Zionism by the early thirties had undergone some changes. It was still essentially what it had been in the first days after the war, idealistic, modernist, devoted to liberal and socialist beliefs, opposed to violence. But a spirit of bitterness and hardness was growing in the movement. Hitherto the wrangles of the Zionist organization and the Palestine administration had not been as ferocious as might appear from a recital of political conflict: it was more like the incessant disagreement in Great Britain at the same time between (for example) British agriculture and the British government. Agriculturists of all kinds accused the government, with good reason and perfect conviction, of short-sightedness, incompetence, and even betrayal, but this did not mean that they wanted to overturn the form of government in Great Britain or felt any weakening of their allegiance to the sovereign. Hitherto most Zionists, for all their murmuring against the regime, respected the mandate and even felt some gratitude for its work on their behalf. The events of 1929 changed this. Jews found it hard to maintain the former loyalty to a regime which, moved to action by a bloody aggression against Jews, had ended by trying to limit and (to their minds) to cripple Jewish endeavor in the Jewish homeland.

Hitherto Jabotinsky and his followers could be accurately described as wild men on the fringe, but after 1929 the Jabotinsky spirit became an integral part of Zionism in action: not a decisively influential part by any means, but a real part nonetheless. Its influence spread very slowly and was not strong enough, until a much later period, to resist serious and even radical setbacks to its career from within Zionism. But from 1929 onward there was a distinct general change, for the worse, in Jewish-Arab and Jewish-British relations. The genuine wish of many Zionists for a sensible accord with the Arabs became more and more a matter of isolated preference and initiative, and less and less a part of Zionist policy. There were no more speeches by Dr. Weizmann to Jewish audiences to be compared with the one he gave in 1923 in America, and which has been quoted. It has been said, with melancholy justice, that he ceased to have an Arab policy.[26] If this was true of the gradualist leader of Zionism it was yet more true of most of his followers and colleagues.

Jewish-British relations were not restored to what they had been in Plumer's time by MacDonald's repudiation of Passfield. The Slavonic majority of Zionists had always been suspicious of all authority and this had always made for some atmosphere of distrust. As mentioned already it had led to something in the nature of mass delusion about Ronald Storrs. The example of Lord Plumer had diminished this distrust, but it now returned, grew in strength, and was never again to be overcome. An ugly little incident of this time shows the bitterness of the new feeling. At the massacre of Hebron (as has been mentioned) the Arab police hesitated to act against fellow Moslems and when ordered to shoot aimed over the heads of the crowd.[27] But the young British police officer in command "held the mob at bay for hours,"[28] almost alone, until reliable reinforcements arrived. It is calculated that by his tenacity and courage he saved six hundred lives. If something like this had happened ten years earlier the name of this young man would have become honored and famous in Zionist history, and would have been handed down from father to son, doubtless with embellishments to the tale. But in 1929, not only was he little regarded but to quote Albert Hyamson, "he was subject to sustained attack by the survivors and their friends for his failure to save the lives of the

[26] Weizmann Biography.
[27] Evidence taken before the Shaw Commission.
[28] Hyamson, op. cit.

seventy victims of the Arab onslaught." Calculated and totally one-sided propaganda was taking over. The deed and the man are not mentioned in Israel Cohen's definitive study, and not even in the more generous pages of Dr. Weizmann's autobiography. He rendered great service, but all the same he was a political inconvenience in 1929.[29]

The new ideas informing Zionism were, like many forceful political ideas, narrow ones which saw extravagant idealism in extravagant self-interest. But these ideas, it can be said to the credit of human nature, did not overcome the old liberal tolerant ideas with which Jews had become associated. When in June, 1933, the wise and moderate Chaim Arlossoroff, one of the ablest men in the Agency, was mysteriously murdered, as it was then mistakenly thought by Revisionist fanatics, there was a shocked Jewish reaction against extremism which opened a noble chapter in the history of modern Palestine. But amicable Jewish-British relations were never restored, not even when the British government and the administration followed an actively Zionist policy in the midthirties.

If Zionism was a slow starter, so also was Arab nationalism in Palestine. In the last year of the war and those succeeding it, the Palestinian Arabs had a clear cause from which they expected unimaginable bliss and which consequently commanded their loyalty. For a brief time the cause was given a feeble semblance of reality during Feisal's reign over the Kingdom of Greater Syria. That dream had been shattered, not only by French imperialism but by the establishment of the emirate of Transjordan under the rule of Feisal's brother. By and large, his accession met the wishes of the people. This was all very well for the little new emirate, but not for Greater Syria of which Transjordan was now a detached part. By 1930 the shattered dream only survived as useful material for nagging at Frenchmen and Englishmen.

This left Arab nationalists of Palestine without an idea to encourage them, or rather without a positive idea. They were reduced to the negative mental activity of hating the Zionists and consoling themselves by inventing fantastic stories about Jewish malpractice. The leadership was still in the hands of the worthy and inept Musa Kazim who by 1929 was nearly eighty years old. But, as mentioned already, it was at this time that, partly due to fortuitous circumstances, the leadership went, first in effect and later in theory too, to Haj Amin el Husseini, an abler and more deter-

[29] There is no reason why his name should not be mentioned here. It is that of Mr. Raymond Cafferata, a member of the well-known and long established business family of Liverpool. He remained in the Palestine Service till after the Second World War, but retired before the end of the mandate.

mined man. He gave Arab nationalists a positive idea: Jehad, Holy War.
He did not waste his time over "the sacred frontiers of the fatherland"
and was not particularly interested in Greater Syria, though he said he was
when it suited him. He was interested in religion. Though a man of great
slyness and skill in argument he did not make the common mistake of
sophisticated leaders by giving his followers a complex program. He gave
them one of the utmost simplicity: Down with the infidel! In Palestine, as
in most Moslem countries, there was no great anti-Jewish feeling, and an
Arab could be anti-Zionist without indulging further enmity to Jews.
Under the Mufti's influence this was all changed. The enemy was the
Jewish people. To be a Jew was in itself an offense. Arab nationalism
adopted anti-Semitism on the coarsest European model.

The Mufti also put an end to cooperation with the administration as a
feature of Arab nationalism. Knowing that there was much sympathy for
the Arabs among the British, and influenced by the exaggeration of this
by Zionist propaganda, the Arabs had not lost hope that the British would
join with them in crushing Zionism. The Mufti knew better. He taught
his followers to regard the British as an infidel tyranny in alliance with
other infidels against Islam. He had the advantage of holding his beliefs in
complete sincerity.

His ideas did not spread immediately to a great majority, and it naturally took time for Semites to accustom themselves to radical anti-
Semitism of the German kind. But his teaching showed substantial results
early on. Hebron was not a Zionist but a Jewish stronghold. Before 1929
it would have been impossible, or at least extremely difficult, to organize
an anti-Zionist massacre there. And yet this had happened. That was one
rewarding portent. And then in October, 1933, there was an Arab rising
which, for the first time in the history of the mandate, was directed exclusively against the British, a rising that was to lead to greater violence soon
after.

The main achievement of the Mufti in giving a new direction to Arab
nationalism was that he thus revived the interest of the whole Moslem
world in the fate of Palestine, a result which led in time to the signal
though transient success of his cause.

It should be added that the ideas which gave courage to the Arab cause
were not all fanatical or despicable. By giving the people simple objectives
that they could understand, Husseini canalized the natural desire of all
men to live in their accustomed land. The strongest impulse of the nationalists was this one which they shared with all other nationalists or

patriots, good and bad, the love of home. Without this all his skill and political perspicacity would have been ineffective.

There was another, more distant, though discernibly active influence at work on the Arab nationalists, one that has appeared already in the story and seems to have had some effect on Zionists too: the now assured and triumphant career of Mustafa Kemal Ataturk.[30] He had been opposed by the greatest powers of Europe and had forced them to do what he wanted, to acquiesce in the defeat by himself of the Greek army, to agree to the merciless expulsion of Greeks from his territory, and to abandon all notion whatsoever of a dismemberment of Turkey. He had also given a new prestige to the ideal of the small state and homeland patriotism. From the most ghastly of defeats he had made Turkey modestly prosperous, progressive, and self-assured. He gave Oriental people from the Mediterranean to India a new sense of equality with the West, and it is no exaggeration to say that the influence of his career on Asiatic ideas was similar to, and as important as, that of the Russo-Japanese war on the preceding generation. He was looked upon, and rightly so, as the marvel of Asia.

Arab and Jewish nationalism both had the advantages in spiritual resource of new faith firmly built on old faith. The third party, the British, had nothing so stimulating. Apart from a very few enthusiasts, they considered (as mentioned already) that they were there as a result of some complicated political juggling, which they would not have understood, even if it had been explained to them, which it never was. They concluded that the only rational reason they were there was "to look after the Canal," and though one can imagine Rudyard Kipling writing one of his stirring popular poems on this theme, it was of itself insufficient to give men a sense of dedication and perennial inspiration, especially at times when no one in particular was threatening the Canal. The unchanging duty of British officials in Palestine in normal times was to prevent the people there from doing what they wanted most passionately to do, to organize a state in their homeland. Ronald Storrs left Jerusalem in 1926, and nearly ten years after he wrote: "In a sense I cannot describe there is no promotion after Jerusalem." The phrase dates him as belonging to the hopeful days.

Most of the British, especially in the junior ranks which make opinion,

---

[30] British Intelligence reports of the time in the Israel State Archives make frequent reference to the influence of Ataturk's example on Middle East nationalism. See also Sir John Glubb, *Britain and the Arabs*, London, 1959, for the influence of the exchange of population on some Zionist thinking.

felt unloved and miserable. For every one of them who shared something of Ronald Storr's romantic delight there were a hundred who only looked forward to the day when they would "get away from this bloody country." If an Englishman mixed with the people he had to endure long tales of woeful reproach about how the British had betrayed whatever people his companion belonged to. The alternative was to confine himself to the dismally limited world of the Europeans. The commonest complaint of those who were posted to this most famous of historical lands was of insufferable boredom. The task of the mandatory in Palestine was beyond human ingenuity and most British people responded to this challenge by doing their duty mechanically. In the junior ranks the commonest subject of conversation was leave of absence.

British official policy showed a bulldog tenacity in one respect. In spite of growing evidence that such a thing had no chance of practical success, all British governments from 1917 to 1948 based their policy on the belief and hope that the two nations would in time "sink their differences" and advance together to the delights of an independent state shared in common. The proposition appears so utterly unreal in the lurid light of what happened that one may be inclined to ridicule it as the kind of thing that only a humbug or an advertising poster artist could contrive. But in fact it was not so ridiculous as it appears to hindsight. There were both Arabs and Jews (more of the latter) who not only shared this hope but worked for it regardless of the unpopularity it brought on them, and these few souls were among the finest spirits to be found on either side. It would have been most wrong to ignore the claims of such people. But even when that was admitted, the fact remained that nationalistic enthusiasm in both parties was so extreme that the chance of success of a binational policy was negligible, and those who urged such a policy could never be more than a moderating influence. Government surely should have faced this fact. It may be that the success of the Irish settlement misled them here. It is a natural fault of imperial administration to overgeneralize.

Though this policy was persisted in to the end, with only one temporary deviation, it was always liable to be shaken by the requirements of party program. As time went on, Palestine and its problems were treated more and more as vote-catching devices in the course of party political warfare. After 1930 this became common political form. Since there was no Arab or Arab-connected vote in Great Britain the opposition, except in isolated cases, took up Zionist grievances and even extreme Jabotinskyish Zionist claims (depending on the state of things in Palestine and of Jewish opinion in the electorate), thereby raising Zionist hopes which the same party, if voted into office, was bound to disappoint. Until the end British politicians considered this a perfectly reasonable and responsible mode of behavior, as part of that "in-fighting" inseparable, as they say, from healthy democracy and political robustness. It is curious that not until the years after the Second World War did the Zionist leadership detect the game that was being played. Up to the last stage they put their disappointment down to that preference for Arabs over Jews which was shown by many British people in the administration, especially in the junior ranks.

The preference was undoubtedly there, and it probably exercised strong influence over the attempted pro-Arab policy of 1930. The Jews, who were understandably and deeply hurt by such a disposition, tended (as said) to exaggerate its importance. They usually ascribed it to contemptible motives; to relish of Oriental flattery, to the sense of mastery given to British officials by the servile conduct which often came naturally to former Ottoman subjects, to a shallow delight in picturesque clothes and old-fashioned manners. In his autobiography Dr. Weizmann was particularly scathing about the last of these, surely the least disreputable. There was undoubtedly much in these accusations, but there was one stronger and more respectable reason for the preference which was overlooked by critics. The administration left much to be desired, as all administrations do, but it was far the best that the Palestinians had had since remote times, and many of the unpolitical mass of the Arabs liked it. True, the Arab habit of hiding from government persisted so strongly that in many departments, especially in land survey, administration simply could not function with a minimum of essential efficiency, but that did not prevent a considerable contrary movement toward trust, all expressed with engaging Oriental fantasy. Among Arabs of the unpolitical mass an official might sometimes have the agreeable impression that he was doing some good. The unpolitical mass of the Jews was a small minority of the Jewish people, and it followed that the same official, working among Zionists, would not often receive that agreeable impression. People like to be liked. It is not a crime.

The preference certainly did harm in leading to the extraordinary British misconception of the Mufti's character, an aberration of judgment that continued for many years. This, in so far as it was the Mufti's work, was in all probability a triumph of discretion and personality. He was an impressive man to meet and he had an infectious personal charm. He did not appear to be secretive and left whomever he met in no doubt that he would strive to the last for the preservation of Jerusalem and Palestine as a Moslem city and land, first and foremost. It was impossible not to believe in his sincerity. He had natural dignity. He was handsome though very slight in build, and, an Oriental of Orientals, he never wore European clothes but the becoming habit of a Moslem doctor of Theology. His voice was soft and he had the trick of sitting as still as a statue. He never gesticulated or raised his voice. He made other people seem vulgar. It was difficult to think of him as bloodthirsty. He did not deceive only British people. The Arab apologist George Antonius (who died in 1942), one of the most cultivated of men, never wavered in his belief that Haj Amin was a saint.[31]

British belief in Haj Amin's moderation helped on the attempted Passfield policy more than any other single factor. If the belief was true the policy made some sense, if not it made none. The policy, for all its harshness in penalizing the wronged people, should not be too severely condemned: 1930 was very different from 1939. The world of Western civilization, and especially the German-speaking world, was still abundantly a land of opportunity for Jews, and to curb or attempt to curb without compensation the Zionist expansion in Palestine was to inflict pain on Zionists but was not to deny the right to live to the Jews. It did not mean inflicting a wound on the soul of the people. At worst it was to play a party false. Not many Jews outside that party interpreted Passfield's action as an insulting affront to themselves; not many of them regarded MacDonald's letter as an act of reparation to all Jewish people, wherever they might be. They had other interests. The Depression would not last forever. The majority opinion in most civilized countries was that the solid good sense of the Germans would triumph over the fanatic parties then aiming at power, and that the German Republic would be preserved. There was plenty of evidence for optimism at this crossroads of the whole world.

[31] The writer used to meet the Mufti at George Antonius' house in 1936. They could converse in Persian.

7 THE DECLINE OF THE WEST

In the middle of the 1930's, it looked for a short time as though the British government had been alarmed into attempting a radical solution of the problem which Arthur Balfour had set them in Palestine. The most distinguished of the numerous royal commissions to visit the country set out in the autumn of 1936 and remained there till the end of January, 1937. The work which it accomplished outshone that of its predecessors and of the many commissions to be sent to Palestine in subsequent years: it can be said, in proof of its merits, that the report which it made is the best of all contemporary accounts of Palestine in the first phases of British mandatory rule. As with most other such commissions, its recommendations were ultimately rejected by the government which had initiated its labors, but it cannot be said, as with the others, that its recommendations came to nothing at all. Its influence is discernible in later events including the ultimate solution.

The occasion of the commission's being sent was the Arab rebellion of 1936, a rebellion that was in part the result of political development elsewhere in the Arabic-speaking world but was mainly caused by a Zionist revival in Palestine. The revival in turn was the result not of events connected with the country but of the most devastating breakdown in European civilization since the Thirty Years War. The circumstances should be briefly remembered.

Europe's black day was the 30th of January, 1933, when the old President of the German Republic, Field Marshal von Hindenburg, reluctantly, and against his better judgment, appointed Adolf Hitler Chancellor of the Reich. The Nazi revolution, the most retrograde of modern times, perhaps of all historical time, then began its short destructive course. The world was to have a new master, a man whose mind though fourth-rate was united to an unconquerable will, the equal of Napoleon's, and to a genius for political maneuvering not inferior (in the short term) to that of the greatest statesmen of any time. To millions of his countrymen, driven to despair by the incompetence of the democratic parties, he seemed a heaven-sent savior. They are not to be absolutely condemned for feeling thus. Hitler had promised that if he achieved power he would solve the German unemployment problem, whose figures in 1932 threatened to overtop the seven million mark. When his moment came, he contrived, by means of the Todt Organization, the Labor Corps, the rearmament program, and Dr. Schacht's economic policy, to be as good as his word. It was a wonderful thing for Germany. It can be said of Hitler that to do a great wrong he did a little right.

Concerning Nazism this study is occupied only with that side of the movement in which Hitler's character and rule showed themselves to be most sordid: his beliefs and policy regarding the Jews.

There is much paradox in Hitler's character. He was among the greatest liars in modern political history, and yet he confused the world by an astonishing habit of literalness. The fierce polemics in his book *Mein Kampf* and his public speeches were not fiercer or more shocking than the ordinary polemics of ordinary political speech-making. The difference was in this: that in the speech-making to which political audiences all over the world are accustomed, savage denunciation in which, for example, an opponent is likened to the infanticide King Herod,[1] or large numbers of the speaker's fellow men are described as "lower than vermin"[2]; such out-

[1] Lord Randolph Churchill on Mr. Gladstone!
[2] Mr. Aneurin Bevan on the Conservative party, on the occasion of opening a hospital!

pourings are accepted as being no more than figures of speech, vote-catching flourishes calculated to suggest to audiences that the speaker maintains in political life the admired "robust" attitude. But with Hitler they were considered statements. When he described non-Nordic people and especially the Jews as sub-men (*Untermenschen*) he meant what he said literally, and he meant it so literally that he acted precisely on what he said. This was something new which it took his audience (world-wide thanks to radio) some time to get used to. The fact can explain why for several years many people inside and outside Germany were able to console themselves in all sincerity with supposing that Hitler was no more dangerous than any other radical politician.

It has been justly said that hatred of Jews was one of Hitler's very few sincere emotions.[3] The process by which he became an anti-Semite has been traced with a fair degree of certainty, though without detail. When he was in Vienna from 1909 to 1913,[4] he lived close to starvation level in a city in which Jews shared a disproportionate amount of talent and the reward of talent, its use and its abuse. The gaunt unhappy young man with his long dark hair, long *Kaiserzeit* mustache and shabby clothes, and with his inner belief that he was destined for great things, was a natural prey to persecution mania. The cast of his mind being what it was he was prone to belief in ideas which by exciting the imagination could both soothe and inflame the hate in his deprived being. Inevitably he was drawn to the anti-Semitic teaching and ideas which had been prevalent in the German-speaking world since the 1870's and which, at that time in Vienna, had an able spokesman in Karl Lueger, the popular leader of the Catholic party. Lueger was a man imbued with Austrian charm and he occupied a prominent position as the mayor of the capital: he was a highly influential and effective public speaker.

Then, during Hitler's miserable Vienna period, a pamphlet appeared which gave even more extravagant expression than that of Karl Lueger to anti-Semitism. This was *The Protocols of the Elders of Zion,* first published in Russia in 1905. The *Protocols* acquired fame slowly and began to be widely read in the German-speaking world at just about the time that Hitler was first occupying his mind with ideas about the Jews. It is not known when he read the *Protocols,* but a reference in *Mein Kampf* makes it clear that when he did he enthusiastically accepted them as true. This picture of the role of the Jews in the world, of an evil people secretly

[3] Alan Bullock, *Hitler: a Study in Tyranny.* London, 1952.
[4] Hitler's Vienna dates are uncertain, but 1909–13 seems to be the time when he lived there consecutively as a Viennese. Bullock, *ibid.*

united and vowed to the destruction of all Gentile civilization, and the enslavement of all Gentile peoples, remained his for the rest of his life, literally till his last hours, for he repeated the main gist of the nonsense in the will he dictated before committing suicide. This is a very odd fact of history. The *Protocols* had been shown up as a forgery by Philip Graves in 1921, before Hitler was fairly set on his career; the mechanics of the forgery, and the exact details of how it had been contrived by Russian police agents in Paris, were brought to light in the course of evidence taken during a famous legal action in Switzerland. The case occurred in the days of Hitler's rule, in 1934 and 1935. But this massive disproof never even faintly qualified Hitler's devotion to the proposition of the great forgery. It seems reasonable to suppose that the *Protocols* suited his hate-driven mind too well to be forgone, that they expressed the burning faith which had sustained him as he trudged the streets of Vienna as a failure and outcast. He had hugged that faith as a solace in his wretchedness, and he hugged it with no less devotion in his triumph and his fall.

Though Hitler was perhaps the greatest destroyer of orderly life and "the rule of law" in the whole history of civilized Europe, he usually took pains to give his actions the look of being legal. This conduct paid him well as it gave an excuse to escapists. He followed it carefully in his prewar Jewish policy. When he became Chancellor there was no German legal discrimination against Jews. Beginning with a racial "Law for the Restoration of the Civil Service" in April, 1933, the new government made haste to remedy this anomaly by means of a legislative program which terminated Jewish participation in a large area of professional, commercial, and cultural life. In the summer of 1933, however, the Nazis appear to have taken fright at the foreign reactions to their career of atrocity; there was no further anti-Jewish legislation for two years and the Führer even went so far as to publish assurances that the Jews would not be called on to suffer any further diminution of economic opportunity. Many people, including Jews, believed that the nightmare had passed. The lull continued till the 15th of September, 1935. On that day, while attending the annual party rally, Hitler convened the Reichstag in a concert hall in Nuremberg. He invited the deputies to ratify three new laws: one, that the German national ensign should in future be the swastika-adorned red flag of the party; two, that German citizenship was to be confined to Aryan persons while non-Aryans of Germany were to be reduced to subject status; and three, that sexual relationships, marital or otherwise, between Jews and Germans should be forbidden, with a rider (borrowed from a former Austrian code) that German women under the age of forty-five were not to be employed as servants in Jewish houses. The Reichstag obediently voted the measures. There was no dissent. After the passage of these "Nuremberg Laws" thirteen additional anti-Jewish decrees were passed during the next years until by 1938 it was virtually impossible for a Jew to earn his living in Germany except in the lowest occupations, and then only with difficulty. But neither the Nuremberg Laws, nor those that had gone before them or came after, represented any departure in policy. To a varying extent they all had this in common: that they regularized a situation which already existed, thanks to the license Hitler accorded his following. From the moment that he became Chancellor (to quote an authority) "the bullies of the S.A. were enjoying 'the freedom of the streets' for which they had so long clamoured. They lost no time in settling accounts with their enemies and their rivals, those they hated, those they envied and those that they feared. The blood-letting and the terrorism began almost at once; they were to continue, with only minor interruptions, almost to the day of Germany's surrender twelve years later."[5]

The Europe which included Hitler among its heads of state was a new world. By reason of the anti-Semitic impetus that was half the new German driving force, no place felt the weight of change more immediately or more catastrophically than Palestine. The British mandatory authorities were not heedless of new obligations put upon them, but, in common with many other people in the world they, and their home government, did not see the drastic enormity of the change wrought by Hitler's achievement of power. This was pardonable enough at first but became less and less so in the course of years. They do not seem to have faced the fact at any time that a great revolution had occurred, and that to meet its consequences new methods must be adopted and that the old methods were of no avail.

When the British government in the years after 1929 gave thought to Palestine, they remembered the peaceful days of Lord Plumer. The Prime Minister discussed the matter with Dr. Weizmann. "I would like to appoint a General," said Ramsay MacDonald, "but one who does it with his head not his feet."[6] He searched for another Plumer and his choice lighted on a distinguished officer who not only enjoyed a professional record of successful command and great personal courage, but had some experience of civilian administration. He was Major General Sir Arthur Wauchope. He did not prove to be a second Plumer, but the fault was not

[5] D. C. Watt, *History Today*. March, 1963.
[6] Chaim Weizmann, *Trial and Error*. London, 1962.

with him, but with the times in which he lived. He took the oath of office on the 19th of November, 1931, in Jerusalem. He was probably the best choice that could have been made at the time.

He was involved in the problem of massive immigration almost from the first days of his term of office. The Jews of central Europe tended to take a tragically complacent view of the danger in which they stood, but in the year before Hitler became Chancellor a sufficient number of them read the signs of the times for the weight of displacement to be felt in the small and vulnerable area of Palestine. The Jewish immigration figures for 1931 showed the slight but continuing decline noticeable since 1929, but in the next year they rose from the 1931 figure of 4,075 souls to more than double: 9,553. In the next year, the fatal 1933, these figures were more than tripled, the total of Jewish immigrants amounting to 30,327. The British government and the High Commissioner received many warnings that they were walking into great peril [7] but (very much to their credit) they insisted that the need of the Jews demanded that they be allowed to take full advantage of the existing regulations. These were not altered in any way so that in 1934 the figures rose again, this time to 42,359, the largest immigration into Palestine ever recorded up to that time. But in 1935, the year of the Nuremberg Laws, even this figure was surpassed by a grand total of 61,854 Jewish immigrants, nearly all from Europe.[8]

Zionist leaders had often insisted that in demanding a National Home the Jews were not asking for a luxury but the satisfaction of a vital need. The point was never difficult to argue, but, in the more normal years from 1917 to 1933 (years which the abominations of the thirties soon made normal by contrast), counterargument was never difficult either. But after 1933 the need of the Jews for a National Home, their need for a state in which they could take pride, became completely and rapidly self-evident to many Jews who had doubted it before, and to their sympathizers. But the implications of the fact were so embarrassing to any practical administration in Palestine that those responsible found the temptation to escape from it too strong to be resisted. After this year the "Palestine

[7] And the warnings were handed on to the Jewish Agency. On one occasion (a friend of Dr. Weizmann's relates) Sir Arthur Wauchope asked Weizmann to urge a policy of moderate immigration on the Jewish Agency, adding that to build slowly was to build surely, to which Weizmann replied to this effect: "I appreciate the sagacity of your advice and we might follow it if it were not that at this moment we are being harried by the Furies."

[8] Statistics in Israel Cohen, *The Zionist Movement*. London, 1945.

problem" proved to be entirely beyond any peaceful solution, and looking back now it is clear that after 1933 it could never be so solved in Palestine but (if at all) only by strong pro-Jewish countermeasures throughout the world.

Too late, too ineffectually, such a policy was in fact attempted. But that is to look to the end of the thirties. What should be remembered, if the midthirties situation is to be understood, is that the National Home suddenly became an urgent, pressing need to thousands of European Jews, and, as well as that, a symbol of self-help and self-respect at a hideous moment of national degradation when such things meant all that they can mean.

There was no more moving sight in those days than the arrival at Haifa or Jaffa of a Mediterranean ship carrying Jews from Europe: the spontaneous cries of joy at the first sight of the shore, the mass chanting of Hebrew hymns or Yiddish songs usually beginning raggedly over all the boat and sometimes swelling into a single harmony; the uncontrolled joy of these returning exiles (for so they thought of themselves); a man seizing hold of a stranger and pointing with tears of joy to the approaching land crying "Zion! Zion!" and "Jerusalem!" Such scenes made many of those who saw them recognize as never before that the human spirit cannot be destroyed, and that the Jewish inspiration is among the sublimest expressions of the unconquerable soul. Zionism showed itself at its very finest in these years. Enthusiasm went hand in hand with practical sense. The Zionist remembered how the mass migrations of the midtwenties had endangered their purpose, and they succeeded in settling the thousands of newcomers with extraordinary skill. Unemployment crises inevitably arose on several occasions, but they were always kept under control, and the control was largely Jewish. Palestine was the answer to Hitler!

The Arabs looked on with dismay. Seen through Arab eyes, this great work of rescue and redemption had nothing beautiful about it and seemed on the contrary to be a stark act of oppression against themselves. To them it was the beginning of the fulfillment of Jabotinsky's dreams of conquest, and in their official conduct of policy the Zionists were at no pains to disabuse them of such an idea. The Arabs noted that these phenomenal increases in the Jewish population were not regarded by the Zionist leadership as abnormal or satisfying. They were never the subject of gratitude, and the Jewish press continued to complain of British obstruction and niggardliness regarding the number of immigration permits allowed. On one occasion Zionists of Tel Aviv even staged an anti-British riot on the subject.[9] All this suggested to the educated Arabs, and from them was communicated to the illiterate majority, that the Jews were using Nazism as a means of setting up a Jewish State at Arab expense, and that to see in it a work of mercy was to misread what was happening.

There was a great measure of truth in what the Arabs suspected, and they were not (as often before) merely indulging hate dreams about the Zionists. A curious fact about the new exodus seemed to them from the beginning to *prove* that the Jews were less interested in humanitarian succor than in political power-seeking. It was to be supposed that the bulk of those coming to Palestine from Europe in the years 1932–1935 would be Germans, but in fact the exiles from Germany made up a little less than an eighth of the total, while those from Poland made up a little less than half (approximately 43 percent), and these figures showed only a small departure from the proportions of former times. It seemed that the main Jewish effort was decidedly not concerned with the new drift of affairs in Germany.

Part of the explanation for this puzzling state of affairs is certainly to the discredit of the Jewish Agency. The fact was that most of the Jews in Palestine were Slavs and, as the choice of immigrants was democratically controlled, it followed, more or less inevitably even if ignobly, that the Slav majority saw to it that Slav preponderance was not lost in the suddenly changed circumstances of the Nazi era.[10] Palestine Zionists saw a threat and made haste to counter it. Of course if they had known what Nazism was they would almost certainly have acted otherwise, but the grim fact remains that the new victims of anti-Semitism had not only to confront the brutality of autocratic tyranny but the ugly selfishness of well-organized democracy.

It should be said that there were other more reputable and perhaps equally important reasons for the continuing high proportion of Slav over German Jews. Zionism had never meant as much to Western Jews with their long tradition of assimilation as to Eastern Jews with their long

[9] Albert Hyamson, *Palestine Under the Mandate*. London, 1950. From the thirties to the present day it has suited Zionist propaganda to play down the enormous immigrations of 1932–35 in order to concentrate attention on the British restrictions on immigration imposed later. Israel Cohen is a classic example. The propagandists succeeded in their aim and the whole period of the thirties in Palestine has come to be thought of exclusively as one of persistent British anti-Zionism, a view even shared to a large extent by so neutral an authority as Herbert Agar.
[10] Hyamson, *op. cit.*

tradition of escape from persecution, and it was not usual then for a German Jew, when confronted by the sudden cruelty of modern progress, to seek Palestine first and foremost and instinctively as his refuge. One must remember also the muddle-headed character of German policy toward the Jews in the years before the logic of the "final solution" clarified Nazi minds. Until then, Hitler and his followers could never decide whether to expel the Jews or imprison them and meanwhile clumsily attempted to do both. S.S. leaders such as Eichmann were to be heard yelling at the Jews to leave Germany,[11] while the same men and organizations were busy putting prohibitive economic obstacles in their way. But the most telling of the indirect reasons for a Slav majority of immigrants is in the very nature of what had happened not only in Germany but in Europe. As said, Hitler had opened a new age. When he screamed: "People call us barbarians—Yes! We are barbarians and we regard the name as an honorable title!" his words had the deep appeal of all liberators who set men free from inhibiting customs. He found admirers and imitators abroad, and some of the neighboring governments, especially to the east, found it tempting to follow Nazi-style policies even if not descending to his depth of crime. In Poland and southeastern Europe, where the economic slump still persisted, there were active anti-Semitic phases of policy, and the economic situation of the Jews there in the years 1932–1935 was little better than that of their German brethren.

None of this was of interest to the Palestinian Arabs who only saw in the small proportion of German immigrants proof positive of what they feared: that the Jews were intent on one thing alone, the seizure of Palestine. This was their continuing belief, their main preoccupation during the Nazi years. It had this important element of truth: that from the very beginning of the Nazi disaster the Zionist leadership determined to wrest political advantage from the tragedy. Where such advantage might lead none of them could tell, and it is wrong to think of their decision, as the Arabs did, as an elaborately planned conspiracy. But it is true that, once having made the decision, the Zionists, in spite of radical internal differences as to how it should be implemented, remained true to it during the remaining years of the mandate. In the unforeseeable future it did in fact lead them to the forcible occupation of most of Palestine.

The decision was heroic, such as could only have been taken by a great people. It was fatal in the sense that it removed still further from reality the possibility of a peaceful solution. It meant the discredit of Zionist gradualism and a rapid heightening of the Arab sense of injustice with

[11] Herbert Agar, *The Saving Remnant*. London, 1960.

which Arabs found sympathy among many British people both in Palestine and England. The Arab case against Palestine as the answer to Hitler was strong. It should be remembered.

Arabs who were in contact with Europeans frequently reminded those who implored them to lay aside their hostility to the Jews that they, the Arabs, were not Europeans, that they had no influence on the general course of European policy, that Arabs had left their mark nowhere on recent European history, and were thus in no sense responsible, even in the smallest way, for the breakdown of civilization in Germany which had resulted in the revival of persecution. The British on the other hand undoubtedly were Europeans; they had exerted major influence on the recent history and policy of Europe, and even if wholly innocent of direct responsibility for modern Jewish suffering, they certainly had indirect responsibility for the state of things in which that suffering had come about. On whom lay the duty, if there was a duty, to relieve that suffering? Surely on the Europeans. Yet while the Palestinian Arabs were expected, as a result of Europeans crimes, to make room in their very small country for nearly 145,000 Jews, the British in the same space of time, from 1932 to 1935, had only made room in their very much larger and richer country for less than 3,000 Jews!

Arguments in this sense were often to be heard from Palestinian Moslems in those days and were also put forward by many Europeans who took their side.[12] In the long run this undoubtedly strong argument prevailed enough with the British to influence their conduct, this in spite of the fact that in putting it forward many Arabs in characteristic fashion embellished it with elaborate and incredible fantasies. The idea that Hitler was himself a Jew working (in an admittedly roundabout way) for the triumph of Zionism first rose (it would seem) in Palestine where it was often to be met with in those years.[13] It went along with an intensified version of another familiar Arab idea which has already appeared in this book, namely that for unfathomable motives (such for example as are alleged to have driven Bacon to write Shakespeare) the British Secret Service forced Zionism, sometimes against its will, into adopting its frequent anti-British character, while at the same time this dark-minded

---

[12] J. M. N. Jeffries, *Palestine the Reality*. London, 1939. The present writer is guided here by personal recollections of Palestine in 1933 and 1936. He heard most of these opinions from George Antonius and his friends. They are reflected in the articles of the founding protocol of the Arab League.

[13] For details of this contribution to historical theory, *vide passim* the works of Mr. Douglas Reed, a fervent believer.

British organization was maintaining a large, hidden, and dominating hand in the career of Hitler and the new Germany. The latter idea, like the somewhat similar ideas about the secret elders of Zion, proved so popular that it has survived to the present time and not only among Arabs. It may be that the embellishments that some Palestinians dreamed up from the ascertainable facts did no great disservice to their cause. Men like mad ideas.

While the pressure of Nazism deeply intensified the political and racial conflict in Palestine, other events outside the country, but within the Arabic-speaking world, added substantially to the difficulties of maintaining a Palestinian peace. The trouble was that during this period when Arab hostility to Zionism inevitably rose to a new height of intensity, the French and British governments became seriously involved in attempts to placate and honor pledges to Arab nationalism elsewhere in mandated territory.

The first movement in this direction had been in Transjordan years before. In that country the exercise of mandatory powers was little resisted because little resented, and the tasks confronting those in authority were essentially simple for all that they were exacting. In Transjordan the British government could and did pursue the liberal policy to which it was committed, and if the process of realization was extraordinarily slow this was almost entirely due to the political situation brought about by the fall of Abdullah's father in the Arabian peninsula and the rise of ibn Saud. An Anglo-Transjordan agreement of 1923 was transformed during Plumer's peaceful administration into a treaty, in 1928. The main term was that the United Kingdom recognized (within limits prescribed by the Mandate) the sovereign independence of the Transjordan emirate on condition that its government be constitutional. It followed that by the 1930's the emirate had a functioning democracy of a sort, and a real measure of national independence, quite as much as any Transjordan leader wanted. With ibn Saud as their neighbor, these Arab politicians were not anxious for the total isolation that can go with total self-reliance.

The most remarkable event in this liberal movement within the mandatory system was the signing in 1930 of the Anglo-Iraq treaty by which the mandate in question was entirely abolished in favor of an alliance which gave Iraq independence to a degree acceptable in those times. The treaty was ratified in 1931. In return for conceding independence the British government exacted a position of privilege, especially in matters relating to imperial defense. The resentment felt by many nationalists at this continuing British privilege was largely appeased by the introduction of Iraq into membership of the League of Nations by the former mandatory. By and large it can be said that with all its imperfections the Anglo-Iraq treaty was an edifying proof that the idealism behind the mandate system was not all the sham that cynics alleged then and still allege today.

The events of 1930 in Baghdad naturally gave fresh stimulus to nationalist activity and ambition in the French mandated territory of Syria and Lebanon. Since the extinction by the French army of the Syrian rebellion in 1927, French policy had taken a more conciliatory turn but had lagged a long way behind appeasement of nationalist demands. This was not wholly the fault of the French but was due also to the party divisions within Syria arising from the country's complicated ethnological and social structure, and from the main division of interests between Syria and Lebanon. These played into the hands of the French whether they liked it or not. On the whole they liked it very much.

After 1930, however, though the road to a satisfying measure of emancipation was to remain beset with difficulties and to lead to another anti-French rising, French policy was compelled to pay something more than lip service to the League ideal of preparing mandated territory for democracy and independence. In June, 1932, a constitutional government came into office in Damascus. The President of the new Syrian republic was a nominee of the ruling power, and the members of the Chamber of Deputies were only in the feeblest sense representatives of the people. But for all that, nationalism had made an important gain. There was such a thing in the world now as a Syrian republic; there was a President, there were deputies. If there was not yet the reality, there was at least the machinery of self-rule.[14]

Inevitably these things affected Palestine.

Since their last boycott of the constitutional issue, when they refused Dr. Weizmann's proposal in 1930 for a conference, the Arab leadership in Palestine, seeing the checkered but definite rise of democracy all round them, began to entertain doubts as to whether they had acted wisely in this matter. In 1931 when the Anglo-Iraq treaty was ratified their doubts were increased. They felt themselves, and with abundant reason, to be in an

---

[14] Lebanon had been declared a republic in 1926. Ten years later the Franco-Syrian treaty was followed by a parallel Franco-Lebanese theaty. Events in the largely Christian Lebanon never made much impression on the Moslem-dominated Arab national movement.

utterly humiliating position: they were the only Arab community without any vestige of self-rule except in municipal affairs. They included men who had been considered worthy to hold high office in the affairs of the vast Ottoman Empire, and they were now subjected to arbitrary rule such as is only suited as a normal polity to the most primitive of people. Perhaps the source of their most bitter thoughts was to be found not so much in the genuine emancipation of Iraq nor in the establishment of a republic of a kind to the north, but in the fact that next door, national self-governing institutions were enjoyed by the Transjordanians[15]—a people whom the *effendis* of Jerusalem and Haifa regarded as crude, unsophisticated beings, illiterate nomads who were totally unfit for the responsibilities and niceties of politics.

The Arabs had the sympathy of Sir Arthur Wauchope. He took the reasonable Western view, namely that a country suffering from intense inner conflict could not safely be governed by arbitrary methods. It was his fixed determination from the start to exert his influence on the British government toward the establishment of self-rule in Palestine. So far as influence went, he quickly succeeded. The Zionists knew what he was doing and what the government consequently intended. They took immediate action, and at a meeting in London the Executive of the Jewish Agency told Wauchope, who was present, that they disapproved of his revival of the constitutional issue and (with doubtful sincerity) warned him that the foundation at that moment of a Legislative Council in Jerusalem would be as much against Arab as Jewish interests.[16]

Sir Arthur Wauchope was a broad-minded man who was accessible to different ideas originating from different points of view, but he had as well a vein of Scotch tenacity which came out strongly in this first major dispute of his term of office. He pursued the idea of the Legislative Council as obstinately as he believed in its efficacy. Within days of his meeting with the Jewish Agency in London, he made a deposition on the 10th of November, 1932, before the Mandates Commission of the League of Nations that he intended on the authority of his government to institute a representative council in Palestine. The first stage of this democratizing process was to lie in the enactment of a new local government ordinance.

He persisted in the attempt for over three years, and the more the proposal led to rage and discord and even bloodshed in Palestine the more sure he seemed to be that Palestine needed a parliament.

In the year 1933, the first year of the new mass Jewish immigrations,

---

[15] An opinion expressed in the Peel Report.
[16] Cohen, *op. cit.*

the dominant element in the Arab coalition was the Supreme Moslem Council, and the Mufti became more and more openly the nationalist leader. In March he attended a large and representative meeting in Jaffa organized by the Executive Committee, which resolved to refuse all cooperation with the administration and to boycott the purchase of "British goods and Zionist goods." [17] The boycott was to some extent effective,[18] but it was secondary in the new program. Haj Amin was intent on educating his followers into an antigovernmental state of mind. His argument seems to have been as follows: that without government support Zionism was helpless and therefore the immediate need was to concentrate the attack not on the Jews but on their British supporters. Then both would fall. The results of his teaching were clearly visible when the long-threatened explosion at last occurred in October.

Twenty-six Arabs were killed and 187 injured in riots which took place at the end of the month in Jaffa, Nablus, Haifa, and Jerusalem.[19] One British man was killed, and twenty-six injured, but there were no Jewish casualties. The riots were directed exclusively against the British. This was something new to the administration, though they were still unwilling to make it the occasion of a reappraisal of the Mufti. It was in fact his first bold essay in political action, and it was a fitting if tragic irony of this rising that among the people hurt in the Jaffa riot was his kinsman, the venerable Musa Kazim. He was still the president of the Arab Executive, in name but not in effect. After October he retired. His day was over. A few months later he died, probably as a result of his injuries.

It was in the same month of October that the Zionists of Tel Aviv staged their riot, a restrained and minor affair, to protest against the allegedly small scale of Jewish immigration allowed by the government. Some Jews and British were hurt, but there were no fatalities. It was dismissed as the folly of people in a state of desperation, but hindsight can show that it was a portent.

The Arab leaders had taken notice of Sir Arthur Wauchope's devotion to the parliamentary ideal, and for the present they pursued a constitution with the same insistence as they had boycotted one before. A deputation of mayors waited on the High Commissioner in Jerusalem a fortnight or so after the October riots and urged that a Legislative Council be established immediately. Presumably they hoped that recent events might be made to scare him into an immediate move, but Wauchope refused to be hurried.

[17] *Ibid.*
[18] Hyamson, *op. cit.*
[19] Figures from Cohen, *op. cit.*

He said that the new municipal law must first come into force and municipal elections be held. But he still maintained his course toward the only possible solution that he could see.

The year 1934 was relatively peaceful by Palestine standards and extraordinarily so when the enormous immigration of that year is taken into account. The new municipal law was duly enacted; elections were duly held; municipalities were constituted except in Jerusalem where the election had had a disquieting and significant result. A vigorous nationalist, a member of the Khaldi family, had defeated an Arab moderate and family opponent of the Mufti's, Ragheb Bey Nashashibi. In these circumstances, the reestablishment of the municipality was deferred till the next year, but everywhere else appointments followed election in the normal course. Municipalities formed the only area in mandated Palestine where Arabs and Jews sometimes worked in political cooperation. In spite of political breakdowns and waves of mutual boycotting, it remains true that in some places, notably Haifa, they even achieved some temporary measure of political harmony. Sir Arthur Wauchope proceeded confidently toward his goal.

When the situation of the Jews in the world was happy compared to what it had become in the thirties, the Zionist leaders had risked the success of their great enterprise, certainly on two occasions, possibly on a third, by their loyalty to the liberal traditions of world Jewry. As said, it took great moral courage on the part of Dr. Weizmann and his colleagues to agree, in earlier days, to some kind of self-governing regime in Palestine. They could hardly avoid the first occasion when Winston Churchill proposed a Legislative Council, nor the second when they cooperated in the original Advisory Council plan. The third occasion, when Dr. Weizmann proposed a conference on the subject, might have been avoided. His overture was not without risk but possibly not so critically dangerous as the previous ones.

In 1934 the Jews of Palestine were in a more precarious position than at any other moment in recent times, and their situation in the world threatened to become infinitely worse. It was not a time when they could afford to take any more risks, even for the most high-minded reasons. And the risks were plain. The Arab nationalists led by the Mufti can at least be credited with a measure of frankness. They made no secret of the fact that given any sort of political power they would use it not merely to modify the National Home, nor merely to prevent its further growth, but to annihilate it. Though they sincerely wanted some form of legislative chamber, they did nothing to lull Jewish suspicions. Not surprisingly the

Jews decided that this time any boycotting would be done by themselves.

In the summer of that year, 1934, the Jewish Agency once more informed Sir Arthur Wauchope that they were totally opposed to constitutional reform in the direction of self-government. They perhaps weakened their case by again urging it with arguments more suited to propaganda than to serious negotiation, again putting forward objections of unlikely sincerity and occasional inconsistency,[20] and taking no pains to throw the whole blame for their refusal (as they easily could have done) on the extreme intransigence of the new Arab leadership. They used this as a secondary, not as a main, argument. They did not deter Sir Arthur Wauchope from his task of parliament-building which he pursued with the full support of his home government.

It can be imagined how the enormous and unprecedented Jewish immigration of 1935 aggravated the ill-feeling of this dispute, especially when it was learned that there was in addition to the admitted numbers a considerable illegal immigration. The latter made no important difference to the balance of population, but the facts were exaggerated by rumor in a country that traditionally took its news from rumor. When a Jewish attempt to smuggle arms[21] was discovered by the coast-guard police in October of 1935, the hysteria rose appreciably.

Earlier in that same autumn the Nineteenth Zionist Congress had met in Lucerne and the delegates, acting in the name of world Zionism, took the occasion to pass a resolution against the proposal for a Legislative Council. They somewhat carelessly described it as "contrary to the spirit of the Mandate." The Jewish Agency formally communicated the decision to the High Commissioner. The boycott was now official.

The Arab party ran true to form. Their countermove was as ill-calculated as any they had undertaken. They had not troubled to find out the state of opinion and feeling in England; they overlooked the fact that they needed the sympathy of the House of Commons at a moment when the events of the world had made British opinion in general sympathetic to the Jews. When, in November, 1935, an all-party Arab delegation headed by the Mufti asked Wauchope to make their demands known in London, they put forward a program which was wholly uncompromising. They asked for a sovereign parliament, reflecting the Arab majority. As regards Zionist enterprise, they wanted a ban on all further land sales to Jews and an immediate and total cessation of Jewish immigration. Whether they put these proposals forward as a piece of horse trading, or

[20] They are summarized in Cohen, *op. cit.,* p. 206.
[21] Probably by Revisionists. The facts of the case were never established.

whether they really thought that the British government would accept them, is impossible to know. Their hopes of acceptance may have been high. It has been rightly pointed out that the Arabs (like the Jews) greatly exaggerated the pro-Arab bias of the administration and built absurd hopes on it,[22] and though the Mufti was combating this tendency, it was probably particularly strong at a time when it was known that the High Commissioner was seeking something which the Arabs wanted and the Jews did not.

While the Arab proposals were being studied in London, Sir Arthur Wauchope formally conveyed the latest constitutional offer of the government to the Arab and Jewish leaders in December, 1935. It was a slightly liberalized version of Winston Churchill's 1922 offer: the government would "throw open to the Council a wide field of debate"[23]; the Chamber itself would have parliamentary powers of a somewhat late Tudor character, which could also be said of the ruling powers to be retained by the High Commissioner. The Council was to debate and amend government bills and was free to introduce bills of its own, but, although it would debate the annual budget, it was not to have the right of introducing money bills on its own initiative. The main right of the proposed Council was freedom of speech, though to this there were two important limitations. It was to be out of order for members to abuse foreign states or rulers, and (more importantly for the Arabs) it was forbidden to question the legal validity of the British mandate. The Council was not to assume a parliamentary right to govern. The High Commissioner was not to be under any obligation to regulate his actions or policy in accordance with its resolutions. The composition of the Chamber was to be as follows: five members who were officials of the administration: three Moslem, four Jewish, two Christian members who would be nominated by the High Commissioner together with two members representing "commercial interests"; twelve elected members in the proportions of eight Moslem, three Jewish, and one Christian. The Speaker, known as the President, the Rais and the yoshev-Rosh, was to be "appointed from outside Palestine."[24]

For three years the Arab leadership had shown a united front in pursuit of democracy and the strain was beginning to tell. Their best course, as is easy to see today, was to accept this Elizabethan-style parliament in which they would enjoy a majority, and make something of it if possible. But

[22] John Marlowe, op. cit.
[23] Sir A. Wauchope's address in presenting the offer. 22nd December, 1935.
[24] Cmd. 5116 of 1936.

they hesitated. It was natural for them to do so. When confronted with so much concession they grew uncomfortably aware of the contrast between daylight reality and their dreams. To accept meant giving up a cherished and major item of their program against Zionism: their contention from the beginning that the mandate was legally invalid. To accept the constitution meant that they accepted the mandate, and to accept the mandate meant that they must accept the Balfour Declaration, not in the same sense as Zionists accepted it, of course, and possibly obtaining advantages from the clause concerning non-Jewish communities, but it meant an abandonment of their simpler and more heroic attitude of absolute rejection. They were protagonists in a national struggle, and nationalism needs the heroic. Their dilemma was a real one. They argued it among themselves while precious time went by.

The time was occupied by the Zionists in rallying their supporters in England, and in the state of feeling at that time they met with easy but nonetheless remarkable success. Zionist sympathizers in the House of Commons put questions to the Colonial Secretary, J. H. Thomas, on three occasions during February and March of 1936. The proposed constitution was debated in the House of Lords on the 26th of February, and in the House of Commons on the 24th of March.

This famous debate was not one of those occasions when the British Constitution may be said to have blazed its wisdom to the world. It was on the contrary a clear illustration of British escapism, a reluctance to face distressing facts. It gave no lead to the government or to the administration in Palestine. People said afterward that this was an occasion when the Arab case went by default.[25] This was not quite true. Several members put it forward but they did so ineptly; it received in fact almost as slovenly treatment as the Zionist case, in support of which most of the speeches were made. The whole debate was marked by repeated assertions that the Arabs had no real quarrel with the Jews, and insistence on the long-lived delusion that it only required firm administration and more encouragement of Zionism for Jews and Arabs to sink their differences in their common Palestinian patriotism. Owing to the continuing hesitation of the Arabs, the anti-Council speakers, the majority, could argue that it was foolish to force a parliament on to people who did not want one. The Jews had emphatically refused it and the Arabs seemed the reverse of eager to accept. The most intelligent speech was made by the Liberal leader, Sir Archibald Sinclair. He also made the usual remarks about the delights and

[25] Ronald Storrs, op. cit. London, 1937. The Peel Report contains expression of the same opinion.

benefits which Arabs were receiving from Zionism, but he alone pointed out the real weakness of the constitutional proposition, namely that no parliament can possibly survive party differences without a certain basis of shared consent, and that this would be quite impossible to attain in a chamber where half the deputies accepted and half rejected (whatever they might say) the established form of rule in the country. He reminded the House that the Irish members had in recent times nearly wrecked parliamentarianism in England. Mr. Winston Churchill gave the Zionist cause a characteristic burst of his eloquence, and he recalled his own settlement of 1922, mentioning at one moment that "the Emir Abdullah is in Transjordan where I put him one afternoon in Jerusalem"—a version of the event that he may have come to believe. J. H. Thomas, no longer in the prime of his remarkable ability, was unable to defend his policy. His speech was constantly interrupted and made no impression. The government had clearly misjudged the moment and decided to retrieve the position.

In the meantime the Colonial Secretary had replied in January to the proposals transmitted through Wauchope by the all-party Arab delegation in November. "There can be no question," the British government informed them, "of the total stoppage of Jewish immigration," the main Arab request, but the reply did propose that legislation should be introduced with the object of preventing such sales of land as would cause distress to the occupants, and an invitation was extended to the Arabs to send a delegation to London for discussion. The invitation was accepted, but the Arab leaders continued internal discussion on whether to accept the constitution. They also began a fresh argument about how to compose a delegation. There then occurred the debates in Parliament after which the government decided to drop the constitution scheme altogether. The decision was made public by Thomas in the House of Commons on the 8th of April,[26] by which time the Arabs were inclining toward acceptance though they had not yet decided whom to send to London. Ten days after

[26] In a round-about answer to a question by Josiah Wedgwood.

The Colonial Secretary said: "Since the recent debate in the House I have reason to believe that the representation of the Arabs in Palestine would welcome an opportunity to state their case to His Majesty's Government. Having regard to the fact that I received a few weeks ago a formal deputation representative of Jewish interests it is natural, therefore, that the Arabs should have an equal opportunity of stating their case. I have accordingly instructed the High Commissioner to invite the Arab leaders to send a deputation here. This he has now done and the invitation is accepted. In the interval no further steps towards the establishment of a Legislative Council are being taken."

this it was too late to send any delegation and the last slender chance for representative rule in Palestine went for good. The Arab rebellion had broken out.

The debates in Parliament and the withdrawal of the British government were without doubt contributory causes.[27] There was also the fact that the Italian war in Ethiopia had disrupted trade in the east Mediterranean and as a result the recent prosperity of Palestine was in sudden decline. This naturally affected the socially incoherent Arab working class far more than the socially organized Jews, and as a natural result rancor and mutual hatred increased. They were encouraged to increase more by the newly instituted Arabic broadcasts from Fascist Italy. But the overriding cause of the rebellion was unquestionably the immigration of Jews during the last three years, and the accompanying Arab fear of yet vaster immigrations to come, a fear which most Jews in the country did nothing to diminish, and everything to stimulate.

In the first two weeks of April, 1936, there were ominous atrocities. Some Arab highwaymen stopped a bus and robbed the passengers. When they found that two of their victims were Jews they murdered them. The next night two Arabs sleeping in a hut near the scene of the hold-up were murdered, and this was believed to be a Jewish act of revenge. These two crimes had a sudden and probably quite unpremeditated effect on the country. In many places, far apart from each other, Arabs began to molest their Jewish neighbors, usually in the form of wrecking their property, uprooting crops or destroying orange groves by night. On the 15th of April two Jewish men were murdered in a street of Jaffa. At their funeral on the 19th in Tel Aviv there were anti-Moslem demonstrations and these turned into a riot, the worst that had been seen since 1929. Twenty Jews were killed. Then the rising spread wider and more horribly, and atrocities multiplied. A cinema crowd was raked by fire in one place, in another the nurses and patients in a Jewish clinic were butchered *en masse,* and there were sickening obscure untraced murders of Jewish children. In the same month of April the newly formed Arab Higher Committee (representing the four Moslem and two Christian Arab parties) declared under the leadership of the Mufti for a six months' general strike which was to be called off whenever the British government should suspend Jewish

[27] The Peel Report, Hyamson, Marlowe, and most non-Zionist authorities. The fact comes out very clearly in the evidence of Arabs before the Commission. (Minutes of Evidence Colonial No. 134 of 1937.)

immigration, and was possibly to be extended if Jewish immigration remained unchecked. Armed bands, largely recruited from the mass of unemployed caused by the general strike, began to form and were led by bandits and soldiers of fortune. Among these the most prominent was a certain Fawzi el Kawakji, a ruthless man who did not scruple to add to the murder of Jews the murder of Arabs who were suspected of half-hearted sympathy with his cause. The armed bands became increasingly independent, being united only by, their common strategical aim which was the wrecking of roads and railways and telegraph services, and in the north the cutting of the pipeline bearing oil to Haifa. The Higher Committee lost control early on, but all the evidence points to a close secret understanding between Kawakji and the Mufti. This appeared 'in the policy of the rebellion.

The first phase of the 1936 rising was, as noted, anti-Jewish in character, but after the first weeks its character changed and while the attack against the Jews became weaker, it intensified against the British. It was in this connection that the Arab victims of these embattled patriots started to multiply. They were usually people friendly to British rule.

Sir Arthur Wauchope was much criticized both by his own subordinates and by Jews for not showing firmer handling at the beginning of this great rising. He was a dedicated man who acted as though under a vow to bring peace to the Holy Land, and he hesitated, unwisely as it seemed, to shed blood. His military and police forces were restricted to a defensive role, and even when reinforcements came they were rigidly confined to keeping communications open and to guard duty. They were not authorized to go over to the offensive against the rebels. This was regarded as inept weakness. But there may have been wisdom in Wauchope's policy. The rebellion was even more than it seemed and to crush it thoroughly at this time might have meant a terrible campaign against the mass of the population, an offensive movement which would probably not have been supported by the home government or British opinion. The underlying facts of the rebellion have been well described (with aid from a historian of England) by Mr. John Marlowe:

Although instigated, to some extent guided and certainly used by the political leaders of Arab Palestine, the Arab Rebellion was in fact a peasant revolt, drawing its enthusiasm, its heroism, its organisation and its persistence from sources within itself which have never been properly understood and which now will never be known. Like Feisal's revolt in the desert, it was one of the blind alleys of Arab nationalism doomed, like the desert revolt, to failure,[28] and destined, unlike the desert revolt, to oblivion for lack of a Lawrence to immortalise it. One is reminded of G. M. Trevelyan's words about another peasant revolt: "the readiness of the rural population to turn out and die for their faith was a new thing . . . The record of this brief campaign is as the lifting of a curtain; behind it we can see for a moment into the old peasant life. In that one glance we see not rustic torpor, but faith, idealism, vigour, love of liberty, and scorn of death. Were the yeoman and farm servants in other parts of England like these men of Somerset, or were they everywhere else of a lower type? The curtain falls and knowledge is hidden for ever." [29]

The rebellion and the strike persisted throughout the summer. There were over 1,300 casualties including 305 killed.[30] The most serious aspect of this rising (the greatest by far that had been seen in Palestine in the twentieth century) was that it drew strength from abroad and began to show signs of becoming a general revolt throughout the Arabic-speaking world against the British mandate. Most of the guerrilla leaders were from outside; Fawzi el Kawakji for example was a Lebanese, and there was little doubt that these foreign nationalist volunteers enjoyed the support either of their governments or of clandestine parties tolerated by their governments. In May the British government promised that a new royal commission of inquiry into the "causes of unrest" would be sent to Palestine as soon as order was reestablished, but by 1936 the Palestinians, Jewish as well as Arab, were beginning to get tired of royal commissions and to lose faith in their healing powers. The rebellion went on. The career of J. H. Thomas came to its melancholy end, and when he was succeeded by Mr. William Ormsby-Gore,[31] a known enthusiast for the Zionist cause, the anger of the Arab nationalists took on new life.[32] Nevertheless the High Commissioner and the moderates of the Arab Higher Committee sought for a compromise line of policy which would enable the strike to be called off without loss of face. For long they did not succeed and the forces which had been let loose remained beyond all control. In July the compromisers made another move. The Arab case was

[28] In the sense, presumably, that independent Hashemite lordship over the Arabian peninsula and Syria was not realised.
[29] Marlowe, *The Seat of Pilate*, pp. 137-138. See also the same author's *Rebellion in Palestine*.
[30] Total casualties 1,351 including 187 Moslems, 10 Christian Arabs, 80 Jews, 28 British personnel killed. Annual Register.
[31] Later Lord Harlech.
[32] Jeffries, *Palestine the Reality*.

presented to Wauchope again in a carefully worded and scrupulously moderate statement signed by 137 Arab officials of the administration.[33] This document was sponsored by Emir Abdullah and the foreign minister of Iraq, Nuri es Said, both proved friends of Great Britain; but the move lacked popular support and had no immediate effect.

In the autumn, however, the rebellion at last gave way to pressure, and it seemed, on the surface, that the Palestine administration had emerged victorious from the struggle. In September reinforcements amounting to a division arrived in Haifa from Great Britain. Shortly after, the ruling princes of Iraq, Transjordan, Saudi Arabia, and Yemen (certainly with the connivance and possibly at the suggestion of the British government[34]) appealed to the Arab Higher Committee to abandon the strike and to have faith in "the good intentions of our friend Great Britain who has declared that she will do justice." This was a friendly reference to the fact that when the names of the members selected to serve on the new royal commission had been announced on the 29th of July, the British government had published their instructions in a manner likely to appease Arab feeling. The commission was ordered "to ascertain the underlying causes of the disturbances which broke out in Palestine in the middle of April; to inquire into the manner in which the Mandate of Palestine is being implemented in relation to the obligations of the Mandatory towards the Arabs and the Jews respectively; to ascertain whether, upon a proper construction of the terms of the Mandate, either the Arabs or the Jews have any legitimate grievances upon account of the way in which the Mandate has been or is being implemented; and, if the Commission is satisfied that any such grievances are well-founded, to make recommendations for their removal and for the prevention of their recurrence."

The reinforcement of the garrison, together with signs of an appeasement policy toward themselves and the appeal of their supporters without, finally persuaded the Arabs to give up the rigors of rebellion, for the time being at any rate. The strike was officially called off by the Arab Higher Committee on the 12th of October. A month later, on the 11th of November, the new commission arrived in Palestine under the chairmanship of Lord Peel.

As was usual in the case of such commissions their instructions amounted to a request that they solve the problem. Whatever may be said of other occasions, it is beyond doubt that the commissioners of 1936 and

[33] Jeffries, *op. cit.* Peel Report.
[34] Marlowe, *op. cit.*

the government which sent them were perfectly sincere in their hope and their resolve. The Peel Commission came as close as any royal commission to finding a way out of the political tangle in Palestine. Even so, it is not harsh or unfair to say that they came nowhere near their goal. They were too late. The problem may have been utterly beyond solution from the beginning, but, however that may be, it had become infinitely harder of solution now that the problem was not only concerned with reconciling two nationalisms in a single territory, a daunting enough task by any reckoning, but was newly and directly conditioned by a decline in those standards of Western civilization on which the ruling power depended.

8 PEEL TO THE RESCUE

The six members of the commission had all had distinguished careers, most of them in British overseas administration and two of them in the law. Their leader was Lord Peel, a grandson of Sir Robert Peel the Prime Minister. Early in life he had left the Bar for politics where his most remarkable services had been in Indian affairs. He was Secretary of State from 1922 to 1924, and again from 1928 to 1929. He was a member of both the India and Burma round table conferences from 1930 to 1933. He had served on many commissions of inquiry. He was a large genial man of strong personality, a first-rate administrator, and an ideal chairman whose main virtue was a common sense that did not exclude imagination. In 1936 he was in his seventieth year. His health was beginning to fail though this did not affect the vigor of his mind.

His vice-chairman was Sir Horace Rumbold, who had recently retired from the diplomatic service. In appearance Sir Horace was a caricature of the old-style British military commander or Colonial Governor, but most men who served with this portly monocled ambassador agree that he had shrewdness and wisdom under a manner and exterior which suggested qualities the reverse of intellectual. The peaks of his career had been in 1920 when he had been appointed British High Commissioner in Constantinople; in 1923 when he had headed the British delegation at the Lausanne Conference leading to the long-delayed peace treaty with Turkey; and in 1928 when he was appointed British ambassador in Berlin. He had remained in this post till August, 1933 and was thus the first English envoy to be accredited to the Nazi court, a position which he resented as humiliating. His detestation of the Nazi party was extreme and he warned his government [1] that the advent of Hitler to power was a catastrophic event whose dangers could hardly be exaggerated. His personal feelings were closely involved for his response to life was far more emotional than people usually supposed. At this time he was sixty-seven years old and with Peel's frequent absences from sessions he often presided.

Sir Lucas Hammond, like Lord Peel, had Indian experience. He had been chief secretary to the government of Bihar and from 1927 to 1932 he was governor of Assam. He had recently served as chairman of the Indian Delimitation Committee. Sir William Morris Carter and Sir Harold Morris were both lawyers. The former had had a long and successful career in Africa, where he had served twice as chief justice and once as an acting governor. In Africa he had also served on commissions of inquiry. Sir Harold Morris was at this time the Recorder of Folkestone.

It seems agreed by everyone who has written on the subject of the Peel Commission, or was in Palestine in those days, that the most influential member was Professor Reginald Coupland of All Souls College, Oxford. He was at this time the Beit Professor of Colonial History in the university and he had served as a member of a royal commission on Indian civil services in 1923. Apart from this he had no direct experience of political and public life, but he had been the editor of the influential political quarterly *The Round Table* from 1917 to 1919. He was a man of determined ideas and if he had an intellectual fault it was undoubtedly that he tended sometimes to fall in love with theory and to force his observation of fact to suit the object of his passion. He had remarkable powers of persuasion and since his ideas were all the consequence of long, gifted, and systematic thought he often succeeded in imposing them. Judgment of the Peel Commission largely centers around the question of whether Coupland's ideas were good or not.

[1] Lt. General Marshall-Cornwall in the *Dictionary of National Biography*.

As said, people in Palestine had grown tired of royal commissions and did not welcome this one. Its origins in a policy of appeasement toward Arab nationalism and its support of Arab rulers inevitably aroused the suspicions of the Zionists, quite needlessly.

The Jews overlooked two things, the sympathy with their plight that the Nazi regime had brought about in England, and the impression made on civilized opinion by their own policy, known in Hebrew as that of "Havlagah," meaning "self-restraint." This was one of the most extraordinary manifestations of the Jewish spirit to be seen in Palestine at any time and it should be briefly considered.

The legal position of the secret Jewish army, Haganah, had been extremely ambiguous from its beginning in the early 1920's. Haganah had no official existence in the official eyes of the mandatory and yet its existence had been officially condoned and even approved on more than one occasion as a necessary measure of self-defense. The confusion arose from a contradiction of theory with fact. The mandate tried hard to be faithful to one principle: that no action should be taken that might lead Arab-Jewish rivalry to Arab-Jewish combat and bloodshed. The logical conclusion was to forbid arms to both Arabs and Jews, a prohibition which could not be carried into effect. Both parties already had arms, and in Samuel's time, when the Jews were first forming their secret army, the Colonial Secretary (the Duke of Devonshire) instructed the High Commissioner to allow the Jews what arms they needed so as to avoid the greater evil of a clandestine Jewish military force,[2] but this policy, never taken up with any vigor, was not persisted in after Devonshire left office. The secret army was formed, was officially condemned, while the right to Jewish self-defense was recognized. Legal Jewish self-defense consisted of wholly inadequate supplies of arms which were allowed to be used under a complicated and impractical system of British supervision. Haganah to some extent saved the British from their own unworkable regulations, from having to make use of the nonsensical security measures which they had evolved from the anomalous circumstances of Palestine. Court decisions occasionally recognized the fact.[3] It followed that by 1936 the question as to whether Haganah was or was not illegal might have taxed the most astute legal mind. On the other hand membership in Haganah did not weigh on the conscience of the most law-abiding Jew.

The outbreak of the Arab rebellion naturally fired Haganah with a wish to reply to Arab aggression in kind. The Jewish Agency were alive to

[2] Dr. Yehuda Slutzki, *History of Haganah*. Jerusalem, 1954.
[3] Slutzki. A communication.

the feeling of the people and they acted quickly. They proclaimed Havlagah: there was to be no armed operation by Jews against the rebels. Among the colonists and townsmen of the National Home, especially the members of Haganah, this decision was extremely unpopular, and it is a matter for much surprise that the leadership was able to force the decision against exasperated opposition, and without causing any new or more radical split among the Zionists. The achievement was probably due in part to the prestige of Dr. Weizmann, who (after four years out of office) had returned to the presidency of the Zionist organization, though the decision was by no means his alone. The policy was not resisted within the Jewish Agency and was supported by the socialist Mapai party and the left-wing opposition, the Hashomer Hatzair party. With so much support in the leadership the policy went through virtually unopposed, and this was largely due to the fact that, for all its unpopularity, it found an echo in a Jewish tradition which dated back to the early Jewish settlements of fifty years before and almost certainly originated in ancient lore. By this tradition Jews believed that on the holy soil of the promised land their arms must remain "pure" ("tahor"), that is to say, they must not be stained with the blood of anyone whose enmity had not been proved. Such beliefs were easily conjoined to the Western liberalism of the German immigrants, though it seems agreed that Western liberalism was never comparable as a force to tradition.[4]

The object of the Havlagah policy was both idealistic and tactical. There was a genuine wish among most Zionist leaders to lessen the gulf between Arabs and Jews at this crucial moment. The views of such a man as Dr. Judah Magnes, the president of the Hebrew University, who went so far as to advocate a binational state, found little agreement among the Jews of Palestine, but if his policy was rejected and even resented, the pacific spirit of his teaching had a deep influence. It was reflected in the more moderate idealism of some classic Zionists.

The tactical purpose was to obtain the goodwill of the British. The policy ended in confusion and this makes it tempting to say that in its tactical purpose it failed. Yet this needs much qualification. In the years of the Peel Commission the policy made a deep and extremely favorable impression not only on British opinion but—a matter of distant but great importance—on American opinion. The civilized world was still in a pacifist mood and pacifist gestures could still have decisive moral effect. For a short while this gesture was effective and it added to a disposition to sympathize with Zionism. It was an ironical consequence of this that the Peel

[4] Dr. Yehuda Bauer. A communication covering the subject of this paragraph.

Commission, which had its origins in an attempt to conciliate Arab nationalism, came to be looked on as the most favorable to Zionism of those sent in prewar years. A small incident was said to have had a considerable emotional effect on the commissioners. They were being conducted around a Jewish agricultural settlement when Sir Horace Rumbold noticed a man working in a farmyard. He thought he recognized him and when he asked his name he found it was that of a once well-known German musician who had played in his Berlin embassy. He went over and spoke to the man, saying something sympathetic about his mournfully "changed circumstances." The musician replied: "My circumstances are changed indeed. I have escaped from Hell into Heaven." [5]

The Commission held sixty-six meetings, of which thirty-one were public. The first sessions were secret and were spent in hearing evidence from British officials, after which most of the succeeding sessions were taken up with hearing evidence from Jews. Dr. Weizmann opened the Jewish evidence by his memorable appearance before the eighth session, the third public one, held on the 25th of November. No Arab witnesses were heard until the fifty-sixth session on the 12th of January, 1937. This was because the Arab leadership, in spite of the support given to the commission by Arab princes and governments, found it impossible to resist yet another essay in their favorite political maneuver. As soon as the commission arrived they proclaimed that they would boycott its proceedings. Not till January were they persuaded by Arab and British supporters that on this occasion, even if on no other, they were in fact only boycotting their own chances of influencing policy.

When Dr. Weizmann presented his evidence in the dining room of the Palace Hotel in Jerusalem (where the public sessions took place) he showed that he was aware that he was discharging a great role before history, speaking to the future both on behalf of his countrymen in Eretz Israel, the "Yishuv," or "the People" as they are known in Hebrew, and on behalf of the Jews of the world. He has been rightly described as one of the supreme diplomatists of his time.[6] Most of his triumphs were achieved through private interviews, where his personal charm could have full play, but on this occasion, one of the most notable of his life, he made all his impression at a large public meeting.

After describing the composition and constitution of the Zionist organization and the Jewish Agency, Dr. Weizmann entered on "a continuous

---

[5] Sir John Hathorne Hall. A communication.
[6] Sir Charles Webster, *The Art and Practice of Diplomacy*. London, 1961.

statement" in which he described the situation of the Jews in the modern world. He summarized the tragedy of his people in one word: homelessness. He recalled the vast migration of Jews from Russia and Poland to America in the thirty years before the First World War and compared the wretched lot of Jews under imperial Russian rule with their worse lot under Soviet rule in which the profession of Zionism was a criminal offense and the Jewish community had been forced into loss of all contact with their fellow Jews outside. He gave expression to that frequent Jewish dread that the Jewish people might lose their identity. From the dismal obscurity of the Soviet Union he turned to the plight of the Jews among Russia's neighbors. He dwelt on the gradual decay of the once modestly prosperous Jewish community of Poland, and the sudden decay of the smaller and far more prosperous community of Germany, numbering about six hundred thousand. Without allowing himself any display of emotion he first indicated how the example of Germany had strongly infected the neighboring states in the Baltic and eastern Europe with anti-Semitism, and he then asserted that Nazism was also slightly but discernibly infecting Germany's neighbors to the west, France and Great Britain. He told how he had seen opposition to Leon Blum in France confounded with an anti-Jewish impetus, and how in Great Britain he had come upon a new and morbid sensitiveness about Jewish matters.[7] He reminded the commissioners that the gates of America were no longer open and that all governments now followed policies aimed at the restriction of immigration. He summed up the situation in a memorable phrase. Referring to the Baltic and the east European states outside Russia, he said: "There are in this part of the world six million people doomed to be pent up in places where they are not wanted, and for whom the world is divided into places where they cannot live, and places into which they cannot enter."

He then turned to the history of Zionism and pointed out that it was the crystallization of a long historical process, of a continual Jewish movement of return to their native land, a process which had persisted with only brief interruptions from the time of the Roman Empire. The Jewish immigration and pioneering under the mandate were no new phenomena. He said: "When the Jews were driven out of Spain at the end of the

[7] He used a curious illustration to indicate this. He recalled how in the summer of 1936 a fanatic had thrown a pistol at King Edward VIII as he was riding from a parade and that while the man's name remained undisclosed by the police several friends of Dr. Weizmann's had said to him, "For God's sake, we hope he is not a Jew." Weizmann added, "Now that is typical, that is characteristic of the nervousness there is." Evidence taken before the Peel Commission H.M.S.O. Col. 134.

fifteenth century they wandered over the world. Two hundred thousand of them turned their faces towards the East. We are not unmindful of the reception that was given to us then by the Moslem world. We came to Turkey and from Turkey we drifted to Palestine, and communities sprang up. The City of Tiberias, which was desert and laid waste, was rebuilt in that period by a Jew who became influential at the Turkish court. He rebuilt it and it became something like Tel Aviv to-day—a Jewish city built out of ruins. It was subsequently, one hundred years later, laid waste by Arabs—not unlike what is happening now—and then again, one hundred years afterwards, it was rebuilt by a Jew."

He recalled the long history of what might be called Gentile Zionism in England from the seventeenth century to the time of Arthur Balfour, and he briefly referred to the first encounters of the modern Zionism of Herzl with the British government of which Balfour was the chief and in which Joseph Chamberlain was Colonial Secretary. He told them how Joseph Chamberlain had made the offer of Kenya as a Jewish settlement area and how this proposition had been defeated by representatives of the persecuted Russian Jews, the very people whom it was primarily designed to help. Dr. Weizmann reminded the commissioners of his subsequent meeting with the Prime Minister. He said: "Mr. Balfour, when I had the pleasure of making his acquaintance, tried to understand why we felt like this [about Kenya], and the only reason which appealed to him was when I said to him 'It is not Jerusalem and it never will be.' " [8] Weizmann went on to say, "this steadfastness is, my lord and gentlemen, perhaps our misfortune. If it had disappeared, there would be no Jewish problem, but here we are. It is our destiny."

He went on to describe the origins of the Balfour Declaration, its purpose and its immense and immediate effect on the Jews of the world, a point which he seems to have deliberately exaggerated.[9] He explained that his famous answer to a question at the Peace Conference: that a Jewish National Home meant "to build up something in Palestine which will be as Jewish as England is English," did not mean a regime of domination over Arabs reduced to servitude. He reminded his hearers of his adventures with the Webbs. "Lord Passfield . . . told me 'But Dr. Weizmann, do you not realise that there is not room to swing a cat in Palestine?' . . . many a cat has been swung since then, and the population of Palestine

[8] A full account of Dr. Weizmann's famous interview with Balfour, which occurred during the general election of 1906, is in *Trial and Error* and in Mrs. Dugdale's biography of Balfour.

[9] In private he often lamented that the Jewish response had not been more vigorous.

has increased since that particular talk with Lord Passfield, by something like two hundred thousand."

He described his efforts to conciliate the Arabs and referred as he often did on this subject to his abortive agreement with Feisal. To anyone knowing something of the facts this is the weakest part of Dr. Weizmann's impressive deposition, but he was not challenged and the questions of the commissioners suggest that they were not aware of what had happened on this occasion or its sequel. In his answers Dr. Weizmann made great play with the name of T. E. Lawrence. Passing from this subject he declared that he had reached the end of his introductory remarks and would now turn to practical matters, but in fact the deposition dealt in generalities to the end. He had been briefed by Mr. Leonard Stein but he rarely kept to any brief.[10]

He described the spirit of the incoming Jews, defining two kinds of immigrant in the world; the public-spirited, the pioneers who look to other immigrants to come after them and the egotists, the self-centered who, having succeeded in reaching a country of refuge, are at pains to exclude further immigrants. The Jews of Palestine belonged to the first kind and were at one in wishing for continual increases of Jewish immigration. He insisted on the loyalty of the Jews to the mandatory power and how they had faithfully abided by the 1922 White Paper despite the fact that it disappointed many Zionist hopes. He contrasted the little that the Jews had asked and received from the postwar settlement with the great rise in the world enjoyed by the Arabs, who were now the masters of large self-governing states. He turned to practical matters in his analysis of Jewish statistics, his proposals for Arab-Jewish labor cooperation and his demand for a larger measure of Jewish labor employment in public works. With scrupulous politeness he criticized the administration for lack of dynamism in its conduct of affairs, but he expressed the sense of Jewish gratitude toward England nonetheless. He concluded with some remarks on the difficult question of a Palestine Legislative Council. Somewhat surprisingly he did not insist, beyond a short reference, on the Arab record of boycotting, but contented himself with regretfully pointing out that the present Arab purpose in a Legislative Council was to place obstacles in the way of the Zionists. "I would like to add," he concluded, with studied vagueness, "that there may be forms and there may be conditions, and I hope it will be given to this Royal Commission to formulate such conditions and such forms—I know it is asking a great deal—under which self-governing institutions, and particularly a Legislative Council, could be

[10] Mr. Meyer W. Weisgal. A communication.

initiated, certainly with our consent and I hope with the consent of the population of the country. Complex is the task of the Royal Commission, and it has come at a time when the Jewish position, even in our history, has never been darker than it is now, and I pray it may be given to you to find a way out." It had been a masterly performance and many who were present told later how the three hours which it occupied seemed to pass like a few minutes. Dr. Weizmann had portrayed the Jewish tragedy in the light of history with the zeal and assurance of a great artist.

During the remaining public sessions the commission heard forty other Jewish witnesses. Their names included most of those who were to be the first political leaders of the State of Israel. There was no aspect of Zionist life, organization and purpose which they did not fully describe in the course of question and answer. Inevitably, in the circumstances, some of them overstated the Zionist case, on occasion fantastically, as when it was urged that the phrase "non-Jewish communities" in the Balfour Declaration was not intended to refer to the Arab population but to the religious minorities. But the result of such indiscretions was not so much to irritate the commissioners, though the record shows that they went through moments of considerable exasperation, as to confirm Coupland in a growing conviction that there could be no solution of the problem on any basis of Arab-Jewish fellowship in Palestine. The last Jewish witness was Jabotinsky, who, as an exile from Palestine since 1929, was examined in London. In a long statement he returned to his accustomed theme that a wholehearted pro-Zionist policy and a dominant Jewish population in Palestine would (he believed through intuition) result in a peaceful outcome through Arab acquiescence.

The topic most often discussed in the evidence was immigration. The case maintaining the high Jewish figures reached since 1933, and for diminishing the existing restrictions, especially as regarded the number of relatives allowed to accompany individuals, and the vexatious statistical interpretation applied to the admission of young students, mainly from Germany, was argued with the utmost skill and imagination. Illegal immigration was also touched on and the Zionists astutely made a considerable impression by revealing that the economy of the country was often confused by the growing extent of Arab illegal immigration, a consequence of the economic expansion due to Zionism in action.

When the Arabs had been argued out of their boycotting in January, Haj Amin appeared before the commissioners on the 12th, accompanied by nine members and the secretary of the Arab Higher Committee. He had a formidable task: to impose on the commissioners an impression deeper than that made by the Jewish witnesses, especially Dr. Weizmann. His performance was uneven; at one moment he argued with keen and impressive skill, at another he spoiled the effect of undoubtedly strong arguments on his side by supporting them with weak ones. His first contention was that under Ottoman rule "the Arabs formed an important part of the structure of the Empire," and he drew a comparison with their present lowly status west of Jordan. He traced the Arab independence movement from those days to the Arab revolt and the British undertakings which formed its policy. When, however, he came to show that Palestine was part of the promised area of Arab independence he muddled his case by quoting a remark to this effect made by Lord Allenby speaking in a private capacity, instead of concentrating on the large and convincing official documentation open to him. He recovered ground when he came to argue that the terms of the mandate were inconsistent with the Covenant of the League and he made effective use of the melancholy story of the King-Crane Commission sent in 1919 by President Wilson, after abortive agreement with the Allies, to report on the future of Syria and Palestine. The commissioners tried to show that the anti-Zionist King-Crane report was not acceptable as evidence and the Mufti, at advantage through being better briefed, countered with all his exquisite and quiet debating ability.

He touched on a very genuine grievance when he described how British politicians when confronted by Arab demands tended to refer delegates to the League of Nations as the responsible authority, whereat the League would refer them back to the British government as the responsible authority. But then having established his point, he again weakened the effect by describing the influence of the Jews in England and their ambitions in Palestine in grotesquely exaggerated terms. He referred to "the Jews' ultimate aim" as "the reconstruction of the Temple of King Solomon on the ruins of the Haram es Sharif, the el Aqsa mosque, and the Holy Dome of the Rock." As evidence of such a plan he cited indiscreet but entirely personal proposals made by Sir Alfred Mond for the rebuilding of the Temple, and another proposal to the same effect sent to him (the Mufti) by the chief rabbi of Rumania. He mentioned that Jews had been known to pull down mosques on land which they had bought. When reminded that the mandate was pledged to maintain existing shrines he, like another leading clergyman of Jerusalem many centuries before, unconsciously prophesied. He suggested that the Jews might be able to bring about the termination of the mandate. Pressed by Rumbold to make his meaning clear he added: "I can see and my experience up to now shows that the Jews can do anything so far as Palestine is concerned."

His positive proposals were along the familiar uncompromising lines of Arab policy since the days of the military administration: complete abandonment by Britain of the National Home venture; total stoppage of Jewish immigration and purchase of land; termination of the mandate and its substitution by an Anglo-Arab treaty along the lines of the Anglo-Iraq treaty. He was asked what prospects the Jews of Palestine would have under the sort of state he envisaged, and he countered by reminding the commission that the world of Islam had in previous times been the refuge of Jews from Christian persecution. He stuck to his assertion however that the 400,000 Jews then in Palestine were more than a country of that size could "digest," and when asked by Lord Peel whether in his view this did not mean that in an independent Moslem Palestine some of these Jews would have to be removed "by a process kindly or painful as the case may be," he gave the unassuring and Oriental reply: "We must leave all this to the future."

Sir Laurie Hammond took over the questioning in the last stages of the examination and he got an admission from Haj Amin that at no time had there been anything in the nature of an enforced sale of land by Arabs to Jews. This was always the weakest point in the Arab case and the defense here needed to appeal to a broad understanding of human nature such as was nowhere to be found in the narrow hate-ridden mind of Haj Amin. From this he was led by Hammond, Peel, and an indignant Rumbold to declare that the lot of the inhabitants was far less happy under British rule than it had been under the Turkish dominion against which the Arabs had revolted in the war. Hammond asked whether the people would like to have the Turkish conscription for the army back, to which Haj Amin unhesitatingly replied: "Yes, provided we had our own government." In conclusion he promised to let the commission have a detailed statement of Arab-Jewish land sales, but in a note sent three weeks later he regretted being unable to do this owing to the difficulty in obtaining the necessary information.

Of the fourteen Arab witnesses subsequently heard in public session, none added materially to the Mufti's deposition, though the Arab nationalist point of view was given more sympathetic expression in the evidence of its apologist George Antonius.

The radical uncompromising extremism of the Arab representatives all contrived to strengthen Coupland's position as the policy-maker of the royal commission. To see how this happened one needs to go back a little. A few days before Haj Amin's evidence Dr. Weizmann had appeared before the commissioners in a closed session, on the 8th of January. This was the turning point in the career of the commission. The discussions began with Dr. Weizmann's telling the commission about various approaches which had been made by Zionists to Arab leaders in the hope of reaching some kind of preliminary agreement on which to build. The news had by now been received that Arabs were after all prepared to testify and Dr. Weizmann, after saying that this possibly showed some change of heart, suggested that the commission take the opportunity of forming themselves into a negotiating body. At one moment he said, "The Mufti cannot be allowed to stand in the way of a big thing like peace," and at a later moment he said that he was willing to meet the Mufti in person if this could do any good.

Professor Coupland changed the subject dramatically halfway through the hearing. Many members of the administration favored a policy of cantonization at that time, and with this in mind Coupland said as follows:

Dr. Weizmann, looking ahead and supposing, for the sake of argument, that your hopeful prospect of harmony proves unrealisable in the course of the next five or ten years, what practicable alternative might there be? With that question in your mind, would you comment on this scheme which deserves to be called more than cantonisation; it is really partition on a federal basis . . . meaning that in due course and under a treaty system two blocks of Palestine become independent states of the type of Egypt and Irak in treaty relations with Great Britain. That is really the ultimate point on which I want to get your view.

As an experienced diplomat Dr. Weizmann received the proposal questioningly, pointing out the major difficulty that in no sizable part of Palestine were the Jews a compact majority: the colonies were scattered throughout the land. At the end of the hearing Coupland attempted to summarize the proposal. He said:

If there were no other way out to peace, might it not be a final and peaceful settlement—to terminate the Mandate by agreement and split Palestine into two halves, the plain being an Independent Jewish State, as independent as Belgium, with treaty relations with Great Britain, whatever arrangements you like with us, and the rest of Palestine, plus Trans-

Jordania, being an Independent Arab state, as independent as Arabia. That is the ultimate idea.

Dr. Weizmann answered: "Permit me not to give a definite answer now. Let me think about it." [11]

Outside Dr. Weizmann was joined by his private secretary, Yeheskiel Sacharoff.[12] He told him he wanted to clear his mind by walking on Mount Scopus, and the two set out together. When they were alone Weizmann threw off all his reserve and with deep emotion he told the young man what he had just heard from the commissioners, and he went on to say that the long toil of his life was at last crowned with success. The Jewish State was at hand, his labors and pertinacity had not been in vain, and giving his imagination free play he began to indulge in dreams of the future, describing to Sacharoff the type of polity and organization of the new Israel in detail. Well as he knew him, the young man had never seen "the chief" in so exalted a mood, one in which he could not repress the joy that was in him, in which his voice would be suddenly choked by emotion and his eyes filled with tears. All his love for his people, all his love for England, rushed to the surface.[13]

Professor Coupland was not aware that he had made a convert and he sought a further opportunity to discuss his proposal with Dr. Weizmann. It came at a weekend in the beginning of February, shortly before the departure of the commission, when the two met at a Jewish agricultural settlement and training center called Nahalal in Galilee, a place for which Dr. Weizmann had a particular affection. He went there early in the morning from his home at Rehovoth and Professor Coupland was brought from Jerusalem by Joshuah Gordon, the liaison officer of the Jewish Agency, a fat genial man who both on duty and off duty devoted his energies to tireless propaganda on behalf of the National Home. The meeting was kept secret. The day was cold and rainy and the two men spent it with maps in a hut belonging to the Girls' Agricultural School. And now it was the turn of Dr. Weizmann to convert Coupland, to turn the protagonist of a divided Palestine into an enthusiast. According to his own account Coupland seems, up to this moment, to have been strongly in favor of partition though still open to other ideas. But after this day during which he was exposed to the eloquence, faith, and charm of the

[11] Weizmann Archives and Julian L. Meltzer in Weizmann Biography.
[12] Now Yeheskiel Sachar.
[13] Y. Sachar. A communication.

great Jewish leader, he was no longer open to other ideas; he became absolutely convinced that partition was an urgent necessity and he determined to convert his colleagues to the same view and to make it the main recommendation of Lord Peel's report to the government.[14]

Coupland had reached his idea for a solution by partition through following a principle which he had deduced from his researches into history. It was his belief that no two peoples who had developed national consciousness could live together as equal partners in a single state, though to this he allowed an exception which subsequent events render somewhat doubtful. He believed that the British, by the peculiar circumstances of their origin and history, were capable of such a feat of cooperation, and he pointed to South Africa and the happy mutual relations existing there between English and Afrikaner as proof of this important and flattering qualification. He was convinced, now more intensely than ever, that the circumstances of Palestine, and the Arab and Jewish characters, did not allow for another exception here.[15]

The arrival of Dr. Weizmann and an Englishman, and their long private confabulation together, were noticed by the farmers of Nahalal and toward evening many of them were waiting around the Girls' Agricultural School. They were not disappointed. When the two men and their companions emerged from the hut Dr. Weizmann, perhaps seizing this opportunity to confirm Coupland's adherence to his own plan, addressed the puzzled onlookers. "Today," he said, "in this place, we have laid the foundations of the Jewish State!"

Sir Arthur Wauchope and the higher officials of the Administration had of course been informed about Coupland's partition plans, and they did not like them. They preferred the more elaborate but more flexible and changeable canton system which they had worked out, and which they believed would avoid the full dangers inherent in drawing political frontiers. They urged this most strongly on the commissioners, and by the time the latter left Palestine Coupland had by no means succeeded in persuading his colleagues into total acceptance of his own point of view. This seems to have resulted in a great degree of misunderstanding. The administration felt sure that they had succeeded in impressing their view on Peel and that his report would either recommend cantonization or leave the way open for its adoption. They informed the government that they were in general agreement with the royal commission. They overlooked the force of Coupland's steady and persuasive mind and that

[14] Julian L. Meltzer in Weizmann Biography.
[15] Sir J. Hathorne Hall. A communication.

the commissioners were to be exposed to its influence during a short holiday which they all took in Egypt, and during the subsequent journey home, and during the compiling of their recommendations. By the time they came to sign the report the whole commission strongly favored partition along the lines devised by Coupland.[16]

In July of 1937 the Peel Report was submitted without dissent from any of the commissioners. On the day of its completion Dr. Weizmann was in Paris where he had arranged, by the intermediary of the orientalist adviser to the Jewish Agency, Mr. Eliahu Epstein,[17] to meet the President of the Republic of Lebanon. Dr. Weizmann addressed him somewhat as follows: "At this moment Lord Peel and his colleagues are signing their recommendations for a partition of Palestine by which we, Jewish Citizens of a Jewish State, will be your neighbours." He then described what policy he envisaged in the international sphere. He wanted an enduring alliance of the Jewish with the Lebanese State and from there, by joint Jewish-Lebanese initiative, to found a closely knit community of the Moslem, Christian and Jewish nations of the east Mediterranean, and by this means to bring a final end to Arab-Jewish discord. President Eddé was moved to shake Dr. Weizmann's hand and to exclaim: "I salute the first President of the Jewish Republic."[18] This curious and moving little scene epitomized a transient mood of optimism which for a brief moment, and for a few, lightened the gathering darkness of the Jewish tragedy. The awakening to reality was to be painful in the extreme.

The Peel Report[19] was made public on the 7th of July. It is the only royal commission report on Palestine to have become famous. It has been often and ably written about and need only be very shortly summarized here.

The report opened with its often quoted appraisal of Palestine since the Balfour Declaration. The commissioners reached the melancholy conclusion that "the policy of conciliation, carried to its farthest limits, has failed." They were unsparing in their criticism of the administration, notably on the subject of education where Sir Herbert Samuel's imaginative and adventurous initiative had not only been weakly followed but almost reversed; nevertheless their assessment was more inclined to lay the blame on the very fact of the mandate and on the policies leading

[16] Sir John Hathorne Hall. Sir Horace Rumbold. Communications.
[17] Now Mr. Eliahu Elath, president of the Hebrew University, Jerusalem. He was the first diplomatic envoy from Israel to Great Britain.
[18] Elath. A communication.
[19] Cmd. 5479 of 1937.

to it than on the men in charge. They never said this aloud, so to speak, but continually implied it.

On the assumption that the mandate would continue for many years, they outlined a possible new course in administration, of which the most important details concerned land and immigration. On neither were they encouraging to Zionism. They described the land objective as a measure "to provide for close settlement by the Jews and at the same time to safeguard the rights and position of the Arabs," while remarking that "there is no land available for any experiments in close settlement and mixed farming by the Jews except possibly in the vicinity of Jerusalem." They felt obliged, on this account, to urge the prohibition of land sales to Jews in certain areas. As regards immigration they recommended that the influx of Jews should be confined to a total maximum of 12,000 people a year for five years, after which the position should be reviewed. They added that these (with some minor recommendations in the same section) were the "best palliatives" that they could devise, but they held out no hope that they would "cure the trouble." For that purpose the commissioners proposed and recommended a radically different line of policy, in which the assumption that the mandate would continue was set aside. It was now that Coupland, so to speak, took over.

The main feature of this second policy was to reconstruct Palestine. First they recommended that the mandate should be abolished, at least in its present form. The report said as follows:

> It is manifest that the mandate cannot be fully or honourably implemented unless by some means or other the national antagonism between Arabs and Jews can be composed. But it is the Mandate which created that antagonism and keeps it alive and as long as the Mandate exists we cannot honestly hold out the expectation that Arabs and Jews will be able to set aside their national hopes or fears and sink their differences in the common service of Palestine. That being so, real self-governing institutions cannot be developed nor the Mandate even terminated without violating its obligations, general or specific.

The commission thus made it plain that there was no way out of the confusion of Palestine, not even the way they recommended, in harmony with British pledges.

In the place of the mandate the commissioners recommended the partition of Palestine. They proposed the formation of a small Jewish State, after which the remaining territory would be united to the emirate of Transjordan. But they also proposed that in the midst of the country, and also scattered over the partitioned territory, there should remain small areas which would continue to be administered by the mandatory power.

The proposed Jewish frontiers in the north were less than those of present-day Israel but similar in outline. Within the country the Jews were asked to show great restraint in nationalism. The main towns in the north were to remain under mandatory rule. The new State would not only have been without the valuable port of Haifa, (though enjoying facilities there), but also without Acre, Nazareth, Tiberias, and Safad. The northern Jewish territory stopped south of Tel Aviv, the port of Jaffa being conceded to the Arabs as a purely Arab town, though situated in the mandated area.

Eastward from Jaffa the minute mandated territory was to extend inland. It was to take in the airport of Lydda and to include Jerusalem and Bethlehem, stopping a few miles east of both.

The southern Jewish territory hardly existed. In so far as it did, it consisted of a triangular strip south of Jaffa comprising about a hundred square miles. The towns of Gaza, Hebron, and Beersheba and the whole Negev were to go to the enlarged emirate.

There was one very curious recommendation for which, on the face of it, the commissioners could not conceivably have expected Jewish acceptance. This was to the effect that since the Jewish State would include all the most fertile land in Palestine, and would in consequence be in happier economic circumstances, it should be under obligation to pay a yearly subvention to the emirate next door. The recommendation is best understood as payment for injury. What the commissioners had in mind becomes clearer in the light of another recommendation: that since the Arab minority in the Jewish State would be of great size, a heavy proportion of it should be resettled outside the new State in Arab lands, voluntarily if possible, or by compulsion. This recommendation was undoubtedly influenced by the example of the eviction of the Greeks from Turkey in 1923. The fame and high reputation of Nansen, who, in keeping with the inspiring belief of his life, humanized so far as possible this essentially brutal and conscienceless act, has since his time been often put to perverted use to make similar acts appear respectable. As with Turkey fourteen years before, desperation was the excuse.

There were many other points and suggestions made by the Peel Commission, but these leading partition proposals were the most interesting and, as things fell out, the most influential ones in the long run.

The government, after consultation with Sir Arthur Wauchope, who had come to England on a brief official visit, issued a statement of policy with the report affirming their "general agreement with the arguments and conclusions of the Commission" and proposing "to obtain freedom to give effect to a scheme of partition to which they earnestly hope that it may be possible to secure an effective measure of consent on the part of the communities concerned." The report was debated in the House of Lords on the 20th of July and in the Commons the next day.

Parliament showed no enthusiasm for partition nor did the government give a stimulating lead. Neither the Colonial Undersecretary in the Lords, the Marquess of Dufferin, nor the Colonial Secretary, Mr. Ormsby-Gore, presented their case in telling speeches, and in certain passages, notably when Lord Dufferin appeared to ascribe equal guilt for recent violence to Arabs and Jews, and when Mr. Ormsby-Gore attempted to justify the original Eastern settlement on the plea that everyone concerned had Zionist reservations in the matter (not, unfortunately, conveyed by MacMahon or his successors), both speeches showed an unusual degree of weakness and carelessness. None of the numerous Zionists in the House of Commons gave the report unqualified support and Sir Archibald Sinclair, in the course of one of the most tendentious speeches of his career, eloquently described a very strong and valid objection to confining or attempting to confine Jewish nationalism to the dimensions of the tiny state recommended by Peel. He spoke of the dangers of "two racially totalitarian states side by side in what we now call Palestine; with all the Jews extruded from one state and all the Arabs from the other; with the Jews established along an indefensible coastal strip—congested, opulent, behind them the pressure of impoverished and persecuted World Jewry; in front of them Mount Zion. Mount Pisgah can never satisfy the longings which Mount Zion inspires in the Jewish heart. Obviously the Jewish state will, in those circumstances, be fired by the urge to reach by force or by contrivance the goal of Mount Zion and the Jordan valley." No one in the House of Commons was able to put up a comparable argument in favor of the partition scheme.

In the House of Lords the main apologia for the report was delivered by its author, but even he felt impelled to furnish his argument with comments that suggested some lack of confidence. His main proposition, he said, "abolishes, if you like, Jewish freedom, but it gives them instead something far greater and of far higher status, that is, a Jewish State." He was, of course, speaking of "freedom" in the sense that hitherto Zionists had had the right to colonize wherever they could obtain land west of the Jordan, but the remark reads as chilling nonetheless.

He was answered by Lord Samuel in one of the most important speeches of his political life. It had great influence at the time, and probably accounted for some of the coolness with which the House of Commons treated the Peel Report next day. It seems to have had a decisive effect on some events of the future. It lost him the esteem and affection of many Jews.

In the most important section of this masterly performance he indicated the essential weakness of the partition plan. The population statistics as these stood at the moment revealed a grotesque situation. If the Jews were to accept the Peel frontiers they would have to begin their state-building in an area inhabited by approximately 258,000 Jews and 225,000 Arabs: in an area, that is, where the Jews would constitute not very much more than one half of the people. He dismissed the idea of rationalizing the frontier by a transfer of populations on the Greco-Turkish model. In the early 1920's Greece and Turkey had but recently been in a full state of war, with armies in the field and on the Turkish side what today would be called an active resistance movement. This provided no parallel with the actual state of mutual relations between Jews and Arabs. Nansen had been enabled to organize the Greco-Turkish transfer because the exigencies and horrors of full-scale war provided every inducement for Greeks to escape from Turkey, but as things were in Palestine there was no inducement at all for Arabs to flee the most fertile part of the country, whatever inducement there might be for Jews outside the frontiers to enter the new state. He implied that the transfer could only be carried out by the cruellest means, and he pointed out the absurd inconsistency in the fact that the Peel Report recommended just such a transfer, while at the same time it demanded guarantees for the protection of minorities!

Samuel was scathing about the air of optimism with which the commissioners had put forward their main proposal. It was their contention, he remarked, that the establishment of two states "would free the Jews from the watchful hostility of neighbouring Arab states. On the contrary, will not these Arab states be watching day by day to see what is happening to their irridenta?" He went on to consider the administrative confusion which could surely be expected, especially as regards customs organization at the numerous points of entry and departure around the three areas. In the same context he stressed that the security of Palestine, which it had been the primary task of the Peel Commission to restore, would be made far more precarious along the multiplicity of new frontiers than it had been at any time under the mandate. Political terrorism would find richer soil than before on which to flourish: what easier than for an assassin to slip unseen over the frontier to his crime and then to slip back, not to the life of a hunted fugitive sought by the police, but to the protection of approving authorities?

When he came to constructive proposals, he said that he favored a solution by the opposite method to partition, namely by the formation of a large Arab federation, "not to be built up in a day or a year but gradually, perhaps including Saudi Arabia, Irak, Transjordan, Syria, Lebanon and Palestine as well." In such a confederation the Jews might be enabled to migrate and settle in Transjordan as well as Palestine without exciting Arab nationalist alarm. He urged that the holy places be guaranteed by the League, and that two communal organizations, Jewish and Arab, be granted wide powers including the power, on the Arab side, to prohibit sales of land to Zionists. He pictured a central federal council which would act in an advisory capacity to the mandatory. "Will this be agreed?" he asked, "I doubt it. I should be sorry to prophesy that it would be agreed, but the Arabs perhaps may be brought to recognise that the links of the Jews for four thousand years with this country cannot be broken, and that because they are not economic they are all the stronger. They are intangible links and in the long run spiritual ideas are more potent than material things."

He concluded by saying that if some such suggestion as his was not adopted, then nevertheless the only alternative was partition with all the dangers and disadvantages which he had outlined. This conclusion was not remembered by his critics.

The most influential passage in the speech was one which had occurred about halfway through when he introduced his positive suggestions. It was angrily resented by Zionist Jews at the time and more so afterward. It may be considered influential because it seems to have planted a seed in the collective mind of the government. Samuel's words are reported in Hansard as follows:

The Jews must reassure the Arabs. They must consent to a limitation of immigration other than on the principle of economic absorbative capacity. They must accept the principle proposed by the Commission: that political considerations must be brought in. I see no reason why the figure of 12,000 should be the one adopted. The Commission give no reason for the figure of 12,000. The noble Earl [Peel] said that it is quite arbitrary. Apparently it was chosen because it would just keep the balance of population between Arabs and Jews in the future but they do not say so. The Jews might well be asked to consent to an agreement covering a period of years—it might well be a substantial period—and during that period the Jewish population of Palestine should not exceed a given percentage of the total population, perhaps forty per cent or whatever might be agreed upon, but that is the figure I have in mind.

It was not long before the government began to waver in their support of the Peel proposals, if indeed they had not begun to do so by the time they laid them before Parliament. Previous to these debates, they had heard from Wauchope, and it must have been with dismay, that the Palestine administration was far less friendly to partition than they had supposed, a fact which may explain in part the weakness with which the case was put by ministers before the members of both houses. Samuel's speech was calculated to increase hesitation, for though the government might dismiss his positive suggestion, his destructive criticism was unanswerable and pointed unerringly to the fact that, whatever might be done at other times, the partition of Palestine could not be enforced by a British government in 1937, if it was to enjoy the support of Parliament, the country, and world opinion.

The reception of the Peel recommendations by the Jews was ambivalent. Dr. Wiezmann's attitude was in this respect characteristic. He continued to support the theory of partition, but after his first enthusiasm he looked at the particular scheme put forward by the Peel Commission with critical eyes.[20] He was far less critical than the majority of his fellow Zionists nevertheless, but because he could share their criticism he succeeded in winning a large measure of acceptance from them.

The occasion was the Twentieth Zionist Congress held at Zurich from the 3rd to the 17th of August, 1937. Dr. Weizmann as president of the Zionist organization set himself the task of obtaining something in the way of conditional acceptance of the Peel Report such as would keep negotiations open while strengthening the Zionist position. The point of view opposed to him had an able spokesman in Menachem Ussishkin, the elderly president of the congress and a Zionist of the old guard. Ussishkin wanted a Jewish State which would include the whole territory of Palestine, and he was firmly opposed to acceptance of anything less, if only because such an action could weaken the ultimate claim. When the

[20] In his autobiography Dr. Weizmann gave no indication of his earlier passionate acceptance of the partition scheme.

congress met, his views were probably shared by the large majority. It was Weizmann's task to substitute for this stiff-necked Jewish attitude one more pliable, and by the exercise of his great political skill he succeeded. By a majority of 142 out of 458 votes, he obtained the adoption of the following resolution:

> The Congress declares that the scheme of partition put forward by the Royal Commission is unacceptable. The Congress empowers the Executive to enter into negotiations with a view to ascertaining the precise terms of His Majesty's Government for the proposed establishment of a Jewish State. In such negotiations the Executive shall not commit itself or the Zionist organisation, but in the event of the emergence of a definite scheme for the establishment of a Jewish State such a scheme shall be brought before a newly elected Congress for consideration and decision.

The congress passed various other minor resolutions on the subject of the Peel Report, some of which expressed genuine concern at the recommendations, notably on immigration, and others of which are best described as useful propaganda eyewash.[21]

But on the whole there was much more acceptance than rejection of the Peel Report by this congress. This is surprising when one considers how minute in size and how unsatisfactory in so many other ways the new State would have been. A large part of the explanation may lie in the continuous deterioration of Jewish conditions in Germany; humiliating conditions in which any proposal for a Jewish State, the first Jewish State since Roman days, had a compelling glamor outshining criticism in many minds. Another reason is to be found, strangely enough, in those very objections to partition expressed in the House of Commons by Sir Archibald Sinclair when he said that the proposed little coastal state would obviously be fired by the urge to reach the goal of Mount Zion. It seems that this argument was very perfectly understood by the Zionist leaders themselves, and that they realized how the very force of such a circumstance must render the Peel frontiers temporary. In a press interview the chairman of the Executive of the Jewish Agency, Ben-Gurion, said: "The debate has not been for or against the indivisibility of Eretz Israel. No Zionist can forgo the smallest portion of Eretz Israel. The debate was over which of two routes would lead quicker to the common goal." When Dr. Weizmann was asked about the exclusion from the proposed State of

[21] Vide Israel Cohen, The Zionist Movement, p. 214. London, 1945.

the south and the Negev, he remarked more enigmatically: "It will not run away."[22]

Jewish acceptance, qualified or otherwise, demanded a vote by the Council of the Jewish Agency. When it met, also in Zurich, immediately after the Twentieth Congress, the sense of the meeting was toward acceptance, but there was an interesting objection led by Felix Warburg of the United States, and Judah Magnes, formerly of the United States and at this time president of the Hebrew University in Jerusalem.

Magnes had worked hard for Jewish-Arab understanding. He was the chief personality and a founder of the movement known as Brith Shalom (The Covenant of Peace), which aimed at the establishment in Palestine of a binational state. He was pacifist by inclination and he opposed partition mainly because he believed that it must lead to an Arab-Jewish war, though he also entertained a hope that the fact that both Arabs and Jews were opposed to partition might bring them together to cooperate. He had a sincere and even ardent sympathy with Arab nationalism. His ideas were so out of harmony with Zionist policy that he was usually dismissed by Jewish leaders as a person too far from reality to be taken seriously. The accusation was not an empty one. He had taken several initiatives, especially in the period before the arrival of the Peel Commission, to persuade Jewish and Arab leaders to cooperate, and there were moments when it looked as though some sort of negotiation might be started. The Peel Commission overtook these efforts but it seems certain that they were in fact impossible of success. There were Zionists, Ben-Gurion among them, who were prepared to go a long way with Magnes, but the few Arabs of Palestine who dared to show goodwill toward his attempts to establish peace received no support from the men who held authority, and sometimes ran considerable risk. In the end it was this fact which brought the task of his life to nothing, a task which Magnes pursued till he died heartbroken in 1948.[23]

Strangely enough, however, at this moment of the debate on partition, Magnes showed that his reputation for unpractical dreaming was much exaggerated, and that he was capable of political realism. The Palestine Arabs had had their position enormously strengthened by the intervention of the rulers and government of the world of Islam. Magnes endeavored to bring about something of the same kind for the Palestine Jews. In a

[22] Nevill Barbour, op. cit., and G. E. Kirk, A Short History of the Middle East. London, 1948.
[23] Norman Bentwich in Judah L. Magnes. London, 1955.

letter to the *New York Times* of the 18th of July, 1937, he pleaded for a determined effort not only by Jews and Arabs but by the governments of Great Britain and the United States to negotiate a general agreement on Palestine. He was suggesting that as the Arabs had called in the East, the Jews should call in the influence of the whole English-speaking world. Something like this did occur two years later, in part due to Magnes' activity in London and among League delegates in Geneva, but little came of the attempt and it never received Zionist backing. Any increase in Magnes' influence increased the Zionist opposition to him. At the meeting of the Jewish Agency Council in Zurich during August, 1937, when Magnes pleaded for fresh negotiations with the Arabs, he was "almost howled down," and then ruled out of order by the chairman.[24]

To return to the dilemma of the British government in the summer of 1937, and their weakening support of the distinguished commission whose recommendations they had at first warmly agreed with. These had met unanswerable criticism in Parliament; they were received with disappointment by Sir Arthur Wauchope and those he spoke for; the acceptance by the Zionists could be read as so qualified as to leave the issue in the gravest doubt; and then the League of Nations also proved a discouraging audience. Even so, the government might have continued to want to impose their partition scheme if it had not been that they were disappointed of the one favorable reaction that they thought they had the right to expect.

The moderate counsels and intervention of the Arab rulers in 1936 seem to have given rise to optimistic hopes that an act of state which at last restricted the growth of the Jewish National Home in Palestine would receive the support of those same rulers in 1937.[25] The Arab Higher Committee, immediately on the publication of the report, expressed its total refusal of the policy of partition. It has been suggested that this action inhibited Arab leaders outside Palestine from persisting in a conciliatory policy, but this may be doubted if only on the evidence of an unguarded remark by Nuri es Said in Baghdad. Early on, before the debates in Parliament, he had said: "Any person venturing to agree to act as the head of such a state [meaning the Arab state in partitioned Palestine] would be regarded as an outcast throughout the Arab world." Later he apologized for the indiscretion but the words had been spoken. Anti-Zionism was spreading through almost the whole world of Islam. It found expression at an Arab meeting which was called when the debates

24 John Marlowe, *op. cit.*
25 Bentwich, *op. cit.*

in Parliament and the Twentieth Congress had inflamed anti-Zionism yet more.

On September 8th this conference was held at a place called Bloudan near Damascus. It was attended by four hundred delegates representing all Arab states, including Palestine, with the sole exception of Yemen. The conference was presided over by a chubby red-haired man called Naji es Suadi, a former Prime Minister of Iraq. The major resolutions were unanimous and gave what might be called Pan-Arab expression to the extreme demands of the Mufti and the Arab Higher Committee. Palestine, it was stated, was an integral part of the Arabian homeland and no part of this territory could be alienated with Arab consent. The annulment of the Balfour Declaration was demanded, and with it the abrogation of the British mandate, the latter to be replaced by an Anglo-Palestine treaty which would include (the only concession) guarantees for the safeguarding of minorities. The conference issued a threat: "We must make Great Britain understand that she must choose between our friendship and the Jews. Britain must change her policy in Palestine or we shall be at liberty to side with other European powers whose policies are inimical to Great Britain."

Later the Syrian government lodged an offiical protest against partition with the French High Commissioner, and the Iraq government expressed their disapproval to the League of Nations. Later still the Egyptian government with Iraq support also protested to the League. This was apart from other protests direct to the British government.[26]

Since the publication of the Peel Report in July the Palestine Arabs had again taken to violence. In October this was the cause of a terrible crime. Lewis Andrews, the District Commissioner of Galilee and perhaps the ablest man in the Palestine service, was murdered with his escort outside the Anglican Church in Nazareth. The rebellion flared up again and was answered by the administration with a policy of coercion. In the same month Sir Arthur Wauchope resigned and was replaced by Sir Harold MacMichael. At home the British government decided on a new course which they initiated by the devious method of appointing a new commission whose task was ostensibly to advise on the precise delineation of frontiers and the necessary administrative action required for the implementation of Peel's recommendations. In December the government made public a statement to the High Commissioner that they did not consider themselves bound to a policy of partition. In fact Peel's partition scheme had been buried, though it was not dead, as appears later.

[26] Marlowe, op. cit.

The Peel report has often been mourned as a last missed chance to bring a peaceful settlement to the Holy Land. The literary skill with which it was presented by Coupland, and the fact that it was an earnest attempt by men of outstanding ability to perform a bold act of statesmanship, might have much to do with its high reputation. The sincerity of the Peel Commission has never been in question. Nevertheless it is difficult to believe (in the opinion of this writer) that its recommendations could have succeeded, or have led to anything but violently intensified strife and bloodshed, worse than had gone before, and this at a moment when the chance of a general war was visibly increasing. Peel's partition scheme belongs perhaps to that interesting category of unaccomplished things which often exert a great hold on the affection and the imagination. We win the wars we did not fight, and the peace that was never signed ushers in a golden age.

9 APPEASEMENT

The hopes once entertained by many people that Adolf Hitler was sane were growing weaker as the classic year of appeasement opened. The sick state of mind which had brought the Nazis into power had found no relief in the remedy, and during the last years of peace more and more once-rational Germans eagerly took on the mental habits of the mentally infirm demagogue of genius to whom they had entrusted their future. The likelihood or at least the possibility of war, often joyfully acclaimed in Germany, could not be hidden from any but self-deceivers. It is wholly mistaken to suppose, as its enemies often do, that the British government's policy of appeasement was the outcome of a complacent minimizing of the danger. It was due, with all its mistakes and failures to make ready, to the opposite.

For the Jews 1938 and 1939 were years full of the temptation to despair, but also of momentary hopes which were extinguished with infinite pain to themselves. In the swiftly oncoming night of Western civilization the National Home in Palestine more and more appeared to Jewish eyes as a solitary flame of hope. By an incomprehensible irony, so it seemed to many Jews, those who were solemnly charged by covenant with the duty of tending that flame tried, if not to extinguish it, to force it to burn low. There had often been restrictions on the National Home before. They had been resented as unworthy of a pledge to Zionism. Now they began to look like a conspiracy against the Jewish people, in partnership with their enemies.

Only a very prudish or censorious person would blame the Jews for their self-preoccupation at this moment in their history, when the bloodiest persecutor of their race since ancient or barbarous times was the absolute ruler of one of the great European nations, but the fact of a continually heightened and ever narrower Jewish self-preoccupation in Eretz Israel, brought about by the pressure of persecution, must be noted because it became a factor of enormous importance. The process was slow and by no means consistent, but it began to become a considerable force in Palestine affairs in these years. It was to lead gradually to trials of the spirit of the Yishuv which have left wounds that have not yet healed. The blame for this process and its consequences lies with many people, but perhaps least of all with the Jews themselves.

In Palestine the new administration of Sir Harold MacMichael set about suppressing the rebellion. There was some evidence that Haj Amin and the Arab Higher Committee were in guilty relations with the murderers of Lewis Andrews. The High Commissioner disbanded the Committee and declared that all Arab national associations were illegal. Five of the Mufti's colleagues were arrested and deported. He himself escaped by fleeing in disguise with his cousin Jamal Husseini. But this political action did not, as those hoped who still believed that Arab natonalism in Palestine was a shallow and artificial growth, check the spread or ferocity of the new rising which continued to within a few months of the Second World War. Nor was the rising weakened by the fact that its purpose was not single but diffuse. It was primarily (in conformity with the Mufti's leadership) a revolt against the British mandatory; it was also anti-Jewish, and also an Arab civil war; a feud between the Husseinis and their rivals, especially the Nashashibis, for the national leadership of Arab Palestine. The greatest number of casualties in the last troubled years before the war were Arabs, and about a quarter of the Arabs who lost their lives were murdered by their own people. The Mufti in exile was as powerful as he had been in Jerusalem.

The effect of this rebellion on the Jews in Palestine was crucial. It changed not only their own view of Zionism by intensifying yet more a sense of national mission, but in the end it changed the conduct and tactics of the National Home. One piece of evidence alone tells all that one needs to know about the increase of that intense burning enthusiasm behind Jewish life in Palestine. In the course of the rebellion the Arabs, as before, took to laying waste Jewish cultivated land, and it is estimated that in the course of the rebellion they destroyed about 200,000 trees. It is known that in the same period the Jews planted about a million trees.[1]

The conduct of Zionism was bound to change when the rebellion revived, but few people could have foreseen the extent of the change. The policy of self-restraint now made demands which were beyond human nature and it was inevitable that Havlagah would become modified. Even so it remains a very extraordinary thing that the essential policy was not only retained but was conscientiously adhered to by the Jewish majority. The exceptions, however, were much wider than they had been. The story is complex because of the undefined, or rather the inconsistently and contradictorily defined position of Haganah. There was a small section of Haganah known as Fosh (from Hebrew initials denoting "field troops"), which from the beginning of the rebellion undertook the defense of some Jewish settlements and outlying farms. Their orders from the Jewish Agency confined them to a strictly defensive role, but gradually, and especially during this second stage of the rebellion, they went beyond their instructions, not without encouragement from some of the Haganah ruling committee. Fosh adopted a policy of counterattack which was colloquially described in Hebrew as "Yetzyiah minn ha'gader," meaning "Going beyond the hedge." A leading spirit was a man called Isaac Sadeh who organized patrols known as the "Plugot Sadeh."[2] The development of this policy of "aggressive defense" led to some bold sorties in which Fosh troops, notably the Sadeh patrols, tracked down Arab guerrilla fighters to their hidden centers. These "beyond the hedge" operations were on a very small scale and must not be thought of as typical Haganah activity. The British authorities knew something of what was going forward, disapproved, but took almost no action to stop it.

A major change came when Fosh rose to prominence through the initiative of a young Scotsman who had come to Palestine in 1936 as an

---

[1] Statistics in Israel Cohen, *The Zionist Movement*. London, 1945.
[2] Dr. Yehuda Bauer. A communication.

intelligence officer in Fifth Division.[3] His name was Orde Wingate. He was a cousin of Sir Reginald Wingate, and his only other army service overseas had been in the Sudan. He had been seconded to Fifth Division because he was proficient in Arabic but within a few weeks of his arrival in Haifa he had become passionately convinced of the truth and necessity of Zionism. Like many converts he embraced his new faith with a violent enthusiasm which left many traditional believers behind, and not a little perplexed. At first this Gentile was not readily welcomed by Jews who fancied they saw a one-sided Arab sympathizer in a relative of a famous Arabist, proconsul and empire-builder, but they soon recognized their mistake and he was received among them as one of themselves. He became a close friend of Chaim and Vera Weizmann and in 1937 he proposed to Dr. Weizmann that in the event of partition being carried out he should apply to be seconded to service in the army of the new Jewish State. There was something of Jabotinsky in his Zionism and the dream of this man during the remainder of his short life was to lead a Jewish army to conquest. He never achieved his ambition, but in 1938 he realized a semblance of it in miniature.

He noticed that the remarkable success of the Arab guerrillas lay in the fact that they operated at night, while the counteraction by the British troops in the country was usually undertaken by day with meager results in proportion to the employed manpower. He worked out a scheme for regular night-operations in Galilee with the object of defending the oil pipe-line to Haifa and of tracking down and annihilating the enemy. He planned these operations to be undertaken by a mainly Jewish force with a few British in the ranks, with British and Jewish N.C.O.'s and officers, and himself in command. The plan was vigorously opposed by his own headquarters and the administration, not, as he sometimes believed, solely out of anti-Jewish prejudice but much more because of the fixed policy of the regime to avoid action liable to bring Jews and Arabs into a state of civil war. Several Zionist leaders opposed Wingate for the same reason. However, he succeeded in gaining acceptance. The British Force commander was Sir Archibald Wavell who had already initiated night operations, though not as a regular activity, on somewhat similar lines to those now proposed. He was a man of imagination with a decided leaning toward lone enthusiasts with bold and unorthodox ideas. He gave Wingate the permission he sought.

Wingate made his headquarters at the Jewish settlement of Ein Harod toward the eastern end of the Vale of Esdraelon, the Emek Jezreel. He

[3] Christopher Sykes, *Orde Wingate*. London, 1959.

recruited his following largely from Fosh, and he first took them into action on the 3rd of June, 1938. The Special Night Squads, as he called his force, operated regularly until the following December. After this, with the arrival of large British reinforcements, they were drastically reduced in numbers and had a very minor role. Nevertheless they continued operations till the summer of 1939. Wingate was not habitually modest in his appraisal of his achievements, but probably on this occasion, as certainly with the 1943 Burma expedition which brought him fame, he achieved more than he was likely to guess.

The S.N.S. operations were all on a small scale. At no time did Wingate command more than two hundred men in Palestine. But the significance of his successful actions lay in the very fact that they involved small numbers on his side. The lasting effect which they made was psychological. The process appears to have been somewhat as follows. A high-minded and extremely difficult policy such as Havlagah was not to be had for nothing, and the moral price that the Jews paid for this moral feat was the growth of a certain lack of confidence in their capacity to fight back, a humiliating belief that whatever remarkable abilities Jews had, military skill and perhaps military courage and staying power were not among them. Such ideas had taken hold of many Jewish minds.[4] Wingate, coming from outside with a fresh eye, saw through and beyond this fallacy, instantly recognizing that the people who had the will and energy to build the National Home despite discouragements of many kinds, had it in them to be soldiers the equal of any. He proved his belief abundantly. He showed the Jews that with only a few days' training a soldier of Zion was the military superior of a whole crowd of Arab marauders. It needs no effort of the imagination to grasp what this meant to Jews at the time when these things happened. In Israel today people often describe Wingate as one of the founders of the Army of Israel, and by this they do not only mean that several of their most distinguished military leaders learned their first military lessons in Wingate's headquarters hut at Ein Harod. From the circumstances of the second and more terrible phase of the Arab rebellion the Jews discovered that they were soldiers. Though this was a decisive event, its effect showed much later.

The commission to examine in detail how partition frontiers could be drawn was appointed at the end of February. The Chairman was Sir John Woodhead, a man who had acquired a distinguished reputation as an

---

[4] This was told to the writer by the late Professor Rattner of Haifa. In 1937 he was a leading personality on the ruling Committee of Haganah.

administrator in India. His colleagues were Sir Alison Russell, K.C., Mr. Percival Waterfield, and Mr. Thomas Reid, all, with the exception of Russell, members of the India Civil Service. The commission went to Palestine in April and returned to London in July. They published their report in November. They had interrogated a great number of British and Jewish witnesses. The Arabs had had recourse to their usual tactics, but on this occasion the policy of boycott did them no harm. For the moment things were going their way. The Woodhead Commission opened a road to a British policy which dismissed Peel's recommendations in entirety.

During this spring, summer, and early autumn of 1938, while the Woodhead Commission pursued their labors, and while, strengthened to appearances by his pact with Mussolini, Hitler threw off his fantastical disguise as the peace lover of the West,[5] an event took place in France which should by rights, if rights had been less battered then, have been of great and consoling significance to the Jews.

Five years after Hitler had risen to power, action was attempted which should have been taken in the first year of his rule, and might have been if more people had listened to the enemies of Nazism. There was only one line of action which from the general point of view might have substantially reduced the horrors of the Nazi regime, and, from the British point of view, could have given some genuine hope of solving the Palestine problem. There could be no return to gradualism, such as might conceivably have allowed the National Home to achieve its end in peace, unless some pro-Jewish countermeasure was taken elsewhere in the world, a measure of vigor and scope equal to those of the Nazi persecution. One can say to the credit of Western civilization that such action was recognized as necessary, but one cannot unfortunately say more.

The initiative came from President Roosevelt. In June of 1938 (influenced to some extent by the propaganda of Judah Magnes and his friends) he proposed that there should be a meeting of governmental representatives from all the countries of America and Europe except Germany. He knew little about Zionism or Arab nationalism or the troubles of the mandate in Palestine and he acted at first as though confronted with a relatively simple issue. "Such a conference," he said, "would manifest before the non-European world the urgency of emigration, chiefly to Palestine." The British government took alarm and privately pointed out the danger to them of his proposal as it then stood.

[5] In a curious essay Thomas Mann objected to comparison of Hitler with Napoleon, asserting that "the blackmailing pacifist" was unworthy of association with "that god of war."

They asked that the conference should be confined to representatives of governments prepared to accept immigrants, that the agenda should deal with refugees and not only with the Jewish problem in Germany, and, most urgently, that the subject of Palestine should not be discussed.[6] Roosevelt agreed to all these conditions. The representatives of thirty-one countries[7] assembled in the Hotel Royal at Evian on the 6th of July.

The American representatives were Myron C. Taylor, a former president of the United Steel Trust, and James G. Macdonald, the League of Nations High Commissioner for Refugees from Germany (from 1933 to 1935) and a member of the United States Foreign Affairs Association, who acted as Taylor's adviser. The leading British delegate was Lord Winterton, known in the House of Commons as an Arab apologist, and his junior was Captain Victor Cazalet, also a Member of Parliament and known as an enthusiastic Zionist. Many of the sittings were presided over by the principal French delegate, Senator Berenger.[8] The conference opened with some feeling of optimism because to many people's surprise the Nazi government allowed Jewish delegates from Berlin and Vienna to attend.

Myron C. Taylor made the opening speech for the government of the United States. "Discrimination and pressure against minority groups," he said, "and the disregard of elementary rights are contrary to the principles of what we have come to regard as the accepted standards of civilisation." He dwelt on the iniquity of enforced migrations which he described as something that only intergovernmental action could deal with. "If some Governments," he concluded, "are to continue to toss large sections of their populations lightly upon a distressed and unprepared world, then there is catastrophic human suffering ahead which can only result in general unrest and in general international strain which will not be conducive to the permanent appeasement to which all peoples earnestly aspire."

Over a hundred organizations, mostly Jewish and all representing distressed minorities, had sent spokesmen to Evian. The mere fact of the United States, contrary to its continuing isolationism, having called the

[6] Mark Wischnitzer, *To Dwell in Safety*. Philadelphia, 1948. He quotes a Yiddish authority, "Dos Spiel fun weltmeluches mit unsere flichtingen."
[7] The countries represented were: Argentina, Australia, Belgium, Bolivia, Brazil, Canada, Chile, Colombia, Costa Rica, Cuba, Denmark, the Dominican Republic, Ecuador, Eire, France, Guatemala, Haiti, Honduras, Mexico, the Netherlands, New Zealand, Norway, Nicaragua, Panama, Paraguay, Peru, Sweden, Switzerland, the United Kingdom, the United States, Uruguay.
[8] Norman Bentwich, *A Wanderer Between Two Worlds*. London, 1941.

conference was enough to fill the victims of modern tyranny with what one of those present described as "extravagant and almost Messianic hopes." [9] Myron C. Taylor's words, which were spoken from the heart of a sincere man, roused their hopes afresh. But it was to be noticed that he was not authorized (as he and Macdonald would like to have been) to make any constructive American proposal and his speech amounted to nothing much more than an invitation to the German Third Reich to mend its ways. In this the speech was typical of the conference.

Optimism did not survive for more than a day or two. What came out more and more clearly was that the governments concerned were not prepared to inconvenience themselves for the sake of the Jews or anyone else and that the delegates were not authorized to do more than make edifying speeches in favor of toleration. Some of them did not even trouble to go this far and merely insisted on the danger to themselves of alien immigration, especially when it became clear that the enormous Jewish minority of Poland, reduced to misery by the iniquitous "Government of the Colonels," was also appealing for help. The conference developed "an unfriendly atmosphere of evasions and rationalisations." [10] To add to this prevailing atmosphere the delegates of the distressed, mostly people without political experience, irritated the conference by refusing to combine or to form a united front on any adequate basis. They preferred that so far as possible the separate bodies should be heard individually. As a result, on one afternoon the bored members of the conference committee had to listen to thirty statements of cases. As the hot day dragged on and the drone of seemingly endless depositions filled the room, the committee in desperation made a ruling that each individual address must not exceed ten minutes in length, and later reduced the time limit to five. Outside the conference room, among crowds of journalists and people drawn by curiosity to what they believed was a historic occasion, a curious figure was often to be seen buttonholing conference members and delegates, a Hungarian nobleman called Count Coudenhove-Kalergi who had a plan for solving the problem by setting up a Jewish state in Africa.[11] He was not treated seriously, but at least this picturesque gentleman wanted to do something, and that in itself was unusual.

There was only one really striking exception to the negative attitude of the governments assembled at Evian. It was to be found in the conduct of the Dominican Republic. Although in extent not very much larger than

[9] *Ibid.*
[10] Wischnitzer, *op. cit.*
[11] Bentwich, *op. cit.*

Palestine, this state showed the reckless generosity which alone could save the world at such a moment. The Dominican representative, to the surprise and one hopes the shame of the others, conveyed to the conference the offer of his government to receive a hundred thousand Jews from Germany and Austria, on condition that the settlers were of respectable character and willing to work on the land and that the expenses involved in purchase of land and agricultural equipment for Jewish settlements did not fall on the state. (Compared to other governments represented at Evian the state was not rich.) By German calculation the number of German subjects (mostly Jews) threatened by the Nuremberg laws was about 600,000.[12] If only half a dozen of the thirty-one states in conclave had had the courage, imagination, or sense of responsibility to follow the example of the Dominican Republic, then, in theory at least, Hitler's victims would have been saved, and in practice many more saved than in fact were. When the tragedy was played out in full the statistics of Nazi persecution were, of course, found to be very much greater than was calculated even by pessimists in 1938. To account only for those killed, the prewar figures needed to be multiplied by ten.

The action of the Dominican Republic, described by the *New York Times* as something "rare in this conference," was not wholly ineffective, and some countries took action in the same sense on a proportionately smaller scale. The United States agreed to allow Jewish immigrants in to the limit of the legal quota for Germans which amounted to 30,000 a year. In the three years 1938 to 1940 the American authorities in fact went beyond this figure by a little over 10,000.[13] In the same years Great Britain took in approximately the same number of German Jews as America. British conduct at the conference was much criticized because it was expected that the people who had undertaken responsibility for a Jewish National Home would give a decisive lead. This they carefully avoided doing because it was their belief that if they encouraged immigration to England they would be encouraging Jewish pressure on Palestine. In proportion to their size and economic situation (unemployment still stood at a high level), Great Britain cannot be said to have acted ignobly in the matter, but for political reasons they allowed it to be supposed that they were more indifferent than they were. They only did good in secret, but the need was for someone to do good in public.

It was often said (and is still said) that the wide expanses of the British Commonwealth and Empire should have provided a refuge for many, and

[12] Sir John Hope Simpson, *The Refugee Problem*. London, 1939. Figures for 1939.
[13] Figures in Wischnitzer, *op. cit.*

even a majority of the persecuted of Europe. This was also believed at Evian. As a result of decisions taken, British and American commissions surveyed British Guiana and found it to be a land of scant opportunity for this purpose. There was another objection, one often overlooked in dealing with refugees: the unhappy people did not want to go to this tropical land. Among themselves the Jews used to describe the place as British Gehenna. Another plan was to settle Jews in Northern Rhodesia. This was put forward by Victor Cazalet and enthusiastically blessed and urged on everyone he met by Count Coudenhove-Kalergi, but when a commission paid a visit of inquiry it found stubborn local resistance. Although this territory is twice the size of Great Britain and had then a white population of only 11,000, the local authorities supported by public opinion judged that there was only room for a hundred and fifty new settlers.[14] In the Commonwealth, Australia, after much hesitation, agreed to take 15,000 in the course of three years, but Canada refused to be committed and in the event allowed very few exiles to land. South Africa only allowed Jews to come in who had close relatives there already. Outside the Commonwealth some countries made some minor adjustments to their immigration laws in favor of the persecuted, but some others noted Evian as a danger signal and, so far from allowing refugees in, erected new legal barriers against them. The conference did succeed in instituting a permanent body known as the Inter-Governmental Committee on Refugees, the I.G.C.R., but otherwise, apart from stimulating the United States, and perhaps Great Britain, into more generous though utterly inadequate policies, the Evian Conference failed, and with that failure went the doom of millions of innocent human beings. In the words of Norman Bentwich the meeting had demonstrated that the democracies had "a little conscience but less faith." Official observers from Nazi Germany and Fascist Italy looked on with pleased contempt.

The Zionists, who played no part in the conference, were not worried by its failure. They seem to have expected no great result from it, and gave no expression of embitterment when the result turned out to be negative. From the start they regarded the whole enterprise with hostile indifference. Zionist writers scarcely mention it. The fact is that what was attempted at Evian was in no sense congenial to the spirit of Zionism. The reason is not obscure. If the thirty-one nations had done their duty and shown hospitality to those in dire need, then the pressure on the National Home and the heightened enthusiasm of Zionism within Palestine would both have been relaxed. This was the last thing that the Zionist leaders

[14] Bentwich, *op. cit.*

wished for. As things stood after Evian the outlook for the Jews was black throughout the world except (to quote Norman Bentwich again) "for the bright spot of Palestine and the speck of Dominica." The Zionist leaders preferred that it should remain that way. Even in the more terrible days ahead they made no secret of the fact even when talking to Gentiles, that they did not want Jewish settlements outside Palestine to be successful. They did not want Santo Domingo to become more than a speck. They wanted a Jewish Palestine and the Dominican Republic could never be that.

This outlook and conception of policy, typical of the increasing narrowness of Zionist thinking, may seem horrifyingly party-minded and harsh. It was all that undoubtedly, but it was something more besides. It was not compassionless. The Zionists, both the more large-minded and the most narrow, had a constructive aim. The Zionists wanted to do something more for Jews than merely help them to escape danger. They wanted to help them to overcome their humiliation. They wanted to make them the object of respect, not the object of pity. They wanted to enable them to stop being pathetic, and they conceived that there was only one way to do this, to make them come to Palestine and undertake a fully national life. Since the early thirties there had been much trouble between Jews and the Palestine authorities over illegal immigration, and the Jews had raised the defense, and were to continue to do so, that Palestine was the only country where they could go and be welcome. Before Evian the truth of this Zionist assertion was doubtful, but after Evian it was less so, and the latter state of affairs suited the Zionist leadership. If their policy entailed suffering, then that was the price that had to be paid for the rescue of the Jewish soul.

It is hard, perhaps impossible, to find a parallel in history to this particular Zionist idea which was at the heart of the Zionist accomplishment during the ten years after 1938. That such was the basic Zionist idea is not a matter of opinion, but a fact abundantly provable by evidence. It was an idea in whose reality people outside could not usually believe at first, and which often shocked them when they recognized its existence. There can be no doubt that here again one is confronted with an idea which, even if judged as morally wrong, is such as could only be conceived by a great people. As time went on it grew rather than diminished in strength. It formed another crossroads.

The Woodhead Report was published in November of 1938, two months after the Czechoslovak crisis, and in the same month as the Kristallnacht pogrom in Germany, that first and deadly proof that Adolf Hitler's resounding diplomatic triumph at Munich, far from appeasing German discontent, had whetted Nazi appetites. The report is a curious document, manifestly the product of puzzled and divided minds: the commissioners put forward a new partition scheme but with so much discouragement and qualification that it is not easy to say precisely what they did or did not recommend. Two of them, Sir Alison Russell and Mr. Reid, put reservations on record. Most writers on the subject of Palestine judge the Woodhead Report adversely, but it is difficult to see what useful and positive recommendation the commission could have made. The British government had declared itself against enforced transfers of population, and the Woodhead commissioners pointed out that without recourse to that merciless line of policy, a partition of Palestine into Jewish and Arab territory was simply not possible. Yet they seem to have felt that because they were called "The Palestine Partition Commission" they must somehow advise on some sort of a partition, and the one they put forward to the Colonial Office, with undisguised uneasiness, and with insistence that the partitioned areas could not be independent states although independent statehood was the main object of partitioning them, reserved to the Jews the smallest pale of settlement that anyone had yet devised for them. It was about 400 square miles in extent and only had one large town, Tel Aviv. There was not the remotest possibility that any Jew, even an anti-Zionist, would accept this useless little ghetto.

On the 24th of November the proposal was presented by the Colonial Secretary, Mr. Malcolm MacDonald, to the House of Commons in a speech which was ill received. In an emotional moment he referred to Bethlehem as the birthplace of the Prince of Peace, and several members had the impression that they heard Mr. Churchill say in a loud aside: "I always thought he was born in Birmingham." The Woodhead Report had concluded by urging its recommendations as "the basis of a settlement by negotiation," and the government took this as an opportunity to summon a Jewish-Arab general conference rather than to press for acceptance. The government also found Woodhead useful as a means to push Peel out of the way. Peel had come to look dangerous, especially since the meeting in October, 1938, of the "World Interparliamentary Congress of Arab and Moslem Countries for the Defence of Palestine." From this conference, held in Cairo, further threats of an Arab-Axis alliance had issued, and in the opinion of Orientalists the meeting had been more representative of Moslem feeling and therefore more ominous than its predecessor of Bloudan. Hopes could not be high, but they were centered on some compromise being worked out at the Arab-Jewish Conference. Such a conference had been proposed to Arthur Balfour in 1918 but somehow no one had "got around" to holding it till twenty years later.[15]

Arab delegates from Palestine, Egypt, Saudi Arabia, Iraq, Yemen and Transjordan came to London in the opening weeks of 1939. Many people in England thought that the Mufti should have been invited, but on this Malcolm MacDonald was firm. The Mufti's cousin Jamal Husseini was invited however. The Palestine delegation set the tone for Arab conduct at the conference, and they came to London in order to give another performance of their long-practiced boycott. They refused to sit at the same table with Jewish delegates or even to meet them, and once again these tactics seemed to do them more good than harm because circumstances favored them greatly—for the time being.

From the beginning when the two delegations met the British representatives separately, usually under the chairmanship of Malcolm MacDonald, it was obvious that there was no ground for compromise. The Jews made it clear that the Peel proposals which they regarded as inadequate, were as far as they were prepared to, or indeed could, go in concession if they were to represent Zionism. The Arabs were prepared for no concessions of any kind, and the Palestinians among them acted not only through conviction but at the price of their lives. They demanded total cessation of Jewish immigration and land purchase. But though the positions were irreconcilable, the official Arab refusal to confer with or even meet the Jews did not mean that there was absolutely no Arab-Jewish exchange of views. Some of the extra-Palestinian Arabs did not go along with the fanatical extremism of the Mufti and they had occasional though not very fruitful meetings with the more moderate of the Zionists, notably with Dr. Weizmann. Both sides knew what happened at the others, meetings with the Colonial Secretary. There was no lack of energetic agents and go-betweens who conveyed the minutes of Arab-British meetings to Jews, and those of Jewish-British meetings to Arabs. This continual breach of confidence does not seem to have soothed feelings on either side and was sometimes responsible for dangerous misunderstandings. At one conference with the Arabs, (according to a Jewish authority), Mr. MacDonald was urging a more conciliatory attitude when an Arab delegate said something to the effect that the difficulty was that when a concession was made the Jews invariably treated it as the basis for further demands. Malcolm MacDonald replied: "Such behavior is very typical of that

[15] According to George Antonius, in a conversation with the writer, the 1918 proposal was made by General Clayton and Sir Mark Sykes.

people." The remark was with the Jews shortly after and was taken for a display of anti-Semitism.

There did occur one moment in the conference when it faintly appeared to some that the outcome would not be total failure. This was another of those numerous Palestinian occasions when essentially reasonable and desirable action was attempted long after it might have been of any use. Since the end of the war Arabs and their supporters had complained of the division of Syria by its present lines of partition. A legend had grown up that before 1918 the whole area of modern Syria, Lebanon, Palestine, and Transjordan had been a single and undivided country under one central administration. The British government began to play with the idea that peace might be brought to Palestine by giving the legend reality. It would seem that approaches were made to the French government and, in remarkable contrast to French form in previous times, the suggestion was favorably received. It was not so received by those whom it would most closely affect.

The prospect of the National Home as a canton in a large independent Arab state, once so acceptable to Zionists, and given new expression in 1937 by Herbert Samuel, now filled most of the Zionist leaders with misgiving.[16] They saw stronger Arab pressure on them from a United Syria than they had endured from the Mufti's rebellion. They were in considerable doubt as to how to escape from this untimely gift, but, as on previous occasions, they did not need to place themselves in an unfavorable light by resisting a theoretically reasonable proposition, as the Arabs did the resisting for them.

The irritation which the proposal instantly aroused in Arabs suggests that the longing for a reunited Syria, often expressed by Palestine nationalists, was in fact no very deep-seated passion. Among those attending the conference in an advisory capacity to Arab delegates was George Antonius, whose book *The Arab Awakening* had been published in England shortly before. It remains an important if one-sided account of Anglo-Arab relations, and one of the points he most strongly made was that the Arabs could never be at peace with the West unless the unity of all Syria was restored and acknowledged. It is probable that Antonius' masterly book influenced the present proposal. But when, on official prompting, this proposal was reported in the press, Antonius' anger knew no bounds. He described it as a trick to delude Arabs into a surrender to the Zionists. He accurately reflected Arab opinion which had forgotten this dubious irridentist claim in its growing preoccupations with anti-Zionism. The

[16] A communication in Israel.

United Syria plan was dropped before it had been officially conveyed, and was forgotten.[17]

From the opening of the conference the British government had made it clear that if no compromise was reached then they would impose a solution, not that many people believed that there could be a solution now. Since February 8th, when the conference opened, Mr. MacDonald, the Foreign Secretary Lord Halifax, and the Foreign Under-Secretary Mr. R. A. Butler, had urged the Arabs to accept controlled Jewish immigration and land purchase, and urged the Jews to modify their ambitions in the hope that Arab nationalist resentment would be appeased. They urged both sides to trust Great Britain to safeguard their rights. They urged Jews and Arabs to think in terms of an independent state of Palestine. They urged in vain. The delegates of neither side would (or could) agree to any diminution of their claims. Neither was interested in a binational state. As for trust in Great Britain, both regarded the mandatory power as having broken its word in the most disgraceful fashion.

On the 15th of March the government presented a series of final proposals to both sides, and both sides rejected them. On the 17th the conference came to an end. On the same day the German army invaded Czechoslovakia.

The time had now come for the mandatory to impose its terms, as it had said it would do. Some authorities take the view that the government of Neville Chamberlain retreated from the Peel recommendations, appointed the Woodhead Commission, then called a conference which they knew would fail, in order to be free to do this. It is quite true that the White Paper which they issued two months later did determine policy for the remaining years of the mandate. But to see the sequence of events as precisely logical is to see Machiavellism in Neville Chamberlain, and to ignore the fact that though he was not by any means that total stranger to astuteness that some of his enemies believe, he never quite lost a sincere and naïve belief that all of the problems of the world could be settled by a quiet chat over a cup of tea. Many problems, which in consequence make no great stir in history, have been solved that way, but after the failure of the St. James's Palace Conference, as it came to be known, it was clear that the Palestine problem was not among them. If appeasement was to be practiced here it had to be done at the expense of one party to the dispute. The Government calculated, quite correctly, that in the coming war the Jews would have no choice as to which side they supported, so they decided to appease the Arabs at the expense of the Jews.

[17] Dr. Yehuda Bauer and personal recollection of conversations with Antonius.

As early as the 24th of February Malcolm MacDonald had given the Jewish delegation some warning to expect that this line of policy would be pursued.[18]

The government prepared the way by issuing the first official publication of Sir Henry MacMahon's correspondence with Sherif Hussein.[19] It is extraordinary that no government had done this before, and the present action seems to have been forced on the authorities by the fact that an accurate translation of the letters from Arabic had appeared in George Antonius' book, published shortly before in November. (It will be remembered that the letters had once been published in the *Daily Mail* but this was now quite forgotten.)

In presenting the letters the Colonial Office were at pains to give the impression of an unswerving consistency maintained over twenty-two years in British Palestine policy. Readers of the Command paper were informed in an introduction that "the language in which [Palestine's] exclusion was expressed was not so specific and unmistakable as it was thought to be at the time," a remarkable way of conveying that "at the time" the subject had not been mentioned in the letters at all.[20] A belief that Palestine had been effectively excluded by MacMahon had long been accepted by people who had not read the letters, but when the assertion appeared side by side with the damning evidence to the contrary in what MacMahon wrote, the belief was inevitably shaken and the Arab case appeared at its strongest.

Of some compensatory value to Zionism was the first publication in the same Command paper of Hogarth's interview in 1918 with Sherif Hussein after he had become King of the Hejaz. This might have made a great difference once, but in 1939, thirteen years after the collapse of Hussein's kingdom and more than twenty years after the event, it could have no effect at all.

Shortly before the 17th of May, the day when the government issued their statement of policy, Dr. Weizmann was invited to visit Malcom Mac-

[18] Zionist Archives.
[19] Cmd. 5974 of 1939.
[20] At a meeting with Arab delegates in February, 1939, His Majesty's government produced the most grotesque of all their recorded arguments that Palestine had been excluded. This was to the effect that Sherif Hussein had been warned that his boundaries would be influenced by French interests; that at the time France was laying claim to Palestine, and that when this claim had been successfully resisted by Great Britain, Palestine had been excluded by virtue of having been the subject of an unadmitted claim! The style of thought recalls the Barrister's Dream in *The Hunting of the Snark*. Cmd. 5974.

Donald at his house in the country. He drove down with the same young secretary, Yeheskiel Sacharoff, to whom he had unburdened himself in joy after his crucial meeting with the Peel Commissioners. The young man waited outside for a long time. When Weizmann came out of the house he was pale and trembling with anger. He told the young man that though he had often heard that the English were double-faced and perfidious, throughout his long experience of England and Englishmen he had never believed it, but now he did. He broke into strong, violent, unrestrained language against MacDonald. "That he could do this!" he exclaimed when he was more collected. "He who made me believe he was a friend!" He drove back to London in silent fury to tell his colleagues of the Jewish Agency what had been communicated to him regarding future British policy in Palestine.[21]

The main propositions of the White Paper—the infamous White Paper as it came to be thought of by millions of Jews—were these: there was to be no partition of Palestine; it was not part of British policy that Palestine should become a Jewish State, and this objection was based on the provisions of the Churchill White Paper of 1922; likewise it was not part of British policy that the country should become an Arab State, and this objection was based on a rejection of the Arab claim drawn from the MacMahon correspondence; British policy was based on a "desire to see established ultimately an independent Palestine State" within ten years; in the transitional period Jews and Arabs were to be invited to take an increasing share in the administration; in the same period the expansion of the Jewish National Home by immigration would in principle be limited by Arab agreement to it, but during the next five years Jewish immigration would be permitted, economic conditions allowing, to the extent of 10,000 a year with an immediate immigration of 25,000 refugees in addition to the yearly quota; after this immigration, amounting to 75,000 in five years, no further Jewish immigration would be allowed "unless the Arabs of Palestine are prepared to acquiesce in it"; land purchase by Jews from Arabs would be prohibited in some areas, and restricted in others, in accordance with regulations to be published by the High Commissioner.[22]

The clause in this statement which most disturbed Zionists and Arabs was the provision for 75,000 Jews being admitted in the course of five years. There seems a strong probability that its origin was in Herbert Samuel's speech in the House of Lords in which he criticized the findings of the Peel Commission. Many Zionists, Jewish and Gentile, reproached

[21] Yeheskiel Sachar. A communication.
[22] Cmd. 6019 of 1939.

him after May, 1939, with having done a grave and unforgivable injury to his people. His name was removed from places in Tel Aviv which had been called after him. He felt the insult bitterly. But the injustice to which he was subjected was less an example of political malice than of "the wrong of time." His Zionism belonged to a former generation, and he was a stranger to the narrow mood of uncompromise that characterized the age of Fascism and anti-Fascism; he was a Liberal of the old school whose ideas had not much relevance to the world of 1939. At the same time he suffered the common political misfortune of having certain of his ideas taken up in part. His suggestion that the Jews should form 40 percent of the Palestine population was part of a wider suggestion for a Middle Eastern Union in which Zionism should have room for maneuver. The government reduced his 40 percent to about 33 percent, and took this part of his suggestion without any attempt to make it conditional on the wider one. Samuel had clearly stated that unless the larger suggestion was acted on there was no alternative to partition with all its dangers. It is obviously permissible to consider that his whole proposition was harmful because it was so inapplicable to the conditions at that time, but it is wholly absurd to consider it as a calculated act of treason against that National Home which he had done much to build. Nevertheless, in a world given over to wretchedness and madness, it was a long time before general Zionist opinion could see this.

For the Jewish reaction to the White Paper, in the Zionist world and far beyond it, was almost unanimously one of horror and desolation and a loss of the ebbing but still considerable confidence in Britain as the guardian of Palestine. The commonest description of it by Jews was "betrayal," and it remains so today. It was seen as a gross act of pillage, of an exercise of the ignoble and age-long right claimed by the strong to turn on the weak and sacrifice them to their interests. It was associated with the abandonment by Great Britain of the Abyssinian cause [23] and with the fall of Czechoslovakia in March, and Dr. Weizmann bitterly remembered how the day after the conclusion of the Munich agreement in 1938, Jan Masaryk had told him that this was the beginning of a succession of surrenders of the rights of small states to the violent tyrannies then in the ascendant.[24] This was another case, in the opinion of Jews, of attempting appeasement by dishonorable means, of a cowardly attempt to turn away the anger of men who were intent on violence and lived by murder; the Arabs of Palestine were guilty of rebellion and bloodshed, the Jews were

---

[23] Chaim Weizmann, *Trial and Error*. London, 1949.
[24] Mr. Abba Eban in Weizmann Biography.

not, so the Jews were penalized to appease the Arabs. In Palestine thousands of indignant men and women in Jerusalem, Tel Aviv, Haifa, and the Jewish settlements saw in the White Paper an act of treachery done out of craven fear of the Mufti's gangsters. Seven years later, a Jewish editor with a name for moderation could refer to "the perfidy of the monstrous White Paper, a creature of funk spawned by a Government dominated by a passion for appeasement." [25]

After the German army had invaded Czechoslovakia in March 1939, it was quite clear that the policy of appeasement toward Germany had failed. The government believed that war must come, and most people in Great Britain felt the same though they often tried to believe otherwise. In the face of the disaster it was said (and is still said) that policies of appeasement needed to be abandoned and attempted nowhere again. This became a widely held opinion in reaction to Neville Chamberlain's political failure. As a line of argument it is nonsensically unhistorical. Those who condemned all appeasement forgot that such policies are inherent in the British political tradition and constitute a great part of its claim to respect. Great military and autocratically ruled countries, such as Russia, can maintain themselves without any such tradition, but this is quite impossible to a country whose eminence depends on world-wide commercial interests on a scale far beyond the country's power of military enforcement, and whose stability consequently depends on observance of treaties. The whole temper of British opinion has for long been conditioned by a sense of these facts. A British government that shot down strikers would fall. If the Arabs of Palestine had had no justice on their side, then possibly a bloody campaign against them, swiftly terminating all possibility of rebellion, might have succeeded without revolting home opinion (apart from other opinion) against the government; but since the opposite was manifestly the case, there was no alternative open to a British government except a policy of appeasement to Arabs. An authority friendly to Zionism puts the matter in this way: "From the moment when the Balfour Declaration stated that the rights of the existing population would be safeguarded, it was evident that no final solution was possible while these rights, as the population themselves understood them, were ignored." [26] In Arab opinion, among moderates and the pro-British, just as much as among the extremists, the Fascist-minded and the anti-British, those rights had been ignored.

[25] Gershon Agron, *Palestine Post.* May, 1946.
[26] Dr. J. W. Parkes, *A History of Palestine from 135 A.D. to Modern Times.* London, 1949.

If British tradition had not been weighted with moral considerations compelling appeasement, then, even so, there would have been no alternative to this particular policy of appeasement, once the prospect of war was as close as in the summer of 1939. The concern of the Arabic-speaking world with Palestine was not a chimera imagined by orientalists and Arabophils. It was a real fact and an extremely dangerous one. It tended to make the Arab world friendly-disposed to Nazi Germany, and a large part of the oil resources of Britain were situated in the Arab world. To have opened a major quarrel with Arab states when Europe was moving toward war would have been an act of folly by Great Britain without precedent.

The White Paper was not received with acclaim by the Arabs. The statement that 75,000 Jews were to be allowed to immigrate within five years seemed to the Mufti's party an intolerable condition, and when the Arab National Defense Party signified that they were prepared to accept it, a member of this group was murdered by one of the Mufti's terrorists. The Egyptian government, who had been regarded as counselors of moderation, announced that they "felt unable to recommend that the Palestine Arabs should co-operate with the Mandatory on the basis of the new policy." From no part of the Arabic-speaking world was there any positive encouragement toward acceptance.

Nevertheless it has to be said that the White Paper, though it did not bring about a revival of the Anglo-Arab alliance of the First World War, did succeed, very imperfectly but in the main, in its primary object. It cut the ground away from extremist agitators. Slowly rebellion died away in Palestine, and throughout the war years there was no formidable Arab rising against the British in the country. Egyptian interest in Zionism temporarily faded, and the political clashes, including the most serious in 1942, which occurred between the British and Egyptian governments, were unconnected with and (so far as appears) uninfluenced by the Palestine question. Egypt was not the treacherous ally of Britain that later propaganda has described, and during the most critical phase of the war Egypt and Palestine afforded a tranquil base for British troops in which the number of men who needed to be detailed for security duties was a fraction of those needed in the First World War. The benevolent neutrality of King ibn Saud throughout the war was valuable to the Allied cause in influencing Moslem opinion. The emir of Transjordan proved a staunch ally. The most serious threat to Britain to occur in the Arab world during the war was the German attempt to seize Syria and Iraq in conjunction with Rashid Ali's putsch in 1941. Zionists (including Dr. Weizmann in his memoirs) have pointed to this as proof that the White Paper policy was not only dishonorable but futile. The point to remember is that the attempt and the putsch failed, and it seems beyond doubt that one reason for that failure was that the Germanophil parties were not strong enough, and that both in Syria and Iraq there was a pro-British interest of the utmost value in restraining opinion. If British policy had been as the Zionists wanted it to be, then the circumstances would have been very different, and so might the event.

For all that, no English person can possibly feel proud of the White Paper. If it is morally defensible in the short term it is not so in the long term. Nothing can disguise the fact that there was odious moral cruelty in inflicting so heavy a disappointment on millions of people to whom Palestine was the only hope left on this earth, and in this connection it must be remembered that in Palestine the White Paper policy meant doing the same thing to that part of the population which had remained loyal to Great Britain during the years of rebellion. This moral harshness was all the more atrocious because it meant that British rule became consciously involved in enormous physical cruelty as well. The policy limited yet further what little opportunity existed for Jewish escape from Nazi tyranny, and the most uncritical believer in appeasement could not doubt in 1939 what that tyranny meant to the minorities it disapproved.

The morality of the White Paper cannot be judged without reference to the position of the Jews in the world as a whole. If British initiative had made Evian a success; if moral and political courage had not been left there to the Dominican Republic alone; if under British leadership that attempt at appeasing the anxieties not of the assassins, but of the victims, had been whole-hearted and had had strong positive results, then, bitter as the resentment of the Zionists at MacDonald's policy must still have been, there would have been nothing in the White Paper of which anyone need be ashamed; but after the failure of Evian, and when the need of the Jews of Germany and eastern Europe was foreseeably moving to a state of desperation, to a question (literally) of life or death, then there was much to be ashamed of. In those circumstances it could be defended only as a necessary but ruthless war-measure, and experience and history show that all such measures have to be paid for dearly.

The fault in this act of policy did not lie with Malcolm MacDonald or the government he served, but far back, with the complacency and unseriousness of their predecessors. By 1939 there was no escape from the confusions of so much accumulated folly, and it is difficult to see what alternative line of action MacDonald himself could have taken. That is his strong personal defense. Yet, in the final analysis, the White Paper turned out to be the opposite of what it claimed to be. In the long run it proved to be unrealistic; it relied on people doing what is beyond human nature; it asked the hard-driven Jews to regard their loyalty to Great Britain as its own reward. It destroyed finally (though the process was gradual) the lingering reality of Anglo-Jewish cooperation in the peaceful establishment of the National Home, a cooperation which had often broken down, was never happy except in some early stages, but which had achieved much. It was wholly unjust for Zionists to say, as they often did and sometimes still do, that the White Paper was the work of anti-Semites and was issued in the spirit of Nazis ordering the wreck of Jewish life in Germany, but it is not surprising that in the turmoil and anguish of those hideous years many Jews should have felt as though this was the fact, and as though the whole world was their enemy.

PART

PART

III

10 WAR AND THE WHITE PAPER

In Palestine, as in most places, the declaration of war was received with dumbfounded shock. For a short time even the preoccupation of Zionism took second place in men's minds, and an added reason was that in Palestine the realization of world war as a fact was accompanied by sudden economic disaster. There was financial panic, hoard-buying of essential food stuffs, and with the interruption of Mediterranean trade, a cessation of the building industry, and an immediate decline in the citrus industry. This led to a terrifying and unprecedented rise in unemployment; half the labor force of the country was out of work before the end of 1939, and the Jewish (the Zionist labor organization) unemployment figures in December were calculated by Histadruth at 50,000. Economic collapse was avoided by the energetic action of Sir Harold MacMichael's administration and later by the real though temporary prosperity that comes to any area that has the dubious good fortune to become a wartime military base.[1]

One curious thing was noticed by many people in Palestine during the first part of the war. The economic plight of the country and the immensity of the threat surrounding it had the effect of drawing Jews and Arabs together in many fields, and there was perhaps more Jewish-Arab cooperation, especially in the citrus industry, than at any other time in mandate history. This had absolutely no effect, however, on Arab-Jewish relations in the political field.

In the free countries the feeling of most Jews about the war was straightforward and uncomplicated. They faced a simple situation: Britain and France were at war with the persecutor of their race so, whatever their feelings regarding Palestine, they rallied to the democratic side. In Palestine, inevitably, when the first shock had passed, Jewish feelings remained dominated by Zionism and in consequence were not simple. Zionism had just emerged from its gravest quarrel with the mandatory, and since May the quarrel had in no sense diminished, but had rather increased as the government refused to give way to Jewish representation regarding any detail of the White Paper. In these circumstances a Palestine Jew often found himself troubled in conscience. No Jew in his right mind could possibly carry opposition to Britain so far as to serve the cause of Hitler; yet he found himself asking whether he could, in opposition to Hitler, unconditionally serve the cause of Great Britain, the betrayer of Zion as he believed.

The power of slogans is habitually overestimated, but they occasionally achieve positive results. Early in the war David Ben-Gurion, chairman of the Jewish Agency Executive, gave the Zionists an ingenious formula. In a public announcement he declared: "We shall fight with Great Britain in this war as if there was no White Paper, and we shall fight the White Paper as if there was no war." This openly paradoxical call to arms corresponded exactly to Zionist emotions. Unlike most slogans it exactly defined policy. To fight Hitler and the White Paper became Zionist purposes which were carried through during the war years. Neither purpose was ever laid aside, and it followed inevitably that the Jews of Palestine became people of divided mind.

For that reason the Zionist military record in the war, which is of decisive importance to an understanding of what happened after, is a story of extraordinary complication.

[1] Albert Hyamson, *Palestine Under the Mandate*. London, 1950. Israel Cohen, *The Zionist Movement*. London, 1945.

In terms of logistics the problem appeared simple. The British army needed manpower in abundance; here in Palestine the Jews could provide men who were not only willing, but ardently desirous of fighting Nazi Germany; and yet the Anglo-Zionist debate which opened on how to employ this needed manpower, a debate which on the high political level began even before the war had been declared, was not resolved till seven months before the war's end. An element of divided mind was also found on the British side. The events of 1939 had poisoned and embittered Anglo-Jewish relations beyond repair. It was not long before the British government, the Palestine administration, and ordinary English people on the spot began to pay the price for the White Paper.

Five days before the fateful 3rd of September Dr. Weizmann wrote to the Prime Minister conveying the offer of the Jewish Agency "to enter into immediate arrangements for utilising Jewish manpower, technical ability, resources, etc." in the prosecution of the war. Neville Chamberlain replied with noncommittal courtesy, noting, he said, that Britain could rely "upon the whole-hearted co-operation of the Jewish Agency." It will be seen from this exchange that from the beginning there was some degree of wilful misunderstanding, Dr. Weizmann and the Zionist leaders meant by the words "utilising Jewish manpower" the formation of a Jewish army. Chamberlain contrived to understand that the offer of the Jewish Agency meant "whole-hearted co-operation" and that they would not give any more trouble about the policy of appeasing the Arabs.[2]

It may be the best method, in trying to set forth the tangle of policy which came after, to begin by following from the point of view of official maneuver the fate of the Zionist proposal for a Jewish army. Though it cut across whatever was consistent (which was little) in British Palestine policy, the proposal went a long way to success and in London found many advocates in high places. One of these was General Sir Edmund Ironside who had become Chief of the Imperial General Staff on the declaration of war. Within a week or so of September 3rd he urged the raising of a "Jewish Legion" on the Secretary of State for War, Leslie Hore-Belisha. The latter turned the proposal down "for the present."[3] The C.I.G.S., however, continued to press for the scheme, and in November was still assuring Dr. Weizmann in this sense.[4] But so long as Chamberlain remained in power, and Malcolm MacDonald was Colonial Secretary, the policy of the White Paper was not questioned in Whitehall, and so the

[2] Text in Cohen, *op. cit.*
[3] *Ibid.*
[4] The Diaries of Mrs. Blanche Dugdale.

scheme was not seriously discussed by the government. It had no support in British Jerusalem. The policy in Palestine was to curb Zionism, and so relentlessly was this carried out that in the autumn of 1939 a group of forty-three Jewish young men were arrested and given long terms of imprisonment for drilling in secret, although at their trial no evidence was found to disprove or even throw doubt on their defense that they were only fitting themselves for service in the war. Protest in Parliament and elsewhere, including one from Ironside, were of no avail for more than a year when the sentences were quashed by MacDonald's successor.

When Mr. Churchill became Prime Minister in May, 1940, the Zionists found great cause for hope: they now had friends in the Cabinet, and, at such a moment of tension, even their opponents sometimes proved sympathetic. When Italy declared war on the 14th of June, Weizmann made an official approach to the new Colonial Secretary, Lord Lloyd. His proposal was for the Jews to undertake the defense of Palestine. "We ask His Majesty's Government," he wrote, "whatever they may decide about our offers of help, to allow the Jews of Palestine, under the direction of the Jewish Agency and the Jewish National Council, and under the control of the British military authorities to organise as many military units as they can, and to train their men, as far as possible with the help of the British forces in the country." The Italians had not yet shown their value in world war and Weizmann pointed out that "the annihilation of the half-million Jews in Palestine" might be imminent, and he demanded the "elementary human right" of the Jews "to go down fighting."[5] This was the sort of language to appeal to a man of Lloyd's adventurous spirit. Though as a traditional pro-Arab of the Empire school he was opposed to Zionism, it appealed to his imagination nevertheless.

In July hopes for a Jewish army rose again and again faded. The War Office now took up the idea. Weizmann exerted his diplomatic skill on the Vice-Chief of the Imperial General Staff, Sir Robert Haining, who promised to send instructions to Sir Archibald Wavell (now Commander in Chief Middle East) to organize the training of Jewish military cadres. This seemed a decisive victory, so much so that Mrs. Dugdale, Balfour's niece and biographer, wrote in her diary on receiving the news: "So the walls of Jericho fall at last, with not much blast of trumpets after all!" But almost immediately after his assurance to Weizmann, General Haining had second thoughts. It may be that Lloyd intervened, for Haining could hardly act without consulting the Colonial Office. At all events, the instructions were not sent, and there ensued a period of recriminating ex-

[5] Eban, in Weizmann Biography.

asperation among the Zionists in London[6] such as usually accompanies disappointment. Then there was a sudden brightening of hopes again.

Mr. Churchill had always been a Zionist, albeit of a very Gentile and unorthodox kind, since his days as Colonial Secretary. Unlike other Zionists in Parliament he remained as Zionist in office as he was in opposition. He was not daunted by the immense difficulties of policy which it raised. It was not long before he took action. At this time he was giving leadership to his country such as it had not received since the time of Pitt (possibly not then), so when he intervened in the dispute he could force a solution the way he wanted—for the moment. On the 6th of September, the middle period of the Battle of Britain, he assured Dr. Weizmann of his full and official support for the Zionist project of raising a Jewish army, and on the 13th of September a meeting took place which seemed to decide the issue. Churchill himself did not attend. The conference was at the War Office. It was presided over by the Secretary of State, Mr. Anthony Eden, and attended by Lord Lloyd, Mr. Lacy Begally representing the Foreign Office, and Dr. Weizmann heading a small Zionist delegation. After discussion Mr. Eden officially communicated to Weizmann that "the Government have decided to proceed with the organisation of a Jewish army, on the same basis as the Czech and Polish armies. Its size, to begin with, would be 10,000 including 4,000 from Palestine. They would be trained and organised in England and then dispatched to the Middle East." [7]

"13th September, Friday—and yet a lucky day!" wrote Mrs. Dugdale in her diary. "A great day! The walls of Jericho have fallen, fallen! I looked in at the Dorchester about 5 p.m. and found Chaim [Weizmann] just back from this interview, elated and solemn. He said: 'It is almost as great a day as the Balfour Declaration.'"

For some months the prospect for a Jewish army remained set fair in spite of an early disappointment. From the first moment that a Jewish army was proposed the Zionists remembered Wingate and his exploits with the Special Night Squads. It was treated as a settled matter that when and if the Army was formed he would command it. His friends overlooked the fact that Wingate's Palestine career had given him an unsavory and by no means undeserved reputation in the War Office for political intriguing. He had only recently emerged from a dispute with his former seniors in Palestine on this very matter, a dispute which had seriously endangered his whole career. Two months before the September meeting

6 *Ibid.*
7 *Ibid.*

Mr. L. S. Amery had pressed Wingate's claims for service in the Middle East, and Wavell, whose admiration for Wingate was undiminished, had replied by asking for his services, but only on the strict condition that he was excluded from Palestine. A week after Weizmann's meeting at the War Office Wingate, bitter and angry, left for the Middle East and employment far from Palestine and Zionism, in Ethiopia.[8]

This disappointment did not, however, prove an immediate setback. On the contrary. Dr. Weizmann learned shortly after that on the 2nd of October Winston Churchill had informed the Cabinet that he wished to repudiate the White Paper, and on the 16th of October Dr. Weizmann was officially notified that at a subsequent Cabinet the project for a Jewish army had been formally ratified.[9] It seemed that the Zionists had won their point completely and finally. Yet the walls of Jericho remained standing till 1944 and never fell down in entirety.

The last wholly favorable omen for the Zionists appeared in February of 1941 when Dr. Weizmann was introduced to Major-General Leonard Arthur Hawes, an officer with a distinguished Indian record who had been chosen to command the Jewish army.

At the beginning of the same month Lord Lloyd died suddenly. He was succeeded by Lord Moyne. Whether this made a great difference to the fortunes of Zionism may be doubted, but it is true that though Lloyd and Moyne were both pro-Arab and inclined to anti-Zionism in their political sympathies, there was a romantic strain in Lloyd, what might be called a Disraelian pro-Semitism which made him sympathetic to Zionist ideas, and there was nothing of this in Moyne. Then and later Zionists saw in Moyne an enemy who brought down their most cherished designs. What in fact happened was inevitable, in all likelihood. The decision to raise and equip a Jewish Army had been taken at one of the most stirring moments in English history, a moment when loftiness of spirit seemed capable of sweeping every obstacle aside. The retreat from the decision came in the gray hour which follows exaltation. The Zionist party in the government had to face political and economic obstacles. No decision as to a Jewish army could be implemented without reference to the authorities in Palestine and the Middle East Command. When inquiry was made it was found that the dislike of the Palestine administration for the scheme was fully shared by Sir Archibald Wavell. Winston Churchill was enraged and referred to Wavell's fears of dangerous Arab reactions as "all this stuff." [10]

[8] Christopher Sykes, *op. cit.*
[9] Eban, *op. cit.*
[10] Winston Churchill, *The Second World War,* Vol. III. London, 1951.

But he found and continued to find that he could not override Middle East opposition. The economic obstacle was as grave as the political one. The Middle East Command was short of supplies and equipment, and in addition to his enormous African commitments Wavell had the preparation of the impending Greek campaign on his hands. In such circumstances to raise and equip a new army was literally impossible. Winston Churchill, in a hard note, ordered the Colonial Secretary to inform Dr. Weizman of postponement but not to mention the political reasons.

So Lord Moyne had to play the dismal part of the man who calls with explanation on the morning after the night of proposals and promises. On the 4th of March, 1941, he wrote to Dr. Weizmann:

"I am very sorry to tell you that the raising of the Jewish contingent has to be postponed . . . The Prime Minister has decided that owing to lack of equipment the project must for the present be put off for six months, but may be reconsidered again in four months." [11]

The Zionists assumed that this was chicanery, and not till long after did the truth occur to them that shortage of equipment was the plain fact.[12] By a curious irony the "lost leader" of the Jewish Army, Orde Wingate, had been involved during recent months in a similar conflict in Africa. He was at this moment in the early stages of his astonishing guerrilla campaign as commander of the Emperor of Ethiopia's personal troops. A large part of the preceding autumn in Khartoum had been spent by Haile Selassie, supported by Wingate, in bitter argument with his British allies about the meager supplies of arms and equipment which they allotted to him. Haile Selassie also suspected chicanery, as did all Great Britain's few allies from time to time in those years.

But the Zionist suspicion, unfair as it was at the time, was not ill-grounded. As mentioned, Moyne was under instruction to hide the political objection from Weizmann, and that objection was certainly the more important. To supply a Jewish army would have been no Herculean task in the later years of the war, but the political obstacle was to grow. Zionists were justified in seeing any delay as a fatal obstruction. As soon as enthusiasm on the British side gave way to sober reflections, such as those expressed by Wavell, other sober reflections had time to break in, and these never led to the raising of a Jewish army but away from it.

After March, 1941, the story of the projected force was one of anticlimax. For a long time it was confined to a plan which had been initiated in Palestine in September 1940, the September of Zionist hope. The purpose

[11] Text in Eban, *op. cit.*
[12] Yehuda Bauer, *Scripta Hierosolymitana*, Vol. VII. Jerusalem, 1961.

of the plan was to turn Arabs and Jews into comrades in arms: Jews would not fight as Jews or Arabs as Arabs but both as citizens of their common country.

There was something akin to the theory of artificial respiration in the long-enduring British devotion to the idea that with a little persuasion the Jews and Arabs of Palestine could be brought to look on themselves as Palestinians first and foremost, and as such primarily interested in erecting an independent state which they would happily share. The idea had been proved dead on many recent occasions, and in spite of the courageous advocacy of Magnes and his group, it had at no time shown fully convincing signs of life. It was an unwelcome idea to most Palestine Jews, and utterly repellent to almost all Palestine Arabs. Yet from many points of view, and especially the British, the idea gave expression to a most desirable state of things. Therefore, with bulldog determination, the British, now and for the remaining years of the mandate, persisted in treating this wholly fallacious notion as if it were living and true. It remains very doubtful whether any of them went so far as to *believe* that it was true.

The Palestinian Force plan of September 1940 was put into operation by adding a Palestinian battalion to the East Kent Regiment, "The Buffs." As originally designed the companies of the battalion were to be Jewish or Arab in a precise fifty-fifty ratio, but this proved impractical, largely owing to the greater pressure of recruitment from the Jews and the greater proneness to desertion of the Arabs. In its final form the battalion was enlarged to fourteen companies, and a preponderance of Jewish over Arab groupings was allowed. When it came to action these companies did good work, to the surprise of many who wondered how a unit recruited on the basis least likely to infuse it with *esprit de corps* could have the morale necessary for military valor. The fact is easily explained so far as the Jews are concerned. For most of the war these companies, British as they were in all their forms, were as near to a Jewish Army of Palestine as the Jews could get. When the companies were expanded and designated as the Palestine Regiment in August, 1942, Shertok declared that this was "but a shadow of that which [the Jews] have been urging." [13] But for all that they did not let the opportunity go by.

Here, to avoid a possible misunderstanding, it is necessary to explain that the main soldiering effort by the Jews of Palestine was quite separate from this dispute and maneuver around a hoped-for Jewish army. Great numbers of young men took the simple course of joining the British

[13] Quoted in Daphne Trevor, *Under the White Paper*. Jerusalem, 1948.

armed services. In 1941 they numbered over ten thousand and by the end of the war over fourteen thousand.[14] Many of them served in Jewish units in the British army, navy or air force, but the majority went through the war as individuals. But though their service was unconnected with Zionist politics, many of them retained closer relations with the Zionist leadership than was commonly known. This appears later.

As things turned out, the Zionists would have been much better advised, from their own point of view, if they had encouraged this sort of individual and unconditional service and forgotten the quest for an army, since the latter involved long-drawn negotiations which inevitably tended to delay the flow into army employment of young Jewish men, and the great Zionist need in the future was to be for men with military training. But none of this was possible to see then, and it would have been strange indeed if in the war against Hitler and Nazism the Jews of Palestine had not done all that they could for the right to maintain their own fighting force under their own emblems. As Dr. Weizmann said, this was "an elementary human right."

Winston Churchill remained in the fullest agreement over that right and he never flagged in his endeavors to grant it to the Jews, but even he, enjoying the great constitutional power of a British Prime Minister, and a unique measure of prestige, could not make headway against the political and military forces which opposed him on the matter. In spite of all Mr. Churchill's skill in political maneuver, the opponents of his Zionist policy outmaneuvered him almost until the end.

When six months were up after notification of postponement, Lord Moyne reopened the matter as he had promised. He conveyed news of a further postponement on the 23rd of October, 1941. He informed Weizmann and Ben-Gurion that "since the Government had to give every aid to Russia it would not be possible to form a Jewish Division."[15] And there the matter remained, alleviated only by the expansion of the Palestinian battalion in the summer of 1942, and in spite of the continual protest and pressure of the Zionist leadership, until the last months of the war.

As 1943 drew to a close Zionists began to fear that if the postponement continued much longer there would be little gain even if the permission was granted, because a Jewish army, if formed then, would be too late to take part in the invasion of Europe and the conquest of Germany. On the 26th of November the Jewish Agency made a request for immediate ac-

[14] Statistics in Bauer, *op. cit.,* and Cohen, *op. cit.*
[15] Eban, *op. cit.*

tion to avoid such delay, and significantly they addressed it not only to the British government but to the United States.[16] Still nothing was done. In April of 1944 fifty-three members of Parliament, from both sides of the House of Commons, tabled a motion in the same sense. On July 4th, a month after the beginning of the invasion, Lord Strabolgi introduced the same motion in the House of Lords. The Under Secretary of State for War replied that "the possibility is being very carefully studied." These studies were not completed till two and a half months later, nearly a year after the Jewish Agency's note to Britain and America. The War Office announced on the 20th of September, 1944, that "the Government have decided to accede to the request of the Jewish Agency"—though not to the reiterated request for a Jewish Army, nor to a Jewish Division, but to the formation of a Jewish Brigade Group. This half-loaf measure could be rapidly put into execution because the Group was to include the trained and equipped Jewish companies of the Palestine Regiment. It was ready by the end of 1944, carrying its own standards which bore the mystical sign of the Star of David. But by this time the war was in its last phase and the Jewish Brigade had missed the opportunity for which all Zionists longed: that of fighting the Nazis in crucial battle as Jewish soldiers serving under a Jewish flag.

These maneuverings and negotiations between the Jewish Agency and the British government caused great exasperation to Zionists. To many of them, and to their sympathizers, it still seems today that the obstruction whose strength and origin were undoubtedly in the Palestine administration, and which delayed the formation of the Brigade Group till it was almost too late, and far too late for the realization of the first generously conceived plan, was an ugly illustration of a dull unimaginative mind, typical of British Jerusalem; a mind which could only feebly sympathize with the sorrows of the Jewish people, and indeed could only feebly grasp the fact that the Jews were passing through a tragedy at all; the mind that caused the mandate to end in total failure. Many Zionists would put the matter in stronger and more accusing terms.

It is unquestionably true that as a result of having to deal for years on end with a problem without possibility of solution, there had arisen in the spirit of the Palestine administration a lack of imagination which was often so deadly that it could be mistaken for active wickedness. A single

---

[16] G. E. Kirk, *Survey of International Affairs: 1939–46. The Middle East in the War.* Oxford, 1952. This invaluable, though in places possibly biased, account is used as a reference work throughout the present chapter.

illustration from personal experience can perhaps make the point clear.[17]

In the summer of 1942 when the Afrika Korps under General Rommel had driven the Eighth Army back to El Alamein, and when the possibility of a British evacuation of Egypt was being provided for, several departments of G.H.Q. in Cairo were transferred to Palestine. Some of these departments employed German and Italian Jews, usually as translators. In many cases the officers responsible for the movement of personnel during this time of crisis gave priority to these people, and to their families, in consideration of what might be the fate of captured German and Italian Jews associated with British army work in war. The number of those concerned was not large, possibly a hundred at the most. They were, with few exceptions, Jews domiciled in Egypt who could all, without exception, be vouched for by responsible people. So far as anyone knew, none of them were interested in Zionism, and even if they had been fanatically so interested, this would have provided no excuse for leaving them in danger while their officers sought safety. Such was the sensible and decent view taken by their employers, but it was found impossible to get this view shared by the Palestine authorities. The issue was complicated by the happy excess of zeal shown by a certain transport officer who moved a number of these Jews to Palestine before official agreement to their reception was forthcoming.[18] This was as well for the peace of mind of the Jews since the British authorities in Jerusalem refused to accord agreement. Their minds were stuck in one posture: to watch for infringements of the White Paper, and they detected one here. They spoke of quotas, of waiting lists, of how exemptions might worry Arabs, of the great peril of permitting breaches of the rules. They said nothing about the great peril to which Jews might be exposed in a German-conquered Cairo. This was something outside their experience. Their chief emotion, in that fearful hour, seemed one of pained surprise that members of G.H.Q. could act with so little regard for protocol. In petulant self-assertion they ordered the immediate return of the whole party to Egypt. News of this boneheaded instruction found its way from the Administration office to some of the Jews, whereat an Italian, overcome by panic, attempted suicide. He was discovered and saved. The incident had the desirable result of attract-

---

[17] The experience is personal to the writer.

[18] Despite the exigencies of the Official Secrets Act the name of this admirable officer should be remembered: Captain Albert Nacamuli. He had only been appointed transport officer for the purpose of this movement shortly before. He took many of the people concerned to Palestine himself in his sports car which made some dozen fantastically overloaded journeys between Cairo and Jerusalem in the course of two days.

ing the attention of a senior security officer who was a more balanced man than some of his colleagues of the Palestine service. He looked into the business, and when he discovered the brutal nonsense it was, he took steps to bring it to an end. On condition that they did not claim the right to permanent residence (which none of them had thought of claiming), the Jews in G.H.Q. employ and their dependents were allowed asylum in Palestine. Most of them returned to their homes in Egypt before the end of the year.

It was noticeable that after this shameful sequence of events many of these Jews never felt the same about Great Britain, were never at ease with English people to quite the same extent as they had been before. It must be stressed that their status as confidential employees put them in a privileged position: they had a strong case for preferential treatment, and in addition they were personally acquainted with many British officers who (with one or two dismal exceptions) were prepared to fight their case against the pedantry of stupid officials. It can be imagined how much worse they would have fared if they had come from enemy countries; if they had known no British officers or soldiers or English people of any kind; if there had been plausbile reasons for suspecting artfully smuggled spies among them; if they had been crude people, ignorant of any language in which they might explain themselves to the rulers of Palestine. Such were the circumstances and characteristics of most of the Jewish people who came to Palestine during the war years. They were often met by the same dull mental response, the sort that is best described as flat-footed, the sort that in 1942 did everything that can be done to turn devoted servants who had proved their devotion into implacable enemies. There were in Palestine a lamentably large number of English people who had an unerring touch in the making of enemies.

An administration informed by such a spirit as has been just described, which sought guidance by looking up the clauses of the White Paper in the spirit of a Beckmesser, was not likely to throw itself heart and soul behind the Jewish wish for a Jewish army. But from that point it is easy to fall into a facile generalization. The administration was not only informed by such a spirit, and the opposition to the Jewish army did not only come from fools; the objection was not merely irresponsible or dictated by pedantry or unthinking bias. It was grounded on an opinion well supported by evidence from the beginning, and increasingly so as the war went on. According to this opinion the Agency's purpose in raising a Jewish army would be twofold: to fight Nazis on the battlefields of the Second World War, as the Zionists affirmed, and no one questioned their sincerity; and secondly to compel a Zionist solution of the Palestine problem by force of arms, to threaten and if necessary to attempt the conquest of the country even at the cost of civil war. Zionist authorities, writing subsequently to this time and the establishment of Israel, leave not the slightest doubt that a Jabotinskian policy of this kind was fully intended by the Jewish Agency from the first moment when it pressed for a Jewish army.

One issue dominated Anglo-Zionist relations. Of far greater importance than the harsh land transfer regulations of the White Paper,[19] or even the issue of the Jewish Army itself, was the burning question of permitting Jewish immigration into Palestine from Nazi Europe. Behind this bitter dispute was the hideous conditioning factor of German policy toward the Jews, and the history of this falls into two definable halves: from 1939 to 1942 during which period German policy remained muddled and was further confused, and slightly alleviated, by the corruption of officials; and a second phase from 1942 to the end of the Nazi regime when German policy was clear and intensified, though at occasional points remaining confused, and alleviated, as before, by corruption. Throughout, the reaction of Zionist policy was remarkably consistent. There was much change in emphasis and method during the course of the war, but no change in essential principles, and among these was the unalterable conviction that the clauses in the White Paper limiting Jewish immigration being against both the terms of the mandate and the direction of the League of Nations, were not legally binding.[20] When the Administration described unagreed

[19] They were issued on February 28th, 1940, and barred about 63.4 percent of the total area of Palestine to Jewish land purchase, placed 31.6 percent under restrictions on Jewish purchase, leaving 5 percent free. The regulations were greeted by protest, a brief general strike by Jews, and some serious rioting in which about 400 people were injured and two killed. Yet in spite of the intense, indeed cruel, harshness of these regulations they have never figured as prominently in Zionist literature as one might expect. The reason appears to be that the organization for Jewish settlement called the Keren Kayemeth found ways of circumventing the regulations and obtaining Arab agreement to sale in the restricted and prohibited areas. From 1940 to 1947 the Keren Kayemeth bought about 82,500 acres, nearly doubling their Palestine property, a little under 70,000 acres being outside the free area. (Marlowe.)

[20] The Zionist case that the White Paper was illegal was based on the following: In June, 1939, the Permanent Mandates Commission of the League unanimously reported against it as "not in accordance with the interpretation . . . the Commission has placed upon the Palestine Mandate." A further motion as to whether the interpretation might be so revised as to admit the policy of the White Paper was defeated by four votes to three. By the constitution of the League, the Commission had no veto over the proposals of a mandatory but was responsible for advising the League Council. With the outbreak of the war the Council did not meet and the views of the League were not ascertained. The British government could claim that in these circumstances the White Paper legally remained in force de facto. Zionist

Jewish immigration to Palestine as illegal it was talking nonsense, so ran the argument, and good Zionists henceforth always wrote the word in inverted commas. The Zionists opposition to restrictions on immigration remained absolute and ruthless. It remained so till the end of the mandate.

The situation of Haganah at the beginning of the war was as typically complicated as ever. Since the middle of the thirties the ruling committee had tried to turn Haganah from a mainly left-wing organization into one that was genuinely nonparty and national. Agreement along these lines was reached in 1937, but it was very imperfect; the left-wing element still predominated at the expense of a resentful right-wing, and the party conflict remained acute. It is almost impossible, because of the taste for elaboration that seems part of Jewish psychology, to make a valid generalization about Haganah politics, but the conflict in crude terms can be described as between a moderate and modest right-wing conception of the Haganah role, and the forward policy advocated by the better organized Left groups who represented the political thinking of the Zionist labor organization, Histadruth. The right wing saw Haganah as a fire brigade, as an armed body for use in preserving Jewish lives and property in moments of abnormal threat and crisis such as the Arab rebellion; they saw Haganah as supplementing the role of British troops and police. The left wing wanted to give Haganah a more essential role, that of the armed force of Zion. Their political aim was that Jews should be able to defend themselves against all comers. "They stood for a national, as against a local organization, and by 1939 most of them tended to see in Haganah an instrument of Zionist policy, and not just an organization that answered a certain limited need." [21]

Apart from Haganah there was another more clandestine Jewish force raised by Jabotinsky's Revisionists. They separated from Haganah in 1937, a logical step following the separation of the extreme Revisionist party from the world Zionist organization in 1935. The force they raised was known as the "Irgun Zvai Leumi" (the National Military Organization), called "Etzel" for short. They had little to do with Haganah at this time.

Since the party conflict within Haganah had not abated as hoped since

propagandists spoiled the strong case to the contrary by insisting that the Commission could and did act for the League. They were much encouraged in this argument by the support of Judge Brandeis later. (Kirk, Wischnitzer.)
[21] Bauer, op. cit., quoting "post factum oral depositions" in Haganah Archives.

1937, there was a fresh reorganization in June, 1941, and this remained in force during the war. A ruling all-party committee of eighteen was elected under the Jewish Agency Executive and made responsible for Haganah finance and general policy. This committee of eighteen then delegated its administrative and some of its political authority to a body of eight members. This was composed of three representatives of Histadruth, three of the secular right wing, one representative of the religious group, and the national Haganah commander. The committee of eight was in turn served by a General Staff under the orders of the national commander. In the Zionist fashion these bodies were referred to by strange-sounding Hebrew abbreviations: the command committee of eight was known as Ma (from Mifkadah Artzit), the commander as the Rama (from Rosh Midfadah Artzit), and the general staff as Matkal (from Mateh Klali).[22]

As mentioned in a previous chapter, it was never easy to know precisely whether or to what extent Haganah was illegal or not, but before the war had been going for more than a few months it became literally impossible. The Palestine administration tried to find an answer to the riddle by the formation of a Home Guard, called the Jewish Settlement Police, drawn exclusively from Haganah and nominally under British command, though in effect run by its less respectable parent. In popular speech it was known as "the legal Haganah" and it was a matter of tact in official circles not to stress that this legal body was recruited, administered, and officered by its illegal namesake. But even without the device of the J.S.P. the illegality of Haganah was early called in question by official approaches from British authorities.

The first of these appears to have been made in London in the spring of 1940. A secret department acting with full official authority went into conference with David Hacohen representing the Jewish Agency, and they reached an agreement whose upshot was that Haganah would supply Rumanian-speaking agents for a sabotage role in the Rumanian oil fields. This operation (which Wingate offered to lead) never came to anything, and was probably too ambitious and difficult to succeed without long prewar preparation, but it led to other Anglo-Haganah contacts. The approach to Hacohen synchronized with discussion on the same subject between veiled British authorities in Cairo and the Jewish Agency Executive. This led in turn to British military instructors training Haganah personnel in a variety of military techniques, chiefly those suited

[22] Bauer, *op. cit.*

to raiding behind the enemy lines, a kind of operation which sometimes requires great courage.[23]

By the time of the disastrous Greek and Cretan campaigns, sufficient Haganah men had been trained for numbers of them to take part. In May, 1941, after the British defeat in Greece and while the battle of Crete was still being fought, a group of twenty-three of these trained Haganah men was sent under a British officer on a raid to Tripoli with the object of wrecking the oil refineries. The raid was unsuccessful and the men were all killed, without exception. This was the beginning of the Haganah "Shock Companies," known in Hebrew as Palmah (from Plugot Mahatz), which were formed in honor of the gallant twenty-three.[24] In the same month the same veiled authorities, who to the non-British were indistinguishable from the British Army, led another Palestine Jewish expedition, recruited this time not from the possibly acceptable Haganah but from the decidedly impossible Etzel,[25] with the purpose of seizing the Mufti in Baghdad from where he was helping to direct Rashid Ali's rising in favor of the triumphing Axis powers. During 1941 trained Haganah personnel undertook intelligence and clandestine propaganda missions to Syria and Lebanon, sometimes under British direction and sometimes under that of the Haganah "Haifa Office" in collaboration with the British. The Haifa office was run by Emmanuel Wilenski and a former Rama, Professor Rattner, both of the Haifa technical college. When the British invaded Syria and Lebanon in July, 1941, a Haganah platoon acted as scouts and saboteurs in the van of the army.[26]

After such episodes it was difficult for officials of the Palestine administration to prosecute a man and obtain a sentence of imprisonment against him for belonging to Haganah, yet according to the law they were allowed to do this. Doubtless a few of the more crass kind, the kind that in a mood of pompous regret tried to turn back the unoffending G.H.Q. Jews in 1942, tried to do this too.[27] One must never underestimate the importance of the crass kind in Palestine. They were foundation stones of Zionist propaganda.

[23] Magen Baseter (Secret Defense), a Hebrew record of which Miss Denman translated passages for the writer's Orde Wingate. Also Bauer, op. cit.
[24] Bauer, op. cit.
[25] Arthur Koestler, Promise and Fulfilment. London, 1949.
[26] Bauer, op. cit.
[27] In Promise and Fulfilment, a masterpiece of Zionist propaganda, Mr. Koestler suggests that the two policies, training and suppression of Haganah, were concurrent, but he gives no incident of suppression later than January, 1940, before the opening, that is, of the dubious Anglo-Haganah honeymoon.

Since the Jews wanted a Jewish army it is strange, at first sight, that they did not seize on this Anglo-Zionist military cooperation and build from there. They were, of course, inhibited from pressing a political advantage through the use of publicity methods by the extreme secrecy in which the collaborating departments work, and to which the Jews were committed. One must also remember that though his cooperation, in such striking contrast to the tragic hostilities of postwar years, has been much remarked, it was on a very small scale. But there was another stronger factor against making this the starting point of the Jewish army. Since the British did not hesitate to make the same advances to Etzel as to Haganah a strong military British-Jewish partnership under the present auspices might lead to a diminution of Haganah's carefully built-up authority, and thus to a lessening of the authority of the Jewish Agency itself.

All these reasons and circumstances against exploiting cooperation to the full might have been and probably would have been overcome since the prize of a Jewish army was so great and so desired, if it had not been for the dominating circumstance, namely that since the policy of the White Paper had come into force the emotional disposition for close partnership with the British was not there. The real obstacle was the bitter, hating attitude which the Jews developed toward Britain as a result of the conduct of the mandatory regarding immigration.

The mass movements of the Jews from Germany, and from the Nazi-occupied and Nazi-influenced countries, are part of a chapter which is so disgraceful to Europe that the reading of it can almost excuse the despairing cynicism which refuses belief that there is in fact any merit at all in Western civilization. These movements continued to the end of the Nazi regime, and then persisted under other pressures to the present day.[28] So far as the Nazi years are concerned the largest movements occurred during the later part of what has been described above as the muddled phase of German persecution, when floundering Nazi hatred and hysteria had little defined object beyond ill treatment.[29] In so far as an object did exist it was to make the heartland of the Teutonic ruling race empty of Jews. This at least had one alleviating factor, that there was some sort of encourage-

[28] At the time of writing (1964) the officially acknowledged flow of Jewish immigrants into Israel is calculated at an average of 50,000 a year, but no one appears to question that the real figures are much higher than this.
[29] As early as 1935 a Nazi official told James G. MacDonald: "Do you know that we have arranged to wipe out the entire Jewish population in the Reich? . . . Everything is ready and can be done in a single night." (Wischnitzer.) Nazi conduct from 1933 to 1942 suggests that this enthusiast was expressing the extreme ideas of the party and not a settled policy.

ment for Jews to get out of the European hell. The occasion was grasped by Zionists, by believing Nazis, and by people out to profiteer. In addition to the flow of Jewish refugees from Germany and eastern Europe which had been going on since 1933, a new type of migration, headed toward Palestine, was organized from the ports of the eastern Mediterranean early in 1939. To quote Mark Wischnitzer, the leading authority on this exodus: "In part it was a spontaneous movement; in part it was aided by Palestinian Jews. But to a great extent it was organized by Gestapo agents bent on making Central Europe *Judenrein*." [30]

It is impossible, and will probably remain impossible to know in what proportion these agents of migration operated, and to what extent Nazis helped the migration through genuine belief in the Nazi creed or through corruption, but it is known on ample firsthand evidence how the migrants fared, and that when the Gestapo had a hand in the matter, any alleviating circumstance was remote from humanity. An American correspondent described the traffic in Jews on the Danube: "When passengers are needed (by the boat-owners) Jews are rounded up and threatened with the concentration camp unless they leave Germany. 'Where can we go?' they plead. 'Palestine,' replies the Gestapo. For illegal emigration the Gestapo is ever able to arrange the transfer of funds; visas and exit permits appear magically. The German Danube Steam Ship Company hands the refugees down the Danube to Rumanian ports. Only the worst craft are used[31]; vermin-infested freighters, discarded cattle boats, leaking tankers. Accounts of their voyages read like tales of the old slave trade. Often when a boat that is already overloaded is about to sail, the Gestapo will force another two hundred or three hundred on board." [32] Every passenger had to pay the boat owners exorbitant sums. The traffic seems to have been financially very rewarding.

The boats, the little death ships as Arthur Koestler described them, set out for Palestine where some succeeded in landing their passengers clandestinely by night, but others were stopped and challenged. In accordance with the terms of the White Paper, the Jews were not allowed to land. It was now that they discovered that their visas were forgeries.

When confronted by this new threat to orderly government, the Palestine administration and the Colonial Office did not know what to do. At

---

[30] Mark Wischnitzer, *To Dwell in Safety*. Philadelphia, 1948.
[31] Because, as the writer elsewhere explained, there was little if any prospect of boats returning.
[32] *Saturday Evening Post*, 9th August, 1939, quoted by Mark Wischnitzer. The account is true of this traffic until its virtual cessation after 1942.

the beginning they acted in strict and unimaginative accordance with the rules. The results disgusted opinion. During March and April of 1939 (before the issue of the White Paper in May), a crowd of Jewish refugees arrived off the Palestinian coast on three Danubian boats. Needless to say, they had not got a valid visa between them. They were told to be off. At the end of April the Colonial Secretary was asked by Josiah Wedgwood in the House of Commons what had become of these people. He replied that "he understood" that they had been sent back to "the port of embarkation." "Does this mean," asked Mr. Noel Baker, "that the refugees are in fact being sent back to the concentration camps?" The Colonial Secretary answered that "the responsibility in this matter must rest on those who are responsible for organising this traffic in illegal immigration." Though perfectly correct, the spirit of the reply, when people considered the agony of the return journey, proved beyond bearing, and the government could not risk further episodes of the kind. By an act of unimagination the government had given their critics an opening and to Zionists a weapon which they naturally used to the utmost. But although Zionist propagandists alleged and still allege that there were continued forced returns of death ships to Nazi Europe, no names of boats are given after April, 1939. There seems no reason to suppose that the atrocious episode of that spring was repeated. The Colonial Office and the Palestine administration seem to have formulated a refugee policy after the issue of the White Paper, a policy which they revised in 1940.

The number of illegal Jewish immigrants into Palestine from April to October, 1939, was calculated at 6,323. The economic crisis was sweeping down on the country with alarming rapidity. Jewish unemployment figures were already the highest ever recorded. The administration acted in continual fear of precipitating some uncontrollable economic disaster. They had also another reason to pursue what they called a "cautious" and the Zionists called a "merciless" policy. It was well known that the refugee traffic was run with Gestapo consent, and sometimes on their strenuous initiative. This very strongly suggested a deep-laid Nazi conspiracy, and after the fall of France people more and more connected these forced migrations with the well-attested accounts, then to be met with not only in newspapers but in military appreciations, of German skill in what were usually called fifth-column tactics. There was at that time a great deal of exaggerated belief in German subtlety, especially in turning refugee problems to their account, and this belief, which fitted what was known of the ghastly Nazi philosophy, was shared by all the enemies of Hitler, including Jews. To many sensible people it seemed almost a self-evident conclusion that the migrations were organized with a dual purpose: to cause political embarrassment to the British position in the Middle East, and to introduce in the guise of refugees skilled intelligence agents and saboteurs. In fact this conclusion was fallacious, but it would be absurd to blame the British authorities, in the state of information at that time, for their mistake. The refugee policy in its first form can be inferred from MacDonald's curiously guarded answers to questions in Parliament: it was to the effect that the number of refugees allowed to remain was to be deducted from the 75,000 provided for in the White Paper. The revised policy, influenced by fears of fifth-column tactics, was that the refugees were not to be allowed to land in Palestine. Instead they were to be interned elsewhere in British colonial territory.

In pursuance of their policy "to fight the White Paper as if there was no war," the Zionists represented both policies as an atrocity. They were helped by the fact that owing to their fear that the migrations were in part a Gestapo cover plan, the British were careful not to state their intentions, and it would seem also (though this is not certain) that the British purposely did not discourage hideous rumors that Jewish refugees who came to Palestine from the Balkans were liable to be sent back. They gave orders to the police to fire at ships refusing challenge, and on one ship, the *Tiger Hill*, the police killed two refugees.[33] This of course added to the already bitter rage of the Jewish population. But it was a small incident, clearly not intended, and likely to be soon forgotten. Then in November of 1940 came an incident which, with the abundant help of propaganda, crystallized feelings. There occurred a fatal accident of great proportions, an accident which was entirely the fault of Zionists, but which nevertheless caused a lasting breach between the British and the Jews of Palestine.

The story is well known in outline but must be briefly given again here. On the 11th of November, 1940, two broken-down ships, the *Pacific* and the *Milos,* were intercepted by the British navy off the coast of Palestine and brought into Haifa harbor. Between them they carried over seventeen hundred refugees. The Palestine authorities refused to allow them to land. There were protests throughout Palestine and on November 20th the Jewish Agency tried to force the administration's hand by declaring a general strike. This did have the effect of forcing the administration into an open declaration of policy, and the High Commissioner tried to allay feelings by broadcasting a communiqué. This was declared then and later to

[33] Koestler, *op. cit.* The author adds: "Such incidents became a regular practice." He gives no examples.

be one of the most abominable utterances of a cynical ruler. The text was as follows:

> His Majesty's Government are not lacking in sympathy for refugees from territories under German control. But they are responsible for the administration of Palestine and are bound to see to it that the laws of the country are not openly flouted.
>
> Moreover they can only regard a revival of illegal Jewish immigration at the present juncture as likely to affect the local situation most adversely, and to prove a serious menace to British interests in the Middle East. They have accordingly decided that the passengers shall not be permitted to land in Palestine but shall be deported to a British colony and shall be detained there for the duration of the war.
>
> Their ultimate disposal will be a matter for consideration at the end of the war, but it is not proposed that they shall remain in the colony to which they are sent or that they should go to Palestine. Similar action will be taken in the case of any further parties who may succeed in reaching Palestine with a view to illegal entry.

(The hand of a crass drafter is evident in the allusion to "British interests" in the second paragraph.)

There was a ship of the Messagerie Maritime line in Haifa at the time and this was requisitioned for the journey of the refugees to Mauritius. The ship was called *La Patria.* When the passengers had been transferred from the *Pacific* and the *Milos* a third hulk filled with Jewish refugees was brought in to Haifa on the 24th of November. It was called the *Atlantic.* It was decided to transfer the new arrivals to the *Patria* also. But before this could be done, at eight o'clock the next morning, an alarm was sounded on the *Patria* and the passengers were told to jump for safety into the water. A few minutes after there was an explosion within the boat. She heeled over and sank in one and a quarter hours. Two hundred and forty refugees and about a dozen police were killed by the explosion or by drowning.

The Jewish Agency declared that the sinking of the ship was an act of mass-protest against the inhuman decision of Sir Harold MacMichael, an act of attempted mass-suicide. This official Zionist version was much later given eloquent expression by a famous writer:

> The passengers blew up their ship. They had reached their journey's end. They were not even threatened with deportation back to Europe; only to a tropical island without hope of return. But these people had become

allergic to barbed wire. When a person reaches that stage he is past listening to the reasonable voice of officialdom which explains to him that he should never have escaped, or saved his wife and children, as "a revival of illegal Jewish immigration at the present juncture" was "likely to affect the local situation most adversely." [34]

The book in which this was written was published in 1949. Even so long after the event, the legend was still flourishing, although the evidence all pointed to the unlikelihood of the suicide story. The commission of inquiry, held in the following January, established beyond much doubt that the sinking of the ship was the work of a small determined group working from the shore, and not in consultation with the people on board, except for three or four individuals. It was tentatively concluded, and most authorities have since agreed, that the destruction of the *Patria* was the work of Etzel desperadoes.

But the truth was somewhat more shocking. It was not the wild hotheads of Etzel who made up the minds of the refugees for them, but the supposedly responsible-minded Jewish Agency acting through Haganah. Of course, it must be stressed that the Zionist leadership had no such bloody purpose as to stage a mass suicide. The object of the operation went no further than to disable the engines of the *Patria*[35] so as to keep her and her cargo of wretched humanity in Haifa, and thus to increase the pressure on the administration to allow them to land and remain. When the technician calculated amiss and instead of wrecking the engines blew a hole in the *Patria* and sank her with fearful loss of life, the Jewish Agency hastened to cover up the atrocity with the mass-suicide story which concentrated all indignation on the administration alone.

The story was believed by the great mass of Jews in Palestine, although the survivors of the disaster were allowed to remain in the country and must have told many people something of the truth of the matter. Possibly they told fewer than might be expected because it could be a dangerous thing to do. At a meeting in 1942, the head of the German Jewish community publicly denounced the anti-British policy of the Jewish Agency and hinted, more truthfully than perhaps he knew, that this mass-suicide story was propaganda nonsense. An attempt was made on his life immediately after, on his way home from the meeting.[36] This attempt on a man's life for denying the story can suggest that the real reason it was

[34] Koestler, *op. cit.*
[35] *The Jerusalem Post,* 29th November, 1960.
[36] The writer was in Palestine at the time.

believed was that so many people wanted to believe it. Some light is thrown indirectly on this possibility by the sequel which (in the writer's opinion) is the most extraordinary part of the whole episode. The victims themselves were in time persuaded to approve the ruthless methods employed by the Jewish Agency at their expense. The man who placed the bomb which cost so many innocent lives later became a well-known functionary of the Israeli port of Haifa.[37] No one appeared to bear him any illwill. On the twentieth anniversary of the disaster in 1960 the occasion was marked by a memorial service at the common grave of the *Patria* dead followed by a social meeting at a Haifa Club attended by numerous survivors and representatives of the very organization which bore responsibility for this appalling tragedy.[38] The ceremony and the tea-party were marked by no bitterness. Men can rarely understand a nationalism that is not their own.

The refugee traffic continued throughout 1941. It will never be known how many of the hulks foundered on the way. The deportations of those who reached Palestine went on as before, and as before Zionist propaganda made skillful use of the circumstances. The beautiful island of Mauritius, where Reza Shah Pahlevi was comfortably installed in retirement, was described as another Devil's Island, and the moderate deathrate[39] was described in terms of people who "died of tropical diseases." If some (or possibly many) of the refugees had some sense of gratitude to Great Britain,[40] the fact was artfully hushed up by the never-silent propagandists of the Jewish Agency. In February, 1942, another disaster occurred, closely resembling in some respects the sinking of the *Patria*.

A cattle boat that should have been out of commission long ago, the *Struma*, reached Istanbul in December, 1941, carrying 769 Jewish passengers from the Balkans, overcrowded in the usual obscene way. The

---

[37] Private information.

[38] *Jerusalem Post*, 29th November, 1960.

[39] 1940–44, 18.1 per thousand. Kirk, *op. cit.*

[40] Albert Hyamson gives a propaganda-free account of the relations of refugees sailing to Palestine and British authorities. "The British navy was always on the watch. This was the great safeguard, for it was known that no immigrant ship once seen would be left to sink with its human cargo. At the worst the prospective immigrants would be sent to Mauritius, later to Cyprus, to await there for an indefinite period permission to settle in Palestine." A little later he says of ships making for Palestine: "A short distance from that coast the ship would be detected and escorted into Haifa. Here ended the hazard of the journey. The passengers would be transferred, sometimes after a show of resistance, to a seaworthy vessel or vessels which the government of Palestine provided. It often happened that a few—the sick, pregnant women, perhaps orphan children—would be treated as exceptions and allowed to land."

passengers had, as usual, no valid Palestine visas, in which circumstances the Turkish authorities, as usual, forbade them to the land. The Jewish Agency remembered a similar case fourteen months before when another unseaworthy boat called the *Salvador* had reached the Bosporus from Bulgaria. The *Salvador* passengers had been forbidden to land for the same reason that the *Struma* passengers were forbidden now. The boat set out, presumably for Palestine, but was wrecked in a storm in which 231 out of the total 350 refugees were drowned. The survivors were brought back to Istanbul and the Turks took on themselves the responsibility of sending 59 of them back to Bulgaria. Zionists put the blame on the British as a matter of course. The remaining 70 reached Palestine and were allowed to stay. The Jewish Agency were determined to prevent a repetition of the *Salvador* tragedy in the case of the *Struma,* but they were also determined not to budge an inch from their essential principle: the flow of refugees was to come into Palestine and was to be diverted nowhere else: better that they should die than be so used as to enfeeble Zionist resolve. For two months the Agency argued with the administration over the *Struma,* beseeching Palestine visas which the administration refused to give, and for two months the refugees lived on board their stinking floating prison within sight of Turkish land, victims not only of active persecution, but victims also of the obstinacy of two supposedly friendly organizations.

At length the administration agreed to issue visas to the children on board between the ages of eleven and sixteen. Before arrangements for this were completed the Turkish authorities ordered the boat away from Istanbul and on the 24th of February the *Struma,* having been towed into the Black Sea, sank rapidly after an explosion. What had happened to cause the disaster was never known. There was only one survivor.

The Jewish Agency hastened to declare this another act of mass protest and mass suicide, and they laid all the blame for the disaster on the British administration. Placards in English and Hebrew were to be seen in many towns of Palestine declaring that Sir Harold MacMichael was "wanted for murder." The Agency found Gentile supporters in England. These were moved to action by the fact that there appeared to have been an unaccountable delay between the Anglo-Zionist agreement regarding visas for the children and communication of this to the Turkish authorities. The truth about this allegation is not yet known, and assertion in Parliament by the Colonial Secretary, Lord Moyne, that there was no culpable delay was emphatic but guarded. Zionist apologists overlook what may have been a decisive factor in the tragedy, that under the influence of the strong

German party in Turkey a wave of extreme anti-Semitism was rising in that country. But the point to be remembered here is that total British responsibility for the *Struma* disaster was accepted as the fact by the over-whelming majority of the Jews in Palestine.[41] Ever since the *Patria* episode, resentment against the policy of the White Paper had come to include dark suspicion of British aims; in many cases it now turned into passionate hatred.

The Zionist claim that the Jewish Agency did all that it could for the refugees, while no one else would do anything at all, is manifestly untenable, for if they had (to quote an authority) "concentrated on the humanitarian, instead of on the political and propagandist aspect," [42] it would have been very much easier for the British in Palestine to have saved these *Struma* refugees. But this consideration can again lead to another facile and mistaken generalization: that the narrow-minded Jewish Agency prevented a high-minded administration from accomplishing the deeds of mercy on which its heart was set. To believe that (to remember an utterance of the Duke of Wellington) is to believe anything. To say as much is not to subscribe to any of the fantastic anti-British stories put in circulation by Zionists or other zealots: it is to insist again on the appalling lack of imagination which more and more characterized the bewildered Palestine administration.

Imagination and government rarely go together, and this is as well, for the partnership as often as not results in deeds of hate and cruelty. But the Palestine administration was in a peculiar situation: it owed its very existence to an act of imagination, the Balfour Declaration, and therefore it could only logically fulfill its function in constantly imaginative action. It became the task of Palestine administrators on all levels to apply ordinary prosaic administrative method to the realization of a poetic dream. This impossibly difficult task was beyond them, inevitably. The result was a reaction which took the form of the growth of that large class of the "crass kind," indicated already. These people represented a reaction from the imagination and its burden, resulting in an extraordinary loss of initiative. This loss of initiative was, in the writer's opinion, the basic reason why the administration found itself at a loss whenever it had to deal with the recurrent problem of the refugees.

The administration rightly complained that the Jewish Agency in-

---

[41] The anti-British case in the *Struma* affair is given in Koestler, *op. cit.*, and in Daphne Trevor, *op. cit.* Both writers take no account of the state of political feeling in Turkey at the time. The British case is given in a note in Kirk, *op. cit.*, p. 244.

[42] Marlowe. *The Seat of Pilate.* London, 1959.

creased the difficulty of the task by taking the narrowest political view of the question, but one may well ask why the administration had to follow the Jewish Agency at all. A more virile, confident High Commission would have simply carried out its policy, informing the Jewish Agency and anticipating their hostile propaganda by propaganda of its own. Why did two months have to be wasted in fruitless argument while the wretches on board the *Struma* lingered in bestial misery outside Istanbul? Why could not the Palestine administration have immediately requested the Turks to send the refugees to Haifa and from there dispatch them to Mauritius or other colonial territory? Why did they have to treat the Jewish Agency rather than themselves as the rulers? The administration did not incur a charge of murder. They were guilty of the very different offense of being "wet"; of lacking in mental alertness and in the courage that comes from potent ideas: of acting in the spirit of Evian.

The real dilemma of the Zionists in their attempt to establish a Jewish fighting force may now begin to appear and to be recognized as elementary. They became confronted by the simple fact that it was impossible to conduct the two policies announced by Ben-Gurion with equal success. The fight against the White Paper could not fail to arouse British misgivings about the use to which the Jewish Agency would put a Jewish fighting force, and without British goodwill it was literally impossible to establish the force. The dilemma increased by compound interest. The fierce anti-British propaganda of the Agency had the natural effect of stirring the Yishuv into a Revisionist state of mind which they did not conceal, and this added to British alarm and suspicion, and this in turn made the Zionists more and more uncertain of the extent to which they could rely on the British.

Within the Haganah committee a party division, prompted by the paradox of the situation, formed in the course of the first two and a half years of the war. The right wing and the moderate socialists took the view that the way to obtain a Jewish army was through gradualism and an evolutionary policy. Their argument was that as many Palestine Jews as possible should join the British services, and one result of this would be that more Jewish units would inevitably come into being: the Jewish army would thus become a fact whether it was recognized or not. The right wing and their associates also voiced the common-sense idea that in a war against Hitler it was folly to make conditions about service, and a historian summarizes their view in this way: "If everybody did not pull his weight in the war-effort, which in the last resort was the guarantor of the

Yishuv's security, there would be, after the war, no Yishuv whose future was to be decided." [43]

In a period of Anglo-Zionist accord the right-wing view might have prevailed, and in spite of the intense anti-British mood which affected the Yishuv after the White Paper, it did prevail to a considerable extent, as the number of Palestine Jews who joined the services shows. But suspicion opened the way to a very different point of view which was given expression by the left wing. One of their number put it with admirable clarity. "We were afraid, and we still are today, that those in whose hands we place Haganah, the major part of our defensive strength, will not take us into account when it comes to defending this country. They will make their abstract calculations as to our units, calculations in which Palestine is just one point in a gigantic front line. But for us this point is the centre of the war. I am sure that a Jewish Force will have a different strategy altogether. It will not analyse the value of long or short supply lines in this battle. It will defend Palestine." [44] The words were spoken in the spring of 1942 when Rommel and the Afrika Korps faced the Eighth Army.

This was, of course, the great conditioning factor which gave a knife edge of anxiety to every phase of the debate. The possibility of a large-scale British evacuation of the Nile Delta had to be taken into account, and evacuation of Egypt could well mean a general British retreat from the whole eastern Mediterranean. This terrifying possibility gave ever-fresh urgency to the demand for a Jewish fighting force, and the *Struma* disaster came in the middle of this critical time to give it yet more. Thanks to the skill and violence of Zionist propaganda, Jews of Palestine saw this as a proof that the British would not willingly defend the National Home from the orgies of atrocity with which the Nazis would celebrate so tremendous an ideological prize. In April, 1942, Moshe Shertok attempted to force the issue by addressing a categorical and formal request to General Sir Claude Auchinleck. His main demands were for intensive training for the "Palestine Buffs," the formation of these companies into battalions, the expansion of the "legal Haganah" the J.S.P., and all these measures to be taken in the interests of the defense of Palestine." [45] Shertok addressed similar proposals to the military authorities in Jerusalem, and his efforts were at the same time massively supported in the Diaspora by Ben-Gurion and Dr. Weizmann, who were in America.

In the summer of 1942, while the threat from Rommel and the Afrika

[43] Bauer, *op. cit.*
[44] *Ibid*.
[45] Zionist Archives.

Korps lay over Egypt and the east Mediterranean, it looked as though the Zionists would obtain what they wanted, under the pressure of circumstances and Dr. Weizmann's diplomatic success in Washington. Winston Churchill was there in June, and after the fall of Tobruk to the Afrika Korps on the 20th, Weizmann took the occasion to write him an eloquent letter. He urged "the claim of Palestine Jewry to defend themselves through a single, organised military force of their own, fighting under their own flag alongside the armies of the United Nations." He went on, "At least two and probably three divisions could be raised in Palestine in this way for immediate service. If I may repeat what I said in the critical days of June, 1940, if we go down in Palestine, we are entitled to go down fighting. The Mandatory Power is in duty bound to grant us this elementary human right. I know that I speak for the great mass of Jews everywhere when I say that the refusal to grant this right will never be understood." [46]

Winston Churchill's goodwill toward the idea of a Jewish army was never in doubt and Weizmann, exercising his unique gift of persuasion, succeeded in giving Mr. Churchill added strength to assert his preference against the fears of his Middle East advisers. He obtained important American support from Sumner Welles, from General Marshall, from Henry Morgenthau, and through Morgenthau from the President himself. The latter even concerned himself with details. He telephoned to Sir John Dill, head of the British Military Mission, urging him to seek the appointment of Wingate as the force commander.[47] While these maneuvers were going forward, Shertok maintained the pressure on the Middle East Command and on London from the Jewish Agency in Palestine.

The only result of this activity was the transformation of the Palestine Buffs into the Palestine Regiment. This was as far as the administration would go, and they went thus far reluctantly, to placate Mr. Churchill. At no preceding time had they had such strong incentives against a pro-Zionist policy in the military sphere. As always, they had their accustomed nervousness about Arab reactions, but in addition they were in possession of disturbing information about the direction of Zionist tendencies. The item which caused them and British Army Intelligence the greatest uneasiness was the knowledge that Jews who became members of British services and had formerly been members of Haganah (this was the situation

[46] Zionist Archives and quoted in Bauer, *op. cit.*
[47] Weizmann's correspondence with Miss Dugdale in the Weizmann Archives.

of the majority of serving Jews) [48] remained under Haganah direction and considered themselves under the orders not only of their commanding officers but of the Rama as well. They knew that men serving on lines of communication took the opportunity to secure arms for Haganah, and there were many cases of British soldiers corrupted into stealing and selling arms. There was a manifest influx of extreme elements into the body politic of Zionism and it was known that, in the debates within the Haganah committees, the possibility of using the force against the White Paper-minded British was freely discussed.[49] Such knowledge was all the more alarming as it came at a time when the extremist trend of Zionism had received definitive expression from the Zionist leadership. That belongs to the next chapter. What needs to be remembered here is that for a variety of reasons the administration and the Middle East Command remained deaf to the pleadings of the Jews for an army.

One other reason, unconnected with the foregoing, has been deduced for the failure of this enterprise, so dear to every Jewish heart. It seems that the military necessity to form a Jewish army was unconsciously called in question by the action of the Jews themselves, action which in this case was entirely to their credit. To appreciate how this came about it is necessary to remember again how desperately anxiety weighed on men in the eastern Mediterranean, and most of all on Jews of Palestine, between the beginning of Rommel's counterattack in January, 1942 and Montgomery's victory at El Alamein in October. That Auchinleck by his last masterly action had turned the tide by July was realized by very few. He and his staff had no gift for manipulating opinion, and the strength of the British position was virtually known to no one.

In these circumstances the Jews found themselves unable to play a cool political game. As the danger increased, or appeared to increase, the recruiting figures went up. Between June and October, 5,196 enlisted. The administration and G.H.Q. could well ask why they should run the political risks attaching to the formation of a Jewish army, when Jewish recruiting figures could hardly be higher than they were.

Shertok complained to London[50] that the failure to establish a Jewish force discouraged the Yishuv from giving of their best, but the behavior of the Jews completely contradicted him.

[48] Sixty percent of them according to figures in the *Zionist Review,* 18th June, 1948. Hurewitz seems to go further and speaks of "the enormous majority."
[49] Private information agreeing with Bauer, *op. cit.* and Kirk.
[50] Zionist Archives quoted in Bauer, *op. cit.*

Dr. Yehuda Bauer sums up what happened as a result. "In [normal] times [when German tanks were not standing near the gates of Alexandria] the British had no need for a large number of Palestinian Jewish recruits. In times of stress, when they were needed, they were forthcoming without a Jewish Force." He concludes: "The force was a Jewish, not a British need."

This was the dominating circumstance and, given the surrounding circumstances which emerged more and more clearly from the increasing tension between the mandatory and the Zionists, it explains why, despite strenuous support in the British Government, a Jewish military unit, drawn from the Yishuv in Palestine, did not go into action under a Jewish flag until March, 1945.

11 THE STRESS OF TRAGEDY

The autumn of 1942 was a time of changing circumstances for the Jews, of relief and deepening anxiety, and of new initiative. The victory of El Alamein and the British advance westward along the African shore meant that the Jews of Palestine could at last forget the long-threatening nightmare; no longer did they have to contemplate the possibility of seeing the National Home destroyed by the armies of Hitler. This was a great thing, but it meant little if any lessening of the tension in which Jews lived. Even at the height of the danger the Jewish Agency, and great numbers of their following, had looked to the future and remained preoccupied to an extraordinary extent with political questions; now that they had some leisure to plan for the future they were less disposed than ever to forget Jerusalem. Soon the Jews were oppressed by a new anxiety: it was possible that with the length of time that it would take to defeat the Nazis, the war would be lost, so far as the Jews were concerned, whatever the outcome.

In January of 1942 Nazi policy toward the Jews entered its second, clear, defined phase. A meeting was held in a house in Wannsee near Berlin under the chairmanship of Reinhardt Heydrich. He had been in close session with Hitler and was authorized to express the Führer's will: it was decided that the inconsistencies of German policy regarding racially unacceptable people, especially Jews and gypsies, must be ended. There was to be an *Endlösung,* a "final solution," which would take the form of the systematic slaughter of these people in Europe. This meant killing about eight million people. Such a program required elaborate administrative training, skill, and apparatus. All this took time to acquire. Too severe a shock to feelings was to be avoided in the interests of German morale, and the secret was well kept for over six months. The first reliable and accurate information about the new policy seems to have reached the West in August when Rabbi Stephen S. Wise of New York was told about it by Gerhard Riegner, the representative of the World Jewish Congress in Geneva.

Stories of impending massacre had been coming out of Germany since 1933, and they were treated by anti-Nazis as useful propaganda material but with scepticism. There was reason for this. After the fall of France, for example, it had been confidently reported that the Germans planned enormous million-fold transportation measures whose effect would be to terminate the existence of a nation. Horrible cruelties were practiced on the French but this was not among them. A reluctance to believe atrocity tales had been inherited from the First World War. People remembered how they had been taken in by propaganda about "frightfulness" and they had a dim mass impulse not to be taken in again. Reluctance to believe the incredible worst about the Nazis may be described as the historical revenge of Kaiser Wilhelm II for all the libels put upon that foolish man's name.

But intelligence about the final solution could not be disbelieved for long. Exchanged and escaped prisoners and fugitives, especially those who had been in Poland, brought the story with them again and again. It came to Palestine in November, 1942, with two Jewish women, members of a Zionist communal settlement, who had contrived to get out of Poland in an exchange of internees.[1]

In December of 1942 the fact was officially accepted, and the Allied governments issued a formal condemnation of "this bestial policy of cold-

[1] Yehuda Bauer. A communication.

blooded extermination." This was very proper, but not of any great help. What could they do to help? Not much, in truth, but they could, in any reasonable assessment, have opened their gates wide to any Jews or gypsies who might succeed in escaping. But 1942 was a year of closing doors. The common fear of the time that enemy agents traveled as disguised refugees seems to have led to the harsher visa regulations established in the United States in the previous year, and the example was now followed and exceeded elsewhere in America. In April, 1942, entry was denied to all people, Jewish or Gentile, from the Axis countries into Cuba, Mexico, the Argentine, Bolivia, Chile, Paraguay, and Panama. The only countries to follow a liberal policy in this respect were Ecuador and once again the Dominican Republic. At the other end of the world, the Turkish Government was beginning to put into operation the anti-Semitic policy which reached a climax in 1943, and the mandatory administration found a new problem on its hands when Turkish Jews began to come to Palestine in increasing numbers. Nineteen forty-two was the beginning of a mercifully short period which was probably the most terrible that the Jewish people had to undergo at any time in their history since the Roman campaigns of the first and second centuries. Zion was their only hope.

Before the news of the final solution had reached anyone in the Allied camp, a very remarkable initiative had been taken in America by the Zionist leadership. The event occurred in the Biltmore Hotel in New York where some six hundred American Jews, including some non-Zionists, and sixty-seven visiting Zionists met in conference from the 9th to the 11th of May, 1942. Almost every shade of Zionist opinion in the free world was represented.

Weizmann and Ben-Gurion were both present. They were not in accord; between them there had arisen the familiar and inescapable clash of an older and a younger generation of politicians: Weizmann wanted to continue in patient negotiation with the British government for a Jewish army, and with British and American leaders for a reversal of the White Paper; Ben-Gurion wanted to excite Americans into supporting a swift and revolutionary change of Palestine policy in which the British would be forced to acquiesce. While Weizmann was still thinking in terms of many thousands of immigrating Jews to be slowly built up into a majority according to the old Zionist pattern, Ben-Gurion was thinking in millions, in terms of a modern version of the great migrations of early history, one in which a quarter or perhaps more of all the Jews in the world would make their home in Eretz Israel. Weizmann thought, with justice, that it was folly to risk a breach with England while he was negotiating for a

Jewish army; Ben-Gurion thought, also with justice, that the way to get American support was to "think big" and propose simple, drastic, and stirring programs.[2]

Ben-Gurion decided to use the Biltmore conference for the definition of just such a drastic program as he considered necessary to his purpose, and he did it in such a way that Weizmann was more or less compelled to go along with him. Four months earlier Weizmann had written an article entitled "Palestine's Role in the Solution of the Jewish Problem" for the well-known monthly magazine of New York *Foreign Affairs*. It was not one of his most interesting writings, and did little more than repeat (thereby giving them some official blessing) numerous American Zionist statements of aim calling for the establishment of a Jewish State.[3] In May, 1942, Ben-Gurion used Dr. Weizmann's article as the basis for a resolution to be put to the vote at the Biltmore Hotel meeting. The article suited his purpose well. Weizmann had written that a policy should be announced, and the Arabs "clearly told that the Jews will be encouraged to settle in Palestine and will control their own immigration; that here Jews who so desire will be able to achieve their freedom and self-government by establishing a state of their own." In drafting the resolution based on these words Ben-Gurion was careful not to depart from their sense, but to give them more of an extremist ring. He demanded "that the gates of Palestine be opened, and that the Jewish Agency be vested with the control of immigration into Palestine and with the necessary authority for building up the country, including the development of its unoccupied and uncultivated lands, and that Palestine be established as a Jewish Commonwealth, integrated in the structure of the new democratic world." The resolution was adopted with no contrary vote, though it was not a clear victory. The American Jewish Committee, a formidable body led by Judge Proskauer and credited with much political influence, refused to participate in the conference.[4] More disturbingly, the Mapai delegation from Palestine had abstained from voting. Nevertheless, technically unopposed, the resolution was there to be used.

Dr. Weizmann was exasperated by the action of the conference, and the use by it of what he had written. He made it quite plain in his letters of

[2] Yehuda Bauer, *Scripta Hierosolymitana*.
[3] *Vide* Kirk, *op. cit.* pp. 241-244 for details of the principal statements.
[4] This appears to have been the result of a temporary breach between Proskauer and Ben-Gurion dating from the previous year when Proskauer took some offense at Ben-Gurion's urging him to use the influence of the A. J. C. against American neutralism.

the time[5] that his article in *Foreign Affairs* had not been intended by him as an active political move, but merely as one of those formal statements of the ultimate Zionist aim which had to be reiterated from time to time in order to keep it fresh before the eyes of his followers. He believed that while Ben-Gurion's rash initiative might provide excitement for the Zionists of New York it could only wreck the delicate negotiations he was conducting.

The antagonism between the two men came visibly to the surface. Ben-Gurion, described by Professor Kirk as "the Lloyd George of the Yishuv and like him 'almost monstrously photogenic,'"[6] stood in those days for Zionist democracy. There was little of the democrat about Weizmann. Ben-Gurion urged that a high and active degree of collective responsibility should be maintained in all phases of negotiations, and this was the direct opposite of Weizmann's method. One may suspect a certain class antagonism between the two men. Weizmann, polished and sensitive, at his best when exerting influence in private conference on statesmen of the Whig or Tory kind with whom he shared culture and taste in a somewhat aristocratic tradition; Ben-Gurion, the personification of popular leadership, at his best when he could use the arts of dramatic public speaking which Weizmann despised as vulgar rabble-rousing. In the days following the Biltmore conference sharp letters were exchanged between the two from their hotels in New York,[7] and Ben-Gurion brought the quarrel openly to the conference table, violently criticizing Weizmann's tendency to use his position as president of the Zionist organization as a means of arrogating to himself the right to speak for the Jews of the world, without reference to any other Jew in the world. In the conduct of the increasing dispute Ben-Gurion soon overreached himself. He forgot that however out of tune Weizmann might be with the spirit of Biltmore, his name was a most honored one in the United States, and the new leader's partisan denunciations compared ill with the dignified reserve in public of the older man. American opinion turned against Ben-Gurion, and he soon lost, or rather appeared to lose, at least so far as his personal position was concerned, the whole advantage that he had gained over Weizmann at the Biltmore conference.

But he had one decisive advantage over his great antagonist. He was younger, harder, and therefore freer. Weizmann was sixty-eight, not a man of great age, but one who had grown older than his years. In the

[5] Weizmann Archives. Letters to Mrs. Dugdale.
[6] Kirk, *op. cit.* He quotes Philip Toynbee.
[7] Weizmann Archives.

February of 1942 his eldest son, Michael, had been killed in action, and the blow had crushed him. He still had some great and brilliant services to render to the Zionist cause, but after the death of this young man as an officer in the Royal Air Force, he was never quite the same again. Slowly, often held at bay by this powerful adversary, age nevertheless closed in on him. He suffered ill health and his sight began to fail. People occasionally noticed some weakening of his formidable powers of judgment, and at moments he tended to live unrealistically in the past. He still believed that Zionism should and could grow by gradual and evolutionary stages, and thus in peace, but he did not adequately recognize that after the Biltmore conference he, as the advocate of this belief, had been brought into a radical conflict with Ben-Gurion and that the Yishuv must take sides; he overlooked that to maintain the political ascendancy that was his due from the dispute after Biltmore, he needed to act with the utmost vigilance and alertness.

In these circumstances Weizmann made a fatal mistake: he did not go to Palestine. In Eretz Israel he was becoming a somewhat remote and shadowy figure; he was given honor and respect but more and more in the way that these things are offered to ancestors. The Jews of Palestine, outside the councils of the Jewish Agency, and Va'ad Leumi, knew nothing about the Biltmore conference except that it proclaimed the Zionist aim of a state, and they had no reason to suppose that Weizmann had not led the initiative equally with Ben-Gurion. While Weizmann went to London, Ben-Gurion, the object of vituperation in America, went to Palestine.

The status of the Biltmore resolution was in doubt. On arrival in Palestine Ben-Gurion set to work to give it full and official ratification. He succeeded. From Herzl's day the Zionist organization had been governed by a species of republican two-chamber constitution. A General Council (described from German as "The Greater Actions Committee") was in theory the supreme authority. It gave expression to its policy at the Zionist congresses, and its decisions were then given practical shape by a Central Executive ("The Smaller Actions Committee"). Neither the General Council nor the congresses could possibly meet during the war, so without opposition the full measure of democratic authority became temporarily vested in the Central Executive. In 1942 all the members of this body were Palestinian Jews.[8] At the request of Ben-Gurion they were summoned for the 10th of November.

The rumors of mass slaughter of Jews by the Nazis were receiving continuous confirmation from witnesses reaching Palestine. The resulting

[8] J. C. Hurewitz, *The Struggle for Palestine*. New York, 1950.

climate of opinion has been perfectly described by Professor Kirk: "As the war reached the 'end of the beginning' and the leaderless Arabs were vaguely thinking of the 'day of reckoning,' the Zionists were being irrevocably impelled along the path of political assertion by the mortal plight of their kinsmen and co-religionists in Axis-occupied Europe, and by the realisation that Britain would not compel the Arabs to submit to further Jewish mass immigration into Palestine." [9] After Ben-Gurion had effectively roused the Yishuv at public meetings, the Central Executive met for the purpose of debating the Biltmore program, and, as the new leadership confidently expected, giving it by its vote a complete constitutional character. Yet the task proved more formidable than had been supposed.

Opposition came from several quarters. The German and Austrian Jews had recently founded a party called New Immigration, and their program included total identification of Zionism with the British war effort. They were averse to any policy of fighting the White Paper until Nazism was defeated. They were not moderates in theory. The party's ultimate aim was Jewish sovereignty in a predominantly Jewish Palestine and they feared that any early move to statehood must result in partition to which they were strongly opposed. As the German-speaking Jews formed over 10 percent of the Yishuv their opposition was a serious threat to the Biltmore policy.

During the early summer of 1942 the extreme left faction known as the Young Watchman Party (Hahomer Hatzair) had gone into coalition with a binationalist group led by Chaim Kalvaryski and called the League for Jewish-Arab Rapprochement and Cooperation. Chaim Kalvaryski was a man of seventy-five, one of the pre-Herzl pioneers. He was the spokesman of a genuine and generously friendly policy toward Arabs, and he severely criticized the Jewish Agency for not devoting their efforts to seeking contacts and agreements in the world of Islam rather than in the West. Hahomer Hatzair joined Kalvaryski in a Marxist spirit. They pursued binationalism as part of a program for uniting the workers of the world.

Another binationalist group had formed in September of 1942 and was led by Judah Magnes. It was known as Ihud or Union and had been joined by Henrietta Szold, the foundress of the American Women's Zionist Organization. The protagonists of Biltmore looked with more alarm on Ihud than on any other of their Jewish opponents and the Central Executive even demanded the expulsion of Ihud members from the Zionist organization. The reason for this special hostility would seem to have been that

[9] Kirk, *op. cit.*

since both Magnes and Miss Szold had valuable American connections, the leadership feared that they might deflect the growing American concern with Zionism away from Biltmore.[10]

All this opposition, to which was added a conservative element that looked with disapproval on the new leader who was ousting the venerable old leader, might have shaken the Biltmore policy, but nothing of the kind happened. The reason was the failure of the binationalists. They were the most formidable part of the opposition to Ben-Gurion, but their policy showed no sign of advance or success at any time. In spite of strenuous efforts on the part of League and Ihud members, especially in Syria, there was, as before the war, no reciprocal action from any Arab party or any individual in authority. This fatally weakened all the devoted efforts of Kalvaryski, Hahomer Hatzair, and Magnes.

The administration might have found advantage in the situation, and obtained a moderation of the Biltmore policy, if they could have achieved the very difficult political feat of encouraging the binationalists while remaining friends with the Agency. There is no available evidence that they tried to do this. There is little reason to suppose that they would have succeeded if they had tried.

The Jewish Agency attitude toward the British hardened under the stimulus of dangerous political opposition. They maintained hope, with good reason, that Winston Churchill would honor his pledges to Weizmann for a pro-Zionist policy, but however much encouragement they received from London, the Agency could at no time detect any relaxation in Sir Harold MacMichael's conduct of the administration. This confirmed them in their long-held belief that if they yielded any detail of their case regarding the legality of the White Paper, especially the right of Jews to enter Palestine, the Colonial Office and the administration would seize on their action as an opportunity to confine the National Home within limits which excluded the possibility of statehood, at least in any foreseeable future. The events of 1942 strengthened the growing Jewish resolve to establish Israel in Palestine as soon as conceivably possible. The Yishuv became more and more convinced that this was the only answer to the persecutions. It was the weakness of the mandatory that until the end it could not see the connection between the tragedy overwhelming the Jews in Europe and the intensification, indeed the transformation of Zionism. It was the greatness of Ben-Gurion as a leader that he grasped this fact fully and from the beginning.

So it fell out that when the Central Executive met on the 10th of No-

[10] Hurewitz, *op. cit.*

vember the Biltmore resolution was confirmed by twenty-one votes to four.

Public opinion in England and America was growing restless at the thought of the German campaigns of extermination. It was a time when English opinion was ill-tempered, changeable, and liable to tantrums which could be dangerous to the men in power. Nearly three years of isolation had had their effect, and there was a longing to break out in action if only to get rid of the oppressive claustrophobia which afflicted the besieged. It was the time when "Second Front Now" was chalked on walls, when Russians seemed like nothing so much as great flights of benevolent angels, and the delay of the invasion of Europe caused the immense popularity of Mr. Churchill to give way to frenzied and puzzling bouts of mass dislike. There was a reflection through sympathy of this siege mentality in the United States, and at least one eminent American professor (better not named) was driven to write a book in which he elaborately proved that the reason for the delay of the second front was that Winston Churchill was in close and secret accord with Adolf Hitler for the prosecution of war against Russia. It was a time when even the least Munichois of politicians were well-advised to appease the irrational hungers of popular irritation. After the German occupation of the whole of France, when the area of the extermination campaign had reached its maximum extent, there was much demand to know why the government did not "do something about it."

In these circumstances Lord Halifax, now British ambassador in Washington, approached the American government on the 20th of January, 1943, with a request for some common Anglo-American action to alleviate the distress of the persecuted in Europe. The American government replied a month later with a request for exploratory talks which were held shortly afterward at Ottawa. One result of these talks was most unfortunate. Both governments issued statements about the number of Jewish refugees whom they had received in their territories since 1933, but later research by competent statisticians showed that some of this claim, perhaps the whole of it, was fantastically exaggerated. The main result of the talks was the decision to hold a conference, and this was done in April, 1943. It met in Bermuda from the 19th to the 30th.

In the interests of security the minutes were not published till the following November. They were not found to be very exciting: it was decided to enlarge the Inter-Governmental Committee for Refugees; to guarantee the finances of this body; to endeavor to save persecuted children from France; to maintain refugees who succeeded in reaching neutral territory in Switzerland, Spain, Portugal and Turkey; to approach the French National Committee in Algeria with a request for refugee settlement in Madagascar. Bermuda proved to be another Evian with the difference that whereas at Evian the assembled governments could have done much, at Bermuda there was very little that anyone could do beyond giving sops to opinion. As noted, one of these sops appears to have taken the form of sham statistics.[11]

The conference was not entirely futile. It gave rise to the formation of the United Nations Relief and Rehabilitation Administration, known as UNRRA, and indirectly to the American War Refugee Board (WRB), but so far as mitigating the plight of European Jewry was concerned it was of very little use. Zionist apologists have little to say about it. They have not used it as a subject of reproach, except in one very odd respect. The only really constructive item in the minutes was the decision to obtain French agreement to refugee asylum in Madagascar. This has been criticized on the grounds that shortly before the war a German-Polish commission of inquiry had reported unfavorably on Madagascar as a place for European settlement. Mark Wischnitzer, one of the fairest of Zionist commentators, even goes so far as to describe this effort as "deplorable." The truth of the matter seems clear: the Bermuda Conference undertook humanitarian duties without reference to Zionist political aims, so it was of no interest to Zionists, and its weak result was not regretted by them.[12]

During this year the Zionist new course began to affect Palestine in a way that surprised and alarmed the Jewish Agency. There were signs of a revival of terrorism. The Irgun Zvai Leumi (Etzel) had followed the

---

[11] For details of these statistics see the appendix, p. 377.

[12] Mr. Henry Morgenthau, Jr., reports, according to Wischnitzer, a scandalous case of neglected opportunity: while the Bermuda Conference was sitting, seventy thousand Jews, it is alleged, could have been rescued from Rumania against funds deposited in Switzerland, according to information reaching the U.S. in March, 1943, but after seven months of Anglo-American discussion the project was turned down because of Foreign Office objections regarding the difficulty of settling so large a number. Research suggests that Mr. Morgenthau's facts are incorrect. The first news of the proposed transaction appeared in the *New York Times* in mid-February. Dr. Weizmann officially requested the British Embassy in Washington to explore the matter, and Sir Lewis Namier took a similar initiative in London. After approximately three weeks the British and American governments concluded that the offer was fraudulent, and this was conveyed to Weizmann by the Washington Embassy. Thereafter, so far as appears, the matter was not revived by him or the Jewish Agency. It would seem incredible that the agency would not have pressed the matter further if they had had reason to suppose that the offer was in fact genuine. Private information.

Jewish Agency's lead and had refrained from any action which might hamper the British war effort, but there had been no such self-restraint on the part of a smaller even more fanatic group. These were called the Sternists after the name of their founder, a strange and formidable young man who was somewhat Byronic in character, or rather somewhat as Byron in his Satanic pose liked men to imagine him. He was called Abraham Stern. In his youth he had shown himself academically brilliant and been admired as a student by Judah Magnes. He was a poet whose work, though intolerable rant in translation, has been admired in the original by serious critics. His philosophy, which he imposed on his disciples, was a caricature of Zionism and primitive Judaism, driven on by an almost insane single-mindedness. All opponents of the National Home, so he held, were to be fought *à outrance* all the time; the end justified the foulest means; all compromise was treachery; there could be no radical distinction between German Nazies or the British because both were opposed to the total realization of the Jewish State and there were no degrees in mortal sin. His followers, remembering an ancient hero of the Roman oppression, called him "Yair" or "the Illuminator." He had been imprisoned in 1939 and freed in 1940. His mind was infested with hate and he hated Jews who disagreed with him more than he did any Gentile, and in consequence most of his later career of crime had been directed against Jewish opponents; in January, 1942, the Sternists murdered two officials of Histadruth, and when they fought the police they concentrated their vengeance on the Jewish personnel. In February of 1942, shortly after the capture of twenty of his men, Stern was killed in a police raid.

The whole Yishuv had looked with horror on the Illuminator and his following, and during his lifetime they gave no support to this ruthless fanatic, who in addition to his other misdeeds, came into some sort of treasonable relationship with Italian Fascists. But during 1943, in the changing climate of opinion, this disapproval began to lessen. In the summer of that year the group revived under a new name, that of the Fighters for the Freedom of Israel, the F.F.I. In November they successfully contrived the escape from prison of the twenty Sternists captured the year before.

The Stern group was always very small and its revival by itself would not have meant very much. But it became known during 1943 that the much larger and more important Etzel were preparing to take the field once more. The circumstances were tangled. Irgun had found new allies among the Polish units stationed in Palestine. Many Poles sympathized with Jewish feelings that they had been betrayed by the British, and their

2. *Abdullah ibn Hussein, Emir of Transjordan, with his escort, October, 1922 (above). Radio Times Hulton Picture Library.*

3. *Field Marshal Lord Plumer and Lady Plumer, February, 1924 (below). Radio Times Hulton Picture Library.*

4. Ceremony to honor the founding of the Einstein Institute, Jerusalem, April, 1925. Wearing academic robes (from left): Lord Arthur Balfour; Sir Herbert Samuel; Dr. Judah Magnes; and Dr. Chaim Weizmann.

5. *Lloyd George speaking at a Zionist Federation dinner, 1931.*
Radio Times Hulton Picture Library.

8. *Sidney Webb (Lord Passfield) and his wife, Beatrice Webb, 1929 (above). Radio Times Hulton Picture Library.*

9. *Dr. Chaim Weizmann (right). Radio Times Hulton Picture Library.*

10. *Haj Amin el Husseini, Grand Mufti of Jerusalem, October, 1951 (above). Radio Times Hulton Picture Library.*

11. *Sir Herbert Samuel, March, 1929 (below). Radio Times Hulton Picture Library.*

12. *Viscount William Robert Wellesley Peel, January, 1924 (above). Radio Times Hulton Picture Library.*

13. *Professor Reginald Coupland (below). Howard Coster.*

14. *Jewish immigrant ship entering Haifa harbor, July, 1946.*
Imperial War Museum, London.

15. *Demonstration against the White Paper, Jerusalem, May,*
1939. Banners read: "Honor to Balfour and Noble England."
"We want surrender." "The wicked policy will not be imple-
mented—Jewish Palestine will be built." Zvi Oron.

16. *Ernest Bevin and his wife (far right) at the Labour Party Conference in Blackpool, 1945. Radio Times Hulton Picture Library.*

17. *David Ben Gurion in the Parliament in Jerusalem. Radio Times Hulton Picture Library.*

18. *A Jewish arms cache discovered by British security forces in September, 1946 (above). Imperial War Museum, London.*

19. *Some of the arms found there (below). Imperial War Museum, London.*

20. *Irgun terrorists blow up the King David Hotel, July, 1946 (above). This photograph was taken at the moment of the second explosion. Imperial War Museum, London.*

21. *Jewish immigrants being deported to Cyprus soon after their arrival at Haifa in August, 1946 (below). Imperial War Museum, London.*

22. *Haifa railway station blown up by terrorists, September, 1946. Imperial War Museum, London.*

23. *Menachem Begin (right). By courtesy of Messrs. W. H. Allen, from* The Revolt *by Menachem Begin.*

themselves in public against the reviving terror. It was otherwise in private, but in public they only condemned with caution, and when they expressed disapproval they were always careful to indicate that the ultimate blame lay with the British. By this hesitant conduct the Agency, much against its will, bore a share of responsibility for the increasing record of atrocity.

It is difficult to say whether this particular policy of appeasement toward those whom they condemned in principle was effective or not; a harsh anti-Irgun anti-Sternist movement by the Jewish Agency might have had no more result among the restless Yishuv than to unseat the ruling committee in favor of one in some genuine sympathy with the terrorists, thus increasing the area and scale of their ill-doing; on the other hand it is arguable that it was precisely the morally timorous, tight-rope-walking conduct of the Agency that gave the terrorists the chance they needed, and which they exploited, thus infecting great numbers of the Yishuv with their horrible state of mind. (In the writer's opinion the Jewish Agency, as advocates of a program that had majority approval, could at this time have safely resisted the terrorist revival, but one must not forget that these were years when all minds were to some extent perverted by the familiar violence of war.) What can be said for certain is that evidence for apparent sympathy between the Agency and the terrorists enormously increased the ill-feeling between the mandatory and the National Home.

The first occasion when the administration and the Agency clashed over the new terrorism occurred as early as January, 1943. It is not certain whether Etzel or the Sternists were involved in the incident, or whether it was merely symptomatic of a new and dangerous state of angry feeling. What had happened was as follows: after the victory of El Alamein Jewish recruiting had fallen off, as was to be expected, and gangs of zealots took to visiting the houses of supposed shirkers in order to punish them, all in the style of the early fascist bands and the German Brownshirts of more recent memory. Houses were wrecked, sometimes with bombs, and the traditional horror of tarring and feathering and torture by castor oil were resorted to.[16] The administration issued regulations to prevent this. They expected support from the Jewish Agency, but instead, and greatly to their astonishment, they received protests. Apologists contrived arguments which laid the blame for the persecution not on the persecutors but on the administration which was trying to stop it. Later one Gentile en-

[16] Hurewitz, Kirk, op. cit. Personal recollection: the writer was in Palestine at the time.

thusiast even went so far as to describe the atrocities by the innocuous and almost laudatory term "conflicts of conscience," and expressed the matter thus: "Other nations spared themselves these conflicts of conscience through conscription. It was not the Jews' fault that there was no military conscription." [17] It is a consistent defect of colonial regimes, and one of the strongest arguments against them, that the subject people are induced to lay all the blame for all things on the rulers. In this case the refusal of the Jewish Agency to make common cause against these disgusting practices increased, out of all proportion to a relatively minor episode, the belief that the Jewish Agency and such bodies as the Stern group were at one.

The misconception became stronger later in the same year through an incident that received wide and calculated publicity. As noted already, the British Intelligence departments in Egypt and Palestine were worried by the continual sale of arms to Jews by soldiers in poorly disciplined regiments. In the summer two British deserters were run to ground in Haifa. On interrogation they gave a sensational account of the large-scale arms-trafficking in which they were dealing, and they implicated leading members of Histadruth and Ben-Gurion himself. This provoked Ben-Gurion, understandably exasperated by the publicity organized by British information services, to a violent counterattack in which he asserted that the court had acted under anti-Semitic influence. In keeping with the new spirit of absolute uncompromise, he opened a new phase in Zionist propaganda which lasted to the end of the mandate: henceforth to be anti-Zionist was to be anti-Semitic; to disapprove of Jewish territorial nationalism was to be a Nazi.

The affair was drawn out in an unsuccessful attempt to put an end to Jewish gun-running; the first trial was followed by the trials in November of three Jewish men who were implicated in the traffic. They all received heavy sentences, and this aroused their fellow-Jews to a genuine sense of grievance, for concurrently with these trials cases of gun-running between British troops and Arabs were coming before the courts and being leniently dealt with. As an American intelligence officer justly remarked, the administration was concentrating on the gun-running that was dangerous. If they had concentrated equally on it all they would have had an overcrowding problem in the jails. No Jew could be expected to fall in with this point of view in 1943. Instead they had a sense of injury upon injury. [18]

[17] Daphne Trevor, *op. cit.*
[18] For further details of the arms trials see Kirk, *op. cit.*

248 / CROSSROADS TO ISRAEL

The arms trials, no great event in themselves, brought a new situation to a head. It was well described by the Middle East Commander of this time, Sir Henry Maitland Wilson.

"By January, 1944," he wrote in a dispatch, "the attitude of the Jewish Agency towards the Government had hardened to such an extent that any action conflicting with the Biltmore Programme or for enforcing the White Paper met with opposition and obstruction. The Jewish Agency was in some respects arrogating to itself the powers and status of an independent Jewish Government. It no longer attempted to deny the existence of arms caches, but claimed the right not only to hold arms for self-defence but to resist any attempt on the part of the authorities to locate them."

The White Paper was now being fought with a vengeance, as if there were no war. In this atmosphere the terrorist organizations could flourish and in January of 1944 there occurred a decisive event. Irgun publicly called off the truce with the administration. They did this by means of a widely circulated declaration from which the following is a representative quotation.

Four years have passed since the war began and all the hopes that beat in your hearts then have evaporated without a trace. We have not been accorded international status; no Jewish Army has been set up; the gates of the country have not been opened. The British regime has sealed its shameful betrayal of the Jewish people and there is no moral basis whatever for its presence in Eretz Israel. We shall fearlessly draw our conclusions. There is no longer any armistice between the Jewish people and the British Administration which hands our brothers over to Hitler. Our people is at war with this regime, war to the end. This then is our demand: immediate transfer of power; Eretz Israel to have a provisional Hebrew Government. We shall fight. Every Jew in the Homeland will fight. The God of Israel, the Lord of Hosts, will aid us. There will be no retreat. Freedom or death.[19]

From now on Irgun and the Sternists, though following somewhat different policies, grew to be inescapably allied, in fact if not always in theory. Their major difference in 1944 was on the targets of terrorism. The Sternists, so far as can be deduced, for there is no first-hand record from any of them, favored a policy of indiscriminate atrocity against any British person or establishment of interest. Irgun favored a policy which they took to be a form of self-restraint. They refrained from attack against

[19] Begin, op. cit.

any British military installation, so long as the war was in progress, but concentrated their destructive energies on those civilian installations necessary to orderly rule by the mandatory. They believed that they would thus achieve the double gain of fighting the war and the White Paper simultaneously and without detriment to either cause. With that self-approving naïveté which can so often appall his reader, Begin described this plan as "true political wisdom."

By the early autumn of 1944 the Sternists had, since the beginning of the year, murdered fifteen men, a small number for the length of time when compared with their later performance. Following tradition they had kept to their policy of including a fairly high proportion of Jews among their victims. Irgun in the meantime had wrecked four police stations and the Tel Aviv offices of the Department of Light Industry. The most ambitious terrorist enterprise of this time was an attempt by the Sternists to assassinate Sir Harold MacMichael, an act of no conceivable political purpose as Sir Harold's term of office was about to expire, as had been publicly announced. The attempt was made on the 8th of August. It failed. The High Commissioner was unhurt but three of his staff were wounded.[20]

Knowing of the reluctance of the Jewish Agency to join with the British in action against Jews, Begin, now the Irgun Commander, seems to have thought that if he could meet Ben-Gurion he would be able to talk him into partnership. His record suggests such a line of thought, and his book can be believed at this point where the author shows himself and his following in a deplorable light and the Jewish Agency in a very favorable one. Throughout the spring and summer of 1944 Begin tried to obtain an interview with Ben-Gurion who refused. At length Ben-Gurion agreed to send a Haganah committee member as his representative. This was Dr. Moshe Sneh. He seems to have carried out his mission with great efficiency, putting before Begin the most cogent arguments, and those most likely to appeal to a Zionist, as to why a descent into the nightmare of terrorism was impolitic, to put the matter no higher. He argued in vain.

He opened by reminding Begin of his allegiance. The Jewish Agency, he said, and no one else formed the body responsible for the representation of the Jewish people, to which Begin gave the rhetorical and not very clear reply that this was not so because Irgun had been in the right for longer than the Agency. "We have the consciousness of a mission," he added, "for better or for worse that is how it is." In another part of his record Begin indicates by an epigram the philosophy of life behind his sense of mission: "I fight, therefore I am."

[20] Report to Parliament. Hansard Society for Parliamentary Government.

Dr. Sneh then put to Begin the telling point that he and his Etzel colleagues could not possibly have the information necessary for the formulation of Zionist policy. This seems to have riled Begin who by his own account prided himself on statesmanlike abilities, for he gave the following warm and nonsensical answer: "First of all, we have the information. Secondly, I don't believe in 'deep secrets.' In this era of radio we know enough."

Against this wall of obstinacy and blindness Sneh still retained the patience to try to get through. With some boldness he gave Begin some of the information which Irgun could not at the moment possess: namely that on Winston Churchill's initiative the British government was working out a partition scheme somewhat on the lines of the Peel recommendations. He repeated a remark, which has an authentic ring, supposedly made by Mr. Churchill to Dr. Weizmann: "I carved up Palestine once. I shall unite it again and carve it up a second time." The other asked whether such words meant that Mr. Churchill was prepared to fight for Zionism, and by this he seems to have meant to inquire whether the British government would go so far as to take up arms against those Arabs whom Begin claimed to love almost as much as, if not even more than the British. Sneh explained to him that Mr. Churchill had to count on a great deal of opposition, in Parliament, in the Colonial Service, and elsewhere, but that he was convinced, relying on his prestige, that he could get this new partition scheme accepted, not at that moment but after victory. Mr. Churchill wanted a radical solution, impossible of attainment before a victorious end to the war, "and that," said Sneh, "is why he says he prefers one big fight," meaning the conflict on the mainland of Europe. After some more elucidation by Sneh, all of which seems to have been quite accurate, Begin replied that he had no belief in any solution by partition.[21]

Not long after this encounter, in the autumn, Begin had a meeting with Eliahu Golomb, at that time Haganah Commander, the Rama. Begin seems to have despised him because, during a recent visit to London, the Rama had been impressed by Dr. Weizmann's successful work of negotiation with the British government. The meeting was stormy and, according to Begin, ended with Golomb saying to the terrorist leader: "We shall step in and finish you."

Golomb, according to many people who knew him, was the ablest man to hold the post of Rama, and it is possible that he might have made good his threat. But shortly after this he died. He was succeeded by Moshe Sneh.

[21] Begin, *op. cit.*

The hideous comedy of these meetings between Jewish Agency representatives and the fanatic in command of Irgun were part of a momentous tragedy. To understand the meaning and scope of what was happening it is necessary to go back to 1943 and note a new direction in British policy.

It must never be forgotten in estimating that policy that the imperial idea had been rejected at this time by men in authority, but it had not been totally abjured. It was too difficult a psychological feat to achieve quickly. If it was largely agreed (sometimes reluctantly, sometimes with enthusiasm) among intelligent people that domination by one people over another was immoral, it was not agreed that more progressively successful people should have no right to privilege and special consideration for their wishes in the affairs of the less progressive. This was not a practical idea, but an almost inevitable one. It led British politicians, at first on their own and then with American support, to put forward plans for regulating Arab affairs. So early as May 1941 Anthony Eden as Foreign Secretary had made a public announcement that "His Majesty's Government for their part will give their full support to any scheme [for Arab unity] that commands general approval." [22] He reaffirmed this policy in February 1943 in a statement in the House of Commons. The Arab reaction was at first suspicious and negative, but later, as British fortunes in the war took a turn for the better, a movement towards Arab unity influenced by these statements by Anthony Eden, began to gain momentum. But since the movement had begun in British initiative the Arab nationalist leaders who took part in it felt obliged to avoid most scrupulously any appearance of acting in the British interest. The British were disappointed when they found that the Arab League (not founded till 1945) had a distinct anti-British bias.

As for the Zionists, they looked with considerable alarm at this British attempt to give new strength to Arab nationalism, and it was interpreted by many Palestinian Jews as a subtle move to make Zionism impotent. But in fact these attempts at unity, certainly in their early stages, were believed to be of help to Zionism. From that point of view they were a reversion to Herbert Samuel's idea that the National Home could and would grow with greater ease and in peace if, instead of being an oppressively large area of a small country, it was the small neighbor of a large one. In part the attempt was made in order to give Zionism the room for maneuver which it had lost on the establishment of the Emirate of Transjordan. It needs to be considered along with the very curious and wholly unsuccessful movement, which began in 1939 and continued till the sec-

[22] The Right Honourable Anthony Eden at the Mansion House, 29th May, 1941.

ond half of 1943, to give King ibn Saud large financial backing from Zionist sources, and make of him an "overlord," a species of handsomely salaried President of the United States of Arabia, in exchange for an assurance that he would approve and support the Jewish National Home.[23] The plan was rejected with abhorrence by ibn Saud. Like the notion that a united Arab world would feel the tolerance of satiation toward Zionism, this ibn Saud plan was not realistic; it underestimated the Eastern reaction against Western dominance and ignored the fact that anti-Zionism was the strongest uniting factor in the Arab world. So far as the Jews were concerned none of these movements toward Arab unity were of any benefit.

But however mistaken these plans may have been, they proceeded, contrary to what Jews believed, from a point of view that was highly advantageous to Zionism. There was a large following in Parliament which shared Mr. Churchill's impatience with the White Paper policy. That restless mood which, as has been noted, forced the Bermuda Conference, caused many people to feel shame and irritation at a policy which seemed to penalize the already persecuted Jews in their own homeland. Mr. Churchill took advantage of this mood to attempt a redirection of policy in Palestine. He acted in conformity with Mr. Eden's initiative toward Arab unity.

After the disasters in Malaya, Singapore, and Burma, there was a Cabinet reshuffle in the summer of 1942, and this resulted in Lord Moyne's being replaced as Colonial Secretary by Oliver Stanley, one of the most brilliant men in the Conservative party. Stanley shared Winston Churchill's views on Palestine and before the autumn of the next year he had begun work on a new scheme to replace the White Paper at the end of the war. Dr. Weizmann was kept informed throughout, and as early as September, 1943, Mr. Churchill told him that the Cabinet committee on Palestine had decided to give Jews full sovereignty in one sector of a partitioned Palestine. In the present state of published information not much is known beyond the bare outline of this new partition scheme, but according to Oliver Stanley's account given in the House of Commons in 1946, there were to be Jewish and Arab areas, the latter, if the inhabitants so wished, to be part of "another Arab country" (parliamentary, it would

---

[23] The scheme originated with the late Mr. St. John Philby and received the support of President Roosevelt, Mr. Churchill, and Dr. Weizmann. Lord Moyne attempted a negotiation on this basis in December, 1942. For details see Kirk, *op. cit.,* Chaim Weizmann, *Trial and Error,* London, 1949; and H. St. John Philby, *Arabian Jubilee,* London, 1952.

seem, for Transjordan). There was to be a "Jerusalem enclave" administered by the former mandatory.[24] The scheme appears to have been similar to Peel's but with stronger bias toward the needs of the Jews.

The London office of the Jewish Agency protested against the principle of partition in a memorandum which they sent to the Colonial Office in October, 1944. The document was cogently argued; its two main points of interest were first the contention that Arabs would never consent to a peaceful partition of Palestine, though they would accept "as an accomplished fact" an established Jewish State; and second the fact that the Agency defined the promised land as "Palestine West of Jordan." [25]

A leading authority, Mr. J. C. Hurewitz, considers that the protest of the Agency was "dictated largely by considerations of future political bargaining." This agrees with what is known. It would have been folly to have completely committed Zionism to partition with a Peace Conference mirage-like in sight. It can appear that Churchill and Stanley were in sympathy with the protest, and may have explained to Weizmann that partition was as far as they could possibly go without undoing successful appeasement-work in the Arab countries. The disagreement with the Agency seems to have been of a friendly kind. This comes out very clearly from what is known of what happened on November the 4th of 1944 when Mr. Churchill held a quasi-official conversation with Dr. Weizmann on the proposed scheme. Dr. Weizmann's record of the discussion, which has the full support of contemporary documentation in the Weizmann archives, is the best that is available and should be quoted in full. He tells how he lunched at Chequers with the Prime Minister, his brother John Churchill, Sir John Martin and his secretary Major Thompson.

[Mr. Churchill] spoke of partition, and declared himself in favour of the Negev in the Jewish territory. And while he made it quite clear that no active steps would be taken until the war with Germany was over, he was in close touch with America on the matter of the Jewish National Home. Hearing that I was going to Palestine shortly, he recommended that I break my journey in Cairo to see Lord Moyne who, he said, had changed and developed in the last two years. He asked me whether it was our intention to bring large numbers of Jews into Palestine. I replied that we had in mind something like a hundred thousand a year for about fifteen years. I spoke also of the large number of children who would have to be brought into Palestine. Mr. Churchill commented that it would be for governments to worry about the children, and mentioned financial aid. I

24 Hurewitz, op. cit.
25 Hansard, 31st July, 1946.

answered that if the political field were clear, the financial problem would become of secondary importance.

At one turn the conversation touched on oppositionist Jews, and Mr. Churchill mentioned Mr. Bernard Baruch, among others. I said there were still a few rich and powerful Jews who were against the idea of the Jewish National Home, but they did not know very much about the subject.

When the lunch was over, Mr. Churchill took me into his study and repeated the points he had made in the general conversation. He seemed worried that America was more or less academic in its attitude on the question. He also added that he did not have a very high opinion of the role the Arabs had played in the war.

It was, on the whole, a long and most friendly conversation; it was also one of the rare occasions when Mr. Churchill did not do practically all the talking. I left the meeting greatly encouraged.

Dr. Weizmann had planned to go to Palestine within a few days, and he fell in with the Prime Minister's suggestion that he should discuss matters with the Minister of State in Cairo.

Lord Moyne was a man of attractive character, wholly free from the politician's vice of excessive self-regard. In 1940 when Mr. Churchill became Prime Minister, Moyne had agreed to serve as the joint parliamentary secretary to the Ministry of Agriculture, and gave no thought to the fact that from 1925 to 1929 he had held the post of Minister in this very department. As noted, he became Colonial Secretary after Lord Lloyd's death in 1941. After suffering political reverse following the Far Eastern disasters in 1942 (for which he appears to have been blameless) he thought nothing of accepting the post of Deputy Minister of State in Cairo immediately after having held those of Colonial Secretary and leader of the House of Lords. In January, 1944, when the Minister, Mr. Richard Casey, retired, Moyne succeeded him.

It will be remembered that in his early days as Colonial Secretary he had had to convey disappointing news to the Zionists. From this circumstance they still regarded him as a convinced enemy. Their suspicions were increased by the indisputable fact that the Middle East Office (the Minister of State's secretariat) contained several anti-Zionist members who were capable of influencing policy in this sense, judging, if by nothing else, by a paper prepared in Cairo by the Royal Institute of International Affairs for distribution to the Commonwealth Conference of February, 1945. They maintained liaison through Iltyd Clayton (a confirmed Arabophil and anti-Zionist) with those Arab politicians who were pursuing the cause of Arab unity. A fatal event for Lord Moyne was, in all probability, the meeting of such Arab politicians, including one from Palestine, in Alexandria during October of 1944. It met under the chairmanship of Nahas Pasha, the Egyptian Prime Minister, and issued a statement known as the Alexandria Protocol. This, so far as Palestine was concerned, has been accurately described as "an invitation to H.M.G. to co-operate on the basis of the White Paper, and a threat of non-co-operation if the White Paper was abandoned." [26] It referred to "the promises binding the British Government and providing for the stoppage of Jewish immigration." The conference was only indirectly British-inspired and was not at all British-directed,[27] but it seemed otherwise to Zionists, and to many Arabs as well, and it was taken by many to prove that Moyne was intent on an anti-Zionist intrigue.

In fact he was by no means an anti-Zionist, and if he had been he would never have been appointed by Winston Churchill to the Ministry of State in Cairo, a post invented by the Prime Minister and wholly within his gift. Small incidents can illustrate Moyne's attitude to Palestine. While he was deputy to Mr. Casey he had taken the bold step of meeting one of the leading members of Irgun, and the interview appears to have been a remarkably friendly one, such as opened the eyes of the extremist and gave him a new idea of British intentions toward his people. In early October of 1944 Field-Marshal Lord Gort, who had been appointed to succeed Sir Harold MacMichael, visited Moyne on his way to his new post. The Minister planned to hold a dinner party at which Gort could meet leading Middle East authorities. The name of Iltyd Clayton was proposed as that of a suitable guest, but Moyne immediately vetoed it. Clayton, he said, was far too biased in his pro-Arab views; he might give the new High Commissioner a wrong impression "and it was all-important that there should be fair play." [28]

Lord Moyne was not the sort of administrator whom Zionists could in the normal course of things regard as ideal. He had a typically British compromising mind, devoted to fairness as the supreme virtue which could cure every ill in the world, and it has been remarked earlier in this

26 Marlowe, op. cit.
27 Sir Walter Smart. A communication.
28 These two incidents are mentioned in a letter from Miss Dorothy Osmond to the present Lord Moyne. Miss Osmond was at this time the first Lord Moyne's private secretary. Of the dinner party incident she says: "It has always seemed to me that this incident was the best possible example of the fair-mindedness which your father brought to any problem at all."

book that fairness was of little avail in the affairs of post-Balfour Palestine. But, for their immediate needs, for that political "holding operation"
while the war continued, and before bold new schemes could replace the
White Paper, Moyne was a guarantor of the caretaker service which had
become essential to the Zionist cause. But the new generation of terrorists,
people driven mad by the crimes against them, knew nothing of this and
as Begin's record shows wanted to know nothing about it. Far more than
that, they wanted revenge. Two days after Dr. Weizmann's interview with
Winston Churchill, on the 6th of November, two young men of the Stern
Group murdered Lord Moyne and the driver of his car in a street of Cairo.

The murderers were arrested, tried by an Egyptian court-martial and
hanged.

It seems that Irgun had no part in this atrocity, and had no fore-
knowledge of it. They had not yet abandoned all restraint and all reason.
That was to come. The two young men had acted solely within the even
darker tradition of "the Illuminator."

Some Zionist authorities have tried to depict the murderers as pitiful
victims of brutal British misrule. Their ages, which seem to have been
established by unexceptionable methods when they were arrested, have
been described as less, and again less, by succeeding writers,[29] tending to
heighten the colors of a picture that does not want for sadness. The
younger of the two was called Ben Hakim. Arthur Koestler relates, on the
authority of the young man's family, that in his early youth he saw the
blowing up of the *Patria* off Haifa, saw the people drowning in the harbor, and all the hideous procedure of fishing dismembered corpses into
boats from the sea. It is said that this sight haunted him for the rest of his
short life and that from it sprang a dedicated decision to repay crime with
crime, fulfilled in the murder of this British minister. The story has been
doubted. It is difficult to know what may be imagined, what may be authentic, at this distance. But if the story is true, then it can be said, in the
light of present knowledge, that by this senseless murder the Zionist leadership paid a heavy price indeed, both in guilt and in political blundering,
for their reckless indulgence in propaganda falsehood. Even if it is not
true, then it must still be said that gross perversions of the truth such as
the Agency-sponsored tale of the mass-suicide aboard the *Patria* had
helped to arouse a fanatic spirit of which the murder in Cairo was a nat-

[29] They were identified at the time as 25 and 23 years of age. See Kirk, *op. cit.*,
p. 324 note. A Zionist propaganda account of the crime is contained in *The Deed*
by Gerold Frank published in the U.S. in 1963 and in England in 1964. The British
edition was withdrawn as a result of protest.

ural consequence and expression. Lord Moyne was the victim of propaganda. So were the wretched men who killed him.

Shock at the crime brought a turning point, or rather what could have been a turning point had there been more wish on the part of more people to go a new way. But the estrangement of the Jews and the mandatory had gone too far to allow this to happen, and the consequence of the murder was an armistice that did not lead to a peace. This may have been inevitable.

The Jewish Agency took vigorous action to dissociate the Zionist leadership from what had happened in Cairo and in this they were encouraged by the indignation of those many Jews who held to the long liberal Jewish tradition and who were as a rule little heard in this time of strident nationalism.[30] The Agency's most significant departure in policy was to give the full cooperation of Haganah with the mandatory police against the terrorists. As a result of this, two hundred and seventy-nine Sternists and Irgun followers were rounded up and deported within the next six months. The Agency furthermore appealed to the Yishuv to denounce the gangsters to Haganah and refuse them shelter, but this was an order that many Jews who were far from the spirit of Irgun or Stern found it impossible to obey. They knew that a denunciation to Haganah meant subsequent arrest by the mandatory police, that it meant handing Jews over to Gentile punishment. This went against the deep racial sense of solidarity which is at the very heart of Jewish belief and way of life. In consequence Jews often refused vital help to the police in their campaign against Irgun and the Sternists, and this in turn gave the mandatory authorities, at all levels, an impression that the criminal element was of much larger extent and enjoyed much wider approval and support among the Jewish people than was in fact the case. Among cruder people in the ranks both of the British police and army, this quite inevitably gave rise to ugly phases of anti-Semitism unconsciously influenced, here and there, by the Nazi model.

The show of genuine goodwill and cooperation in governing circles, not fully reflected and sometimes contradicted in the workaday world below, was typical of the new time. It so happened that independently of the cooperation effort by the Agency and Haganah, the relations of the High Commission with Jewish and Arab representative bodies had suddenly improved in the autumn of 1944. As Sir Harold MacMichael's term of office drew to a close, the government, like their predecessor in 1931,

[30] See a quotation from the liberal *Ha Aretz* of 17th November, 1944, in Kirk, *op. cit.*

258 / CROSSROADS TO ISRAEL

looked for some respected military leader who could repeat the happy
Plumer story in Palestine. Their choice was again felicitous. It fell on
Lord Gort who, as the stout-hearted and extraordinarily able governor of
Malta during its long siege, had added to his considerable reputation. Like
Plumer he came from Malta to Jerusalem. Considering the state of Palestine in 1944 and 1945, he may be said to have added to his many titles to
fame that of being a respected High Commissioner in the most difficult of
all posts at the most difficult of times. He had to carry out unpopular
policies, but he was able to retain sufficient personal popularity to maintain a tolerable relationship between the ruler and the ruled. He restored
the contacts that had been broken through the tensions of the last years.
He had the gift of sympathy, and to his initiative was ascribed the decision
(in February) to allow those Jews who had been deported to Mauritius to
settle in Palestine.[31] There can be no doubt that the virtual suspension of
terrorist activity after Haganah had cooperated with the British authorities
was greatly helped by the fact of Lord Gort being the man at the head of
affairs. But his term of office lasted only a year. In November of 1945 he
was discovered to be suffering from cancer and he had to retire at short
notice, a few months before his death. His admirers have urged that with
good health and a five-year term he might have guided Palestine to peaceful adjustment. It is more likely that in the long run he would have failed
like his predecessors. The time had passed when any single individual
could change the course of events. Below the surface there was too much
desperation, and the extremism that comes from desperation, to accept
compromising policy. This was illustrated by the arrival in Palestine, a
week after the death of Lord Moyne, and for the first time since 1939, of
Dr. Weizmann.

His reception has been described by Dr. Abba Eban.

The Hebrew Press poured out its affection in words of stately tribute.
The community surrounded him with the emblems and ceremonies befit-
ting a beloved Head of State. Indeed, anyone reading the newspapers of
that period to-day would find it hard to believe that the Jewish State
under Weizmann's presidency had not already been established. The British High Commissioner, Lord Gort, solemly exchanged visits with him.
School children crowded into the streets to greet his coming. The farmers
of Galilee displayed their smiling fields and plump livestock. At Rehovoth his scientific colleagues of the Sieff Institute saluted him with awe.
The little township puffed out its chest and almost exploded with pride.
A trainload of Jewish soldiers, enlisted in the Brigade Group over which

[31] Hurewitz, *op. cit.* The point is not remarked by all Zionist writers.

he and Sharett[32] had spent so much of their vital force, were shunted on to the Rehovoth platform to parade before the two men who had arduously laboured for their establishment. He was moved by these tributes to the depths of his soul.[33]

This is in no way exaggerated. But the immense and profoundly deserved ovation given to Dr. Weizmann, though it moved him, did not dim the caustic recognition by this scientist of the darker aspects of the scene to which he came. "It was a wonderful homecoming," he recorded in his autobiography, "all that the heart could wish; or rather, it would have been if there had not been certain phenomena which caused me grave concern." In continuation of the paragraph he praised the steadfastness and solidarity of the Jews of Palestine in the war years, but he added:

Side by side with these developments, in some ways linked with them, and in part arising from the bitter frustration of legitimate hopes, there were the negative features I have referred to: here and there a relaxation of the old, traditional Zionist purity of ethics; a touch of militarization, and a weakness for its trappings; here and there, something worse—the tragic, futile, un-Jewish resort to terrorism, a perversion of the purely defensive function of Haganah; and worst of all, in certain circles, a readiness to compound with the evil, to play politics with it, to condemn and not to condemn it, to treat it not as the thing it was, namely an unmitigated curse to the National Home, but as a phenomenon which might have its advantages.

He made more public appearances, and gave more addresses both private and public, than at any other time in Palestine. He was never received other than with love, gratitude, and veneration, but he had almost no political success. He was received, not as a politician, but as royalty, as a "prince of the captivity" who had led his people home. This was not his wish; he wanted to accomplish the hard task he had set himself. His purpose was to assure that the final growth of the Jewish National Home should, even under the stress of tragedy and of newly excited ambition, move by gradualist, self-restrained and peaceful stages, as it had done in better times. He wanted to persuade his people to accept the partition scheme which he had discussed with Winston Churchill. He told his audi-

[32] Moshe Shertok changed his name to a Hebrew form, Sharett, after the foundation of the State. Many of the Yishuv did this.
[33] In Weisgal and Carmichael, eds., *Chaim Weizmann: A Biography by Several Hands*. London, 1949.

ences what he had told Churchill, that a transitional period of at least five years, possibly ten, was necessary before a Jewish Commonwealth emerged, during which time he wanted Jewish immigration at the rate of 100,000 a year.

His whole position as the advocate of this very moderate policy (as it seemed to Jews) had been enfeebled by several circumstances, and the first of these was the murder in Cairo. This made it difficult, even impossible, for the British Prime Minister to obtain the support of Parliament for a bold new pro-Zionist scheme unless he first appeased the just indignation of the anti-Zionists; he felt compelled to say in the House of Commons on the 17th of November (two days after Dr. Weizmann's arrival in Palestine) that if Zionism was to tolerate such crimes he and those like him who had supported the Zionist cause would have to "reconsider their attitude." When, shortly after, Dr. Weizmann told an audience of Palestine Jews that Winston Churchill was "a man who keeps faith with us," [34] the ugly train of events set in motion by the murder took away from the force of his words. Winston Churchill would keep faith with the Zionists if he could, but it was less certain now that he could.

More important than the inevitable weakening of the massive political support that Weizmann had built up in England was the fact that his present proposition did not accord with the spirit of the time. It belonged to the 1930's. It had the appearance of a retreat from the bolder proposition of Biltmore, and what man of spirit was likely to choose revised Peel when he was offered the heroic goal of a Judenstaat? Weizmann was intent on uniting the political leadership of the Yishuv but for all the splendor of his personal position and appeal, he appeared, as a politician, as no more than a spokesman for the minority which opposed Ben-Gurion, the Biltmore resolution, and the victorious majority of the Central Executive. The minority were still in the field, but as routed partisans, and the Agency Executive took the occasion of Dr. Weizmann's unwelcome advocacy of a moderate course, to rout them again. Moshe Shertok made public the fact that the Agency had presented a memorandum to the British government opposing the idea of partitioning the land, and on the 6th of December the Va'ad Leumi voted a resolution in the same sense by an overwhelming majority.[35] The time had passed when Weizmann's opposition to such a resolution could have been effective. It would in fact have been most abnormal if, in the winter of 1944–45, the Jews of Palestine had accepted a partition scheme, no matter how generous. Extremism had

[34] Hurewitz, *op. cit.*
[35] Kirk, Hurewitz, *op. cit.*

received new and unexpected support. In the same month as the Va'ad Leumi gave new assent to the Biltmore resolution, the Labour Party in Great Britain held their annual conference, and Mr. Attlee, on behalf of the National Executive, moved and secured the adoption of a resolution which was to cost the reputation of that party dear indeed. The main and key phrases should be remembered:

> There is surely neither hope nor meaning in a "Jewish National Home" unless we are prepared to let Jews, if they wish, enter this tiny land in such numbers as to become a majority. There was a strong case for this before the war. There is an inevitable case now, after the unspeakable atrocities of the cold and calculated German Nazi plan to kill all the Jews in Europe. Here, too, in Palestine surely is a case, on human grounds and to promote a stable settlement, for transfer of population. Let the Arabs be encouraged to move out as the Jews move in. Let them be compensated handsomely for their land and let their settlement elsewhere be carefully organised and generously financed. The Arabs have many wide territories of their own; they must not claim to exclude the Jews from this small area of Palestine, less than the size of Wales. Indeed we should re-examine also the possibility of extending the present Palestinian boundaries, by agreement with Egypt, Syria and Transjordan.

This proposal had already been made public in the spring, in the annual report of the Labour Party National Executive Committee. Alarmed at its likely effect on Arabs within and without Palestine, the Jewish leaders, including Ben-Gurion, hastened to dissociate themselves from the proposal to organize a transfer of population, but it is quite impossible to suppose that the resolution as a whole, which went far beyond that of Biltmore, was unwelcome to the Zionists.[36] It gave great help to the pro-Biltmore majority; it gave new strength to Ben-Gurion and those who followed him in demanding an immediate commonwealth and the immediate admission of great hosts of immigrants, and it made Weizmann's plea for gradualism sound irrelevant. Ben-Gurion had emphatically won the political leadership of the Jews in Palestine. Everything, for the moment, was going his way.

Dr. Weizmann stayed in Palestine till March of the new year. He returned to London where almost immediately he was overcome by an attack of glaucoma. He became blind temporarily until relieved by a succession of painful operations.[37] It is probable that his continual condem-

---

[36] In private but not in public Weizmann discussed the possibility of a population transfer notably with a fellow Zionist at the end of 1941.
[37] Eban, in Weisgal and Carmichael, *op. cit.*

nation of terrorism while in Palestine had some effect in checking extremism during the months ahead, but that was the limit of the political achievement of the visit. He had wanted much more. He was not a man who could accept the penalty of age with patience.

The temporary cessation under Jewish pressure of the activities of Etzel and the F.F.I., a turn of events over which Begin in his book raised hands of execration and self-pity, occurred in one of the last periods in which there was a genuine degree of Anglo-Jewish cooperation in Palestine. As suggested already, the period was marked by more mutual hostility than could be allayed by the needs of the time, and for that reason the area of cooperation was not enlarged. There was one very curious feature of this temporary alliance, which has drawn much criticism on Lord Gort and his successor, and this was the continuing refusal of the Administration to acknowledge the legality of Haganah. Considering the wartime association of Haganah and the Special Operations Executive, and that the illegality of Haganah was open to question at any time, to continue to regard this Jewish force as outside the law after accepting its help in the pursuit of a common aim was fantastic even by the standards of Palestine. Yet there is a case to be made in defense of this extraordinary procedure.

The argument in favor of recognizing Haganah has been urged by many commentators who point out that only thus would the administration have given strength and support to the responsible elements in Zionism, and from that point of departure the development of Jewish nationalism after the war might have proceeded in at least some degree of harmony with Britain. There can be little doubt that there were influential and moderate Haganah men who thought along these lines at the time and pressed the argument on members of the administration. They did so in vain. As a result (so runs the argument) there was no area for cooperation and no alternative to a state of general Anglo-Jewish mutual hostility.

The argument may be true but is at least open to doubt. Against it can be urged the fact that neither Haganah nor the administration had anything to gain by close association. The British government, no matter what majority or prestige its chief might enjoy, could never go beyond a partition plan such as that of Oliver Stanley, and it would require all the political skill of a Churchill to pilot such a measure through Parliament without being forced into unacceptable modifications. The visit of Dr. Weizmann had in the meantime proved that even without any modifications such a plan would have been rejected by the Yishuv. The Biltmore and Labour Party resolutions had made it impossible, and doubly impossible under Ben-Gurion's leadership, for the Jewish Agency and the ruling committee of Haganah to demand less than an immediate commonwealth, and if, in spite of plain warnings, they had for some reason demanded less, they would quite surely have accomplished nothing more than a division in their ranks and their own fall from power. It is quite impossible that they would have been succeeded by men who were more moderate! There was only one way of avoiding Anglo-Jewish hostility and that was for the British government to base its policy on an extremist interpretation of the Biltmore resolution. This the Labour Party proposed to do. It appears later that no matter how much they may have wanted to carry out their pledge, this was something they could not do.

12 THE HUNDRED THOUSAND

Little has been said of what the Arabs of Palestine had been doing since 1939, since the issue of the White Paper and the fading away of the rebellion. The reason is that there is so little to say, or rather, from a mass of complicated detail, one can extract virtually nothing which made a lasting impression on events.

The trouble with the Arab politicians was the usual one: a disunity which was radical and not to be compared with the party warfare of the Jews. Their position was not easy. The White Paper had taken the sting out of the Arab grievance, and furthermore the changing situation in the world without was, for the moment and with deceptive appearance, taking the sting out of the whole anti-British interest. The loss of this sting meant a great change, for anti-British agitation had been a strong factor in Arab politics everywhere during the last ten years. In the first part of the war the White Paper had, by a narrow margin (and not in Iraq), diminished the anti-British impetus till it stood just below the danger point; but when it became clear early in 1943 that the Axis could not win the war, and that the propaganda talk of brave old Britain beating back the great new powers was not all nonsense after all, then something like a pro-British reaction began to be discernible in Arab lands. The Arabs, it must be remembered, saw and to a limited extent judged the Axis by nearby Italy rather than distant Germany, and they assumed the United Nations victory somewhat prematurely in consequence. All this hampered Palestine politicians. They were in the awkward predicament of losing their enemy.

The Arab population needed leadership, now as always, and they were without it. They had had only one really vigorous leader at any time and that was the Mufti. His pro-Axis leanings had made him to some a popular figure of romance during his days of exile in the early war years, but by 1943 he was (temporarily) discredited in the eyes of most people. He had gone to Berlin; was to be heard broadcasting from Hitler's capital; was compromised with the defeated Axis. He was no longer a safe man to follow to success and prosperity. (One hopes that his popularity would have sunk yet lower if it had been known then how he was occupying his time in Germany as a keen and effective coadjutor in the final solution, protesting successfully to Hitler at some small alleviations in regard to children.[1])

The leaders of the former Istiqlal or Independence party made efforts from the beginning of 1943 to build up a unified leadership. In the summer the three principal movers[2] succeeded in establishing a new party with the direction of the Arab National Fund, but, even so early, hopes of Arab unity within Palestine were thin. The partial success of the Istiqlal men provoked the Husseinis (the Mufti's former associates) and other parties to jealousy. Believing as party politicians do everywhere that they were motivated by nothing so much as public spirit, they prevented unity when it was just possible, and spread the familiar boycotting spirit against coalition. As a result, the preliminary Arab conferences toward the founding of the Arab League, held in July, 1943, and February, 1944, proceeded without any Palestine representative being present.

The purpose of the Husseinis was a simple one: to restore the credit of the Mufti, and not let Palestine leadership go elsewhere. They succeeded. In April 1944 there was something like a Husseini revival operated by a new group called the Arab Palestine Party. They had an able propagandist in a Greek orthodox Arab called Emile el Ghuri, a successor to George

[1] Mark Wischnitzer, *To Dwell in Safety*. Philadelphia, 1948.
[2] Ahmad Hilmi Pasha Abd el Baqi, Awni Bey Abd el Hadi, Rashid al Hajj Ibrahim.

Antonius who had died in 1942. In contrast to Antonius, el Ghuri was of harsh, extremist temper, better suited than his predecessor to the new age. (It is difficult to resist an impression that the Husseini revival was connected with the Zionist terrorist revival.) The leader of the new party was Tewfik Saleh el Husseini, a cousin of the Mufti's. Unlike the Istiqlal party which demanded adherence to the White Paper, the Arab Palestine Party demanded the "dissolution of the Jewish National Home." There was no change from the Mufti policy of the thirties. The revival had the effect of making the political division of the Palestine Arabs complete, and they nearly missed the chance of sending a representative to the third exploratory meeting of Arab states interested in unity, the one that was held in Alexandria in October, 1944. Then, after the formal establishment of the Pact of the League of Arab States on the 22nd of March, 1945, there was a transient prospect of an Arab coalition in Palestine. Mr. J. C. Hurewitz, the leading authority on this tangled and unrewarding subject, describes it as follows: "The leaders took to meeting informally at one another's homes and offices in April 1945 at irregular intervals to discuss local political affairs. This was as close as they came in wartime to forming a new executive for the national movement." [3]

With the end of the war, and despite the fact that the affairs of Palestine had a high priority in the program of the Arab League, the mutual antagonism of the Palestinian parties increased greatly. The result was an odd paradox; the Arab states outside were united on the Arab national cause in Palestine, while the nationalists within Palestine were so disunited that no possibility of a strong Arab leadership in Jerusalem now remained. Efforts by King Abdullah of Transjordan to compose the differences of the politicians were resented. Strangely enough this state of affairs did not weaken but (with most tragic results) strengthened Arab resistance. With the exception of the Palestine representative to the Arab League, Musa el Alami, the politicians on the spot seem to have been short-sighted men of no apparent political ability. In their state of chronic party warfare they could count for little if anything in Arab councils. The initiative passed to more resolute hands outside, and ultimately back to those of the Mufti Haj Amin.

At the end of the war the position of Great Britain throughout the Middle East was spectacular and illusory. The glamor of the old days when Allenby had conquered was back again, but this time it vanished like a

---

[3] J. C. Hurewitz, *The Struggle for Palestine.* New York, 1950. At this time there were in all six Arab parties in Palestine of which Mr. Hurewitz gives details.

morning mist, sooner than expected. However, for a while things looked very good, seen through English eyes. In the Arab world the British name was enjoying the popularity which comes with success. In the same month as the war ended Britain added to this popularity the nobler prize of moral esteem on account of an action which, on the surface at least, seemed to be one of rare magnanimity. Things could look good through Arab eyes too. During the war the British government had given support to the Arab national cause in Syria and Lebanon, and in May of 1945 British troops were sent in to secure the independence of those countries and to prevent the reopening of the Arab-French quarrel. French and Arab cynics prophesied that this would be another case of sending troops in "to restore order," and then staying there for a century or two. But this time the cynics were confounded. In the spring and summer of 1946 the troops withdrew and Syria and Lebanon were left with their promised independence. The Syrian action did not improve British relations with the liberated France of General de Gaulle, but it improved them to an embarrassing extent with Arab countries. It set a standard for British support of Arab nationalism which was not easy to live up to. It is forgotten today how much this action forced Britain into an unwelcome *beau rôle,* gave rise to hopes that took skill and luck to fulfill, and put the British into a position where any minor miscalculation could be followed by major disillusion.

The great *fata morgana* of a triumphant Britain, with the sword sheathed, and with a cornucopia in her benevolent hands, received a new glow in Eastern eyes when Winston Churchill was defeated in the general election of 1945 and the Labour Party came into office under Clement Attlee. In the East, Churchill was admired as strong man, and distrusted as an imperialist. The Labour men were known to believe in an egalitarian philosophy which they were prepared to apply to international affairs as freely as to internal social matters. Everything was hurrying toward the best possible state of affairs in a very good world. Where was the flaw in the picture?

The only people in the East who were equally involved in the West were the Zionists. They could see the state of things through Western eyes. Europe was in ruins; the cornucopia was empty; magnificent as the British position might appear to men living far away from Britain, it was manifestly desperate at home, and to add to its desperation and to diminish the little freedom of action that remained to any British government, the victorious alliance, which had been under strain, was now breaking down. The American lend-lease economic agreement with Great Britain

268 / CROSSROADS TO ISRAEL

was abruptly canceled with results that might have been ruinous. And this was a minor flaw in the alliance compared with the major breach. A third world war between the West and Russia became a close possibility and was perhaps only avoided by a narrow margin. In 1945 generous British plans to anticipate generous treaties and remove all British troops from the eastern Mediterranean became the subject of alarmed second thoughts. The Labour government proved in India that its professions of faith were wholly sincere. In the Middle East it was unable to offer additional proof for the simple reason that the U.S.S.R. was too near. Both Persia and Turkey were under Russian pressure. In Persia the Russians had begun to maneuver with the purpose of making the country a Russian satellite as early as 1942. In 1945 it seemed to any reasonable British minister or service chief as vital as ever it had been to appease anxieties in the world of Islam, and to maintain the British garrisons stationed, or rather left there in force by the accident of war, in Egypt and the Arab lands to the East.

If the Zionists, with their cosmopolitan Jewish connections, were alone able to understand the predicament of the mandatory power in Palestine, they preferred to shut their minds to it. They had no alternative. Though it became official Zionist doctrine that the White Paper had been a hopeless political failure from the British point of view, the Zionist leaders must have known that it had proved a useful instrument in the war, and that if they acquiesced in any postwar pro-Arab British policy, or renounced their own forward policy no matter how temporarily, the detested White Paper would become immutable law. By such a law Jewish immigration would not only decline but would presently cease.

But the Zionists had another reason for taking a self-centered line, one that was little known to Gentiles then and (for reasons of policy one may suppose) has not been much publicized since. As mentioned in an earlier chapter, Zionism was never prone to excessive optimism about Jewish character. In his history of the movement Nahum Sokolov, the chief negotiator with Weizmann for the Balfour Declaration, spoke with contempt of the sentimentalities of "Judeophils," as he called them, and he praised Sir Mark Sykes because, like Arthur Balfour, he harbored no sort of illusions about Jews. The early Zionists were somewhat too liable, in fact, to share the ideas of anti-Semites about the mischievous role which the Jews as a displaced people tended to play in the world. In its inner debate Zionism began as an extraordinarily self-critical movement.[4] It became

---

[4] Lord Boothby has told the writer of an occasion when he was listening to speeches at a Zionist Congress with Dr. Weizmann. The venerable president turned to him

still more so after Zionism, under the stress of tragedy, had grown from a party to a need.

In the immediate postwar period, the reaction of many Zionists to the ordeal of the Jews of Europe was strongly marked by self-pessimism. Most of the European Jews were dead. Statistics vary and will probably never be definitive, but it seems that in the course of the final solution between five and six million people had been systematically murdered, that is, over 75 per cent of the whole European Jewish population. As said earlier, a political result among the survivors was a majority reaction toward Zionism. This of course agreed with the beliefs, aims, and hopes of Zionists, and they did all they could to intensify the impulse yet further, but among themselves there was another and more negative reaction, though of equal force. Many Zionists were overcome with fear as to what might happen to Jews after the experience of the final solution, if they were denied the opportunity of regaining self-respect. Men who knew the degrading effect of ghetto life in countries hostile to Jews, and this was the case with the majority of the Zionist leaders, became obsessed with the idea that the Jewish survivors of the Nazi regime, especially the younger ones, would turn into an enormous criminal class. They apprehended the strange and terrible possibility that the cruelty practiced by anti-Semites on Jews could have so demoralizing an effect on the victims as to make the nonsensical propositions of anti-Semitism come spuriously true. Only a religious impulse could counteract this moral danger left by Nazism, and the impulse was to be found in the modern religion of patriotism. Except through Zionism this religion was denied to Jews as Jews. In fervent acceptance of this belief, a number, perhaps a majority of Zionist leaders, and a large number of thoughtful people in the Yishuv pursued the aim of the State in a new missionary spirit, thrusting arguments against it from their thoughts.[5]

There was no lack of portents in the months after the German surren-

---

and whispered: "This is the sort of speech that brings out all my latent anti-Semitism." The jest is not to be taken too seriously, but it may serve as an interesting symptom.

[5] It is always dangerous to define in precise terms and as an historical fact what was never defined with precision at the time. So far as the writer knows, the state of mind described here, and said to have been a decisive one in shaping Zionist action in postwar years, cannot be proved by reference to contemporary documents. The writer gained the impression that such a state of mind widely existed from independent conversations with friends in Israel, and the terms used here closely follow an elucidation by Dr. Yeduha Bauer.

der to warn the British government anew that unless they followed Labour's extremist statements of policy, a dire struggle with Zionism was on the way. The first portent came in the same month as the German surrender. Dr. Weizmann as president of the Jewish Agency wrote a severely worded memorandum to Mr. Churchill at the end of May demanding on behalf of the Jewish Agency the full and immediate implementation of the Biltmore resolution: the cancellation of the White Paper, the establishment of Palestine as a Jewish State, Jewish immigration to be an Agency responsibility, and reparation to be made by Germany in kind beginning with all German property in Palestine. Weizmann was never a *doctrinaire* gradualist.

Mr. Churchill replied that the future of Palestine could not be settled before "the victorious Allies are definitely seated at the Peace Table." Another memorandum from the Agency followed in mid-June demanding the immediate issue of 100,000 immigration certificates for the use of European Jews.[6] This second memorandum was ill-timed and had no effect. The British coalition government had been dissolved and a general election was in progress. Further to distract attention from Palestine, the British in the Middle East were in the thick of the Syria and Lebanon crisis. In late July the Labour government came into office. Their election victory was joyfully greeted by the Yishuv. It was doubted by some whether the new rulers could in fact go so far as to transpose the Palestinian Arabs to some other territory, but it was not doubted that they would go further than any of their predecessors in carrying out the Zionist clauses of the mandate. There was a brief and ominous quiet in Palestine while men waited for the fulfillment of pledges.

Portents within Palestine had been there in plenty during recent weeks. The most disturbing was a fresh revival of Irgun and the Sternists. Less sinister, though equally disruptive of orderly administration, was the revival of a Haganah organization dating from 1937 and called Mossad le Aliyah Beth (the Committee for Illegal Immigration). With astonishing skill and speed this secret committee raised an effective escape-section known as the Bricha (literally "running") which succeeded in introducing Jewish immigrants into Palestine from central and eastern Europe.[7] During the brief "armistice" Irgun and the Stern Group refrained from action, but the Bricha activity went on. When the armistice gradually came to an end toward the close of September, the gravest of all portents appeared: Haganah went into alliance with Irgun and the Sternists.

[6] Hurewitz, *op. cit.*
[7] Herbert Agar, *The Saving Remnant*. London, 1960.

In the meantime a new and decisive influence had come on to the scene. The government of the United States had grown interested in Zionism.

Considering that the original purpose for which a British government in 1917 became involved in Zionism was to obtain American goodwill; considering too how much the establishment of the National Home owed to President Wilson, and to American personalities such as Louis D. Brandeis and Felix Frankfurter, it is strange that up to the Second World War successive American administrations had practically no interest at all in Palestine. But if this is strange, it is also logical. There was no great American political commitment in western Asia (as opposed to the Far East), none to compare with those of France and Britain, and for an American government to have become concerned in the complicated political maneuvering in and around Palestine would have been a gratuitous offense to that interwar isolationism which most politically minded Americans held as a faith.

The change came rapidly, with great force and from different directions. Before the war the large Jewish population of New York kept America informed about the atrocities of the Nazi regime, and at the same time the Weizmann policy of self-restraint made a deep and favorable impression on a state of opinion that was predominantly pacifist. These two factors prepared opinion for a change of climate which began to be felt toward the end of 1942. At the news of the final solution American opinion reacted with the sudden generous intensity that appears to be a national characteristic. The revival of Zionism among American Jews proceeded with rapid acceleration, and the enthusiasm was echoed and affirmed by the general population. A result was the Bermuda Conference. Isolationism was a thing of the past, and during the rest of the war years there was a steady unrelenting pressure on the government from Congress and public opinion for an American solution of the Palestine question. The first political move in what was to be a protracted political event occurred on the 2nd of November, 1942, when the reconstituted American Palestine Committee, composed of sixty-eight senators and two hundred representatives, issued a statement denouncing the White Paper. The propagandists of Zionism did not neglect so favorable a sign; they exploited it to the very utmost and so successfully that insofar as Americans thought about Palestine, which they did more and more, they thought about it in Zionist terms.[8]

[8] A most remarkable description of the Zionist climate of opinion in the U.S.A. in 1943 and 1944, is to be found in *Dust in the Lion's Paw* by Freya Stark. London, 1961.

At the beginning of 1944 identical resolutions were introduced into the House of Representatives and the Senate which read as follows: "Resolved that the United States shall use its good offices to the end that the doors of Palestine shall be opened for free entry of Jews in that country, and that there shall be full opportunity for colonization so that the Jewish people may ultimately reconstitute Palestine as a free and democratic Jewish commonwealth." If these resolutions had passed, then Congress would have committed itself to the Biltmore program. But the Secretary of War, Henry L. Stimson, intervened with a warning that "further action on [these resolutions] at this time would be prejudicial to the successful prosecution of the war."

The debate did not proceed in deference to the War Department.[9] The truth of the matter was that the American Executive looked with some alarm at the rising enthusiasm for Zionism.

In part this was precisely for the reasons given by Stimson to Congress. In southern England preparations for the greatest and most hazardous operation of the war, the invasion of Europe, were under way, and to arouse Arab hostility at such a time, with the danger of having to divert troops from the great enterprise, was to be avoided at all costs. This was fully appreciated in Congress, and the Zionists of America had the wisdom not to persist "at this time" in the endeavor to obtain congressional endorsement of Biltmore. But military considerations were only part, and of necessity only a temporary part, of the government's distaste for a full-blooded Zionist policy. Of lasting importance was the fact that American detachment from the Arabic-speaking world had come to an end.

The event which caused the change had been the discovery in 1938 of a large oilfield near Dhahran in eastern Saudi Arabia, and the "point of departure" was the subsequent award of the oil concessions to the Arabian-American Company in 1933. Mr. Frank E. Manuel describes as follows the effect on American political thinking:

> During the course of World War II it became increasingly clear that tangible American interest in the Middle East . . . was to be an important new feature of American foreign policy. It has been compared with our nineteenth-century proclamation of a stake in China. Saudi Arabia became a virtual American protectorate. On January 8th, 1946, a concession was awarded to the Trans-Arabian Pipeline Company, a subsidiary of the Arabian-American Oil Company which in turn was owned jointly by the Standard Oil Company of California and the Texas Company, to construct a pipeline from the Persian Gulf across Arabia. The existence

[9] Frank E. Manuel, *The Realities of American-Palestine Relations*. Washington, 1949.

of a United States Army air base at Dhahran highlighted the strategic importance of this greatest single oil area in the world, a barren uncivilised corner of the globe nominally under the power of a desert sheikh called King. The area was no longer a political vacuum and the United States was in the Middle East to stay.

The American government had learned the lesson of imperialism and from the beginning was careful not to assert the "virtual protectorate" but to maintain it by persuasion. In this way circumstances thrust the United States into a pro-Arab line of policy which was eased by the fact that it accorded with what American involvement in the Middle East existed already. This was cultural, for the most part the work of Protestant missionaries whose most notable achievement was the American University of Beirut. Like all Protestant missionaries these had a tendency, through long association and through the interests of a natural school for Orientalists, to regard Islam and the Arab world with sympathy and affection. The new American direction of policy was acclaimed by Americans on the spot, while more and more Americans at home urged on their government a pro-Zionist course which the new friends of the United States would certainly regard as hostile to themselves. The American party leaders believed (quite mistakenly as it turned out)[10] that votes in elections in which sizable numbers of Jews took part would most vitally depend on the extent to which candidates committed themselves to strong Zionist policies. Like the British, the American government soon found that Zionism introduced a distracting dilemma into the task of formulating an Eastern policy. Whatever line they followed was demonstrably dangerous.

President Roosevelt in his last years hit on a simple method of dealing with the dilemma: he gave strenuous encouragement to both sides. During his last presidential election he sent a message to a convention of American Zionists held in October, 1944. "I know how long and ardently," he said on this occasion, "the Jewish people have worked and prayed for the establishment of Palestine as a free and democratic Jewish commonwealth . . . If re-elected I will help bring about its realization." About four months later, when the re-elected President was returning from the calamitous Yalta Conference, he met King ibn Saud aboard an American warship in the Suez Canal. According to the Secretary-General of the Arab League, Abdur Rahman Azzam, Rossevelt gave ibn Saud a pledge that "he would not support the Jews against the Arabs."[11] This

10 *The Forrestal Diaries* (Walter Millis, ed.) make this clear.
11 Reported in a United Press dispatch from an interview with Azzam, 25th August, 1945. Manuel, *op. cit.*

may be somewhat exaggerated, but the memoirs of Edward R. Stettinius certainly indicate that the President was impressed by the anti-Zionism of the Arabian king, and American authorities make it clear that he promised to act in accordance with Arabian-American friendship.[12] It is the fact that he informed Congress when he returned to Washington on the 1st of March, 1945: "Of the problems of Arabia, I earned more about the whole problem, the Muslim problem, the Jewish problem, by talking with ibn Saud for five minutes than I could have learned in exchange of two or three dozen letters." His words rejoiced the Arab world and depressed the Jews, but about a fortnight later he reaffirmed his Zionist pledge of October to Rabbi Stephen S. Wise of New York, and about three weeks after that, a few days before his death, he reaffirmed in a personal letter to ibn Saud his promise to him of February. He defined it as follows: "Your Majesty will doubtless recall that during our recent conversation I assured you that I would take no action, in my capacity as Chief of the Executive Branch of this Government, which might prove hostile to the Arab people."

On the 12th of April, 1945, Roosevelt died and was succeeded as President by Harry S. Truman, a very different and straightforward man. But no amount of straightforwardness could disentangle Mr. Truman's double-charactered inheritance in the field of Eastern policy. He found himself forced into dubious ways that repelled his sense of honor, and into acting an anti-British part of whose danger in face of the growing Russian threat he was painfully aware. It has been said, notably by Mr. J. C. Hurewitz, that if Roosevelt had survived into the postwar years, then, with the immense prestige which he enjoyed in the world, he might have imposed a solution. This is surely to overestimate Roosevelt and his position. On the problem of Palestine there was no solution that could be peacefully imposed, and the late President's tendency to sophisticated maneuver and intrigue might have hideously complicated the problem yet further. Mr. Truman added nothing to its complications, though the latter involved him in tortuous intrigue. He was forced by circumstances to continue Roosevelt's game of encouraging both sides,[13] but it can be said of Truman that, from his accession until May 15th, 1948, he never lost sight of two simple principles: that the United States must not be involved in Palestinian strife, and that action must be taken with the object of giving a chance of new life to as many as possible of the survivors of Nazi barbarism. It was the second of these principles that caused trouble, but it can

[12] Harry S. Truman, *Years of Trial and Hope*. New York, 1958.
[13] For some details see Bartley C. Crum, *Behind the Silken Curtain*, London, 1947.

be seen now (what was admittedly not easy to see then) that if the British government had taken Mr. Truman's lead in the matter they might well have saved themselves from humiliation and disaster. But apart from the fact that this was obscure, Mr. Truman had to deal with a man who became a problem on his own. The difficulty with Ernest Bevin was that when he had made up his mind he was unable to reverse the process.

As in the first days, so in the last stages of the mandate, Palestine became the responsibility of the Foreign Office, in effect if not completely in theory. The two postwar Colonial Secretaries, George Glenvil Hall and Arthur Creech Jones, remained responsible for the administration in Palestine, while the Foreign Secretary, Ernest Bevin, undertook the task of resolving the problem in the international sphere. The two functions could not in fact be separated and Palestine came under dual control, but, however it may have been below, on the surface this difficult arrangement seemed to work smoothly. With the access of increased American interest and influence in the affairs of Palestine the major role fell inevitably to the Foreign Office, and since the new Prime Minister left most of the initiative for Palestine to his Foreign Secretary, it followed that till the end of the mandate the dominating personality on the British side was Ernest Bevin.

In a moment of tragic irony Bevin declared that he staked his "political future" on solving the problem of Palestine. He is usually held to have handled the problem with greater ineptitude than any of his predecessors, not even excluding Lord Passfield. The judgment is harsh and has led to others: he has been described as an anti-Semite and an ignorant blunderer. The charges are not baseless but they need qualification. For example, his ignorance has been exaggerated. He had some experience of Zionism at the time of the second Labour government, when the Zionists were protesting against the Passfield White Paper. At that time the representative of Histadruth in Great Britain, Dov Hos, called on Bevin as a fellow Trades Unionist for help, and according to the account of Mr. Ben-Gurion, he gave it abundantly. He assured Dov Hos that "our boys," meaning the Trades Union Members of Parliament, would vote against the measure and that he would warn Ramsay MacDonald of the parliamentary dangers that he was walking into; "Don't worry" he said, *"I'll* tell the old man." It was the belief of Dov Hos that Bevin's intervention was decisive.[14] In the light of after events this episode can indicate where Bevin's weakness lay. He believed that his many, remarkable and successful years of service in

[14] Mr. Ben-Gurion in an interview with the writer. He was uncertain of the nickname employed by Bevin for Ramsay MacDonald.

the Trades Union movement had taught him all he needed to know for the management of affairs. His first biographer shrewdly remarks, "like most men self-educated by experience Bevin tended to underestimate what his own experience did not make intelligible." In the past, he had had trouble with Jews who were in a state of feud with Catholics in the Transport and General Workers Union, and he had succeeded in disciplining both out of their tendency to weaken solidarity. He had had more experience than most men of Jewish religious grouping but he had none of Jewish nationalism, and when he met it he refused to accept that this was not the thing he knew.

These obstinate limitations to a mind that was otherwise perceptive and capacious did make him accept too eagerly advice that was learned and agreed with his prejudice, and such advice he found abundantly in the Foreign Office,[15] Preoccupied with the new threat from Russia and anxious to preserve the good will of the Arabic-speaking world which Bevin, in common with most other Labour men, had never studied. With his want of patience and with his easily aroused feelings, he gave way in the end to extravagant delusions. In the last phase of the mandate he came near to anti-Semitism; not to the thoroughgoing racial superstition, but to grotesque belief in world-wide secret Jewish plots against his country and himself. It was a lamentable case of the "infirmity of a noble mind," but when judging Bevin it must always be remembered that in dealing with Palestine he was dealing with a problem that had no solution, in which he was often opposed by the most repulsive form of gangsterism, and that even had he pursued a policy ten times more liberal than the one he did, he must always have appeared as a dishonest evader in Jewish eyes, loaded as he was with the vote-catching folly of party politics.

Bevin's failure, along with that of many of his predecessors, can be interpreted as a "failure of communication." He and the Jewish leaders could never see Palestine through the same eyes, and when they did exchange spectacles both parties shuddered and asked for their own back. The British view took no account of the spiritual depth of the disaster from which the Jews of the world were emerging, of the extent of psychic damage, of the extraordinary measures needed to restore spiritual health; in the British administrative view the Jews appeared as presenting a problem similar to that of the bombed-out citizens of London or Coventry: to deny them sympathy would be inhuman; to assist them to find new "living units" was a positive duty; to allow them to criticize rehabilitation plans through appointed authorities was in accordance with respectable

[15] Richard Crossman, *A Nation Reborn*. London, 1960.

democratic procedure; but to tolerate their noncooperation in an hour of need was mere weakness, and to allow them to combine for purposes of rebellion was to endanger those very principles of the rule of law for which the war had been fought. The Jewish view (as this seems to the writer) has been described already in this book. It was focused on one thing: the need for redemption. In the postwar years it showed an added virtue in recognizing this as a supreme purpose, but it also showed in heightened form its perennial defects. From the very beginning, from the days of Herzl, modern Zionism showed a feeble awareness of the claims of the people inhabiting Palestine. They were called Arabs; more precisely Syrians of Palestine; more precisely descendants of ancient Canaanites, Hebrews, Greeks, Romans, Arabs, Crusaders, Turks, Egyptians, and other nationalities of more recent times. They spoke Arabic and thought of themselves as Arab nationals, so they had and have a respectable historical claim to be thought of as Arabs. To the Jews they were an obstacle, and when chicanery and self-deception were laid aside were not thought of as anything else. The binationalist party survived to the very end but never received the smallest support from the Jewish Agency. All the wrong was not on Bevin's and the British side.

The problem, then, was an insoluble one. But means came to hand in the first days of the Labour government which could have diminished the problem (though for how long it is hard to say), and through diminution might conceivably (though this is not to suggest probabilities) have allowed some return to gradualism. The chance was resolutely set aside, less through ignorance than through knowing too much. The story, followed from its beginning to its shadowy end, is curiously illuminating. It concerns the proposal to allow one hundred thousand of the Jewish survivors of the final solution to enter Palestine.

The proposal was first raised by Dr. Weizmann and the Jewish Agency in their May and June memoranda, as mentioned already. Later, in June, 1945, Mr. Truman took a fateful initiative. He instructed Earl G. Harrison, the Dean of the University of Pennsylvania Law School and the American representative on the Intergovernmental Committee on Refugees, to furnish him with statistics of "displaced persons," especially regarding those Jews who were considered "nonrepatriable." He was determined to do something to help such people. He was sceptical (so he recorded afterward) of the views on such questions that he heard from the "striped-pants boys" in Washington. "It seemed to me," he said in his memoirs, "that they didn't care enough about what happened to the thousands of displaced persons who were involved." In the meantime the new

President had affirmed his predecessor's Zionist and Arabian policies. He attended the Potsdam Conference from July 17th to the 1st of August. The Palestine question was not on the agenda, but the President took the occasion to tell Mr. Churchill and Mr. Attlee (after his accession in late July) that he hoped that as many Jews as could be peaceably settled in Palestine would immediately be allowed in. Both Prime Ministers wanted to know whether they could count on American help if this was agreed. Mr. Truman, faithful to his Arabian inheritance, answered no. On his return from Potsdam Mr. Truman held a press conference in the United States in which he made public his agreement with "the American view . . . that we want to let as many of the Jews into Palestine as it is possible to let into that country," adding, "I have no desire to send 500,-000 American soldiers there to make peace in Palestine." [16] As a result of these encounters in Potsdam and this press conference Mr. Attlee and Mr. Bevin seem to have developed an attitude of some distrust toward the President.

On the 1st of August a World Zionist Conference (not to be confused with a Congress) met in London. Dr. Weizmann spoke cheerfully of Zionist prospects with a Labour government in Britain, but Ben-Gurion expressed a more typical Zionist view when he warned against optimism and urged "passive and active resistance to the implementation of the White Paper policy in its present form or in any modified shape." As Professor Kirk remarks: " 'resistance,' 'battle,' 'offensive,' and 'struggle' were key words." The august head of the Zionist Organization of America, Rabbi Abba Hillel Silver, hinted that virtue might lie in violence and asserted that it might be "the height of statesmanship to be unstatesmanlike." This seems to have been aimed at Weizmann's persistent belief in the merits of diplomatic negotiation. Silver may not have perfectly realized to whom he was giving encouragement.

The immediate upshot of this conference was that Ben-Gurion led a Zionist delegation to the Colonial Office and put forward a demand in the strongest terms that 100,000 immigration certificates should be immediately issued for the use of European Jews, and that Palestine should be declared a Jewish State. Within ten days of reaching office the Labour Party were asked to cash part of the enormous check that they had made out to Zionism in a flourish of excitement. The Colonial Secretary was very shocked and said that the behavior of his visitors "was different from anything which I had ever experienced." [17] He did not return an official

[16] Truman, *op. cit.*
[17] Hansard, 23rd April, 1947.

answer till the 25th of August by which time he had received a warning from the London office of the Arab League saying that the latter would never accept Palestine as a Jewish homeland. In mid-August Azzam, speaking officially on behalf of the Arab League, declared in Cairo that Western support of Zionism could cause "a new crusader's war." Mr. Glenvil Hall's answer was, in consequence, one of studied moderation. He proposed that the 2,000 immigration certificates remaining from the White Paper quota should be made immediately available to the Jewish Agency, and that Arab agreement should then be sought to a further monthly immigration of 1,500.[18] This proposition was indignantly rejected.

At about the same time, in the second half of August, President Truman received the findings of Earl G. Harrison. As regards the Jewish nonrepatriable population, still remaining in wretched conditions in the same camps where they had suffered, he calculated the number at 100,-000. He was aware, as mentioned in his report, of the Zionist demand to the Colonial Office for this number of Jewish immigrants, and he made no secret of the fact that this had influenced his calculation, but later estimates show that it was also an objective one. The most important point that Harrison made from a political point of view was that "for some of the European Jews, there is no acceptable or even decent solution for their future other than Palestine." "They feel," he wrote in another passage, "that only in Palestine will they be welcomed and given an opportunity to live and work." He strongly recommended that the demand of the Jewish Agency should be allowed. "There is no question," Harrison said, "but that the request thus made would, if granted, contribute much to the sound solution for the futures of Jews who . . . do not wish . . . to return to their countries of nationality. No other single matter is, therefore, so important from the viewpoint of Jews of Germany and Austria . . . who have known the horrors of concentration camps as is the disposition of the Palestine question."

Mr. Truman decided to give full encouragement to Harrison. His first move was to send the report to Mr. Attlee with a long letter recommending British action in conformity with its findings. Mr. Attlee's reply[19] was given in two installments. It was not cordial. Referring (presumably) to the recent rejection by the Jewish Agency of Mr. Glenvil Hall's offer, he

---

[18] Kirk, Hurewitz, op. cit.

[19] Given in paraphrase in Truman, op. cit. Kirk and Hurewitz both refer to reports that Mr. Attlee made acceptance conditional on American cooperation, but this is not mentioned by Mr. Truman.

told the President that the Jews were not at the moment making use of certificates available to them. He pointed out that the demand for an immigration of 100,000 was not an isolated attempt to rescue deserving cases of hardship but part of a general demand for the total abrogation of the White Paper, made without the slightest regard for the consequences in the Middle East. He reminded the President of the assurances given by both their predecessors that before any radical action was taken in Palestine the Arabs would be consulted. He would endeavor to obtain facilities for immigration but he asked that no major policy should be initiated before "the United Nations could assume charge of the situation." [20]

September was a month of increasing and conflicting tensions. The British government was in no mood to welcome the American President's latest intervention which coincided with the arrival of intelligence reports that under the new Rama, Moshe Sneh, Haganah was negotiating an alliance with Irgun and the Sternists, and that the brief and uneasy armistice between the new active post-Biltmore Zionism and the recklessly pledged Labour government was likely to come to an end in weeks or perhaps days. The Labour Party at the same time was threatening to split over the Palestine question, between those who were shocked at the apparent disregard of the pre-election pledges and those who recognized that these could not be carried out in the face of the hostility of Russia and the strategic needs which they suddenly imposed.

In America the strains of disagreement were even more strongly in evidence because they involved activity at the highest political level. Mr. Attlee's dry and discouraging letters in answer to Mr. Truman's plea were to the taste of the State Department who (in Truman's words) "continued to be more concerned about the Arab reaction than the sufferings of the Jews." In mid-September Harrison's report was made public by order of the President and with the clearest indications that he supported the proposals. According to Sumner Welles the President's political gesture, on this occasion, was largely dictated by party interests. In the presidential election of autumn, 1944, Governor Thomas E. Dewey had sought votes by proclaiming as part of the Republican program "the reconstitution of Palestine as a Jewish commonwealth," and, in the opinion of Sumner Welles, Mr. Dewey at this time planned to seek advantage, in the course of interelectional maneuver, by making some Palestine immigration proposal far in excess of Harrison's. Mr. Truman therefore, according

[20] Kirk, *op. cit.,* indicates that even at this early stage the British government were believed to be planning the handing back of responsibility for Palestine to U.N.O. as the successor of the League of Nations.

to this interpretation, anticipated Governor Dewey, on the advice of party managers. The facts, given the authority, are almost certainly correct, but they should not obscure a certain obstinate, decent, inalienable conviction in Truman's mind that, no matter what the political arguments for and against different policies, the broken people surviving in Himmler's concentration camps must be given their chance to remake their lives. He was in 1945 in a position of enormous strength as a President of the United States, and of enormous weakness as a Vice-President who had automatically succeeded without massive electoral support. He had the odd but inconveniently long-term advantage of being universally underestimated. He could not insist on policy beyond a certain point, and when he was pressed by his advisers he felt obliged to agree to the request of the State Department that Roosevelt's last letter to ibn Saud should be published in September.[21] The split mind of American policy on Palestine was now there for everyone to see. Confidence in him declined accordingly. And yet Mr. Truman persisted in his determination that somehow or other those hundred thousand lost human beings would get where they wanted and needed to go.

During the month of October in Palestine, the last month during which Lord Gort was High Commissioner, there were preparations for battle on both sides; some skirmishes, some bloodshed, but still a lingering hope that the British government might yet contrive a policy in conformity with their pledges. As a guarantee of security the 6th Airborne Division arrived during this month. It was one of the most distinguished units to have arisen from the Second World War, and was now detailed to a frustrating, repulsive, and desolating task. The clandestine broadcasting station of Haganah, known as the "Voice of Israel" (Kol Israel), was heard in Palestine, with great effect, for the first time since 1939. But these were lesser matters compared with the rise of illegal immigration.

The activities of the Committee for Illegal Immigration and especially of the Bricha increased greatly because they could call on the services both of the mobilized and demobilized men of the Jewish Brigade, and many Zionist sympathizers, Jewish and Gentile, in the UNRRA organization. The Second World War, with its swift and elaborate development of resistance forces, of escape routes and spying networks, had evolved techniques for clandestine movement that left the prewar methods of illegal immigration into Palestine far behind. The Mossad le Aliyah Beth and the Bricha gained two important and unexpected new allies in the immediate postwar months. The famous American-Jewish charitable organization,

[21] Truman, *op. cit.*

The Joint Distribution Committee, commonly known as "The Joint," had always been scrupulous in abiding by the spirit and letter of international law, but, in the course of 1944, its directors had been stung by Zionist accusations that in maintaining their correct attitude in a lawless age they were failing their brethren. For the first time, so far as appears, they actively defied existing law in Palestine, taking as their justification its doubtful validity in Jewish eyes.[22] They lent their massive aid to the smuggling of Jews from a devastated central Europe where homelessness was almost the common lot, into the land "promised of old to Abraham and his seed for ever." The other unexpected ally was to be found in numerous French people in official employment who liked to help Zionists in a high-minded operation which they reckoned might be as disagreeable to the British as the recent high-minded British operation in Syria and Lebanon had been to the French.[23] It is believed that 8,000 illegal immigrants or would-be immigrants passed through the Jewish Brigade lines in the course of seven weeks in the summer of 1945.[24] But none of this Mossad action was commensurate with the need, as the Jewish Agency saw it, of the Jewish people.

As early as September 23rd the new Rama proposed that the forces of Haganah in conjunction with their terrorist allies should undertake a vast sabotage operation, described as "a single serious incident," which would be publicized as widely as possible with the object of serving as "a warning and an indication of much more serious incidents that would threaten the safety of all British interests in the country." (The term "British interests" included plans already under way to use Palestine as a major military base in preference to Egypt.) Dr. Weizmann, Ben-Gurion, and Moshe Shertok were all in England at this time pursuing their fruitless negotiations with the government, so the Rama sent the proposal by telegram to the Agency's London office. The telegram was intercepted and deciphered by the British Secret Service.[25] With this information in their hands, British resistance to Jewish demands inevitably stiffened. On receiving Dr. Weizmann on the 5th of October Ernest Bevin opened the conversation by bursting out with : "Wht do mean by refusing the White Paper certificates? Are you trying to force my hand? If you want a fight you can have it!" An idea became firmly implanted in British governmental minds that

[22] Agar, Kirk. Also Dr. Bauer, a communication.
[23] A private communication to the writer in Israel.
[24] *With the Jewish Brigade* by Bernard Casper. London, 1947. Quoted in Kirk.
[25] Kirk, *op. cit.* Agency leaders suggested that this and other telegrams were forged but they did not press the point. Begin, who was closely concerned and who is more prolific than others in anti-British accusations, has no doubt about their authenticity.

the whole Zionist leadership and following were now given to terrorism, and some events of October, a Palmach operation on the 10th in which the Jewish troops liberated over two hundred interned illegal immigrants, a half-day general strike with violent demonstrations, the proclamation of "The Jewish Resistance Movement" by Kol Israel, and the accumulating evidence from further deciphered telegrams all confirmed the idea.

On the night of the 31st of October the "single serious incident" took place. Palmach troops sank three small naval craft and wrecked railway lines in fifty different places; Irgun attacked the railway station at Lydda, and the Sternists attacked the Haifa oil refinery. The attacks were accomplished with great skill and little loss of life, probably none intentionally.[26] The operation had the desired effect of making the British government think seriously about Palestine, but it also had the effect of solidifying yet further Bevin's resistance.

When in doubt in former years the British government had always done the same thing, they had invariably appointed a royal commission of inquiry. They did the same in the October of 1945, but with a difference. It was essential, after President Truman's interventions and in view of the dependence of Great Britain on the Anglo-American alliance, and on an American loan, to have American cooperation. So instead of the classic Royal Commission an "Anglo-American Committee of Inquiry" was instituted. There were delays in its formation, apparently due to the stresses of party politics in America, and the announcement of its mission was not made till the 13th of November. The terms of reference were concentrated on two essential points: "to examine political, economic and social conditions in Palestine as they bear upon the problem of Jewish immigration," and "to examine the position of the Jews in those countries in Europe where they have been the victims of Nazi and Fascist persecution."

The Committee was composed of twelve members, six American and six British.[27] Great hopes centered on them.

Mr. Bevin had by now moved into an uncomfortable position which

[26] The Irgunists and Sternists needed to make a favorable impression on Haganah in this first large combined operation.

[27] The American members were: Professor Frank Aydelotte (Director of the Princeton Research Institute); Editor Frank W. Buxton; Senator Bartley C. Crum; Judge Joseph C. Hutcheson (American Chairman); James G. MacDonald; Ambassador William Philips. The British members were W. F. Crick (economic adviser to the Midland Bank); R. H. S. Crossman, M. P.; Sir Frederick Leggett (Deputy Secretary of State, Ministry of Labour and National Service 1942–45); R. E. Manningham-Buller, M.P. (now Lord Dilhorne); Robert, Lord Morrison (former member of the House of Commons); Sir John Singleton (High Court Judge and British Chairman).

had been tenanted by several Colonial Secretaries and High Commissioners. An impression, a fixed idea had made itself felt among many Zionists that he was a dedicated enemy. It followed that whatever he did or said was found to suggest horrible meanings. The critical moment when this view of Bevin came into definitive focus seems to have occurred on the 13th of November, and his reputation as a maniacal anti-Semite largely rests on the angry interpretation by Zionists of the remarks he made when announcing the Anglo-American Committee to Parliament, and at a subsequent press conference. In his speech in the House of Commons he said that the government "would not accept the view that the Jews should be driven out of Europe or that they should not be permitted to live again in these countries without discrimination." It was on this occasion that he said: "I will stake my political future on solving this problem," adding, "but not in the limited sphere presented to me now," meaning not in Palestine only.

But the gravest imputations were deduced from what he said at his press conference afterward. When he was asked for his opinion of the Zionist plans for increasing the natural resources of Palestine, he replied that he considered them "eighty percent of propaganda with twenty percent of fact." He probably had in mind a book called *Palestine, Land of Promise* by Dr. Walter C. Lowdermilk of the American Christian Palestine Committee in which the author claimed that, following the example of the Tennessee Valley Authority, Palestine could hold a population of approximately six million.[28] Lowdermilk was hailed as a prophet of Zion, and this remark about eighty percent propaganda was thought offensive enough, but the utterance which (invariably quoted out of context) is to this day held against Bevin with feelings of anger and disgust, and which Dr. Weizmann three years after described as "gratuitously brutal," occurred when he endeavored to sum up his speech for the press in the sort of honest, matey, no-nonsense language that people expected of him. "I am very anxious," he said, "that Jews shall not in Europe over-emphasise their racial position. The keynote of the statement I made in the House is that I want the suppression of racial warfare, and therefore if the Jews, with all their sufferings, want to get too much at the head of the queue, you have the danger of another anti-Semitic reaction through it all."[29]

[28] The book was not published in England till 1946 but had had a world-wide sale from America in the war.
[29] The offense caused by this remark may have been through a fancied reference to American anti-Semitic witticisms to the effect that Jews behave unfairly in queues. The joke is not known in England and Bevin was certainly alluding on this occasion,

One can imagine Arthur Balfour making the same sort of point in fastidious, careful, round-about and stylish language, and being quoted with approbation after by his Zionist friends. But Bevin had become a propaganda target and whatever he did was held to be bad.

The next day Kol Israel made what was probably the first public Jewish comment on what Bevin had intended as an appeal for moderation: "What Hitler did in his murderous blitz against the Jewish people is now being repeated in the form of slow, grinding, political policy by the democracies. We are being condemned to live in an intolerable ghetto so as not to deprive Europe of its Jewish talents. The new proposals are anti-Jewish and inhuman etc., etc." [30]

At the time when Bevin made these remarks, the hope for moderation was not only weak on the Jewish side, but even lower among the Arabs. A few days before there had been a rising in Tripoli, on the 5th of November, and this had turned into a massacre in which about a hundred Jews had been killed. There was plenty of reason for supposing that a pro-Zionist policy by Britain would set aflame the whole Arabic-speaking world, and perhaps the whole Islamic world. It was possible, even probable, that the United States would relapse into isolationism, as strongly hinted by Mr. Truman's remarks at Potsdam.[31]

November and December of 1945 passed in much the same way as October had done, so far as Palestine was concerned. There was no further pretense of an armistice between the Zionists and the British; disorders (notably a rising in Tel Aviv in which British official buildings were burned and British shops looted) grew more savage in character; the illegal immigrations grew in number and in skillful management, obtaining such general assent as even included that of so moderate a man as Judah Magnes; Zionist propaganda progressively succeeded in transforming hatred of Nazism into hatred of Bevin, and children in communal settlements were taught a "spitting drill" to be used against British soldiers amid screams of "English bastards" and "Gestapo" with the object, sometimes achieved, of goading them into "incidents"; yet in spite of a continual increase of tension, the state of Palestine during the remainder of

---

and in a good-humored way, to the distressing amount of queueing necessitated by shortages in England.

[30] Quoted in Kirk, *op. cit.*

[31] Richard Crossman, *Palestine Mission*. London, 1950. This book contains not only the best account of the Anglo-American Committee but of the relevant state of political feeling in England at that time.

1945 remained far from that of warfare.[32] A change of policy by the British government in conformity with their pledges could have had the effect of a complete change of attitude in the Yishuv, especially at a time when the deep psychological wounds of recent suffering had had the effect of making them extraordinarily liable to sudden reversals of feeling. But the British government saw no way to effect such a change without endangering the whole Western position. For all Winston Churchill's close sympathy with Zionism, it is hard to believe that a Conservative government would have acted very differently. For the moment the hopes of the Jews and British, but not those of the Arabs, were centered on the Anglo-American Committee.

They did not begin work till the last days of 1945. In the meantime Mr. Truman took action in the hope of reducing the tensions of the last months. As may be imagined, American conduct over Palestine since the end of the war had not made for much love of America in Great Britain. Mr. Truman's policy was certainly open to the uncomfortably telling charge that the United States, largely for reasons of internal politics, was contributing a great deal of advice and moral exhortations to the problem of Palestine but nothing whatsoever in the way of practical help. America, to many eyes, was playing an ignoble part. The State Department was conscious of this and warned the President of the adverse effects that might come from uncritical support of Zionist claims. "No Government," a memorandum of September had stated, "should advocate a policy of mass immigration unless it is prepared to assist in making available the necessary security forces, shipping, housing, unemployment guarantees . . . In view of the foregoing, the United States should refrain from supporting a policy of large-scale immigration into Palestine. . . ."[33]

Mr. Truman could not turn back now, especially when he found himself supported in his Zionist policy to an embarrassingly extreme degree. The resolution committing Congress to the Biltmore program, which had been deferred on Stimson's intervention in 1944, was revived at the end of 1945. On the 19th of December an almost identical resolution was adopted, enjoining the United States government to secure the opening of Palestine "for free entry of Jews into that country . . . that there shall be full opportunity for colonization and development, so that they may freely proceed with the upbuilding of Palestine as the Jewish National Home" (not "a national home *in* Palestine").

In these circumstances Mr. Truman made an immediate endeavor to

---

[32] Kirk, *op. cit.*
[33] Quoted in Truman, *op. cit.*

establish that line of policy which, from the very beginning of the European disaster in 1933, could alone have given the Palestine question a chance of peaceful solution. On the 22nd of December the President issued an official statement of policy to the effect that the admission of refugees from Europe into the United States was to be expedited. The administration of this policy was to be in the hands of an interdepartmental committee. A directive in the sense of the President's statement was sent to American embassies and consulates. But Mr. Truman's initiative did not involve a change of legislation, and for that reason it at first failed completely because it went radically against twenty years of fixed American policy. As Richard Crossman pointed out: "The quotas were designed and administered not to assist but to prevent the entry of precisely those homeless, helpless Jews and non-Jews of Eastern Europe who made up the "refugee problem." [34] It was found, ten months after the 22nd of December, that since the President's statement and directive, only 4,767 people had been admitted under the committee's guidance, numbers which were too small to have any influence on the problem. American behavior in this matter was not egregiously contemptible. Amid the social and political difficulties of the unhappy years after the war no nation could face the added difficulty of doing its duty with regard to the victims of Nazism. In the end the American law was modified in the sense of Mr. Truman's statement, but the process was slow and did not become effective till two and a half years later, far too late to save the peace in Palestine. It seems that history will record a regret that the politicians and publicists in America who clamored for an enormous Jewish exodus to Palestine did not give the same support to Mr. Truman's initiative in December, 1945.

On the 27th of December Irgun undertook an operation independent of Haganah: coordinated raids at three points, on two police headquarters and an arms dump, killing nine members of the British forces. According to Begin, Haganah approved the raid.[35] Ben-Gurion and Moshe Shertok informed the new High Commissioner, Sir Alan Cunningham, that they "completely dissociated the Zionist movement" from these crimes but added that any effort by themselves to cooperate against the terrorists "has been rendered futile by the British government's present policy." Such was the background of incident in Palestine against which the Anglo-American Committee started work in Washington.

Zionist activity was running true to form. The committee heard abundant evidence in their first sessions in America, and the British members

[34] Crossman, *Palestine Mission.*
[35] Menachem Begin, *The Revolt.* London, 1951.

seem to have been tempted into a state of anti-Zionism if not worse by the torrents of Zionist anti-British propaganda to which witnesses subjected them. They moved to London in January, 1946, where they heard more evidence and where they had an informal but portentous meeting with Ernest Bevin. He gave them a solemn though unofficial assurance that provided they turned in a unanimous report he would "do everything in his power to put it into effect." [36]

In view of subsequent events, this utterance of Mr. Bevin was extremely unwise. It was held later and very naturally to be a proof of his dishonesty. But a dishonest man would surely have had more guile than to compromise himself in this manner. In the writer's opinion, it seems much more likely that, having been convinced of the strength and importance of the Arab case with which he had acquainted himself in the Foreign Office with all the excitement of learning something new, and now clinging tenaciously to his new faith with all the ardor of a convert, Mr. Bevin could not but believe that when these committee members went to Palestine, when they saw the situation face to face, they would quickly dispose of all this Truman nonsense about foisting a hundred thousand immigrants onto an already densely populated country. He could not believe that a group of intelligent and disinterested men would take a view very different from his own.

From London the committee divided into separate parties to visit Poland, Czechoslovakia, Germany, and Austria, meeting again in Vienna in February. They came to the conclusion that as to the numbers of those in need the request of the Jewish Agency and the findings of Earl G. Harrison were based on sound statistics. They found that the numbers of Jewish survivors in the "assembly centers" of Germany and Austria amounted to some 98,000 people, most of them Poles. Mr. Crossman later recorded: "Even if there had not been a single foreign Zionist or a trace of Zionist propaganda in the camps these people would have opted for Palestine." He had a horrifying meeting with a boy of about sixteen who acted as "camp policeman" in a small center on the Austrian-Italian frontier. "His had been the survival of the fittest," wrote Mr. Crossman, "of the personality able to cajole, outwit or bribe." His mother had managed to reach America and of her this youth said: "I have cut her off, root and branch. She has betrayed the destiny of my nation. She has sold out to the Goy. She has run away to America. It is the destiny of my nation to be the lords of Palestine. It is written in the Balfour Declaration."

The committee learned how the organizing bodies elected from among

[36] Crossman, *Palestine Mission*.

the survivors successfully blocked plans made by UNRRA for settling orphans in Switzerland and other European countries, and perhaps even their thorough researches did not give the committee the full measure of the spirit of uncompromise here. The Jewish leaders of the survivors sometimes went beyond what the Jewish Agency itself considered tolerable in this matter. In November of 1945 the British government had conveyed to the Zionist organization that they were prepared to admit a thousand Jewish orphans into England. The organization accepted with thanks and sent an emissary, Adler Rudel, to Germany to negotiate with the relevant body which was known as "The Central Committee of Liberated Jews of Bavaria." To Rudel's shocked amazement the committee absolutely refused to cooperate. They told the emissary that humanitarian effort could not be dissociated from politics. They put it this way: "Why turn these children from being assimilated Diasporites in Germany into being assimilated Diasporites in England? We want them in Palestine as Jews." They refused to yield either to Rudel's pleadings or to his indignation.[37]

From Europe the committee went to Cairo in order to hear evidence from representatives of the Arab League. They heard a unanimous opinion from many different witnesses that the only rights that Zionists could claim in Palestine were those of a minority in an Arab State: they had no claims whatsoever to Palestine. There was no shift in Arab opinion since the earliest days of the military regime. During these Cairo sessions, however, the committee did hear far the most eloquent plea against Zionism delivered at any time by an Arab nationalist. It had been urged that since Jews and Arabs had a common Semitic origin the Arabs should be more accommodating to Zionism, and to this Abdur Rahman Azzam gave a reply that has been widely quoted [38] and should be remembered again here.

"Our brother," said Abdur Rahman, "has gone to Europe and the West and come back something else. He has come back a Russified Jew, a Polish Jew, a German Jew, an English Jew. He has come back with a totally different conception of things, Western and not Eastern. That does not mean that we are necessarily quarrelling with anyone who comes from the West. But the Jew, our old cousin, coming back with imperialistic ideas, with materialistic ideas, with reactionary or revolutionary ideas and trying to implement them first by British pressure and then by American pressure, and then by terrorism on his own part—he is not the old cousin and we do not extend to him a very good welcome. The Zionist, the new Jew,

[37] A report of Adler Rudel's meeting shown to the writer in Israel.
[38] Twice by Richard Crossman, in *Palestine Mission* and *A Nation Reborn*.

wants to dominate, and he pretends that he has got a particular civilising mission with which he returns to a backward, degenerate race in order to put the elements of progress into an area which has no progress. Well, that has been the pretension of every power that wanted to colonise and aimed at domination. The excuse has always been that the people are backward and he has got a human mission to put them forward. The Arabs simply say 'No' . . . We are not going to allow ourselves to be controlled either by great nations or small nations or dispersed nations."

This is perhaps the clearest and most convincing statement ever made of Zionism's misfortune that, by an accident of time, its development depended on imperialism, when imperialism was waning.

From Cairo the committee traveled to Jerusalem on the 6th of March. The situation in Palestine was the dreadfully familiar one with the familiar increase in tension during the last months. One the 17th of January, 1946, Mr. Bevin had informed the United Nations General Assembly that Great Britain intended to recognize Transjordan as an independent sovereign state in the near future. The British government could hardly do anything else if it was to abide by the pledges of the League mandate, or retain the good will of Abdullah who had been Britain's only active Arab ally in the war, but this liberal move, of which the arch enemy was the spokesman, was quickly interpreted by Zionists as an act of oppression subtly planned to act as a check to the natural growth of the National Home. During this same month the new High Commissioner, Sir Alan Cunningham, tried strenuously, and of course in vain, to obtain Arab agreement to a monthly Jewish immigration of fifteen hundred. Then in the last days of January the High Commissioner attempted to appease both sides simultaneously by large-scale concessions, and to assert the authority of the mandatory against repeated acts of terrorism and sabotage. On the 28th he promulgated severe emergency laws which among other provisions ordained death as the maximum penalty not only for taking part in a terrorist raid but for belonging to a terrorist society. Two days later he announced that Jewish immigration might proceed up to 1,500 a month despite Arab objections and on the same day he permitted the return to Palestine of the Mufti's cousin Jemal el Husseini, Haj Amin's close associate both in the rebellion and the Rashid Ali coup d'état. These measures failed to appease. The Arabs replied to the restoration of Jemal with a general strike and the Jews to the concession regarding immigration with renewed acts of resistance in successful defiance of emergency laws which were too extreme to be put into operation. Three big sabotage operations were carried out between the 20th and 25th of February, only a week before the committee arrived in the country.[39]

The committee heard many Arab and Jewish witnesses in Jerusalem. Most of them on both sides talked, as expected, according to an agreed party line and in a somewhat more conformist spirit than could be taken seriously by anyone used to freedom of speech. There were terrorists on both sides who had proved that they had no scruple about killing deviationists. A high pitch of farce was reached on the 11th of March when Ben-Gurion was asked to give evidence about Haganah. His replies were so evasive that he appeared to be saying that he was wholly ignorant of the existence of a military body described by that term. He insisted that there was a Hebrew word "Haganah" meaning "defense," but whether this word was used in connection with a legal or charitable or insurance society or with something else, he seemed all innocently not to know.[40] A few of the witnesses, however, spoke their mind with candor and made a correspondingly deep impression, notably Dr. Weizmann. So long as there were commissions of inquiry there remained more need of his negotiating skill, than of party-line assertion, in serious discussion.

Some of his statements on this occasion are of lasting interest. When he was asked how the establishment of a Jewish State could eliminate the evil of anti-Semitism, he replied: "We appear to the Gentiles as a peculiar people, suspended between heaven and earth. We must explain ourselves, and everyone who does that is condemned in advance." He nodded slowly in the affirmative when it was put to him that he considered that Europe could no longer be a homeland for Jews, and when someone asked the shocking question whether Hitler had, in that case, won the war, he said: "Hitler may be said to have lost the war, but, so far as the Jews are concerned, he won a complete victory." [41] After their European tour of inspection the committee were united on one thing, that the original proposal for 100,000 Jewish immigrants from Europe should be agreed to immediately. When the committee asked Weizmann whether he considered that the figure was a practical one for immigration in one year, he paused and said that the figure seemed to him reasonable, adding "that he did not know whether it would take one or two years to bring these people in." [42] Such honesty and truth came as a breath of fresh air. His politi-

[39] Kirk, Hurewitz, *op. cit.*
[40] Public hearings before the Anglo-American Committee. Quoted in Kirk.
[41] Crum, *op. cit.*
[42] Crossman, *op. cit.*

cal colleagues looked agitated. Jemal el Husseini was sitting a few rows behind him.

The Arabs of Palestine did not recognize the validity of the Anglo-American Committee but they did not boycott its sessions. Without exception the Arab witnesses stuck rigidly to their classic role of uncompromising opposition to any increase in the Jewish National Home. They did this sometimes with persuasion and skill, as in the case of Mr. Albert Hourani, or with grotesque ineptitude, as in the case of Jemal el Husseini. Their case was difficult to answer, especially when it returned to the familiar central argument, namely that the present plight of the Jews was not brought about by Moslem Arabs but by Christian Europeans, in spite of which the Arabs, not the Europeans, were being asked to provide relief. No one ever found a reply to that, and even Mr. Bartley Crum who made no secret of total sympathy with Zionism, and who had swallowed much propaganda nonsense in America to the effect that Jewish-Arab hostility was the unnatural result of a British conspiracy, found himself momentarily disturbed in mind by this aspect of the situation.

Repeatedly the members of the committee put before witnesses the proposition for the immigration of 100,000 Jews. They could get no sort of assent from Arabs. From the Jews they obtained a large measure of assent, but usually guarded. From Judah Magnes, testifying on behalf of Ihud, they heard a very unusual plea for the immigration. "Our view," he said, "is based on two assumptions: that Jewish-Arab co-operation is essential, and that the alternative is strife and bloodshed. The Jews want Jewish immigration. Give it to them and they will forget the Jewish State. The Arabs want self-government. Give it to them and they will forget their fears of Jewish immigration." He pointed out that the proposal for 100,000 would result in a smaller proportionate increase in the numbers of the Yishuv than had been envisaged in the Peel proposals. "Let the one hundred thousand in," he said, "even if it means strife. I am going to give you an extreme answer. Even though that were the only way [in the sense of 'strife being the only possible consequence'], I would bring them, but that is not the only way." [43]

The Zionist press in America and Palestine had for some time been inveigling against Magnes as a Jew false to his people, and there were further and more bitter press denunciations of him after the public session at which he made these depositions. He was sixty-eight years old at this time, of frail health, nearing the end of his life. With a determination that was heroic he clung without compromise to all that was finest in the pa-

[43] Crum, *op. cit.*

cific teaching of Judaism, but he wanted for spiritual comfort. The gigantic wickedness of the Nazi regime had shaken his former easy acceptance of his faith; he found himself tempted to doubt the goodness of God and to believe rather in blind forces. He was a lonely man struggling against despair, and in that moment of spiritual crisis, his people called him a traitor.

The committee traveled widely in separate parties, visiting Syria, Lebanon, Iraq, and Saudi Arabia. They traveled all over Palestine too and were served by an efficient fact-collecting secretariat. They determined to make recommendations that were fair to both sides. For this purpose they went to Lausanne on the 28th of March and spent three weeks in discussion and drafting. Mindful of what Mr. Bevin had said to them in London they produced a unanimous report.

Like most of the reports of most of its predecessors this one was still-born. The recommendations, for that reason, need not be closely examined. Partition was rejected as unpractical and so was the proposition that Palestine should be a Jewish or an Arab State. The positive recommendation was binationalism. The committee, in the words of Professor Kirk, "clung to the hope, against all the experience of the past ten years, that somehow the two communities might be induced to live together in peace." They made the familiar mistake of supposing that fairness was relevant to post-Balfour Palestine. In recommending binationalism they proposed the following main conditions: first that the mandatory power should immediately issue 100,000 immigration certificates, in order to settle in Palestine all the Jews in the assembly centers of Europe, and in addition should "facilitate further immigration under suitable conditions"; that Palestine should continue under a system of trusteeship which, since the American members of the committee had made it abundantly clear that the United States would not take an active part in the administration meant an extension of the British mandate; that the restriction on Jewish land-purchase ordained by the White Paper should be withdrawn; finally, and as a measure to gain Arab good will, that it should be illegal to exclude Arab labor in enterprises financed by the Jewish National Fund.[44]

The report was made public in Britain and the United States on the 30th of April, 1946. The British government had in the meantime subjected the findings to critical examination by Foreign Office officials and their service chiefs. They had in consequence and under advice come to the conclusion that the report was an abomination. They thought this not (as would have been reasonable) because binationalism had never

[44] Anglo-American Committee Report.

worked and had no glimmer of a hope of working, but because the report was held to be too conciliatory to Zionist and American ideas and neglectful of British interests. Mr. Bevin refused to meet any of the British committee members on their return, and when Mr. Crossman obtained an interview with Mr. Attlee the encounter was harsh and disapproving on the Prime Minister's side. He told Mr. Crossman that he had "let us down." [45] What Britain wanted in Palestine, now that Egypt was to be evacuated of British troops, was a secure base and the lesson had not yet been appreciated that a base is not secure in a chronically rebellious country. The British political imagination remained beguiled by a nineteenth-century dream of British garrisons circling the world to ensure that "imperial communications were kept open." It lingered on in full strength long after garrisons had lost most of their political validity and was as strongly impressed on the minds of Labour ministers as on those of the sternest die-hard Tory.

But the anger and disapproval of the government before publication were as nothing to the explosion of wrath with which British ministers met the reception of the report on the 30th of April in America. It was published with a covering statement by Mr. Truman in which he gave presidential approval to the pro-Zionist items, notably the immediate admission of the 100,000, but said of the other recommendations that they were "questions of long-range political policies and questions of international law requiring careful study," etc., etc. Even so fair a judge as Mr. Crossman regarded the presidential move as "lamentable." As for old Ernest Bevin he was flung into what his biographer, Francis Williams, no doubt accurately described as "one of the blackest rages" of that not unwrathful man's career.

It is easy to blame these socialist ministers who pledged themselves to Zionism for their short-sighted conduct of Palestine affairs, but the surrounding circumstances must be remembered. Even the most emotional subscriber to the *New Statesman* and its relations was beginning to have reasons to doubt the doctrine of Stalin's far-sighted idealism by this time, and the need to keep the Islamic world south of Russia friendly to the West was being slowly recognized by progressives as something more than the class-fad of a section of the Conservative interest. The Russian conspiracy in Persia was moving toward fulfillment. At the same time British negotiators were in session with United States representatives for a loan to rescue Britain from disaster. Lord Attlee has pertinently described the situation: "We had to have a loan . . . The Americans thought we'd

[45] Crossman, *A Nation Reborn*.

overstated the case. We had not. You can criticise the loan and the arrangements surrounding it—and we fought inch by inch throughout the negotiations—but the fact remains that we could not do without it." [46] In the bitter and often humiliating circumstances of British bargaining from poverty it was very easy to fancy slights where there were none, and to imagine that the rich opponent was putting on gross pressure at all times. There was a natural inclination in a large field of activity toward Anglo-American hostility and it had effect on the reception of the Anglo-American report.

There were these general reasons for the report (which followed American rather than British lines) to be ill received by the British government. But there was a strong particular reason too. Five days before its publication the Stern group in Tel Aviv had raided a military car park which was guarded by two British noncommissioned officers and six men of the Airborne Division. The purpose of the attack seems to have been solely that of mass murder, and of the eight men on guard the Sternists killed seven. [47] The effect of the news on Parliamentary and public opinion in Britain was one of intense anger against Zionists in general, and people remembered with renewed indignation the continual refusal of the Jewish Agency to cooperate thoroughly in the suppression of the terrorist organizations. People heard without surprise or regret that the Divisional Commander had rejected the condolences of the mayor of Tel Aviv on the grounds that "as representative of the community of Tel Aviv" the mayor "could produce sufficient information to lead to the arrest of the criminals instead of which he had, in common with other Zionist officials, adopted an attitude of neutrality." [48] The atrocity of the 25th of April was followed by a counteratrocity on the night of the 26th. Hitherto the discipline of the British troops in the country had been exemplary in the face of provocation, but now there was a serious breakdown in Tel Aviv. At a nearby Jewish village troops took the law into their own hands and wreaked their vengeance on the innocent population, breaking up twelve houses and brutally maltreating numbers of Jews.

Amid such circumstances, the anger of British people at American intervention for the immediate admission of 100,000 is understandable enough, ill-judged as it was. The reaction of the government was immediate—and fatal. While Ernest Bevin appeased his black rage by sending a

[46] Francis Williams, *A Prime Minister Remembers*. London, 1962.
[47] R. D. Wilson, *Cordon and Search*. Aldershot, 1949. The author of this book was an officer in the division.
[48] Kirk, *op. cit.*

vigorous protest to Washington, the Prime Minister gave a statement to the House of Commons on the 1st of May. He sharply criticized Mr. Truman's intervention in favor of the Zionist recommendations, and said that he was curious to know whether such action denoted American willingness to share in the enormous cost and the consequent military commitment entailed by the proposed mass movement. He then made a statement whose effects were described without exaggeration by Mr. Crossman as "catastrophic." He said that there could be no question of admitting so great a number as 100,000 until and unless the "illegal armies," Jewish and Arab, within Palestine surrendered their weapons and disbanded. If he had said that the terrorists must be disbanded as a preliminary to the immigration, then it is possible that he might have had the cooperation of the Jewish Agency. But it was here that the government were betrayed into unwise courses by knowing too much. The clandestine deciphering of Jewish telegrams between Palestine and London had been going on and the government were well aware, unfortunately well aware, of the collusion between Haganah and the terrorists, and this stiffened their attitude when it should have been relaxed. It led them into demanding the disarmament and suppression of Haganah. This was something that no Zionist, and not many non-Zionist Jews could possibly accept. It was most unlikely that even the most ruthless and determined administration would be able to enforce such a measure and, as was pointed out by several critics of the government, the expense in men and resources needed for the abolition of Haganah would be greatly in excess of those needed for supervising the immigration of 100,000, violent as Arab reaction might be. But the government, and especially Ernest Bevin, shocked by the extremism of postwar Zionism, and angered at what they took to be Jewish ingratitude (not wholly unjustly for the government were maintaining a Jewish immigration of 18,000 a year, a fairly high figure by prewar averages) stuck obstinately to their conditions.

What no one in authority seems to have realized then was that the Jewish leaders, acting most honorably from an appalled sense of immediate need, had made a considerable political blunder in asking for 100,000. It is true that they had from the beginning explained that this demand, if agreed to, was not to be the end of immigration, and an immediate acceptance by the Foreign and Colonial Offices might have landed the British government in great difficulty for that reason. But by May, 1946, the simple idea had taken general hold that the Jewish leaders were asking for one thing, for 100,000, and the British were grossly refusing that one humanitarian and necessary demand. Zionist propaganda which, during the last years of the war and the first months after it, had shown amazing skill in England and America, had overreached itself. It had spent so much energy on condemning the refusal of the British government to the admission of 100,000, on painting a picture of Ernest Bevin and his colleagues as another Hitler and his Gestapo,[49] that it had let most of the Biltmore program go by default; it was allowing people to lose sight of the demand that Jewish immigration into Palestine should be limited only by Jewish Agency veto, and that the major purpose was the establishment of a Jewish State. They allowed the world to see the whole problem in terms of 100,000 only.

If Bevin had had the foresight to be true to his promise to back a unanimous report, he must surely have gained a striking victory over the Jewish Agency. After acceptance of the 100,000, any further demand by the Jewish Agency would have been extraordinarily difficult to press home with popular support. With the problem of the displaced Jews in the assembly centers solved there could have been a swing toward moderation among Jews far in excess of what the Jewish Agency under Ben-Gurion wanted. An eminent Jewish authority, Dr. Abba Eban, makes this point. He refers to the fact that Dr. Dalton, according to his autobiography, would have accepted Mr. Truman's proposal had he been Foreign Secretary, and Dr. Eban goes so far as to add: "The irony is that if this friendly inclination had been put into effect the problem would have lost its unendurable tension and it is doubtful if the State of Israel would have arisen."

Dr. Eban's view is not merely a piece of wisdom after the event. There were a number of British Jews who believed at the time that acceptance of the proposal for 100,000 immigrants was the only hope for a gradual and therefore peaceful solution. They put the case for acceptance to men in power without result. The writer remembers being told about these moves by a Jewish friend who at that time served on various refugee committees. He was as well-informed as anyone could be, at that time, about the statistics of displaced persons and prevailing opinion among the Jewish populations of survivors. No one in England, he said, seemed to realize that though the Jewish leaders were putting forward their demands in a polemic and often offensive way, the demands themselves were in fact as

---

[49] On the occasion of General Sir Frederick Morgan's asserting that Haganah were operating in the interest of illegal immigration into Palestine from Europe, an assertion whose truth is not doubted, the Jewish-American entertainer Eddie Cantor took a page in the *New York Times* and devoted it to anti-British governmental propaganda under the title "I Thought Hitler Was Dead." The even less respectable propaganda maneuvers of Mr. Ben Hecht are well known and best forgotten.

moderate as they could make them. As it was they were having difficulty with some of their followers, since to a true dyed-in-the-wool statist Zionist, 100,000 was about a tenth of the immigration considered necessary.[50] Admittedly this opinion seemed to the writer a very biased one at the time, and so presumably it seemed to officials and members of the British government.

The rejection in May of the immigration proposals of the Anglo-American Committee and the offended refusal to agree with Mr. Truman's admittedly undiplomatic action, seems to have been the last occasion when a constructive effort could have been made to reach accord between the mandatory and the Jewish Agency with some slender hope of ultimate Arab acquiescence. This is by no means to say that such an effort would have been successful. It does seem reasonable, however, to say that here was one of the few points where within uncomfortably narrow limits, and facing alternatives which without exception involved considerable risk, the British government had some choice of policy. After this the situation in Palestine sometimes became worse, and momentarily became happier, but it is difficult to see another opportunity which gave any freedom of action within the terms of the mandate. For the British government this was the last crossroads.

Neither the British nor the Americans were in any hurry to proceed to the next stage. Not till three weeks after the 1st of May did the two governments invite formal comment from each other and from Arab and Jewish representatives, and not till three weeks after that did Mr. Truman set up a Cabinet Committee to guide American policy on Palestine. This resulted in one sensible American initiative. The justice of Mr. Attlee's caustic inquiries as to what help America was prepared to give on settling the 100,000 seems to have been admitted and an official offer to finance the transport was conveyed from the American to the British government. The Cabinet Committee was empowered to negotiate with a corresponding British body but the negotiating mission did not arrive in London till the middle of July, 1946. By this time many things had happened to alter the scene.

While the Jews had given the findings of the Anglo-American Committee partial acceptance, much as they had done to the Peel recommenda-

[50] The point was made in the House of Commons by Mr. Ben Levy on 25th February, 1947, that 100,000 was a small number compared to former Jewish aspirations but he made the mistake of supposing that after the Nazi massacres this was the limit of immigration attainable by the Jews.

tions, the member states of the Arab League had rejected them completely and with alarming threats to the American government about the possible suspension of trade between these states and the West. Ibn Saud sent a particularly strong note. As for the Arabs of Palestine, in their elation at Bevin's reaction to the report, they returned to the delights of party wrangling, and it was now that the leadership was taken out of their hands definitely and for good.

At the end of May, 1946, the Mufti arrived in Cairo. He came from France where he had been imprisoned since the end of the war. He is said to have eluded his captors by a crafty disguise, but some authorities consider it not impossible that he received help from French officials.

In mid-June the Labour Party held its annual conference at Bournemouth and for the first time since the great Socialist victory Ernest Bevin had to meet the angry criticism of those many party members who looked with shame and indignation at his policy. They were led by the party chairman, Harold Laski. He deplored that the proposed 100,000 should be made "victims of timidity and hesitation," and spoke of the unsocialist policy of sacrificing "the Jews who escaped from the tortures of Hitlerism to the Arab leaders."

Bevin replied to these strictures in what Professor Kirk has described as his "pragmatic if sometimes barely coherent manner." No surrender, no appeasement—this was the tone of his reply on the 12th of June. As obstinate men will, he saw whatever stood in the way of his goal in wildly exaggerated form. He asserted that to admit 100,000 Jews into Palestine would cost Great Britain another army division and £200,000,000.[51] Abandoning diplomatic niceties he gave full rein to his "black rage" against American interference. It was at this conference that he made an accusation against the United States which was not forgotten or forgiven by Americans in his lifetime: the reason, he said, that there was so much United States pressure for the admission of Jews into Palestine was "because they don't want them in New York." It is known that the remark caused personal distress to Mr. Truman,[52] then vainly battling to soften the American immigration laws, and it fairly drove the New York population mad with indignation. When Bevin went to America later for a meeting of the United Nations, the dockers of New York refused to

[51] Bevin has been much ridiculed for this statement. It expressed an opinion widely held, sometimes in more extreme form, by pro-Arab Englishmen. *Cf.* Sir John Glubb, *A Soldier with the Arabs* (London, 1957): "It was a question of how many divisions of troops would have been necessary to fight a three-cornered civil war against Jews and Arabs simultaneously."

[52] Manuel, *op. cit.*

handle his baggage, and at a baseball match the demonstrations against him were so violent that the authorities feared for his safety and smuggled him out of the stadium.[53] The American press helped on a wide-spreading opinion that between those anti-Semite criminals Ernest Bevin and Adolf Hitler there was little if anything to choose. But as Mr. Maurice J. Goldbloom, an American Jewish correspondent to the Labour Party Conference noted, Bevin's attack was in large part resented because it "contained some uncomfortable grains of truth: many of the most enthusiastic Congressional supporters of Jewish immigration into Palestine were equally enthusiastic advocates of limiting immigration into the United States." [54]

The force of the rank-and-file protests at the Labour Party Conference was weakened by the fact that they synchronized with a new sabotage program in Palestine conducted by the terrorists in conjunction with Haganah. Nine bridges, including four railway bridges and the Allenby bridge across the Jordan, were demolished on the 16th of June. Then followed another period of typical paradox: in Palestine terrorist activity reached a climax; the administration attempted forceful repression, and at the same time in London and Washington the British and American governments initiated a new attempt to solve the insoluble problem.

On the 29th of June, 1946, the administration did something which dramatically illustrated the pass to which Anglo-Jewish relations had come: they ordered the arrest not only of members of Palmach but of the Agency leaders, including Shertok. Ben-Gurion was in Paris, or he would have been taken with rest. There were widespread searchings by the military for Haganah, and especially Palmach arms. Weizmann and the Zionist leaders in Britain and America protested, and the Zionist propaganda machine went into action with stories of atrocities wreaked by the British troops on Jewish settlers, some of which stories were true, most of

---

[53] Williams, op. cit.

[54] Such persons seem to have been adequately represented on the Anglo-American Committee. Vide Sir John Glubb, A Soldier with the Arabs: "A sub-committee of the Anglo-American Committee visited Transjordan. I was present at a reception given in their honour . . . One of the Arabs inquired why the United States did not herself accept some of the 100,000 Jewish immigrants of whom Mr. Truman had spoken. 'There are limits to kindness,' replied the American dryly . . . The United States is the most generous of nations. He could truly have quoted the immense benefits which America had already conferred, as an excuse for her inability to do more. 'If there are limits to American kindness, there are presumably no limits to Arab patience,' retorted one of the Jordanians hotly."

which were exaggerated, and many of which were invented.[55] There was a moment of quiet when it looked as though Zionists of all shades had been stunned into inactivity by the arrests; then, a little over two weeks after the 29th, Irgun went into action with the greatest of their atrocities to date. They blew up a wing of the King David Hotel in Jerusalem, a floor of which was used as British Army Headquarters. Ninety-one persons were killed and forty-five wounded. There were British, Arabs and Jews among the victims.

This gigantic crime was carried out by Irgun alone, though no doubt remains now that Haganah was closely implicated; they were not in agreement over the timing of what was done but had no quarrel over the principle. The evidence of later events strongly indicates that this horrible atrocity sincerely shocked the Jewish Agency as a whole, but for the moment, pursuing their desperate struggle for a Jewish State, for the salvation of their people, they sought for means to divert indignation from themselves and on to the new enemy. Zionist propaganda soon found what it required in the reactions of the commanding officer in Palestine, Lieutenant-General Sir Evelyn Barker. At that time a grotesque policy, modeled on Nazi ideas of racial segregation and known as "nonfraternization," was being attempted (most unsuccessfully one may say to the honor of ordinary men) in Germany, and General Barker in a confidential order to his officers commanded its adoption by the British military toward the Jews. In his fury the General expressed himself in anti-Semitic terms, referring to his plan of "punishing the Jews in a way the race dislikes—by striking at their pockets." As with the truthful remarks of General Sir Frederick Morgan when in late 1945 he asserted the Haganah was taking part in illegal immigration, and the tactless but defensible remarks of Bevin about "the head of the queue," these foolishly ill-considered orders of General Barker were blown up into atrocity-proportions by skillful propaganda maneuvers. In Palestine, Europe, and America the orders were given well-planned publicity which resulted in Barker's minor misdemeanor completely overshadowing Irgun's major one. The newspaper-reading public forgot the multitude of innocent slain.

While these things were happening, an American mission under Ambassador Henry Grady, and deriving its authority from the Cabinet Committee in Washington, had arrived in London to confer with a similar British body. Bevin was ill at this time so the British minister in charge was Mr. Herbert Morrison. The result of the conference was yet another proposed solution which was to follow its many predecessors and a few

[55] Kirk, *op. cit.*

successors into limbo. It was made public on the 30th of July, 1946, and is usually known as the Grady-Morrison plan. The debate on the subject in the House of Commons on the 31st showed that this was in fact an alternative plan to partition devised under Oliver Stanley's secretaryship. It was described as a "provincial autonomy" scheme and it proposed a Jewish boundary not dissimilar from that recommended by Peel except for a large subtraction north of Acre. The rest of the area of Palestine except for a Jerusalem-Bethlehem enclave and the Negev, both to be directly ruled by Britain, went to the Arabs. The autonomy of the two provinces was far removed from independence, even as regards Jewish immigration, and the whole scheme was hedged about with conditions which the leaders on neither side were in a position to accept. It was a reduced version of the Peel recommendation put forward ten years after Peel could have been effective. But the Grady-Morrison plan contained one very interesting detail: it was proposed that within a year of its being accepted 100,000 Jews should be admitted to Palestine. In other words, the British government gave way completely on the one issue which they most blamed the American government, and Mr. Truman in particular, for supporting uncritically. What is equally curious is that this sudden change of mind made so little impression on the course of events, or on public opinion. The proposal for 100,000 was already out of date by July, 1946, though it was to make two more appearances.

Mr. Truman was willing and even anxious to accept the provincial autonomy plan, mainly perhaps because it would carry out Earl G. Harrison's original recommendation for relieving the Jewish refugees of central Europe, but this time he found Jewish and pro-Zionist opposition too strong for him.[56] It seems that the Jews had by now recognized their mistake. Mr. Truman rejected the plan and this meant that the United States did not take part directly in the next episode. This was an attempt to hold a Jewish-Arab-British conference in London, with the provincial autonomy plan as the first subject on the agenda. Both the Palestine Arabs and the Jewish Agency asked for conditions as to representation which the government was not willing to grant, so the conference was confined to the British government, the Arab League states and the Arab League secretariat. They met in the first half of September. The result was an Arab demand for a self-governing Palestine in which the Jews were to hold a third of the Parliamentary seats, Jewish land purchase was to be restricted as at present, and further Jewish immigration to be totally prohibited.

[56] Kirk, op. cit.

When the conference adjourned for two months, there was no prospect of any advance toward agreement.

At this moment, however, both the British government and the Jewish Agency were making genuine efforts to reach a compromise. It seems likely that the appalling crime of the King David Hotel and the continual rise of terrorism with its mounting statistics of murder shocked the Agency leaders back into their former moderation, and it seems too that the complete deadlock in Anglo-Zionist relations following on the arrest of the leaders made the British government and even the intractable Bevin conscious that they may have mishandled their Palestine policy. In August, 1946, before the Arab conference, the Executive of the Jewish Agency (those still at large) met in Paris under the chairmanship of Ben-Gurion who was living there in voluntary exile to escape imprisonment. They drew up a plan which showed a considerable retreat from the official Zionist demands of the Biltmore conference. They proposed a partition of Palestine. The Jewish frontiers they suggested were very similar to those of the present-day state of Israel, with only one large difference, that no claim was laid to Jerusalem and there was thus no "central triangle." The plan was flown to the United States for Mr. Truman's approval and then on the 15th of August pressed on the Colonial Office by Weizmann and two American members of the Agency Executive. But the British government refused to alter the agenda of the forthcoming conference with the Arab League. If they had included this item it is unlikely that there would have been any conference at all. But they noted the change of mind which was not only affecting these leaders but Haganah as well, and when the conference adjourned, conversations were resumed between British ministers and Dr. Weizmann.

With the help of Richard Crossman, Ernest Bevin seems to have forced his mind some way open and he proposed to Weizmann that Palestine should be ruled on a basis of trusteeship for a period of between three and ten years as part of an advance to self-government. To encourage Jewish confidence in the good faith of the British government Mr. Attlee appointed Mr. Arthur Creech Jones, the strongest Zionist sympathizer among the Labour leaders, to the post of Colonial Secretary. Mr. Bevin claimed afterward that these conversations were going so well that by the 3rd of October he was nearing agreement. And then, so went his story, once more that unwelcome untutored transatlantic voice pealed over the waves and shattered the exquisite achievement of his diplomacy. What happened was that on the 4th of October, 1946, the eve of the Jewish Day of Atone-

ment, Mr. Truman gave in to the request of his party political advisers
that he should issue a statement in favor of a radical Zionist solution of
the Palestine problem. Mr. Truman immediately informed the British
Prime Minister of his proposed statement, and Mr. Attlee, after consulting
with Mr. Bevin, earnestly implored the President not to issue the statement or at least to postpone it. But it was an election time in America and
Mr. Truman felt obliged to make the statement as otherwise he would be
outbid in the same matter by his leading Republican opponent, Governor
Dewey of New York. Mr. Truman made the statement, not very
willingly[57] and against some advice. His statement amounted to an expression of support for the Jewish Agency partition plan and a renewed request for the admission of the 100,000.

Authorities deserving of all respect differ as to whether Ernest Bevin
was justified in his belief that this intervention destroyed promising negotiations. It is difficult not to sympathize with his feelings in the latest black
rage which overcame him; one needs only to imagine what the American
reaction would be if United States negotiations on some difficult matter
with Mexico were to be the subject of continual interference by British
politicians in London, made not with regard to Mexico but to British
local elections in which much depended on Mexican voters in London.
But the real question is as to whether Bevin was in fact approaching
agreement. The answer seems to be that he was not. He appears to have
been unaware that the Jewish Agency's partition proposal was as far as
they could conceivably go if they were to retain leadership. Even if he did
realize this, his perception could not help him because as a British Foreign
Secretary in 1946 he was powerless to implement partition of any kind.
As officially reported, he described his situation with terse accuracy. "The
Arabs won't accept partition," he said. "Am I to force it on them with
British bayonets?" There was no other way for him to meet Jewish wishes.
But to look at the other side. Whether or not the Zionist leaders recognized Bevin's dilemma, they saw refusal of their offer as crucial. At a
meeting in Paris the quorum of the Agency decided that if refusal proved
final then they must abandon the British connection and move toward
partition with other help if it was there, or by themselves.[58]

Mr. Bevin, confused by opposition, much of it invisible, floundered like
a stranded whale. He put the blame for what was happening on Mr.
Truman, and "in rage struck wide." It is extraordinary that in his speech
in the House of Commons on February 18th, 1947, he laid stress on

[57] Kirk, *op. cit.* and suggestive passages in *The Forrestal Diaries, op. cit.*
[58] Bauer. A Communication.

the President's supposed indiscretion in having once again pleaded for the admission of 100,000, since this had so recently been conceded in the Grady-Morrison plan, but Bevin gave the impression that this was more important than American support of the partition plan itself. It appeared for a moment after the breakdown of the conversations between Bevin and Weizmann as though the final climax was at hand, but it was delayed.

In spite of the Anglo-American quarrel in October, during which the Jews of New York had again come in for some denunciation from the raging Bevin, and in spite of the Agency's decision in Paris, there was a brief period of relative calm in Palestine under the stimulus of the appeasement policy of the new Colonial Secretary. In November the Agency leaders were liberated and 2,800 illegal immigrants detained in Cyprus were allowed into Palestine. Haganah dissociated itself from the terrorists and signalized the end of the alliance by issuing propaganda against them. The Central Executive of the Zionist organization condemned terrorism and called on the Yishuv to take action against the criminals. There was relief of tension, but nothing more; the big questions remained unanswered. In December, 1946, an event of solemn importance to the Jews of the world took place. The Twenty-second Zionist Congress assembled, the first since the outbreak of war. The meeting place was Basel.

If Anglo-Jewish relations had been what they were shortly before, this meeting must inevitably have been an occasion for a general condemnation of Great Britain leading to angry reactions on both sides. As it was, the state of feeling in this respect allowed the moderates to make their impression. But the congress was confused, inevitably, since it had so great a tide of history to consider and had to make the difficult decision between remaining faithful to Biltmore, and accepting the new Jewish partition plan. It could have no clear result and could give no clear leadership to Jews.

This was one of the last occasions when Dr. Weizmann reappeared as the Zionist leader in all his old vigor and moral splendor. He made a last valiant effort to guide Zionism toward peace. He spoke his mind against the terrorists and declared that the murder of Lord Moyne by the Sternists was "the greatest disaster to overtake us in the last few years." He had hard words, harder than Bevin's, for the American extremists and he castigated the leaders, Rabbi Silver and Emmanuel Neumann, for encouraging a Jewish revolt in Palestine to which, they asserted, American Jews would give "full political and moral support."

Weizmann said as follows: "Moral and political support is very little when you send other people to the barricades to face tanks and guns. The eleven new settlements in the Negev have, in my deepest conviction, a far greater weight than a hundred speeches about resistance—especially when the speeches are made in New York while the proposed resistance is to be made in Tel Aviv and Jerusalem."

All the antagonism of the Yishuv toward the Diaspora was in his words and Emmanuel Neumann, not very aptly, cried out, "Demagogue!" It is recorded that there was a long and painful silence at this insult to the venerable old man. Owing to his failing eyesight he could not see who had attacked him thus. He answered as follows:

Somebody has called me a demagogue. I do not know who. I hope that I never learn the man's name. I—a demagogue! I who have borne all the ills and travails of this movement. The person who flung that word in my face ought to know that in every house and stable in Nahalal, in every little workshop in Tel Aviv or Haifa there is a drop of my blood. You know that I am telling you the truth. Some people do not like to hear it, but you will hear me. I warn you against bogus palliatives, against short cuts, against false prophets, against facile generalisations, against distortion of historic facts. If you think of bringing the redemption nearer by un-Jewish methods, if you lose faith in hard work and better days, then you commit idolatry and endanger what we have built. Would that I had a tongue of flame, the strength of prophets, to warn you against the paths of Babylon and Egypt. "Zion shall be redeemed in Judgment"—and not by any other means.

Dr. Abba Eban describes the sequel to this great utterance:

Between the rows of applauding delegates standing in awe and contrition he made his way, painfully, gropingly, into the street. A few days later he reappeared to make a short farewell: "If I have said harsh things to anyone, I did not intend to hurt. The Jewish people, especially those waiting in the camps, look to you to open the gates. I thank you all."

The delegates arose, this time without exception and sang Hatikvah. Weizmann, the Zionist, had left the Congress arena for ever.[59]

Weizmann did not achieve anything resembling a triumph of moderation. There was too much tide running the other way. He had been re-

[59] Eban, Weizmann Biography. He gives the official version of Weizmann's speech which is somewhat differently quoted in Kirk. Hatikvah ("The Hope") was the Zionist, and is now the Israel, national anthem.

elected President at the beginning of the Congress only by the narrowest
margin; he was not re-elected at the end, though out of respect for him the
post was left vacant. The lesson of the Congress for the British was surely
very plain: that the moderates could lead Zionism but that they needed all
possible support. The Colonial Office under Mr. Creech Jones, and even
the Foreign Office under Mr. Bevin endeavored, for a while, to practice
such a policy as would give the moderates the success they needed, but
they could never go as far as support for the Jewish partition plan, and
anything less was useless.

The winter of 1946 and 1947 was one of double crisis for the British
government: the negotiations for a treaty with Egypt were at an extremely
difficult stage over the question of the Sudan, and in Persia the long Russian attempt to seize the Northwest province with the aid of quislings was
nearing the climax and, as seemed possible then, swiftly moving to a crisis
between West and East which could lead to the outbreak of a third world
war. If ever there was a moment when Great Britain needed to enjoy wide
support in the world of Islam it was in this second winter after the war. It
was no chicanery when officials of the Colonial, Foreign and India Offices
in London said that the Palestine business was a grave difference between
Britain and that world, though there was undoubtedly exaggeration in the
opinion often found then among civil servants and journalists that this
difference was effective in Moslem India and Persia. It was confined to the
Arabic-speaking world, but there it was strong—and Egypt was known to
be aiming at its leadership. It followed that the government, even if it had
been pro-Zionist, could not have given effect to measures which could
meet the needs of the moderate party. Mr. Creech Jones's appeasement
policy, proceeding as it did with lame footsteps, could only provide a
breathing space, and that breathing space was marred and then shortened
by the conduct of affairs in Palestine.

In spite of the condemnation of terrorism by the Central Executive and
by the Twenty-second Zionist Congress, terrorism still flourished in Palestine and it has been authoritatively estimated that Irgun had doubled its
numbers during 1946.[60] By the end of the year this organization and their
Sternist allies could boast, and they were the kind who boasted about murder, that they had killed 373 people in Palestine, of whom 300 were
civilians. By the emergency laws still in operation the Army was empowered to administer the country within its sphere, and this sphere was now a
very large one. They could arrest without reference to the police and could
try cases which would normally have gone to the civil courts by courtmar-

[60] Kirk, *op. cit.*

tial.[61] Exasperated by the crafty malignity of the terrorists whom they could defeat in the straight combat which for political reasons was denied them,[62] and forced to endure defeat and humiliation while keeping order during a time of undeclared war; subjected to continual mockery and misrepresentation and frequent efforts to goad them into misconduct, the Army became an emotional dispenser of justice. Following a grotesque and repulsive British tradition inherited from public school education, the Army took to inflicting corporal punishment on arrested terrorists. The Irgun organized equally repulsive retaliations on kidnaped Englishmen and the practice stopped, after providing a further occasion for riotous attacks on innocent Jews by British troops. One may marvel that such crass ignorance was ever allowed to have its way. A yet greater folly came soon after. Forgetful of the history of Ireland, a special unit was raised whose object was to fight terrorism by means of counterterrorism. One of the principal officers was Major Roy Farran, a young man who had been twice decorated with the D.S.O. in the war. His mission ended in a mysterious case in which he was alleged to have done a young terrorist to death. The truth was never known, but the point is that, under the pressure of an army driven to extreme and sometimes mutinous impatience, a policy which can only succeed under a totalitarian government was thoughtlessly adopted, and the gallant career of an exemplary officer allowed to end in wretched confusion.[63] This foolish policy, begun during this winter, did not reach its end and anticlimax till the spring, but in the meantime, in January of 1947, the army, and through them the administration and the government, became involved in another case, of more regular legal character but equally exacerbating in its course.

In spite of the quantity of sabotage and assassination, no death sentence had been carried out against a Jewish terrorist in Palestine. On the 24th of January, 1947, sentence of hanging was confirmed by Sir Evelyn Barker in the case of a young terrorist called Dov Grüner, who had been involved in the murder of a policeman. Irgun immediately organized a reprisal and kidnaped a British judge and a civilian from Tel Aviv. The High Commissioner announced that unless they were returned within two days Tel Aviv would be placed under military occupation, and at the same time a stay of execution was granted while an appeal went forward to London.

[61] Richard Graves, Municipal Commissioner for Jerusalem 1947–48, in his book *Experiment in Anarchy* (London, 1949) remarks on this evil.
[62] Wilson, *op. cit.*
[63] "With all their great experience of governing other people, the British here made the classical error of antagonising the entire population in the attempt to subdue a small terrorist minority." Jon Kimche, *Seven Fallen Pillars*. London, 1950.

The hostages were duly returned. This case continued for nearly three months, and during that time poisoned an already overcharged atmosphere. For the sake of preserving the calmer mood brought about by Mr. Creech Jones's appeasement policy, it would obviously have been better to have commuted Dov Grüner's sentence at least, but the kidnaping action of Irgun had made this impolitic as it would now appear as a surrender of law to violence. Dov Grüner and his associates became popular heroes and the episode led to another bout of mutual reprisal and atrocity.

A very remarkable thing about the persistence of terrorism, and the continuing refusal of the Va'ad Leumi to help to curb it, is that this did not lead to any considerable outbreak of anti-Semitism in England. It almost certainly would have done so but for a very unusual circumstance, namely that the abnormal cold in England during January, February, and the first part of March had led to a fuel crisis which occupied the minds of most people to the exclusion of nearly everything else. If one looks through the British newspapers of that time it is extraordinary how little mention there is of Palestine, either of the things that were happening in the country or the political debate at home. As said, Palestine had never interested the strongly philistine British. This was, one may legitimately guess, a main reason why at this moment they merely found the Jews incomprehensible and could rarely be bothered to read about their misdeeds toward their British benefactors, or the misdeeds of their benefactors toward the Jews. This was a very fortunate turn of events which must not, however, be put too much to the credit of the British.

On the 27th of January, the same day as the kidnaping took place in Tel Aviv, the London Conference resumed its sittings. This time the Palestine Arabs were directly represented from the Arab Higher Committee operating under the direction of the Mufti in Egypt. The Arab League Council had made over to him all League funds intended for Palestinian purposes and from this he was now in a stronger position than he had enjoyed since his pre-war heyday. It followed from the influence he could exert that the attitude of the Arab delegates was unbending.[64] The Jewish Agency refused to attend the conference but, as before, held separate conversations with Mr. Bevin and Mr. Creech Jones. Their attitude was not pliant: they had gone as far as they could in the retreat from Biltmore; but in that mood of reflection which had come over them in the midst of the horrors of the year before, and in spite of the drastic resolution of August, 1946, to which they still held, they endeavored to make agreement with the British possible. This they did, so far as appears from the

[64] Hurewitz, op. cit.

available accounts,[65] by proposing a species of *Havlegah* in respect of the Jewish State: they would "forgo mention of a Jewish State as the goal, and leave the outcome to time," provided that the mandatory agreed to the full Jewish immigration program and to the removal of all restrictions on land purchase. It seems that they put this to Bevin after he had announced that Britain contemplated the abandonment of the mandate. So far as meeting Arab proposals, and reaching an Arab-Jewish understanding, this offer of restraint, which was the limit and perhaps beyond the limit to which the Jewish representatives could go, had no practical value at all. The new Palestine Arab policy directed by the Mufti was concentrating on the prevention of all land sales to Jews, while Jewish immigration of any kind remained the Arab bugbear.[66]

On the 7th of February 1947, Ernest Bevin made a last effort to save the conference. It took the form of a compromise offer. It is unlikely that anyone concerned had any hope of its effectiveness. He put forward a modified version of the Grady-Morrison plan. Palestine would be divided into Arab and Jewish provinces following the same borders as in the former plan. The provinces would enjoy local self-government. Britain would remain as the mandatory for a period of five years' trusteeship. For two years immigration would be permitted at a rate of 4,000 a month, thus bringing in 96,000, a little short of the long-debated 100,000. After this, further immigration of Jews would be allowed after consultation with Arabs (which now meant the Mufti), though the ultimate decision in this matter would remain with the High Commissioner and the Trusteeship Council of the United Nations.

The Arab and Jewish delegations both rejected the offer and unconditionally, so much so that little if any effort seems to have been made to make them change their minds. To the end the government had clung to binationalism, to a wishful picture of Jewish and Arab workers and politicians blithely hand-in-hand. Mr. Bevin could never see why the two peoples showed no wish to fulfill that dream, and he seems to have thought that it only needed persistent persuasion, such as he had practiced successfully elsewhere, to bring it about. In his somewhat pathetic apologia for his Palestine policy in the House of Commons on the 25th of February, 1947, he seemed bewildered that he had not succeeded in this endeavor. "If I could get back," he concluded (forgetting earlier remarks about £200,000,000 and a division), "if I could get back to the contribu-

---

[65] Harry Sacher, *Israel, the Establishment of a State,* London, 1952, and Kirk, *op. cit.*

[66] Hurewitz, *op. cit.*

tion on purely humanitarian grounds of 100,000 into Palestine, and if this political fight for a Jewish State could be put on one side, and we could develop self-government by the people resident in Palestine, without any other political issue, I would be willing to try again." The Parliamentary debate on the 25th of February was the last that was heard of the 100,-000, and of Bevin's plan. The latter did not even acquire a name. It was not widely commented on in the popular press. It aroused less interest than any predecessor. Though it was not ungenerous, in mandate terms, it embodied an offer that was made a little less than a year too late.

The last stage of British rule in Palestine had now been reached. Lord Peel and his colleagues had stated in the similar but easier circumstances of the 1930's that the mandate was unworkable. The assertion was open to question then but not now. The British government had now no alternative but to surrender authority when their policy failed. Bevin's Palestine performance was in many respects gross and ridiculous, and his refusal to the end to recognize that Jewish nationalism was something more than a New York plot provided a grotesque illustration of how men cling to fixed ideas, but that does not mean that if he had known and understood all that he should have done, and if he had been another Arthur Balfour in adroitness, he would have fared much better. In the end defeat had to be met, with face-saving skill or with Bevin's crude blind lurchings, but either way defeat could not be escaped. There was no way of reconciling Britain's Moslem interests (now entering a difficult liberalizing phase which restricted British initiative) with the ambitions of the Zionists which had grown in size as they became Jewish necessities. The mandatory had to go because Britain's presence in Palestine had become harmful. It is not possible to imagine a practical alternative. The predicament that faced the British in 1947 and 1948 was not one that called in the power of choice, but the courage to follow a difficult road which they had chosen. The government under Ernest Bevin's influence did not find that courage. The difficulties thereby added to the never simple act of disengagement can be outlined in the penultimate chapter. There were a few more crossroads for Jews, Arabs, and Americans, but none for the British.

PART

IV

13 FINALE WITH CHAOS

The conduct of the British government in the last months of the Palestine mandate should never be judged without remembering that 1947 was the year of the settlement with India. The verdict of history is likely to be very favorable to that British act of state. The suffering and bloodshed that it entailed were appalling, but the alternatives would almost certainly have carried with them much worse consequences. The essence of the operation was to proceed without hesitation, with a rigid fixity of purpose toward the goal of Indian independence, if possible without partition, but if necessary with it. Any serious relaxation of the tempo (so ran the argument), no matter for what high-minded reasons, was likely to involve the whole subcontinent in a long and devastating civil war which might well take the form of an Anglo-Indian war. Lord Attlee, with characteristic brevity and crispness, described the policy in later years:

I had come to the conclusion that it was useless to try to get agreement by discussion between the leaders of the rival communities. Unless these men were faced with the urgency of a time limit, there would always be procrastination. As long as Britain held power it was always possible to attribute failure to her. Indians must be faced with the fact that in a short space of time they would have responsibility thrust upon them.[1]

There were parallels between the situation of India and Palestine: two communities, divided by religion and to some extent by race, which both rejected pleas for cooperation, which both demanded national independence on their own terms and on no one else's, and whose political leaders had in common only one idea: distrust of Britain and her habits of imperialism. It seems likely that these resemblances drew attention from the differences and led the British government into attempting the same bitter operation in Palestine as they had successfully carried out on India.

The differences were enormous. The Palestine administration contained men such as Richard Graves who loved and revered the Holy Land, felt inspired to give of their best, and left a memory that stands their country in good stead many years after, but they were not a Palestinian type in the way that their opposite numbers in India were. The general spirit of the Palestine administration was very different from that of the Indian Civil Service. There was nothing in Palestine like the Army of India which, under its last Commander-in-Chief, during the disasters of 1947 and 1948, gave the world an astonishing example of the highest form of patriotism. The agitation about Indian independence spread to the whole of Asia and to the whole English-speaking world, but that fact did not greatly inhibit British initiative, given the Labour Party policy. That is to say: an anti-independence policy would have been very restricted in initiative, but the independence policy could proceed according to British decision with little active interference from without. The interest in Palestine was even more world-wide and in consequence the authority for what was done became increasingly international in the postwar years, giving less and less scope for uninhibited British initiative, no matter what the policy was: pro-Jewish, pro-Arab, or neutral. This was largely the achievement of Jewish negotiating and propaganda skill; the fact can give an opening to anti-Semitic ideas, but should not be slurred over for all that; it was an incredible achievement. The point made here is that since Palestine had become an international interest, there was no way of conducting Palestine policy except in accord with whatever international political organi-

[1] Clement R. Attlee, *As It Happened*. London, 1954.

zation existed. Then, as now, this could only mean close cooperation with the United Nations Organization.

There was a last difference which was a source of the utmost danger if the British government followed any line of conduct which was not integrated with U.N.O. Since the Arab League had taken up the cause of Palestine, Great Britain could not, on her own, act as a neutral in any conflict between the Jews and the Arabs without putting herself into a perilously invidious position. Britain was in treaty relations with all the League member-states, and in the case of Egypt, Iraq, and Transjordan, these involved defense obligations and the supplying of arms. In Transjordan the military forces still contained many British officers. So Great Britain, acting on her own, could only operate an arms embargo by breaking her treaty obligations to the member-states of the League, and this at a time when the Persian crisis had been overcome (in December, 1946) with what appeared to be a close risk of war; when negotiations for a new Anglo-Egyptian treaty were near to breaking down, and when the British position in the Arabic-speaking and indeed the whole Moslem world was assured nowhere, except possibly in Transjordan. On the other hand, to supply arms to both sides was to increase the risk of an Arab-Jewish armed conflict in which British officers would take part in a war against British-protected Jews. Also to follow such an immoral policy could enrage opinion in Britain to such an extent as to destroy the government. Since the mandate was unworkable, there was no alternative but full cooperation with U.N.O. But this was something that no one on the British side could face, though the government admitted the necessity throughout.

On the 14th of February, 1947, Mr. Bevin announced that the mandate was to be referred back to U.N.O. by the British government without the latter's recommending any particular solution. He repeated the announcement to the House of Commons on the 18th and it was debated on the 25th. As early as this, evidence appeared that the government were in a state of divided mind; Mr. Creech Jones's winding-up speech in the debate was not entirely consistent with Mr. Bevin's opening speech. The Foreign Secretary had let it be understood that the British government would approach U.N.O. in order to surrender the mandate, a proposal first put forward (oddly enough) from the Conservative side by Mr. Churchill the year before. But Mr. Creech Jones now stated that the government did not intend to surrender the mandate but to seek advice from U.N.O. on how the mandate could best be administered or amended. The government were divided over Palestine as they were not over India. There was a withdrawal-party, a strategic stay-at-any-price party, a gradualist party and its opposite. Mr. Bevin's own mind seems to have been radically divided. He pressed for withdrawal with more definiteness and vigor than the Colonial Secretary, and yet later in 1947, at the Labour Party summer conference, he told his fellow members that he would not feel himself bound by the advice of U.N.O. unless it took the form of a unanimous U.N.O. decision, a most unlikely occurrence. It has been calculated that what was really in Mr. Bevin's mind and that of his advisers was a belief that no matter how hard they urged the policy of withdrawal "the Jews or the Arabs, or both, would ask the British to stay on and save the country from chaos." [2]

On the 2nd of April the British delegation to U.N.O. asked for a special session on Palestine. This was held on the 9th of May and resulted in the appointment of a United Nations Special Committee on Palestine, known as UNSCOP. The Russian delegation was showing considerable interest in Palestine and so to prevent Russian participation, U.N.O. excluded members of the Security Council from UNSCOP membership. In the end the members were drawn from eleven states: Australia, Canada, Czechoslovakia, Guatemala, India, Holland, Persia, Peru, Sweden, Uruguay, and Yugoslavia. From the beginning of the UNSCOP enterprise the representatives of the Mufti-dominated Arab Higher Committee of Palestine made it clear that they would give no concession and were out for another boycotting exercise. Emile el Ghuri, the Mufti's new fiery propagandist, acted as spokesman in America. He told a U.N.O. committee: "It is the determined and unequivocal will of the Arabs to refuse to consider any solution which even implies the loss of their sovereignty over any part of their country, or the diminution of such sovereignty in any form whatever." [3]

Mindful of the stalling in Westminster that had followed the Anglo-American Committee, UNSCOP were anxious to know whether the British Government would abide by the recommendations of the new inquiry. The chief British delegate, Sir Alexander Cadogan, confined himself to two principal statements. He said: "If the United Nations can find a just solution which will be accepted, it could hardly be expected that we would not welcome such a solution." He added to this: "We [the British] should not have the sole responsibility for enforcing a solution which is not ac-

---

[2] Jon and David Kimche, *Both Sides of the Hill*. London, 1960. This book contains the most interesting account available of the British and other political divisions on Palestine at the time. The authority is stated to be the author's personal and professional acquaintance with many of the principals.

[3] J. C. Hurewitz, *The Struggle for Palestine*. New York, 1950.

cepted by both parties and which we cannot reconcile with our consciences." [4] This second statement suggested more willingness to cooperate than in fact was found to exist. The American Government, as divided
in mind as the British, stressed their neutrality. Mr. Truman, still in part
the prisoner of his officials, did not break out with a new intervention.
With small hope of success UNSCOP went to Palestine where they arrived at the beginning of June. They saw the country undergoing the first
stage of the final chaos.

The breathing space was over and a revival of terrorism, beginning in
the first week of March, had led to a state of affairs in which atrocity was
an every-day occurrence, and counter-atrocity, from being a rare exception
to the rule, was becoming alarmingly more frequent. Irgun Zvai Leumi
and the Stern Group were not the only murder organizations in the field:
with the heightened tension since the war, with the Mufti's recovery of his
authority, Arab terrorist societies had inevitably grown up. They spent a
certain amount of their time in disciplining the Palestine Arab community, a characteristic example of their method being the murder of an
Arab notable who delivered an address of welcome at the founding ceremony of a Zionist village.[5] The two main organizations, the Mufti-led Al
Futuwwah (meaning something like "Young Chivalry" and founded by
Haj Amin in the thirties) and the independent Al Najjadah ("The Helpers") had wasted much energy in fighting each other. A third organization
whose headquarters were in Egypt, the famous Ikhwane Muslamin, the
Moslem Brotherhood, also provided terrorist groups to Palestine, and under their influence, with the blessing of the Mufti, something resembling a
united front of Arab resistance had been formed under the title of "The
Youth Organisation." [6] This had happened shortly before UNSCOP'S arrival. The Mufti had already succeeded in directing the combined terrorists into an exclusively anti-Jewish action.

But the main conflict in June of 1947 when UNSCOP arrived was
Anglo-Jewish. Since the best that the British government could possibly
offer the Zionists was a long way from the most moderate proposals that
the Jewish Agency could and had put forward, there had been the expected defeat of moderation. To retain the leadership Ben-Gurion had
(however reluctantly) to speak the language of extremism and as early as
April, in a speech to the Va'ad Leumi, he had described the object of
British policy as being "to liquidate the Jews as a people, and to recognize

[4] *Ibid.*
[5] *Ibid.*
[6] Hurewitz, *op. cit.*

only the existence of individual Jews who could serve as objects either of pogroms or of pity." He even went so far as to hint that the British were organizing the terrorist campaign. Some journalists, he said, "openly assert that there are contacts between the police and the terrorists. Without suggesting any motive, it is clear that the present regime derives concrete advantage from terrorism." [7] The British government were not behindhand in claptrap of the sort. The official information services in England produced never-verified and almost certainly invented stories about non-Jewish gangsters being recruited for terrorist purposes from the refugees of Europe; about Jewish "strikingly inhuman kidnaping rings" in Hungary who tore Jewish children from their parents to swell the numbers of illegal immigrants,[8] and there was no official contradiction of the opinion often found in the press of that time that the Zionist movement was part of a general Communist plan run from the Kremlin. Mr. Bevin himself seems to have genuinely believed the latter story. In this atmosphere violence flourished. On the 4th of May Irgun with Stern help broke open the prison at Acre, liberating forty-one terrorists with over two hundred common criminals, and, by way of diversion, throwing grenades into the wing where lunatics were confined. This was in revenge for the execution of the canonized Dov Grüner. There were at this time various atrocities, some on a large scale, whose perpetrators and object remained mysterious. While UNSCOP were taking evidence in Jerusalem Major Farran fled the country (to give himself up later), and the case was thereon made public. Shortly before this three terrorists were condemned to death for taking part in the Acre attack. The Jewish Agency made skillful propaganda use of both these events.[9]

But the most remarkable event of UNSCOP's visit to Palestine was the arrival under naval escort in Haifa of a boat crammed with about 4,500 Jewish refugees who clamored to be allowed to land as immigrants. The arrival of this boat, originally called the *President Warfield*, now renamed *Exodus 1947*, and recently bought by Haganah sympathizers from an American line, may have been contrived to occur while UNSCOP were in Palestine. Whatever the truth of that, the Jewish Agency exploited the propaganda value of the overloaded ship's arrival. The opportunity was immense, for since the bitter memories of the *Patria* and the *Struma*, refugee-boats could rouse Jewish feeling as nothing else, and this was the

---

[7] Reported in the Zionist Review 11th April, 1947.
[8] Hurewitz, *op. cit.*
[9] Crossman, Kirk, *op. cit.*

largest and most crowded ever to have been seen in Haifa. Bevin fell into the trap. The clever thing to do was to allow the refugees to land as an exceptional concession made in exceptional circumstances, a procedure which the presence of UNSCOP could make perfectly natural and acceptable. The normal routine thing to do was to intern the refugees in Cyprus until such time as immigration vacancies should occur. What Bevin, aroused to another of his black rages, did do was to use the *Exodus* as a means "to teach the Jews a lesson," and he ordered the boat back to her port of embarkation, Sete, a little town eighty-five miles west of Marseilles.

The Zionists had developed what may be called a boat-propaganda technique which was skillful but often erred on the side of excessive zeal. In his book Major R. D. Wilson, referring to a previous boat incident, tells at first hand "of the exhibition on one occasion of a one-year-old child who died at sea some days previously, with the statement to the press: "The dirty Nazi-British assassins suffocated this innocent victim with gas." (Major Wilson goes on: "The *sotto voce* remark, 'It's not against you, it's for the Press,' made by one of the more moderate passengers to some of the troops hardly compensated.") As with other boat-propaganda-ventures this one also was largely done by fraud, but as with most very successful propaganda-efforts it was based on a large measure of truth. Haganah activists, by stirring the passengers to a wild mood of resistance, and threatening those who hesitated, were able to represent them as unanimous in their demand to be landed in Palestine and nowhere else, but the desperate fighting which marked the end of the voyage in Hamburg shows plainly that there was no great reluctance to follow the advice of the agitators.

The passengers were transferred to three British boats and ordered back to France. Substantial guards were posted on each boat. They arrived at Port de Bouc near Marseilles on the 29th of July. The British requested the French government to take them into France, to which the French agreed but on the strict understanding that no one was obliged to land. This gave the Haganah activists their chance, and gave French officials with still rankling memories of Syria and Lebanon the chance to help the activists. (The French press of the time made no bones about this.) From the shore, and from launches equipped with broadcasting machinery which circled the three boats riding at anchor, a propaganda bombardment was aimed by Haganah agents at the passengers who replied by hanging Union Jacks decorated with swastikas out of the portholes. The British Consul-General in Marseilles went aboard and endeavored to reason with the passengers in vain, and he never succeeded in making contact except with the Haganah men in charge.[10]

What little hope there was of an official change of mind in London regarding *Exodus 1947* vanished when, on the 31st of July, the bodies of two British sergeants were found hanging from a tree near Tel Aviv. They had been murdered by Irgun. As an embellishment of this atrocity one of the bodies had been loaded with an explosive booby-trap. This was a reprisal for the execution of the three terrorists captured after the Acre jail attack. There had been many more extensive atrocities but none that caused such a revulsion of feeling. It may have been that the hideous touch of macabre farce in booby-trapping a corpse gave men a sudden close glimpse of the repulsive terrorist mind, but the reaction was appalling. Several Jews were murdered by British police in counterreprisal and there were also and inevitably cases of troops who ran amok in fury and inflicted casualties on the innocent. The rage was not confined to Palestine; there were anti-Jewish disorders, some of serious proportions, in several British cities.[11]

In the meantime except for some invalids, the *Exodus* refugees in Port de Bouc refused to disembark on being given an ultimatum with a time limit, and the three boats sailed in the last week of August. They were directed to Hamburg, the plan being to land the refugees in the British zone of Germany. This has been considered as an act of brutal spite on the part of Ernest Bevin, but the allegation is probably a libel. Once the decision had been taken not to land the refugees in Palestine or anywhere near it, and once the French authorities had collaborated with Haganah, there was nowhere else that the British authorities could send them except to England, and after the outbreaks following the affair of the two sergeants that would clearly have been an act of folly.

The last voyage of the *Exodus* refugees was not wanting in unexpected pathos. During the original voyage out the activists had, in the way of all propagandists, overpainted the picture they wished their hearers to accept, and they had described British troops as monsters of cruelty similar in character to the vilest of Himmler's rank and file. During the long voyage back to Europe they had found that British working-class men in uniform were very different from these advance notices and there grew up a genu-

[10] R. D. Wilson, *Cordon and Search*. Aldershot, 1949. Mr. Donald Mallett. A communication. He was present as information officer in the British Embassy, Paris. He arranged for a representative of Reuters to sail on the final journey to Hamburg as an independent reporter in order to forestall further propaganda efforts.
[11] Kirk, Hurewitz, *op. cit.*

ine comradeship between the guards on the boats and the survivors of the German concentration camps. Many of the Jews aboard felt obliged to tell the troops that the demonstrations they would make on reaching Germany would be against the British government and not against them. This fellow-feeling made little difference to the result. The ugly scenes of compulsion, resistance, and combat at Hamburg were so violent that the troops had to call for reinforcements.[12] Haganah had won the day. *Exodus 1947* was among the most immense propaganda successes that pre-Israel Zionism achieved at any time. It became the subject of saga-making; long after a book and then a film, bearing about as much resemblance to the fact as Homer's Iliad probably bears to the facts of the siege of Troy, achieved overwhelming popularity. When these things happened the incident gave rise to a general and uncritical sympathy with Zionism and an extravagant notion of English cruelty. Bevin had fallen into an enormous trap indeed.

UNSCOP produced their recommendations on the 1st of September. The report was not unanimous; three of the eleven (India, Persia and Yugoslavia) dissented and one (the Australian delegate) abstained. Their plan was a fantastic partition scheme which, it is safe to say, could never have been put into successful operation. It represented a serious diminution of the Jewish Agency's partition proposals of August 1946, but favored Zionist ambitions more than any other partition proposals offered from the Gentile side by allotting most of the Negev to the Jewish State. Though it did not grant Acre to the Jews it gave them the Arab town of Jaffa. It was by no means a plan that any Jewish radical could accept with enthusiasm. In a new form it revived one of the most unrealistic propositions of the Peel and Woodhead commissions, and this has been admirably described by Professor Kirk as follows: "The impracticability of this 'death by a thousand cuts' was emphasized by the provision that the Arab and Jewish states, each consisting of three segments and entwined in an inimical embrace like two fighting serpents, should attain their independence only when they had signed a ten-year treaty of economic union with provision for subsidising the economically weaker Arab State from the more favoured Jewish State." If both the Zionists and the Arabs (of Palestine and the League) had been strongly binationalist in tendency this plan might in operation have conceivably served as a starting point to an independent Palestine, but there was the time-honored snag. Even at this late date there was still a considerable binationalist Jewish party on the Zionist Left Wing, completely overshadowed by the more thorough nationalist school, it is true, but in existence nevertheless,

[12] Wilson, *op. cit.*

while there was no binationalist Arab party at all, and not many binationalist Arab individuals by this time except among the illiterate peasantry.

UNSCOP also turned in a minority proposal known as a "Federal State Plan." This gave much more territory to the Arabs and was designed to act as some basis for compromise. It was even more unpractical than the majority scheme in that it went back to the canton plan and the Jewish and Arab areas were both fragmented. There could be no question of Jewish acceptance of the minority proposal, and as the Arab authorities turned it down as unconditionally and emphatically as they rejected the majority plan, it quickly vanished from the scene. The "fighting serpents scheme" remained alone. As it was never acted upon, its details need not detain the reader. Of more interest are the political maneuverings to which it gave rise.

The inclusion of the Negev with the town of Beersheba in the majority plan, it quickly vanished from the scene. The "fighting serpents scheme" in session in Zurich. Influenced perhaps by the surprising fact that the UNSCOP report had been received with public rejoicing by the Yishuv, the Council accepted it in principle though they made it clear that they were not to be held as committed until the General Assembly of U.N.O. had cast their votes. When this body met on the 23rd of September it was guided by the Secretary-General, Trygve Lie, into putting the matter into the hands of a special committee on Palestine. This was agreed and its proceedings were opened on the 26th by Mr. Creech Jones. He made it clear that the UNSCOP scheme was not approved by his government, that Britain would not impose it by force, and that "in the absence of a settlement [the British government] had to plan for an early withdrawal of British forces and of the British administration from Palestine."

This is a point where the influence of the India policy can be deduced. When Mr. Creech Jones made the statement, when the India policy was not visible clearly from a distance, it was assumed that he was lying, for it was hard to believe that a British or any government would choose to leave an area of rule "in the *absence* of a settlement." But when the High Commissioner in Jerusalem repeated on the 8th of October that Britain intended to withdraw in the near future, and when people remembered that this improbable course of action had actually been taken by Britain in India, (though not "in the absence of a settlement" it is true) the possibility that Mr. Creech Jones was telling the truth began to make itself felt. In the course of the committee's meetings the Jewish Agency gave effect to the resolution of the Zionist General Council and formally accepted

UNSCOP's majority partition plan. This resolution and ratification represent the boldest essay in moderation (if such a contradiction in terms is allowed) that the Zionist ruling body ever made, and events subsequent to this decision emphasize the tragedy of British policy moving slowly under Bevin's confused leadership.

As the Arabs had refused to compromise in any way with the Jewish National Home for nearly thirty years they could not, except with great humiliation to themselves, publicly retreat now. To their rejection of the UNSCOP schemes they could only add dire threats of warfare. Shortly before the General Assembly met in September the Political Committee of the Arab League held a three-day conference at a place called Sofar in Lebanon. They issued further threats which were well summarized by the Cairo newspaper *Al Ahram*. "The Palestine Arabs will launch a relentless war to repel this attack [the UNSCOP partition plan] on their country, especially as they know that all the Arab countries will back and assist them, supplying them with men, money and ammunition." [13]

The Palestine problem was becoming more complicated in the international sphere than at any other time since the confusions attending the settlements after the First World War. Mr. J. C. Hurewitz describes what was happening in a telling sentence: "The Palestine issue in the fall of 1947 was an Arab-Zionist contest within an Anglo-American controversy about to be drawn into the Soviet-American cold war." In these circumstances it was easy for men to lose their way. The Jewish negotiators in America never did this, not even when the accepted UNSCOP plan, after passing through the elaborate machinery of three subcommittees of the Palestine Committee, was modified in a sense favorable to the Arabs, in the hopes of meeting Moslem objections. The UNSCOP partition scheme as finally passed by the General Assembly of U.N.O. at the end of November, 1947, reduced the proposed Jewish State by approximately 500 square miles and subtracted the town of Beersheba from the Jewish Negev area. Very surprisingly the Jewish negotiators accepted even this hard condition.

This is taking the story forward to November, 1947. In the meantime the British government had been behaving in a peculiar way which perplexed its friends and enemies. Their attitude after submitting their difficulties to U.N.O. became more and more one of refusal to cooperate with U.N.O. Their initial reaction was deserving of some sympathy. The British Ministers had been Members of Parliament at the time of the Peel plan,

[13] Kirk, *op. cit.*

which the UNSCOP plan somewhat resembled, and they all remembered its condemnation by Lord Samuel and by others in a position to judge. It is understandable that they were reluctant to put this twined-serpents scheme into operation, but if they refused help, it could be justly asked, what had they to put in its place? The answer (in the present state of information) appears to be nothing at all beyond imitating that dog-in-the-manger boycotting response which had brought the unfortunate Palestinian Arabs to their present state of helplessness. There was no attempt to help U.N.O. to evolve a plan that might work; indeed it was not long before the government began to look on U.N.O. with positive hostility. And yet after the appeal to U.N.O. there was no way of Great Britain acting independently. When reading of the events of that time, it is easy to suppose at moments that the government was seized with a nihilistic impulse to subvert order, or that they were overcome by one of those strange fits of group-madness such as appears to have afflicted the Austrian government in 1914, or the French at the time of the Dreyfus affair.

In fact this impression of unreason and hysteria can be very misleading, especially in the first part of the last phase. The researches of Jon and David Kimche[14] have given some shape to what before seemed to be purely incoherent, and if the British Government still cannot be regarded with deep respect, in the light that these investigators have thrown, it can at least (in the first part) be acquitted of a charge of insanity, though in the final episodes even this faint honor cannot be accorded with any fullness or certainty.

All three parties in Palestine, the Arab, Jewish, and British, were inclined to indulge the same delusion: that in fact there would not be an Arab-Jewish war. The evidence for this belief was striking and had been known to the Jews and the British since the second Bloudan conference which had taken place as long ago as June, 1946. From that meeting, of the political leaders of the Arab League, held at Bloudan near Damascus it had become clear that the brave words of the nationalists meant very much less than they said. The Arab League was united on anti-Zionism but not on anything else, not even on what should be done to oppose the emergence of the Jewish State, not even on whether or not to oppose it fully in the sense of armed attack or resistance, or even of economic sanctions. Two years after Bloudan, the delegate of the Government of Iraq to the conference, Dr. Fadhil Jamali, described the state of political feeling on the subject of Zionism among the leaders of the Arab member-states:

14 Kimche, *op. cit.*

Irak had shown more concern than any other Arab state for the future of Palestine. After her, came Syria and then Lebanon, but these were still young states and fearful of complications with either Britain or the United States. Egypt had not yet been convinced that she must show more enegry; she was content with offers of moral help. But most negative of all was the stand of the Saudi Arabians; they showed how little there was to the report that King Ibn Sa'ud and his family were prepared to sacrifice themselves for the sake of the Palestine Arabs. Transjordan and the Yemen showed enthusiastic sympathy for the Iraki stand, but were too poor to help in any other way.[15]

During 1947, as the prospect of a Jewish State grew nearer, there was still no move toward any greater or more effective degree of Arab unity. On the contrary, in the course of five meetings of the League or its political committee held in Egypt or Lebanon between the middle of March and the end of the year, the differences that Dr. Jamali had remarked at Bloudan persisted, and to them was added a new and crucial one. The astute and mildly ambitious Abdullah had determined that he and his emirate, now a kingdom, should be the beneficiaries of any division of Palestine. The Syrians and perhaps the Lebanese might have a little share of Palestine in the north, perhaps the Egyptians something in the south, but the main Arab core and the holy city of Jerusalem would go to the Hashemite Kingdom. Such was Abdullah's plan. In making it he showed not only a capacity for self-interest but for common sense. If left to themselves as citizens of an independent polity, the Palestinian Arabs would fare ill in the minute country to which their homeland must be reduced by partition. Their only hope for prosperity lay in union with their reasonably well-run neighbor. But the plan did not suit the Mufti. Was it for this that he had endured exile, defeat, execration, prison, the perils of escape—merely to be Abdullah's chaplain-in-chief? He thought not. He pressed his interest with energy. In his later years he remained devoid of breadth of mind. In this crisis of Arab nationalism he continued to think in family terms.

Abdullah's ambitions were disturbing to Egypt which under King Farouk was in the middle of the first Egyptian move toward the new Egyptian goal, the leadership of Islam, a *de facto* caliphate. There is no town comparable in Islamic holiness to Jerusalem within the Egyptian frontiers, and the Egyptian king and government (but the king more than the government) considered the prospect of Abdullah as the royal guardian of the Mosque of Omar with distaste. But since the Egyptian government was

[15] In a deposition to the Iraq Parliament, 1948. Quoted in Kimche, *op. cit.*

not yet strongly committed to a pan-Islamic ideal, the effect on them of Abdullah's ambitions was not to make Egypt press for counteraction but to confirm Egyptian reluctance to enter the fray in Palestine.

The Iraq government had no territorial ambitions in Palestine but a stronger dislike of Zionism than any other independent Arab state. In the course of Arab League maneuvering the situation gradually came about that the Iraq and Transjordan governments had a clear program in common: to occupy Arab Palestine and hold it against Jewish encroachment, in the interest of an extended Hashemite Kingdom. The Syrian and Lebanese governments (the Lebanese more than its neighbor) [16] vied with the government in Baghdad in fervid nationalist proclamation, but they continued to show extreme reluctance to commit themselves to action.[17] The reasons suggested by Dr. Jamali after Bloudan for Syrian hesitancy are probably quite valid, but this is a point where one should also remember that many Syrians, though by no means all, held golden opinions about the British on account of their action at the end of the war which allowed Syria to become independent without a long wearisome colonial war as had to be endured later in Algeria. However, the Mufti enjoyed wide support in Syria where Abdullah's original Greater Syria plans were remembered. He was still the most determined nationalist on the Arab side, but his "little Palestine" form of nationalism began gradually to appear more and more out of date in the second half of 1947, or so the course of events suggests. He took an active part but less of a leading one in the course of the next six months. The initiative passed into Transjordanian and Iraq hands, so it seemed.

The trend suited British policy very well. Abdullah was a proved friend, and not only through prejudice British people considered him to be a man of balanced judgment. He was the only Arab ruler to take a realistic view of Zionism. He regretted the establishment of the Jewish National Home as much as any of his subjects, but he knew that it could not be removed. He wanted to compound with it. Here was the ideal man for the British government to have on their side and through whom to put into effect an Arab-Palestine policy which would make sense. And the

---

[16] This might possibly be attributable to the influence of the Lebanese Fawzi el Kawakji.

[17] Sir John Glubb tells an interesting story of the first President of Syria discussing with a British officer the maintenance of a tank regiment. The President was shocked at the cost of accessories. The officer explained that without them the tanks would not "remain long in the field." "In the field?" replied the President. "I don't want them in the field! I want them to drive down the Boulevard on Independence Day." *A Soldier with the Arabs.* London, 1957.

evidence is that the British government attempted to do this, with success, in the early autumn of 1947. The only authority for the episode is to be found in the deposition of a Palestinian Arab (unnamed but quoted by the Kimche brothers) in whom the king confided. According to this account he said:

> The English have agreed to my requests, the most important of which was to increase the supply of arms, including armour and ammunition. I will not let others precede me in the capture of the strategic positions in Palestine, but that does not mean that I intend to act all alone.
>
> The Mufti and President Kuwatly of Syria want to set up an independent Arab state in Palestine with the Mufti at its head. If that were to happen I would be encircled on almost all sides by enemies. This compels me to take measures to anticipate their plans. My forces will therefore occupy every place evacuated by the British.
>
> I will not begin the attack on the Jews, and I will only attack them if they first attack my forces. I will not allow massacres in Palestine. Only after quiet and order have been established will it be possible to reach an understanding with the Jews.

Abdullah is reported to have said this on October 1st, 1947, five days after Mr. Creech Jones had announced to U.N.O. the impending British withdrawal from Palestine. As noted, there was much disbelief of the announcement in U.N.O., and this was also the common reaction of Arabs and Jews in Palestine, but there is no reason to suppose that Abdullah was in any doubt. He had good English friends in Sir John Glubb and Sir Alec Kirkbride who could keep him correctly informed. Besides he was acting with British encouragement. But here one meets a new British mystery. If the British government supported Abdullah's ambitions, and it was the only sensible thing to do, one may ask in bewilderment why at the same time they evolved the one principle of rule that was likely to frustrate them: during the last months of the mandate the government remained consistent in preventing any other authority, Arab or Jewish or international, from taking over responsibility before the withdrawal. Exceptions had to be allowed, but the principle was adhered to as much as possible, and the more it was adhered to, the more certain was war.

It is possible to make out plausible reasons why the British government did not openly support Abdullah when he was doing what they wanted. The motive may have been of the same kind as that which (in the writer's opinion) accounted for the extraordinary secrecy that was allowed to hide Hogarth's crucial interview years before with King Hussein: namely, not to make a disclosure that might impair the popularity of an allied Arab sovereign. To do so might be dangerous. Abdullah's only certain Arab ally was the Iraq government and, though remote from the scene of action, the anti-Zionism of Iraq was as strong or almost as strong as the anti-Zionism in Arab Palestine. The reason for this seems to be clear: that in Iraq there was settled a very large and ancient Jewish community, the descendants of the Babylonian captivity, a far larger community than was to be found in any other League member-state. Zionism had made these people suspect to their Moslem neighbors, and the traditions of independent Iraq as regards the treatment of minorities were not liberal ones. If it was publicly known that Abdullah was proposing to take a leading role in a Palestine partition acceptable to the Jewish Agency; if it was known how far he had gone, and, for example, that on the 27th of November he had had a secret meeting with Mrs. Golda Myerson[18] (representing the Agency) in which he had disclosed his plans and referred to the Mufti as the "common enemy," then the consequences in Baghdad might have been terrible to the Jewish community, destructive to the Iraq alliance with Transjordan, and harmful to the British government which was then in the middle of hopeful negotiations for a new Anglo-Iraq treaty.[19]

But the strongest reason for British behavior at this moment was probably to be found in that belief, well backed by the best that official representation could supply, that in spite of numerous League pronouncements of the most bellicose kind there was no likelihood of war, and from that it was easily argued that the least wise course was for Great Britain to be stampeded into "premature" surrenders of authority. She would withdraw as it suited her and when she had packed her bags, and she would pack them in a seemly manner as befitted a time of anxious peace, but not one of chaos and warfare. Many people in or near Palestine then would have found this a sensible point of view.

There were, however, a few people who could see the danger of what was happening. One was Sir John Glubb who had asserted as early as eighteen months before November, 1947, that on the Palestine issue all Arab "friendship and co-operation will be turned into hatred"[20] and that the problem could set all the Moslem world in flames. Another was the Secretary General of the Arab League, Abdur Rahman Azzam. On September 15th, 1947, Azzam told a press conference in London that he gave

[18] Later known as Mrs. Meir. She succeeded Mr. Moshe Shertok as Israel Foreign Minister. Kimche, *op. cit.*
[19] Kirk, *op. cit.*
[20] Glubb, *op. cit.*

"a solemn warning that any attempt to impose [UNSCOP's] recommendations, or any similar scheme, would be implacably resisted by the Arabs. Let there be no doubt that the Arabs, if compelled, would fight for Palestine." He repeated his warnings to members of the Jewish Agency a few days later.[21] Another who saw things as they were was David Ben-Gurion. He was surrounded by colleagues who, from numerous contacts in Lebanon, Egypt, and Transjordan, were (quite rightly) convinced that the Arab leaders did not wish to go to war. But Ben-Gurion and some of the Haganah commanders felt (no one could know) that what the leaders wanted was not necessarily the same as what would happen. Even so, most of the Haganah leadership was thinking in terms of an enlarged version of the Arab rebellion of 1936–39 when Wingate first led Jewish soldiers to victory.[22]

This optimism in face of a terrible and impending reality was a curious episode such as often overtakes a situation which is overburdened with negotiation, investigation, diplomacy and advice. Ordinary uninformed people who read the popular press in England assumed that on Great Britain's withdrawal from Palestine there would be immense Arab-Jewish fighting. It is arguable that they could see straighter than the informed for the good reason that from here on events were to a great extent formed by ordinary uninformed people—by men in the street. In a sense both the Jews and the Arabs were prisoners of men in the street, as usually happens to people who overindulge in the dubious art of propaganda. If the Zionist leaders had made a deal with Abdullah, it is very doubtful that, after the reckless encouragement they had given to extremism, they could (no matter what the deal) have kept the Yishuv sufficiently in check to maintain the peace. On the Arab side it is forgotten that most Arab countries are extremely democratic, not in the way that modern Scandinavian countries are, but in the way that ancient Rome was. From the beginning rabble-rousing was the way to power in Arab politics, and hired mobs were as often as not a decisive element. People who hire mobs sometimes forget that when a mass of men is paid to run riot screaming that So-and-so Pasha is worthy of death, though the constituent individuals may begin with little interest in the matter beyond the mob-wage, in the end they will kill the pasha with genuine hatred. The mobs of the principal Arab cities had been aroused against the Jewish National Home for more than twenty years. This left the leaders little choice when the promised day of action drew near.

21 Kimche, *op. cit.*
22 *Ibid.*

It seems that the British government was quite confident that the UNSCOP plan would come to nothing. In addition they regarded it as impossible that Russia and the United States would vote together on this matter. They felt this in spite of the known fact of the powerful Zionist lobby in America and the recent support of Zionism by the U.S.S.R. (support, that is, in U.N.O. and Palestine, not in Russia where Jewish nationalism remained execrated and persecuted). But the incredible happened, and in November, 1947, America and Russia voted together for the UNSCOP plan. Still there was no sign of British awareness of the need to cooperate with U.N.O. and (for example) obtain U.N.O. support for Abdullah; instead with pointless obstinacy the British government resolved to "go it alone" to the bitter end. The fact that the leading ministers had been in office since 1940, the possibility that the strain on their nerves and abilities in undertaking the India settlement had temporarily exhausted them —such things should not be forgotten. But when all allowance is made for frayed nerves and the weariness of long service in years of strain, it does seem that after November, 1947, an element of embittered cussedness, and the madness that goes with it, became a part of British policy.

Almost as soon as the news broke that on the 29th of November the General Assembly of the United Nations had voted for the UNSCOP partition plan, the war broke out in Palestine. The Jewish leadership had at first a single aim, to hold their allotted area; the Arab leadership were nearly all in a state of hesitancy and bewilderment, except Abdullah, who was biding his time. The leaders on both sides had a wrong estimate of the strength of their enemies. Most of the Arabs thought the Jews were stronger than they were, except the Mufti who underestimated Haganah. Again out of date in his ideas, he seems to have remained deceived as to Jewish character by his memories of the self-restraint policy of twelve years before. He alone among the leaders wanted hostilities, and he supposed that no more was needed for Arab victory than a renewal without British interference of the guerrilla-type operations of the Arab rebellion in the thirties. But he had few followers in the Arab League, and, as said, if the matter had lain with the leaders there might not have been a war. The decision lay elsewhere. As soon as the news of UNSCOP broke, the mobs came out.

The prognostication of Glubb Pasha that Zionism could set the Moslem world aflame was found to be correct. On the 30th of November, the day after the U.N.O. vote, there were Arab attacks on Jews, with considerable loss of life, in Haifa, Tel Aviv, Jaffa, Lydda, Jerusalem, and on the roads.[23] This was to be expected perhaps, but concurrently there were more alarming symptoms. There were riots that caused the shedding of Jewish blood in Damascus, Aleppo, Baghdad, Beirut, even in distant Aden. In Aleppo some three hundred houses and eleven synagogues were destroyed by fire, and in Aden the number of Jews killed was officially estimated at seventy-six.[24] The professors, the *Ulema,* of the al-Azhar Moslem University in Cairo declared a Holy War against the Jews, and from Damascus the Mufti ordered a three-day general strike in Palestine to open on the 2nd of December. This stimulated the continuing Arab attacks on Jews in many parts of the country, and, as the disorders increased, a new and most disturbing phenomenon began to appear. British police and troops in the area of conflict looked on, sometimes with undisguised approval, as Arab mobs looted Jewish shops and burned Jewish buildings, only intervening after the rioters had wreaked damage and injury which prompt British action could easily have prevented.[25] In trying to carry out an incomprehensible and impossible task even the best of the British troops began to be demoralized, and the daily abominations of the Jewish terrorists had embittered thousands of them against the whole Yishuv.[26] This was part of the price that innocent Jewish men and women had to pay for the Agency's needless act of desperation in combining with these repulsive secret societies and refusing to cooperate in their suppression. But while such reflections may go far toward explaining ignoble British conduct, and even toward excusing the reactions of uneducated men in the ranks, they cannot disguise the fact that the conduct in question was ignoble and, no matter what the difficulties of the British task in Palestine, utterly unworthy of a government with mandate responsibilities. Behavior of this kind by British troops all too faithfully reflected British policy.

It can be objected that in this connection the words "British policy" are a contradiction in terms. That may be so. In the present state of information it is impossible to know whether or not there was any deliberate plan behind the five-and-a-half months of blundering that remained to the mandatory after the 29th of November, 1947. Zionist apologists, with

[23] Dov Joseph, *The Faithful City.* Tel Aviv, 1960. This is a detailed account of Jerusalem during the Arab-Israel war written from a strictly Zionist point of view by Mr. Dov Joseph who was the Israeli military governor of the city. Though the book makes no secret of Zionist bias, it is not unfair.
[24] Kirk, *op. cit.*
[25] Richard Graves, *Experiment in Anarchy.* London, 1949. Many other authorities can be quoted in support.
[26] Kimche, *op. cit.*

good reason, see British policy as clearly motivated by a wish to soothe Arab exasperation at UNSCOP and indeed at the whole past thirty years of Zionist increase under British protection; they see Britain as helping the Arabs to thwart the rise of a Jewish State and to keep the National Home small and manageable, in the interests of the British Empire and its oil supplies. Arab apologists, also not without reason, see British policy motivated by a wish to keep on good terms with international Jewry and for that reason anxious to prevent the Arabs from gaining more than a token area of their despoiled heritage: to oppose UNSCOP, but not so much as to exasperate dangerously the Jewish lobbies in England and America.[27] The Zionist theory is probably nearer the truth than the Arab one, but in all likelihood both represent elements of the fact rather than the fact. What the policy was remains a mystery and may have been one to the men responsible and those who carried it out. In the writer's opinion the most likely clue to what it was lies in the India and Pakistan settlement, and the belief that the same techniques could be applied to Palestine.

In the debate in the House of Commons on the 25th of Februay, 1947, Mr. Crossman made an interesting remark which may be a pointer to subsequent events. He said at the conclusion of his speech that he wished to make a "harsh" recommendation. In industrial disputes there came a moment, sometimes, when no amount of negotiation, arbitration and even goodwill was of any avail. The dispute could then only be settled by a strike, and it was far better, in such circumstances, to clear the air by means of strife rather than to try in vain to reach agreement through diplomacy. So it was, he believed, at that moment in Palestine. The words described what was being attempted in India, and they were such as could especially appeal to Ernest Bevin. Strangely enough Mr. Crossman, who usually acted toward Bevin as an unwelcome corrective, seems on this occasion to have fallen into one of Bevin's most erroneous ways of thought. British trades unionism and labor disputes were no guide to national antagonisms, least of all to that in Palestine. If Mr. Crossman's comparison could be defended in the case of India this was by coincidence and not because of a genuine similarity of India with British industry. Taken as a matter of principle, arguments for proceeding to the bitter extremity of a declared strike would lose much of their validity if it was known that both sides were armed and inflamed to the last degree of fanaticism, that many among them thirsted for bloodshed and neither side

[27] Sir John Glubb summarizes the Arab point of view with detail and great perspicacity in *A Soldier with the Arabs, op. cit.*

was above the massacre of women and children. It would be a case not of clearing the air by means of strife but of calling in a large strong police force quickly. Whether or not Mr. Crossman gave the cue, the behavior of the British government was as if they had decided to withdraw authority and let the two antagonists fight it out. It should be remembered that when these things happened the war had ended only two years before and men were living in its aftermath during which brutal deeds on a large scale were daily items of news. Men had supped full with horrors. "Radical solutions," no matter what suffering they entailed, were often admired by people who had not seen what such euphemisms hide.

All this is a matter of opinion, but there is no disagreement that the result of British policy or nonpolicy was chaos through indecision. A narrowly Zionist authority, like Mr. Dov Joseph, and a frankly anti-Zionist one, like Sir John Glubb, reach the same conclusion. Mr. Joseph says this: "Our final fight for freedom, after two thousand years of exile, came at a moment when a war-weary nation, unwilling to go on paying the price of empire and unwilling to give it up, was capable only of a kind of massive, wavering indecision." Sir John Glubb describes the day-to-day life of Palestine in the last winter of the British mandate in one memorable sentence: "With the machinery of the Palestine Government still in position, with officials still going to their offices every morning, with the police still in the streets and a considerable army still in its barracks, raging battles were going on in the country almost unhindered." In the propaganda-infested atmosphere of late-mandate Palestine and of Zionist and anti-Zionist circles of those and subsequent years, only moderate-minded accounts are worth any attention. Among them the British student seeks in vain, even from records such as Major Wilson's *Cordon and Search* that takes pains to stress the British case, for a ground of defense for the British government of those years insofar as Palestine was concerned. The most he can hope for is a reminder of the state of affairs in the world in general: the dread of Communist-inspired revolution in France, Italy, and Germany; the Communist seizure of Czechoslovakia in February, 1948, and fears of a Communist victory in Islamic Asia. These can be advanced as mitigating factors but no more. It has been noted that the Zionist theory of British policy in this confused time may contain the larger element of truth, but the anti-Zionist theory, whatever its weaknesses, certainly shows that British political conduct in 1947 and 1948 was quite fatuous from the Arab point of view. The Palestine Arabs could at least demand of the mandatory protection of at least the eastern part of the UNSCOP Arab area. They could justly demand of the mandatory that this be given in as firm and orderly a manner as possible. British policy denied them this and thus made disorderly protection and war inevitable.

When one compares the British and French records in protectorate administration, the advantage to a fair-minded person (and the point is conceded by many Frenchmen) is strongly in favor of the British, but there is nothing in the French record in next-door Syria comparable in mischievous incompetence to the British record in Palestine from November, 1947, to May, 1948.

It is outside the purpose of this book to retell the story of the Arab-Israel war. Its course, and concurrent British action, till the proclamation of Israel, need only be indicated here. On the 11th of December, 1947, Mr. Creech Jones announced in the House of Commons the date when the Palestine mandate would be terminated: the 15th of May, 1948. Again he was generally disbelieved. During this month of December there had been widespread attacks on Jewish settlements by Arab guerrilla bands who appear to have acted without plan and without coordinated leadership. It was another "peasants' rising." Haganah was alerted. It had already been mobilized in October, 1947, or rather the order for mobilization and the first steps toward it were already in train. Haganah's war preparation had to be done in secret and, as a result, notice of duty, assembly, organization, distribution of weapons and such-like had to follow roundabout and therefore tardy and inefficient means. Even after the U.N.O. vote on UNSCOP, and after Mr. Creech Jones's second declaration of withdrawal, British searches for Haganah arms, and navy patrols against illegal immigration continued. This is a strong argument in the Zionist case. It must be remembered, however, that this was not a purely anti-Jewish measure. It was part of a policy to disarm both sides. The policy was only half-heartedly adopted, and without doubt usually applied to the disadvantage of the Jews, but it is fair to remember that much later, in May, it was operated to the disadvantage of the Arabs against the Transjordan forces, the best by far on the Arab side. The usual anti-Jewish character of the disarmament policy was motivated by the hatred of Zionism to which terrorism had given rise in the British army, but still more from a British overestimate of Haganah. It was commonly believed that if they were given the opportunity these supposedly Communist forces could and would overrun the whole of Palestine up to the Jordan and perhaps go farther.[28]

In fact these tales of formidable Haganah power were a long way from the truth. A large proportion of their arms had been smuggled from

[28] Kimche, *op. cit.*

abroad, stolen or illegally bought from Allied troops. The amount of equipment that can be amassed by such methods is very meager compared to what the smallest regular arms industry can produce. Ben-Gurion had seen the danger as long ago as the summer, and in November he had dispatched one of the most skillful workers in Mossad le Aliyah Beth, a man called Ehud Avriel, as head of a mission to America and Europe to buy arms in large quantities by any means he could devise. In December he was in Paris in the early stages of his search. The arms were still a long way off and the threat to the Yishuv was increasing every day.

As the year drew to an end the character of the struggle began to change, especially in the north where it moved from indiscriminate raiding and counterraiding to more calculated attack and atrocity. In the northeast of Palestine, in the country of the Huleh valley there was continual sniper activity. In the little town of Safed, northwest of the Sea of Galilee, fighting of a more serious kind broke out, and in turn this led to a hideous reprisal on the Arab village of Khissas farther north near the Syrian frontier. Something of the evil spirit of the terrorists was entering Haganah at this time. A small detachment made its way into the village at night and with grenades and machine-gun fire murdered ten Arabs and injured five others. It is believed on unprejudiced authority that this crime was in no sense the sudden deed of hotheads but part of a considered policy which had been preceded by debate, and was finally ordered by the highest authorities of the Jewish Agency and Haganah.[29] It is possible that this Haganah crime (no Irgunists or Sternists took part in it) precipitated the next phase of the war. Among the ten murdered at Khissas were two Syrian and two Lebanese visitors. About three weeks later the first Arab armed bands entered the country from outside.

In the early days of January, 1948, the political temperature, and with the temperature the quantity and cruelty of the mutual bloodshed of Jews and Arabs, rose swiftly especially in Haifa and Jerusalem, and around the Jewish settlements in the Jordan valley.[30] On the 9th Arab volunteers who had joined up in Damascus and Beirut came over the northern frontier. British troops intervened and prevented them from attacking two Jewish settlements, and the British government formally objected to the Syrian government against a violation of Palestine soil. This diplomatic protest seems to have been completely unserious. No attempt was made to eject the invaders, and about ten days later no objection was raised when further and more formidable armed bands came in from Syria. These were

[29] Kimche, op. cit.
[30] Graves, op. cit.

trained soldiers commanded by regular officers of the Syrian army.[31] The British insisted that the geographical complication of the north Palestine frontier made supervision impossible. To some extent the excuse (which was not new) had always been valid, but least so at this time when Great Britain had a large force in the country, capable of dealing swiftly with any except minute secret bands. Nearer to the truth, in all probability, was the remark of the Iraq Prime Minister in an interview with the Egyptian newspaper *Al Misri.* "The Arabs ought not to be afraid of the British. I can assure you that the British forces in Palestine would not try to oppose or fight the Arabs, because Britain is a real friend of the Arabs." [32] The policing of Tel Aviv and Jaffa had been handed over to the Jews and the Arabs respectively, which meant Haganah, Al Futuwwah and Al Najja-dah, and the Tel Aviv authorities were not slow to complain that in the quickening battle the supposedly neutral British forces invariably inter-vened in a way that was beneficial to the Arab interest and disadvantage-ous to their own. It is unlikely that this was an imaginary grievance.

The war was still undeclared. January, 1948, was still a time of prepa-ration and of signs of what was to come. Soon after the second infiltration of armed men from Syria, the commander-in-chief of these forces now known as the Arab Liberation Army, arrived in Palestine on the 25th.[33] He was Fawzi el Kawakji. There were now three principal commanders on the Arab side in Palestine: Kawakji, who acted with the authority of the League; Glubb Pasha in command of the Transjordanian Arab Le-gion; and Abd el Kader Husseini commanding Arab forces in the Jerusa-lem area and deriving his authority from the Mufti's Higher Committee. The Arab Legion was well-trained and had shown its quality in the cam-paign against Rashid Ali, but, owing to its British origin and part-British officer personnel, owing also to the close relations between Britain and Transjordan, the Legion could not defy mandatory orders and wishes in the way the Liberation Army and the Mufti's men could and did. As a result, the effectiveness of the Arab Legion was diminished by becoming involved in the flounderings and confusions of the Foreign and Colonial Offices. Abd el Kader was the ablest and the most courageous of the Arab commanders. He was hampered by the enmity of the Arab Liberation Army whose commander even intrigued against him with the Jewish

[31] Wilson, *op. cit.*
[32] *Al Misri,* 11th February, 1948. Quoted in *A Political Study of the Arab-Jewish Conflict* by Rony E. Gabbay. *Etudes d'Histoire Economique, Politique et Sociale.* Geneva and Paris, 1959.
[33] Kimche, *op. cit.*

Agency.[34] Kawakji had shown ruthlessness and dash in the guerrilla operations of ten years before, but he had always had much of the charlatan
about him. Every battle in which he took part was represented as an Aus-
terlitz of which he was victor, and in his later years his weakness showed
in ever stronger colors while there was a corresponding diminution of his
never large capacity for achievement.[35] A good deal of luck was on the
Jewish side.

The most serious Jewish disadvantage remained shortage of equipment,
and it was galling to the Zionists that British official policy seemed designed to correct any want of balance in favor of the Arab invaders. On
the 12th of January the official Foreign Office spokesman announced that
in conformity with treaty obligations Egypt, Iraq, and Transjordan were
all being supplied with arms by Great Britain. Here was that dilemma
which was bound to make nonsense of British policy as soon as the latter
turned against U.N.O. after appealing for U.N.O. help. It can be said by
way of excuse that evidence was still accumulating that there would be no
war in Palestine. The great Kawakji was not at all keen to fight. He did
not only enter into secret agreements with the Jewish Agency but with the
British High Commission as well,[36] assuring both that he would not be the
first to move. But Kawakji with many others had forgotten the raging
nationalism of the ordinary Arab rank and file. It has been suggested by
the Kimche brothers that the ease with which units of the Liberation
Army entered Palestine, and the reluctance of the British to interfere with
their movement, and their established headquarters at Thebeg or Tubas
only forty miles north of Jerusalem, encouraged the activist elements. At
all events, once arrived, the Liberation Army soon took to warfare. Unless
the mission of Avriel succeeded, the Jews could not meet their enemies on
equal terms. The United States government, the great source and hope for
arms for Zion, had decreed a total arms embargo which applied to both
sides.

Avriel did succeed in his mission, perhaps one of the most crucial in
Jewish history. While he was in Paris in December he found that the
Czechoslovak government took a broad-minded view about the sale of
arms. Under an assumed name and carrying dubious credentials Avriel
posed as the agent of a South American State anxious to buy arms in
Prague. The Czech authorities were fully aware of the identity and purpose of "Mr. Ueberall," but for the sake of lucrative trade they accepted

[34] Gabbay, op. cit.
[35] Sir Alec Kirkbride, A Crackle of Thorns. London, 1956.
[36] Kimche, op. cit.

the polite fiction about his South American responsibilities. The Russians (preparing their February coup d'état) were also aware of what was going on and their approval had to be sought. The U.S.S.R. had voted for UNSCOP, but Russia remained basically anti-Zionist and was ruled in 1948 by the most capricious of her tyrants since the Emperor Paul. Here was a danger which was confronted and overcome in America by Moshe Shertok. He undertook negotiations with the Russian delegate Andrei Gromyko, and Gromyko obtained approval for the deal from Moscow. Avriel and his mission were able to buy about 10,000 rifles and 450 machine guns from Prague. If these arms could be got to Haganah they would keep them going. They were smuggled into Palestine under the direction of another major artist of the Mossad le Aliyah Beth, a man called Yehuda Arazi.[37] But it took a long time to arrange this and there was no immediate relief to the Jewish armed forces.

When the British heard about the arms traffic in Prague they sent notes of protest to the Czech government, and these, we are told, "only caused them amusement." The Czechs had indeed much to tickle them. They were not only making generous profits out of the Jews but out of the Arabs as well. Shortly before the arrival of Avriel they had received a Syrian mission to Prague headed by the Prime Minister's nephew, Major Fuad Mardam Bey. With him they had concluded a deal for arms worth eleven million dollars. If this consignment reached the Arab troops in Palestine the advantage which Avriel had obtained for Haganah would be reduced to very little. Once again Arazi and his colleagues of the Mossad went into action, and after a series of brilliant and incredibly complicated sabotage maneuvers (related in detail by the Kimche brothers) the arms found their way to the Army of Israel, as Haganah by that time had become. After this, in the later stages of the war, when it was becoming clear who was going to win, Czechoslovakia became the Zionist arsenal. It has been said that Czechoslovakia saved Israel, but the honor to the former country was not much. They were further to redress the balance in the next decade by supplying arms to Gamal Abdel Nasser.

This obtaining of arms was (in the writer's opinion) the most fateful of the crossroads which the Jews had to pass in the painful last stages of their journey toward the State of Israel. It was perhaps the most dangerous that they had encountered at any time since the opposition long ago of Asquith and Edwin Montagu. It is unlikely that the Jews would ever have been totally defeated. The unpreparedness, disunity and even mutual hostility of the Arab forces, in contrast with the single-mindedness of their

[37] Kimche, *op. cit.*

enemies, ruled out the possibility of their victory. As Musa el Alami
sagely remarked: "It was obvious that our [Arab] aims in the battle were
diverse, while the aim of the Jews was solely to win it."[38] But merely to
win would not serve the Jewish need: to reach their goal they had to
achieve a decisive victory. Nothing less would do. Nothing short of defeat
was more dangerous to the Jewish cause than partial victory or prolonged
indecisive engagements. Such a circumstance would have opened the way
to a revival of British or international Palestine trusteeship (to which the
Jews were soon to find themselves perilously near), and it could shut the
open door to statehood.

Jewish victory was not yet visible: till the end of February they remained on the defensive, with few exceptions, and those horrible, as for
example another terrorist venture by Haganah—this time in a remote
Arab village called Sassa.[39] The main points of struggle were on the roads
between Tel Aviv and Jerusalem where a Jewish community of about
100,000 was in danger of being cut off.

It was here in Jerusalem that the confusion of British policy was most
painfully manifest. Zionist authorities often accuse the last administration
of callous indifference at this moment to the fate of the Jerusalem Jews,
but in this instance there was a case against the Agency which has been
largely forgotten. The Agency had definitely taken its stand on UNSCOP.
It had accepted its plan with its disadvantages. Jerusalem was outside the
Jewish area of the UNSCOP partition, where it figured as a neutral area,
whatever that might mean. Yet Haganah in Jerusalem and Jewish settlements to the north and south of the Holy City were active in the conflict,
sometimes brutally so.[40] Jerusalem remained the responsibility of the High
Commission, and if the Jews stood by UNSCOP they should have completely made over the defense and administration to the mandatory. That
is the case against them. Yet can anyone blame a Jewish authority who
refused to do this because of a loss of trust in British good intentions? At
this moment, in January and February, UNSCOP at Lake Success were
requesting that a U.N.O. mission should be allowed into the country to
take over authority by stages from the mandatory, and, true to the one
strongly held principle of the decaying administration, this was emphatically refused.[41] It can be argued on the British side that the proposed five-

38 Quoted in Gabbay, *op. cit.*
39 Kimche, *op. cit.*
40 Glubb, *op. cit.*
41 Kirk. It was refused on the grounds that in the then state of Palestine the safety
of commission members would be in jeopardy.

power commission included a delegate from Czechoslovakia, and it was known that that country was planning to play a sinister role in the settlement of Palestine. But again it could be asked—who was Britain to throw stones with her recent announcement of plans to supply arms to those countries who were at that moment reinforcing alien Arab armies on the soil which the mandatory was under solemn obligation to protect? The situation was rapidly passing out of the stage of logic and civilized negotiation and pledge and moving into that of force and violence. Were Jews to blame if they also appealed to the argument of force? Especially since they understood how to use it better than their opponents?

In February two events occurred to influence the Arab cause in Palestine. One hindered and one helped it. The first concerned Iraq whose government had been negotiating a treaty with the British government since July, 1945. A succession of Iraq governments and the regent, Prince Abdul Illah, favored a continuation of the close Anglo-Iraq accord envisaged in the original treaty of 1931, the famous act of state which had proved to many the sincerity of the League of Nations. But a new generation had grown up to whom the concessions of 1930 were contemptible in the light of modern nationalism. They wanted total independence as a matter of course, and they had the national humiliation of 1941 to forget. Against their political influence, which was felt more and more from the end of the war to 1948, the regent and his Prime Minister, Salah Jabr, strove in vain. In mid-February of 1948 a draft treaty, believed on both sides to meet modern nationalist demands was signed by Ernest Bevin and Nuri es Said in Portsmouth, U.S.A. It was greeted by rioting in Baghdad and the fall of the Iraq government. The regent hastened to join the popular side, and the feeling in Baghdad was that the change of government was a triumph for nationalism. Nobody in Iraq seemed to notice that this was a considerable setback for the anti-Zionist campaign. The clauses in the draft treaty relating to the supply of military equipment to the Iraq government became automatically invalid.[42]

The second event occurred at the end of the month. King Abdullah sent a mission headed by his Prime Minister, Tewfik Pasha Abu Al Huda, to London. Glubb Pasha accompanied them, as military adviser, also acting on occasion as translator to the Prime Minister. The official object of Abdullah was to obtain some modifications of the Anglo-Transjordan treaty of 1946. This was accomplished without difficulty. Then Tewfik Pasha requested an interview with Ernest Bevin. He pointed out to him that on the British withdrawal either Haganah would yield to the tempta-

[42] Kirk, Kimche, op. cit.

tion to occupy all Palestine up to the Jordan, or the Anglophobe Mufti would attempt to set up an unviable state in the area allotted by UNSCOP to the Arabs. He proposed that instead the Arab Legion should on the withdrawal occupy the east Arab area, thus avoiding an unviable Mufti-controlled state and providing efficient administration. To this the Foreign Secretary replied: "It seems the obvious thing to do."

Prompted by Glubb, Tewfik Pasha added that the Legion would not be able to occupy the southwestern and northwestern Arab areas which were not contiguous with Transjordan frontiers. Bevin repeated: "It seems the obvious thing to do," and added: "But don't you go and invade the areas allotted to the Jews." The Prime Minister said that he had not the military force to do this even if he wanted to.[43] Assuming that King Abdullah was correctly reported by his Palestine friend (quoted on page 329), it would seem that Bevin officially endorsed to this Transjordan mission a line of policy secretly agreed with the king some months before.

For a moment a gleam of political common sense illuminates the story of British conduct in Palestine. Unfortunately it is only for a moment. This sensible arrangement with Tewfik Pasha, this "obvious thing to do," was not carried out on the British side with resolution or realism. The benefit to Palestine's future was lost.

By the end of February the Arabs seemed in a better military position than the Jews. The Zionist settlements north and south of Jerusalem had both been fiercely attacked by Arabs, and though neither had been conquered, the attack led by Abd el Kader on the southern settlement, Kfar Etzion, had resulted in the whole of the Palmach force moving to its relief being killed. The psychological shock of this disaster to the Yishuv was immense.[44] Against this the Jews had the example of Tirat Zvi where the Liberation Army under Kawakji had attacked a Jewish settlement in the Jordan valley with total failure. But the Arabs held the initiative in the country-wide battle of the roads and on this the outcome of the struggle depended. In the eastern area the Arab Legion were taking over the garrisoning as the mandatory troops slowly withdrew. The Jews, contrary to what most non-Jews thought, were still desperately short of arms. Even without this knowledge, it still seemed to many people that, given some resolution, unity and leadership, the Arabs would defeat them. In fact the Arabs never had a hope.

[43] Glubb, *op. cit.* Sir John gives no date; it is supplied as late February by the Kimche brothers.
[44] Kimche, *op. cit.*

March saw the turning of the tide of battle in favor of the Jews, who at the same time were faced by new and formidable political dangers.

Since the United States had voted with the U.S.S.R. for UNSCOP in November of 1947 the Zionists had enjoyed a fruitful spell of American favor. It was time for the pendulum to swing: for American policy to show its other face, the oil-conscious one. The anti-Zionist interest had never been quiet in Washington, or at Lake Success where U.N.O. was holding its meetings. As J. C. Hurewitz remarks of this period with enjoyable irony: "The hesitant unfolding of United States support of partition suggested that Washington was experiencing difficulty in reconciling the traditional pressures."

The pro-Arab pressure, which was traditionally the more ancient, and was now the most commercially powerful, had recently been greatly strengthened by American political decisions. The Marshall Plan for the recovery of Europe, perhaps the most important and statesmanlike action of modern times, depended for effectiveness on immense American commercial success, and as regards oil it had been originally calculated that it required the oil companies in Asia to supply a million barrels a day. This estimate was drastically reduced in February, 1948, to 200,000 barrels.[45] But it was agreed that below this enormous output the Marshall Plan could fail. It was strongly and logically concluded that for America to open a quarrel with the world of Islam was not merely to jeopardize the wealth of American oil interests but was to endanger the supreme purpose of American policy in the world. A political campaign against American involvement in UNSCOP had begun to get under way in January. On the 21st Vice-Admiral Robert B. Carney (Deputy Chief of Naval Operations for Logistics) testified to the House Armed Services Committee: "In the event of serious disturbance in the Middle East, there is cause for grave concern for the fortunes of American oil facilities throughout that area, and to those who might desire to deny the oil of the Middle East to us [by which he clearly meant the U.S.S.R.], such disturbance could afford nice opportunities for interference." [46] Vice-Admiral Carney and those in Congress and the Pentagon who felt with him received strong backing from James Terry Druce, the Vice-President of the Arabian-American Oil Company, and his fellow directors who looked with dismay at the drift of American policy in Palestine and prophesied evil consequences from it. The United States government began to wilt under the accumulation of

[45] Frank E. Manuel, *The Realities of American-Palestine Relations*. Washington, 1949.
[46] *Ibid.*

pressure. Secretary Marshall, it was noted in February, referred to the American commitment to UNSCOP in terms of studied vagueness. "Until the Security Council," he said on one occasion, "has received and studied the report of the Palestine Commission on security and enforcement and has reached a decision, it is not possible for this Government to determine in advance the steps which may be necessary to carry out such a decision." Senator Warren Austin, United States Ambassador to U.N.O., made his government's position somewhat clearer in the course of the debate on Palestine held by the Security Council on the 24th of February, 1948. In the official American view, he said, the action of the Council should be strictly confined to preserving international peace. He said: "The Council, in other words, is directed to keeping the peace and not to enforcing partition."

American policy on Palestine was becoming almost as complicated and self-contradictory as that of the erratic mandatory. In March it became incomprehensible. On the 5th the Security Council adopted a proposal put forward in February by Ambassador Austin that the Security Council should consult with themselves as to whether there was a threat to peace in the Palestine situation, a proposition which reads somewhat as though they should discuss whether or not the earth was spherical. It seemed to many a further sign that the American government was having second thoughts about its Zionist policy. Yet to those who protested that this was part of an American retreat from UNSCOP, denials were forthcoming from Ambassador Austin, Secretary Marshall, and the President himself. The doubters were reassured when on March 14th the Council passed a United States resolution that "the Security Council will do everything it can under the charter to give effect to the recommendation of the General Assembly." Once more the United States and the U.S.S.R. voted together. The resolution was taken to mean a halt to the retreat and a renewed American decision to implement the UNSCOP plan.[47] But the surprises of March, 1948, were not yet in their stride.

The center of the enigma was Mr. Truman and his curious relations with Dr. Weizmann. He had met Weizmann once, in November, 1947, and he had not only been fascinated by his personality but had allowed himself to be influenced by him. As a result Weizmann had been enabled to render a great service to the Zionist cause: the United States government at that time planned to accept the UNSCOP plan but with the subtraction of the Negev from the Jewish area. Weizmann persuaded Mr. Truman that since this would deprive the Jews of a Red Sea port it would

[47] *Ibid.*

place them at an unfair and grave disadvantage, and as a result of his representations the United States accepted virtually the full UNSCOP area. This was a considerable achievement for Zionism, but in his old age Weizmann was soon to render another even more remarkable service to his people.

It seems that in the winter of 1947-48 Zionist propagandists were once again overplaying their hand. As a result they were rapidly losing the sympathy of Mr. Truman. "I do not think," he states in his memoirs, "I ever had as much pressure and propaganda aimed at the White House as I had in this instance. The persistence of a few of the extreme Zionist leaders—actuated by political motives and engaging in political threats—disturbed me and annoyed me . . . Individuals and groups asked me, usually in rather quarrelsome and emotional ways, to stop the Arabs, to keep the British from supporting the Arabs, to furnish American soldiers to do this, that and the other . . . As the pressure mounted, I found it necessary to give instructions that I did not want to be approached by any more spokesmen for the extreme Zionist case. I was even so disturbed that I put off seeing Dr. Chaim Weizmann who had returned to the United States and had asked for an interview with me."

Dr. Weizmann had returned to the United States at the urgent request of his political colleagues as long ago as the 4th of February, 1948, and from the Waldorf Hotel he witnessed with dismay the signs of an American retreat from partition. In vain he tried to see the President. Then on the 14th of March a most extraordinary event occurred. A man called Eddie Jacobson, a non-Zionist Kansas Jew, called on Dr. Weizmann in his hotel where he was confined ill in bed. Mr. Jacobson had known President Truman since the days of the First World War, and had afterward been his partner in an unsuccessful clothing store. In spite of the fact that he was not a Zionist Mr. Jacobson had a boundless admiration for Dr. Weizmann, whom he had never seen. Hearing from a Jewish friend of the anxieties of the Jewish leaders in America and the irritation of the President, he sent a telegram to Mr. Truman asking him to receive Dr. Weizmann. The President sent him a polite and vague reply. Thereupon Mr. Jacobson went to Washington and called on Mr. Truman at the White House on the plea of personal business. When Mr. Jacobson told him his real intention the President was not pleased. He explained coldly that he respected Dr. Weizmann but that a meeting "would only result in more wrong interpretation."

Mr. Jacobson then played his masterstroke. He nodded to a statuette of

Andrew Jackson that was in the room, and addressed Jackson's successor as follows:

> He's been your hero all your life, hasn't he? You have probably read every book there is on Jackson. I remember when we had the store that you were always reading books and pamphlets, and a lot of them were about Jackson. You put this statue in front of the Jackson County Court House in Kansas City when you built it. I have never met the man who has been my hero all my life, but I have studied his past like you have studied Jackson's. He is the greatest Jew alive, perhaps the greatest Jew who ever lived. You yourself have told me that he is a great statesman and a fine gentleman. I am talking about Dr. Chaim Weizmann. He is an old man and a very sick man. He has traveled thousands of miles to see you, and now you put off seeing him. That isn't like you.

According to Mr. Jacobson's account,[48] this utterance was followed by a long silence during which the President looked out of the window. Then he turned to Mr. Jacobson and said: "All right, you bald-headed son of a bitch, you win. Tell Matt [the appointments secretary] to invite Dr. Weizmann here." Mr. Jacobson was now in New York in order to tell Dr. Weizmann that he was expected at the White House on the 18th.

The meeting was secret and described thus by Mr. Truman:

> We talked for almost three-quarters of an hour. He talked about the possibilities of development in Palestine, about the scientific work that he and his assistants had done that would sometime be translated into industrial activity in the Jewish State that he envisaged. He spoke of the need for land if the future immigrants were to be cared for, and he impressed on me the importance for any Jewish State of the Negev area in the south . . .
> I told him as plainly as I could, why I had at first put off seeing him. He understood. I explained to him what the basis of my interest in the Jewish problem was and that my primary concern was to see justice done without bloodshed. And when he left my office, I felt that he had reached a full understanding of my policy and that I knew what it was he wanted.[49]

On the next day, March 19th, 1948, the United States delegation to U.N.O. astonished the world by declaring a complete reversal of American policy. Ambassador Austin announced that his government would

---

[48] Given by Dr. Abba Eban in Weizmann Biography.
[49] Truman, *op. cit.*

like action on partition suspended and that the General Assembly should be summoned to discuss the establishment of a temporary "trusteeship" to be exercized by U.N.O. over Palestine "without prejudice to the character of the eventual political settlement." In other words, the UNSCOP plan was dropped, once and for all it seemed, by the government which had formerly been its most ardent champion. This was a major defeat for Zionism. The Jews of Palestine and Zionists throughout the world were overcome by a sense of betrayal,[50] and on the 23rd of March the Jewish Agency and the Va'ad Leumi condemned the action of the United States. Inevitably grave suspicions arose regarding Mr. Truman's honesty, among the few who had heard about Dr. Weizmann's visit the day before Ambassador Austin's announcement. The extraordinary confusion of these events perplexed those who studied them for several years, and Mr. Frank E. Manuel (writing in 1948) described the dilemma: "The historian is faced with a choice between the following two interpretations of the reversal [of policy]: either President Truman was deceiving Weizmann or, what seems to be the fact, he was not informed by his own State Department of the import of the orders which had been issued to the United Nations delegates."

It is now clear from a biography of Mr. Truman published in 1950 by Jonathan Daniels, and from the former President's own memoirs, that the second explanation is the true one. On the morning of the 20th the President was thrown into a state of agitation when he read the news of what had happened at Lake Success. He asked his administrative assistant: "How could this have happened? I assured Chaim Weizmann that we were for partition and would stick to it. He must think I am a plain liar." In this, however, he was wrong. Dr. Weizmann himself, though he was an emotional man liable to pass from a mood of optimism to one of black despair, had no doubt at any time that Mr. Truman would keep faith with him. He alone among the Jewish leaders showed no sign of anxiety.[51]

In fact what had happened seems to have been the best possible thing from the Zionist point of view. Mr. Truman, as he makes abundantly plain in his autobiography, was throughout dissatisfied with the Eastern-oil-dominated policy of his State Department and the American armed services, and he followed their guidance restlessly and often with exasperation. He had had enough of being the prisoner of the White House and this high-handed American action at U.N.O., taken with no reference to

---

[50] Eban, Dov Joseph, *op. cit.*
[51] Eban, *op. cit.*

himself, seems to have determined him to throw off his shackles, at any rate so far as Palestine was concerned. He wanted to see the refugees allowed in and he did not want to be thought a liar by a man whom he respected. Ambassador Austin had forced his hand. But the result did not appear till two months later.

At the end of March the first consignment of Haganah arms from Czechoslovakia, artfully stowed away in food cases, agricultural machinery and such-like, arrived in Palestine. Avriel and his helpers had now organized an irregular but considerable supply of arms from Prague paid for by the subscriptions of American sympathizers. The Jews now took the initiative in a bitterly fought action which lasted from the 31st of March to April 9th. It was fought for possession of a hilltop village called Qastel, about five miles west of Jerusalem, and the purpose was to open the road from Tel Aviv. It was on the last day of this battle that Abd el Kader was killed leading a charge. The purpose was only temporarily and fitfully achieved, for Jewish Jerusalem was to remain besieged till June, but the moral effect of a Jewish victory in the technically impregnable position of Qastel was to shake the confidence of already disturbed and disillusioned Arabs. Napoleon's famous epigram to the effect that in war moral considerations are three-quarters of a combatant's strength was wholly true of Palestine in 1948.

On April 4th Fawzi el Kawakji, hoping to satisfy his activists and to restore his reputation after the contemptible defeat of Tirat Zvi, launched a vigorous operation against the Jewish settlement of Mishmar ha Emek which is situated twenty-seven miles southeast of Haifa and whose capture would effectually threaten the Haifa-Tel Aviv road. Kawakji's assault, made with a numerous force, lasted from April the 4th to the 12th, and was renewed on the 14th before his final and total defeat; it was followed according to his custom by a proclamation of a colossal Arab victory.[52] Concurrently the Druze battalion of the Liberation Army attacked a settlement called Ramat Yohanan which, like Mishmar ha Emek, lay near the roads linking Haifa and Tel Aviv. This attack was also repulsed. There was a great difference between the successful resistance of these two settlements and that of Tirat Zvi. These April successes were positive in result, included counterattack, and resulted in the seizure of territory. The Jews were to make many mistakes in the forthcoming weeks and to suffer some severe setbacks; to the very end of the war they suffered from short-

[52] Kimche, *op. cit.*

ages of arms, and these became intermittently desperate, but after these three actions their victory was in sight. It took them to the April of 1949 to achieve it.

In this April of 1948 a terrible event helped to solve in crude and possibly disastrous fashion one of the major problems of the State of Israel which, while the mandate slowly went down in chaos, was even then visibly emerging. In January the High Commissioner had first reported a considerable emigration of Arabs, principally of the middle and propertied class.[53] Gradually this exodus increased as life in Palestine became more unbearable during February and March. There was substantial precedent for such a movement, possibly connected with Arab familiarity with nomad ways. It has been calculated that during the Arab rebellion of 1936 to 1939 some 40,000 Arabs left Palestine, the majority of them to return when peace was restored.[54] To flee the wrath to come is an Arab way. In the chaotic conditions of the failing administration the numbers of those who now went was inevitably much larger than on any previous occasion. There is a certain feudal dependence in Arab life, and more than in any Western society men tend to follow the example of the mayor and the notable and the local clergy. When these local leaders sought safety outside the country, many humble people had a scared longing to do the same, and the local leaders were not encouraged to stay when they found that a large proportion of the professional classes, the rich, the municipal authorities and the members of the Arab Higher Committee itself were intent on flight. Arab commanders were known to take flight when the battle turned against their side and this happened even in large-scale actions such as those fought at Tiberias, Acre, Haifa, and Jaffa later on in the war.

The kind of racial conflict to which the Palestinians were growing accustomed was such as to spread panic. There was no question of combat being strictly confined to armies.[55] The Arab Legion provides an exception, but prisoners were not often taken in skirmishes, or when taken they were as often as not done to death. Both sides were guilty of such horrors. Rage at them may be the real explanation of the Haganah atrocities in the villages of Khissas and Sassa. While the battle of Qastel was being fought,

[53] Kirk, op. cit.
[54] Gabbay, op. cit.
[55] "This will be a war of extermination and a momentous massacre which will be spoken of like the Mongolian massacres and the Crusades." Abdur Rahman Azzam Pasha at a Cairo press conference, 15th May, 1948.

the most ghastly of all these acts of cruelty took place at the nearby village of Dir Yassin. Patrols of the two terrorist societies, Irgun Zvai Leumi and the Sternists, seized this village on the 8th of April, 1948.[56] The inhabitants of Dir Yassin were said to be neutral and to have refused shelter to the Mufti's armed bands, but it is alleged that on this day the village had been seized as a headquarters post by a group of Abd el Kader's men preparing an attack on Jerusalem. That may be true. The assault party are said by their chronicler Menachem Begin to have suffered severe casualties, four killed and forty wounded. The commander of the combined force went further in an address given in New York (!) and claimed that eight men were killed and fifty-seven wounded.[57] Begin, who in his record always shows angry sensitiveness about being described as a terrorist, makes much of the fact that the attacking force is alleged, probably with truth, to have appealed to the inhabitants to leave before the action. When it was over, the Jewish authorities endeavored to prevent an impartial inspection. A policeman reported one Arab killed. On the 10th, Monsieur Jacques de Reynier, the chief Red Cross representative, paid the first of the four visits to Dir Yassin which he made in the course of the next two days. He discovered the corpses of two hundred and fifty-four men, women, and children. There were some survivors. A courageous and anti-Zionist woman named Mrs. Vester, who was in charge of the Anna Spafford Child Nursing Home in Jerusalem, took in some forty orphaned children. When she approached one little boy he screamed, "She is one of them," and fell down with a heart attack from which he died soon after.[58]

The Arabs hastened to organize a counterreprisal. Three days later, on the 12th of April, a convoy traveling under Red Cross badges to the isolated Jewish Hadassah Hospital and the Hebrew University was ambushed and seventy-seven doctors, nurses, university teachers, and students were killed. The justification given by the ambuscade party was that the convoy was being used to carry food and relief personnel to the Jewish troops in the Hadassah Hospital. The excuse appears to be true.[59] To add to the shame of this horrible incident, it occurred about two hundred yards from the British military post responsible for the safety of the road. The

[56] The date is given variously. The writer follows the chronology of M. Jacques de Reynier in "A Jerusalem un drapeau flottait sur la ligne de feu," *Histoire et Société d'Aujourd'hui,* 1950.

[57] Kirk. The address was reported in the *New York Times* of 30th November, 1948.

[58] Begin, Gabbay, Graves, Kirk, Reynier. Bertha Hedges Vester, *Our Jerusalem,* London, 1951.

[59] Reynier. There is a confusing reference to this aspect of the case in Dov Joseph, *op. cit.* p. 74.

attack began soon after 9:30 in the morning, and in spite of appeals for help from the victims and by telephone from Judah Magnes to the British commander, no British military intervention occurred till the midafternoon, and the Arabs were not driven off till half past four.[60] This most hideous achievement of the "crass kind" leaves perhaps the worst blemish on the tarnished British military record of that time.

The counteratrocity was again answered in kind seventeen days later when after a Haganah attack on Katamon, an Arab-European suburb of Jerusalem, there was a massacre of Arab soldiers and their women.[61]

Ben-Gurion showed moral courage amid these crimes. On hearing the news of Dir Yassin he telegraphed to King Abdullah an expression of apology for such deeds by his own people, an action on which Menachem Begin comments with characteristic indignation and self-pity. But however much Ben-Gurion may have wished to extricate Haganah and the Jewish Agency from the contamination of the terrorists, it was hard to do so now. The moral eminence of Ben-Gurion's action is diminished by the fact that on the very day that Monsieur de Reynier reported the facts of Dir Yassin, the Zionist General Council ratified an agreement for cooperation (drafted before the 9th of April) between Irgun Zvai Leumi and Haganah.[62] But the purpose here is not to dwell on terrorist crime but to consider the results of the type of conflict in which civilian massacre was a prominent part. Both sides inclined to indulge in atrocity propaganda for which both sides had ample material, but the danger of this kind of propaganda had been appreciated by the Jews, and was never appreciated by the Arabs. The Jews did not give excessive publicity to such disasters as the Hadassah ambush. The transmissions from Kol Israel, run by people with experience of the morale-building techniques evolved in the war, concentrated on tales of strength and success and largely avoided subjects of grief.[63] The Arab radio-propaganda dwelt on atrocity stories and exaggerated them. Unknowingly, the Arab propagandists did the work of Irgun and the Sternists for them. The aim was to inflame men with hatred of the Jews; the effect was to fill them with terror of the Jews, and the terror was all the more because many Palestine Arabs had a bad conscience about atrocity toward Jews. The readiness to take to flight (which, easy to see both then and now, the Arab authorities should have been at the utmost pains to prevent) became greater every day after the news of

[60] Dov Joseph, *op. cit.*
[61] Reynier, *op. cit.* He quotes a report from one of his staff.
[62] Kirk, *op. cit.*
[63] Gabbay, *op. cit.*

Dir Yassin had been first broadcast. It was repeated with inflated figures and invented vileness in excess of the vileness of the deed itself. Coming as it did, at a moment of growing Jewish armed success throughout Palestine, the terror effect turned the already large exodus of the Arabs into a mass migration. The thousands turned into tens of thousands. The Zionists believed on rough calculation that by the last week of April the Arab refugees from Palestine numbered 150,000.[64] A new possibility came to the minds of many men: the Jewish State as outlined by UNSCOP might not, after all, have to contend with its most obvious and insurmountable disadvantage, an enormous non-Jewish minority. Before the end of April about thirty purely Arab villages in the area of the UNSCOP Jewish State had been completely abandoned.[65]

In after years Arabs and Jews accused each other of having caused this new and terrible emigration by calculated measures. There is an element of truth in the charge either way, but the basic charge seems to be empty. There is good evidence that there were some and perhaps many ruthless-minded men among the Jews who hoped that the terrorists might succeed in panicking the Arabs into mass flight; there is also evidence that there were some Jews, including influential ones, who had hopes that a population-transfer policy, such as had been carried out between Greece and Turkey, might be forced on the Palestine Arabs.[66] But there is no evidence of a long-standing and agreed Jewish policy to evict the settled population; on the contrary in the first half of 1948 there is considerable evidence that the Jews tried to prevent the flight. The case of Haifa is well known. Before and during the battle which ended with the capture of the city by Haganah on the 22nd of April, 1948, an exodus of Arabs, calculated at over 40,000 people, took place. This exodus was certainly in part encouraged by Haganah, who (in the words of Jon Kimche) waged "a psychological blitz" on the Arab quarters by means of vans equipped with loudspeakers.[67] But there was also strenuous Jewish endeavor to make the Arabs stay. The mayor of Haifa, Shabetai Levy, was a Jew and he made violent and even impassioned efforts to get the representatives of the Arab National Committee to use their influence against the hourly increasing exodus of Arabs. The Committee representatives not only completely refused Levy's request but afterward declared that the enomous exodus

[64] Kirk, *op. cit.*
[65] Kirk, *op. cit.*
[66] Sir John Glubb gives interesting evidence on these two points.
[67] Jon Kimche, *Seven Fallen Pillars*. London, 1950. Also Harry Sacher, *Israel, the Establishment of a State*. London, 1952. Koestler, *Promise and Fulfilment*. London, 1949.

from the city was their doing and no one else's. They stated a year later that they "proudly asked for the evacuation of the Arabs and their removal to the neighbouring Arab countries. We are very glad to state that the Arabs guarded their honour and traditions with pride and greatness." [68] When the war was over, Arab journalists and broadcasters asserted on several occasions that the exodus was a planned Arab maneuver, the main object being to clear the land and thus give freedom of action to the invading armies. Statements of this kind gave Zionist propaganda its cue and many Jewish authorities, in perfect good faith, have asserted that the exodus was the result of harangues to leave Palestine broadcast from the radio stations of the neighboring states. It seems much more likely that the Arab claims to have organized the flight of the population are mere boasting. Doubtless there was plenty of encouragement to flee by a great many Arabs, but there seems to have been nothing resembling a public announcement of a policy of flight. The monitorings of Arabic broadcasts and the Arabic press of the time have been searched in vain for official exhortation of any kind. [69]

It can be said with a high degree of certainty that most of the time in the first half of 1948 the mass-exodus was the natural, thoughtless, pitiful movement of ignorant people who had been badly led and who in the day of trial found themselves forsaken by their leaders. Terror was the impulse, by heresy most often, and sometimes through experience as in the Arab port of Jaffa which surrendered on the 12th of May and where the Irgunists, to quote Mr. John Marlowe, "embellished their Dir Yassin battle honours by an orgy of looting."

But if the exodus was by and large an accident of war in the first stage, in the later stages it was consciously and mercilessly helped on by Jewish threats and aggression toward Arab populations. During the first truce which lasted from the 11th of June to the 9th of July, 1948, there seems to have been a new course in Zionist policy. Ben-Gurion appears to have somewhat tentatively initiated it on the 16th of June when he informed his cabinet that after the tergiversations of policy in U.N.O., the new state

---

[68] Quotations in Gabbay, *op. cit.*

[69] This matter was discussed in an article by Mr. Erskine Childers in *The Spectator* of May 12th, 1961, to which the late Professor Leo Kohn (until his death political adviser to the Israel Foreign Ministry and Professor of International Relations at the Hebrew University) replied in an article on June 16th. Mr. Childers' article and later Professor Kohn's gave rise to an interesting and heated correspondence which lasted till the 21st July, 1961. In the writer's opinion the correspondence completely disposed of the Zionist allegation that the exodus was the result of Arab planning. Oddly enough none of the writers to *The Spectator* seems to have read Gabbay.

was no longer under obligation to adhere to the UNSCOP plan, to which, as he reminded his listeners, the Arabs had never agreed: "The situation in Palestine," he said, "will be settled by military power." Of the recent flight of the Arabs from Jaffa he said as follows: "War is war. We did not want war. Tel Aviv did not attack Jaffa. Jaffa attacked Tel Aviv and this must not occur again. Jaffa will be a Jewish town. The repatriation of the Arabs to Jaffa is not justice but folly. Those who declared war on us have to bear the result after they have been defeated." [70] The new policy cannot be shown to have included a plan to expel Arabs, but the effect on Haganah conduct was as if this had been the case. A new ruthlessness soon appeared after the resumption of fighting on the 9th of July. In villages captured by Haganah on the central front east of Tel Aviv the inhabitants were "encouraged" (as the Zionist euphemism goes) to leave and go eastward. Two days after, on the 12th of July, there was stronger encouragement in the wholly Arab towns of Lydda and Ramleh. "From then on," says Mr. Rony Gabbay in his monumental study, "wherever the Israelis advanced into Arab territory the Arab population fled in front of them towards the Arab lines and countries." He explains the meaning of the euphemism: "Jewish encouragement to the Arabs to flee took different forms. It was more often conducted by psychological methods than by open ejection. Although in some cases reluctant Arabs were forced to flee into Arab country, yet in most cases Arab villages were evacuated before the Israeli troops arrived. Looting and pillaging of Arab properties and the commandeering of goats, sheep and mules were not uncommon features." [71] For all its candor this passage still puts the matter in a somewhat favorable light to Zionists. Numerous authorities, including Jewish ones, would prefer to say "many cases" rather than "some cases" of forcible ejection.[72] Subsequent Arab tales of widespread atrocity were officially reported to U.N.O. to be "greatly exaggerated," [73] as was to be expected, but the circumstances of that war were not such as to lead anywhere or even in small measure to chivalry or civilized restraint. What was exaggerated was horrible enough. It is to be noted, however, that where the Arabs had leaders who refused to be stampeded into panic flight, the people came to no harm. The case of Abu Gosh on the Jerusalem-Tel Aviv road is not one in point, as the sheikh seems to have been an unscrupu-

[70] Ben-Gurion in *Be'Hilahem Yesrael* quoted in Gabbay, *op. cit.*
[71] Gabbay, *op. cit.* I have ventured slightly to edit his unidiomatic English.
[72] This comes out in the correspondence in *The Spectator,* May–July, 1961. See also Kirk, *op. cit.,* p. 264.
[73] By Count Bernadotte, 13th September, 1948.

lous Zionist agent, but the case of Nazareth involving a far bigger population, is very much to the point. When the town fell to the Jews the mayor refused to be intimidated, kept his people together and as a result none of the suffering of war came to this community which to this day is the largest and most prosperous Arab one within Israel.[74] But in Nazareth there was what was lacking almost everywhere else: a leading man of public spirit. Elsewhere, sheep without a shepherd "fled the country in total despair. The way in which families dispersed in different directions, in spite of the very strong ties which always exist between members of Arab families, shows the state of mind of these people." The flight would always have been large. Deliberate Haganah policy after the first truce ensured that it was of vast proportions. The precise measure of Jewish blame can never be known. By the end of 1948 the number of Arabs within the area of Israel had diminished from somewhere between 700,000 and 750,000 to about 167,000.[75]

This is to carry the story beyond its terminal point; the establishment of the State of Israel. To remember the last moves and the last crossroads, the story needs to return to the last days of March, 1948, and what followed the astonishing reversal of American policy. On the 19th when the President had made his disagreement and displeasure plain, the United States administration and delegation to U.N.O. reluctantly began the laborious and cumbersome process of turning the ship of state around again, a task which was not undertaken with joy. On the 30th of March Ambassador Warren Austin put a new proposal before the Security Council: he invited them to shelve the trustee proposal, to request the Zionist and Arab authorities to send representatives to a truce parley, and to convoke another special session of the General Assembly. The proposal for a truce was not welcome to either side but was not rejected outright. Both sides stalled, the Syrian delegate agreeing to a new special session but withholding opinion about a truce, the Zionist spokesman, Moshe Shertok, agreeing to a truce but demanding conditions such as the total withdrawal of the Arab Legion, to which the British government could not consent in view of their agreements with King Abdullah, of which the Zionists were certainly aware. Following on this truce proposal, one of the last effective actions of the British High Commission in Palestine was opened when on April 18th, Sir Alan Cunningham proposed a local cease-fire in Jerusalem. The

---

[74] For a severely critical account of Zionist and Israeli treatment of Arabs within Israel the reader should consult *The Arabs in Israel* by Walter Schwartz. London, 1959.

[75] Gabbay, *op. cit.*

Agency agreed, but the Arab Higher Committee, acting as usual under the Mufti's orders, refused. A truce commission was then set up in Jerusalem on the authority of the Security Council. It consisted of the Consuls-General of France, Belgium, and the United States. On the 28th of April they succeeded in obtaining an agreement for a cease-fire in the Old City. The next night Haganah launched the attack on Katamon already mentioned. Two days later, on the 2nd of May, the British authorities roused themselves to order a cease-fire while they attempted to open negotiations for a wider truce. The tide had turned. Arabs had done most of the stalling and blocking hitherto; now it was the turn of the Jews. But during the last six days of the mandate the British did succeed in enforcing a cease-fire over the entire Holy City. It would seem that at the last they showed some sense of shame at the chaos and disaster which British failure of will had helped to bring into being.

In the meantime the political future of Jewish nationalism was passing through many perils. The scene of conflict was U.N.O. in America while British efforts were made to transfer it to London. British confusion of mind was infectious, since it was difficult for anyone to move without consulting the British government. As a result of a melee of conflicting British and American attempts at policy, the last scene at U.N.O. before the declaration of the State is so fantastic in its abundant contradiction that it is not only very difficult to know now precisely what happened, but it was probably extremely hard for the delegates and politicians on the spot then to recognize what kind of drama they were enacting before the world. A dominating factor, in all likelihood, was the growing mutual hostility of Russia and the West then reaching a climax in Berlin, and the belief (chiefly entertained in England) that Zionism had become dominated by communism. There was great British fear, largely shared by Americans, that a victory of Zionism would mean a Soviet victory in the East, and that the Russian aim was to make it concurrent with a Soviet victory in Berlin. Then, less than a week after he had asked the Security Council to shelve the trusteeship plan, Warren Austin put it forward again in a slightly new guise. On April the 5th he asked the Council to adopt an emergency measure with the object of preserving order in Palestine after the end of the mandate. The Trusteeship Council of U.N.O., according to this plan, would administer the country temporarily through a Governor-General until a regime agreeable to a majority of Palestinian Jews and Arabs (that long-lived will-o'-the-wisp) had been evolved. It has been supposed by Zionist authorities, and probably correctly, that Ambassador Austin's proposal had been drafted in consultation with the Foreign Office.[76] What is strange, if true, is that some of the Zionist leaders were apparently in favor of accepting this new compromise.[77] If so, this may be connected with the clandestine negotiations between Abdullah and Mrs. Golda Myerson, though Mrs. Myerson did not meet the king again until a month later.[78]Abdullah was the only Arab chief of state with whom the Jews could conceivably negotiate a tolerable settlement, and they may have looked at his secret overtures and the British plan to make over eastern Palestine to him in an optimistic light. Ben-Gurion and the Agency in Palestine, however, turned the plan down emphatically and so in America did Dr. Weizmann.

On the 9th of April he wrote a letter to the President asserting that there was no solution except partition. He said: "The choice for our people, Mr. President, is between statehood and extermination." While drafting the letter he heard that the trusteeship plan meant a possible continuance of British rule. He added a paragraph: "I would sound a solemn warning against the prolongation of British rule in Palestine. As you may know, I have cherished the British-Jewish relationship all my life. I have upheld it in difficult times. I have been grievously disappointed by its recent decline . . . I tremble to think of the wave of violence and repression which would sweep Palestine if the conditions and auspices of the recent unhappy years were to be continued under British or indeed under any foreign rule. I also know how passionately the British people desire the end of this troubled chapter. Should your administration, despite all this, press for any prolongation of British tenure, it would mean a responsibility for terrible events." [79]

The conduct of the President after receiving this letter adds to the supposition that Austin's proposal of the 5th of April was indeed made after consultation with the Foreign Office. For the moment Mr. Truman held his hand. There are signs that in the last two weeks of April the British government began to consider a change in policy, perhaps influence by the reception of Ambassador Austin's proposal of the 5th, and perhaps also by reports reaching them from the Middle East. It is alleged that British representatives in the neighboring Arab countries, and (according to the Kimche brothers[80]) in Haifa were innocently but gravely misinforming

[76] Sacher, *op. cit.*
[77] Kirk, *op. cit.*
[78] Kimche, *op. cit.*
[79] Eban, Weizmann Biography.
[80] Mr. Jon Kimche states that he saw copies of official British reports from Haifa which had been stolen by Haganah agents. *Seven Fallen Pillars.*

them. In explanation of events difficult to understand it has been asserted that some of the exaggerations about the atrocities of Irgun and the Sternists which were stampeding the Arab peasantry found their way under official cover to London and had something of the same effect on His Majesty's ministers. At all events, an openly expressed anti-Zionist impetus began to appear in British policy. On the 23rd of April Mr. Arthur Creech Jones told the special session of the General Assembly that in his government's opinion the United Nations should aim at "a more modest objective" than partition. The theory put forward by the Kimche brothers is that on this day, which was the one following the capture of Haifa, Ernest Bevin had received a report that Haganah had massacred over 20,-000 Arabs in that town and that, seeing Zionism as a corrupted and criminal power, the government under Bevin's influence were contemplating a reorientation of policy whose grand purpose would be the restoration of most of Palestine to the Arabs, leaving the Jews some such enclave as the Woodhead Commission had outlined. Until further documentation is available it is difficult to accept so fantastic a picture of British policy under so sober a chief as Clement Attlee, but whatever the ultimate truth may be, it does seem incontestable that policy had taken a fantastic turn. A week later, while British troops were being evacuated from Haifa, a cruiser with reinforcements was sent to Palestine! It is alleged that they were sent to preserve Jaffa for the Arabs.[81] They arrived too late to do so, if such was the intention.

This same day, April 23rd, was Passover Eve in 1948 and it was a very important one in the history of Zionism and the Jewish State. A little time before, President Truman had begun to unshackle himself: he had transferred the conduct of Palestine policy in the State Department from the hands of Mr. Loy W. Henderson who had a reputation for anti-Zionism, to those of Major-General J. H. Hilldring, who was not only a Zionist by conviction, but had proved his devotion as an American alternate-delegate to U.N.O. and in public speeches.[82] It is strange that after such an appointment Mr. Truman's attitude to the future of Palestine should have been in much doubt, but so it was. Both in America and, more so outside, men were used to the idea of the prisoner of the White House, and the President seems to have proceeded toward the Palestine policy he favored by cautious moves in keeping with that astonishing gift for diplomatic maneuver and correct timing that his critics throughout the world never suspected until they gained or suffered from it.

[81] Kimche, *op. cit.*
[82] Kirk, *op. cit.*

On the 23rd of April, before setting out to spend the festival with some friends, Dr. Weizmann received an urgent message to go to the apartment of Judge Samuel Rosenman, a friend of Mr. Truman's. He went immediately. Dr. Eban relates that later in the evening Dr. Weizmann rejoined his friends and "sat through the Seder service in a mood of faraway abstraction, and left early." His meeting with Judge Rosenman had been of a kind to affirm and affirm again his trust in Mr. Truman as a human being. The judge had been authorized to tell Dr. Weizmann about an interview not dissimilar to that with Jacobson, which the President had held with this other close friend. Mr. Truman had opened the conversation by telling the other quite simply, "I have Dr. Weizmann on my conscience." He went over the events of the 19th of March, explaining how he was inadequately informed about the United States brief to U.N.O., and, it seems, somewhat blaming himself for the ensuing muddle. He explained that his object now was to get the American position in U.N.O. back to what it had been before the 19th when official American policy was in support of the resolution of November, 1947. If this could be done, he said, and if a Jewish State was proclaimed, he would recognize it immediately. He made one stipulation. He would deal with only one Jewish representative, and that was Dr. Weizmann. Such was the news which Judge Rosenman brought the old man. It was kept a close secret by Dr. Weizmann and his immediate circle and was not divulged till 1962, ten years after his death.

A little over three weeks remained till the end of the mandate. On the 30th of April the Arab League met in Amman under the chairmanship of King Abdullah. The disunity of the member states, and in particular the animosity between the Egyptian and Transjordan governments became intense and visible. With willful optimism Abdullah was still hoping that the end of the mandate would not precipitate the war which was being fought but had not yet been declared. His best hope was manifestly the agreement with the British government endorsed by Ernest Bevin in February. But it was already clear that the British were not going to honor that pledge with any vigor. It was very necessary in the British view to appease King Farouk and the Egyptian nationalists at this moment. The negotiations for an Anglo-Egyptian treaty had passed through a stormy phase in 1947 when the Egyptian government had laid its causes of discontent with Britain before the Security Council in July. This had been followed by a bitter Anglo-Egyptian quarrel about the Sudan and the unity of the Nile valley, reaching a climax in March, but now, in the spring of 1948, there were signs of a welcome and unexpected lessening of the tension, and it appeared that agreement on the Sudan was not far off. These circumstances seem to explain the lack of support which Abdullah received from the British government when he most needed it.

The Arab Legion was in Palestine under odd and unclear conditions. Sir John Glubb explains that in Palestine "they were operating as an allied army with the British Army. The arrangement was a relic of the war when other allied armies, Free French and Poles for example, were also present. Since the war had ended, nobody had been so rash as to attempt any definition of what the role of the Arab Legion had become." It might have been reasonably contended that their role was to act as guarantor of the UNSCOP plan and Bevin's agreement with the King of Transjordan, but at this moment the British government gave the agreement no thought. On the contrary, they made one of their rare anti-Arab moves and insisted to Abdullah that the Legion should be withdrawn from Palestine to east of the Jordan before the end of April. The movement took longer than that and a few elements of the Legion remained in Palestine till after the end of the mandate.[83] Presumably this British intervention was taken, in part at least, to soothe Egypt by not showing excessive partiality to Britain's faithful ally whom King Farouk disliked; it may have been done in belated good faith in the hope of preventing the war by a form of disarmament. It is impossible to be sure of anything in the tangle of failing will and dubious intentions which had become the essence of British policy. While the Arab Legion was being drawn back, no move, certainly none that is recorded, was taken to obtain the withdrawal of the Arab Liberation Army or of its reinforcements from Syria and Iraq. They were basing themselves in Palestine, with, to quote Professor Kirk's ironical phrase, "a large measure of British tolerance."

Throughout the meeting of the League in Amman the Legion was withdrawing eastward, and Abdullah's fellow members saw that the enormous support he was supposed to enjoy from Britain was probably exaggerated. They grew confident in their own more violent councils. Realizing his danger, Abdullah secretly communicated with the Jewish Agency and called for Mrs. Myerson who again came in disguise with a friend, Ezra Danin. The king met them in the house of his chauffeur. He told them that his former hope of a peaceful solution at the end of the mandate had vanished: the Egyptians and the Mufti were now in charge. Yet, he told them, even now he believed that he could avoid warfare if the Jews would strengthen him by agreeing to the elaborate plan which he had already conveyed to the Agency. He proposed that Palestine should

[83] Glubb, *op. cit.*

remain undivided and that the Jews should immediately establish autonomous regimes in the area allotted to them by UNSCOP. For a year no definite constitution would be established, but after this or a suitable lapse of time, the autonomous Jewish provinces would be merged into Abdullah's kingdom. The latter would be extended to include Transjordan and Palestine, would be ruled by a constitutional monarchy based on a half-Arab half-Jewish parliament from which, if possible, a half-Arab half-Jewish government would be drawn, and then the binational state would come into being.

Mrs. Myerson and Mr. Danin assured the king that these proposals were completely out of date. They had conveyed them to the Jewish Agency which had authorized them to express complete refusal. They warned Abdullah of the Jewish resolve to fight. The encounter was firm on both sides but respectful, even friendly. The two envoys left in secrecy, as they had come.[84]

There could, of course, be no question of Ben-Gurion or his colleagues taking the self-denying ordinance implicit in Abdullah's proposals. The time for any such arrangement had long gone by. On Dr. Weizmann's side, after the American President's undertaking, agreement with the proposals would have been an act not only of superhuman but of dangerous restraint. Mr. Truman had only one more year in office before the next presidential election. No one knew of his undertaking except a handful of men in New York and Washington, and its effectiveness depended on secrecy. It would not bind a successor. No further answer was returned to Abdullah.

In the last three weeks of the mandate the politicians and diplomats who were assembled at Lake Success ran true to form. They lived in a whirlpool of contradiction, intrigue, suspicion, and plans which were put forward only to be crushed to death by the pressure of one or another of the lobbies which the insoluble problem had brought into being. The story is told in considerable detail by the intensely pro-Zionist UNSCOP delegate, Jorge Garcia Granados of Guatemala, in his book *The Birth of Israel*. In spite of the extreme and sometimes absurd bias of his account, it is possible to deduce from it an outline of the final chain of events. The difference of objective between the State Department, influenced by the oil lobby, and the President, influenced by suspicion of the oil lobby and by his Jewish friends, persisted nearly to the end. The extraordinary com-

[84] Zeev Sharef, *Three Days*. London, 1962. His account is more definitive than that of the Kimche brothers. Surprisingly, none of the authors refer to the withdrawal of the Arab Legion.

plexity of American political machinery appeared to work against the President until the last moment. Senator Warren Austin, and his successor in the American ambassadorship to U.N.O., Professor Philip C. Jessup, made strenuous efforts to keep the trusteeship principle alive. They tried to convert delegates of the smaller nations, especially those who had been UNSCOP members, to their point of view. There were moments, for example on the 4th of May when a subcommittee was successfully proposed by Ambassador Guillermo Belt of Mexico with the object of organizing an emergency U.N.O. authority in Palestine, and on May 10th, when Mr. Finn Moe of Norway drafted a provisional regime for the country, claiming, and thus gaining American support, that he acted as a member of a wholly uncommitted delegation. The trusteeship plan under a U.N.O. Commission seemed to be back in strength. Throughout Mr. Truman played a sphinxlike part. No one knew what was in his mind. In his autobiography he gave an interesting account of how his mind was working. "There was some tactical advantage to a shift of the debate from the Security Council with its veto, to the Trusteeship Council where decisions were made by majority vote. In addition it was only a matter of weeks [Mr. Truman is speaking of late March] before the British would leave Palestine and thus change the entire situation. There was also a chance that the United Nations might find a solution to forestall the inevitable outbreak of violence so that it seemed worth while to allow [the trusteeship] proposal to be discussed in the meanwhile."

For various reasons—Jewish influence, Russian sabotaging, Arab intransigence—none of the different trusteeship proposals survived the whirlpool. They all went to the bottom. This had the result, as the 15th drew near, of lessening the difference of view between the President and the State Department. By degrees it became a question of when to recognize, not whether to recognize a Jewish State.[85] And here, though they are not recorded as having met again, a difference of view developed between Mr. Truman and Dr. Weizmann. It appears that by the 13th the President wanted the proclamation of the State postponed, and Señor Granados heard that he was prepared to put his personal aircraft at the disposal of the Jewish representatives if they would fly to Tel Aviv in order to persuade Ben-Gurion not to make the proclamation immediately.

One can well understand the President's anxiety. Since March the Jewish forces in Palestine had achieved more than their greatest admirers believed possible. They had captured the main part of Galilee and held Acre, Haifa, and Jaffa. Subtracting a large part of north and central Gali-

[85] Kirk, *op. cit.*

lee, they held an area similar in shape to that proposed in the Peel Report, with the addition of some isolated Jewish areas in the south. But Jerusalem was still severed from the main Jewish territory on the coast, and, though it was an incredible Jewish achievement to have obtained so much, the extent of the proposed state was as yet too small by national standards to be accounted viable. If the tide were to turn back on the Jews it would certainly not be viable. In such circumstances, it was reasonable to prefer to wait on events.

But Dr. Weizmann saw the matter differently. Now was the moment when the Jewish National Home had to declare its faith in itself and its destiny. Now that victory was essential, victory must be helped by giving the Jews the opportunity to fight not as gallant rebels but as the citizens of an ancient state come to a new birth in the family of nations. He had Truman's promise and he decided that it was for him to judge when it should be fulfilled. Secretary Marshall conveyed a warning to the Jewish Agency of the danger of precipitate action. Mr. Meyer Weisgal telephoned to Weizmann from Nice on behalf of Ben-Gurion to know his views. Weizmann's answer was uncompromising: "Proclaim the State, no matter what ensues!" Moshe Shertok flew back to Palestine to advise the rejection of Marshall's well-intentioned advice. Dr. Weizmann went with him to the airfield and his last words to him on that occasion were: "Don't let them weaken—it is now or never." [86]

Ben-Gurion needed no persuasion, and if there had been a split he would probably have gone ahead with a declaration on his own, but he was fortified at this hour of crisis by Weizmann's absolute and unhesitating determination. He could not know one reason for it: the secret agreement with the President.

On the 13th of May, Dr. Weizmann wrote to President Truman informing him that the State of Israel was to be proclaimed on the next day. The letter arrived at the White House on the morning of the 14th. The President discussed it and the situation which it caused with Secretary Marshall, Undersecretary Robert A. Lovett, his naval aide Captain Clark Clifford, his administrative assistant David K. Niles, and other members of the White House staff. [87] During the debate it was realized that Dr. Weizmann held no official position and that therefore no action could be taken officially on his letter. However, there was an official Jewish representative in Washington, Eliahu Epstein, and Captain Clifford was ordered by the President to consult him by telephone. The result was

[86] Eban, Weizmann Biography.
[87] The Forrestal Diaries, Walter Millis, ed., London, 1952.

that Mr. Epstein wrote an official letter to the President signing himself as representative "of the Jewish State." [88] He brought it to the White House in a taxicab. It seems that Secretary Marshall still wished to proceed cautiously and to delay American support of the proclamation for a few days to allow him to consult with the British and French governments,[89] but that the President was now resolute for immediate recognition.[90]

In Palestine the British departure took place a day earlier than scheduled. At nine o'clock on the morning of the 14th of May the last British High Commissioner left the country by the port of Haifa. The mandatory regime first established by Lord Samuel came to an end. The mood in New Jerusalem and Haifa was exalted but somber. Sir Alan Cunningham left Palestine amid silence. Respect was due to a man who had undertaken an office and tasks beyond the power of any human capacity to bring to success, and that respect was given by men who already knew themselves to be the citizens of Israel. The blame for the many sufferings which were ahead lay elsewhere, and in that loftiness of spirit that can animate men in war this was generously recognized and expressed. In Tel Aviv at four o'clock in the afternoon of the same day Ben-Gurion appeared before a specially convened session of the Va'ad Leumi held in the Museum of Modern Art. He gave a profoundly impressive address in which he traced in a few strokes the history of the Jewish people from their mysterious origins in distant antiquity to their sufferings amid the barbarism of modern times. He announced the establishment of a Jewish State in Palestine to be called Israel. He declared certain principles of the new polity, equal citizenship for Jew and Gentile and goodwill towards Israel's neighbors. "With trust in the Rock of Israel," he concluded, "we set our hand on this declaration at this session of the Provisional State Council in the city of Tel Aviv, on this Sabbath Eve, the fifth day of Iyar, in the year five thousand seven hundred and eight."

The vague expression "Rock of Israel" was substituted for the words "Almighty God" in the original draft, in deference to the scruples of Jewish Communists.

Elections were to be held later. For the moment the State was under the rule of an emergency government based on the authority of the Va'ad Leumi.

The news was transmitted by radio to America. Mr. Truman had by now persuaded his Secretary of State that instant recognition was the most

[88] Eban, *op. cit.*
[89] Kirk, *op. cit.*
[90] *Forrestal Diaries, op. cit.*

practical way. It seems certain that a telling argument was that if the United States "beat the Russians to the punch" it would help democratic forces in Israel and assure the electoral support of American Zionists, both Jew and Gentile.[91] So, as soon as he had received the news, the President accorded recognition *de facto*.

The effect of his action has been described by Dr. Abba Eban: "The representatives of the United States in the General Assembly knew nothing of the President's announcement. They were still advocating all kinds of proposals other than Jewish statehood. The news of Truman's announcement broke on them like a thunderbolt: Ambassador Jessup went into a telephone booth to check up with the White House and then read the Truman announcement to an Assembly now plunged in a pandemonium of surprise." The President's own comment on this transaction was entirely characteristic. "The old doctor will believe me now," he said.

Immediately after the British withdrawal, Arab armies entered Palestine. On paper they were powerful; in the field, with the exception of the Arab Legion, they were not, except sporadically. The Israeli military success in the suddenly abandoned country was prodigious but was still hard fought, and checked by serious failures. The most important of these were in the battle for communications to Jerusalem, and in Jerusalem itself. The main Tel Aviv-Jerusalem road remained in Arab hands thanks to the defense of the police-post of Latrun by the Legion. In Jerusalem itself the Israeli authorities were forced with the utmost bitterness to acquiesce in the surrender of the Jewish quarter within the walled city, the venerable area of the town inhabited by Jews since late Roman times and built round a fragment of a wall of the Temple. The Jews overcame the problem of the road by the heroic decision to build a new one, which they did on the foundations of a donkey track bypassing the main road to the south. The Egyptian Army advanced north from their frontier to within nearly twenty miles of Tel Aviv and, on the Jerusalem front, beyond Bethlehem, nearly to the outer suburbs of Jerusalem. The Syrians in the north were halted. The Lebanese offered no serious resistance, but appeared in the field more as a demonstration than for any bloodier purpose. The Iraq army was badly defeated at the crossing of the Jordan east of Beisan, but pushed forward to Tul Karm in the center, only ten miles from the sea, and threatened Hadera which is only two miles from the sea.

In place of the proposed United Nations Commissioner (whose institu-

[91] Kirk, *op. cit.*

tion was rejected by Arabs and Jews), a "mediator" had been appointed on the 20th of May. He was Count Bernadotte, a Swedish royal personage who was president of the Red Cross in his country. With great difficulty he was able to organize a truce on the 11th of June, 1948, to run for four weeks. By this time the Israeli forces had had to leave their settlements in the Negev isolated, and they had surrendered Old Jerusalem, the most distressing of all their reverses, but they had increased their hold on Galilee, and nowhere had the Arabs been able to make a sizeable dent in the main Jewish area, the new State of Israel. The truce was of great benefit to the Jews. At U.N.O., the British had agreed to suspend the supply of arms to Iraq, Transjordan, and Egypt. This was part of an attempt at a general embargo which was harder to operate in the case of Israel's clandestine deals with Czechoslovakia than with the open treaty-controlled deals of the Arab states. Neither side observed the truce conscientiously. Israel increased her superiority in weapons which had hitherto been precarious. Bernadotte attempted to prolong the truce. Israel was willing, so were the Transjordan, Saudi Arabian, Iraqi, and Lebanese leaders, but the Syrians and Egyptians insisted on an immediate resumption of the war. Through their propaganda services they had already proclaimed their victory over Israel. They could not go home with things as they were. They were again fatally caught out by the nationalist fervor they had aroused. The truce terminated on the 6th of July. It was followed by the "ten days' war." In the course of this, Israel's victory became not only certain but was seen to be. In the fighting between the 8th and the 18th the Jewish forces established themselves in almost the whole of the northern territory of modern Israel, the largest exception being an area of about three hundred square miles in Galilee below the Lebanese frontier. The towns of Lydda, Ramleh, and Nazareth fell to them. The communications between Jerusalem and Tel Aviv were restored. The Arabs made minute gains in southern Galilee and northeast of Gaza. The situation in the south remained unchanged. The tide had not only turned, it was now impossible that it would turn back. The Security Council imposed a second truce on the 18th of July.

The mediator, like his seven predecessors in the High Commission, found that his attempts to impose a compromise on this bitter struggle earned him the anger of both sides. Israel was in no mood for compromise just now. Unfortunately Israeli ministers did not hesitate in the heat of the moment to criticize Count Bernadotte publicly. This encouraged the Stern Gang to yet another atrocity. They, or their associates, murdered this admirable and public-spirited man on the 17th of September. The laxity with which the murderers [92] were pursued by Israeli authorities did not justify the accusation that Bernadotte's assassination was a government plot, but it showed the extent to which Zionism had been contaminated by toleration of terrorism. It was almost inevitable that this association, from which Prime Minister Ben-Gurion was now belatedly struggling to emancipate his people,[93] should leave an ugly stain on the early history of Israel. A Mufti government of Palestine was set up by a proclamation on the 20th of September, but on the 1st of October Abdullah obtained a vote by acclamation from five thousand picked notables as the sovereign of Arab Palestine. The Egyptian army in the south gave Israel a needed and sought-for provocation, and the Jewish Army attacked on the 14th and 15th of October. They captured Beersheba on the 21st. The new mediator, Dr. Ralph Bunche, re-imposed the truce on the 22nd, but on the 28th fighting broke out in the north where both sides seem to have transgressed. The result was the final defeat of Fawzi el Kawakji and the capture of the rest of Galilee by the Army of Israel. On the 22nd of December the Israeli army, after a complicated period of skirmishing on the south front, again attacked the Egyptian army in the Negev. This was the last campaign of the war. It was attended by an extraordinary political development, the attempt of Britain to intervene on Egypt's behalf in accordance with the Anglo-Egyptian Treaty of 1936 of which the Egyptians were then struggling to obtain the annulment. The last campaign against the Egyptian army secured the Negev for Israel. A small Palestine police post in the Gulf of Akaba called Umm Rash Rash became the Israel port of Elath.

An armistice was signed with Egypt on the 24th of February, 1949; with Jordan on the 3rd of April (with clauses covering Iraq, withdrawal); with Lebanon on 23rd of March, and with Syria not till the 29th of July, 1949. The delay in the latter case was not only due to protracted negotiations but to internal disorders in Syria which held up the formation of a government sufficiently secure to sign such an instrument.

The war left the Arab states in a mood of embittered humiliation and unforgiveness, but the load of suffering fell yet again on the fellahin of Palestine, especially in the harsh conditions imposed on Abdullah by Is-

[92] It seems that Sternists arrested after the murder were allowed to escape. The head of the Stern Gang was condemned to five years imprisonment on the 10th of February to Parliament, 1949 and released by the simultaneous amnesty. He had been elected and took his seat. (Kirk)

[93] For details of the final and violent struggle for authority between the Provisional government and Irgun, see Arthur Koestler, *Promise and Fulfilment*. London, 1949, pp. 245–255, in which he gives an account of the Altanena affair.

rael when drawing their frontier in the area which runs north from east of Jaffa to the southern Galilee line. The conditions were imposed for necessary reasons of strategy and in no revengeful spirit, but they had the effect of separating many of the Arab inhabitants from their lands and leaving them in danger of complete destitution. Similar circumstances were brought into being in the delimitation of the Gaza strip. All this added to the spirit of revenge which was the main Arab inheritance from the war.

Shortly before the armistice with Egypt, Israel had become a parliamentary state with an elected chamber known in Hebrew as the Knesset. On the 15th of February David Ben-Gurion was confirmed in the office of Prime Minister and, by a unanimous vote, Dr. Weizmann was elected first President of modern Israel. Under the provisions of the State the headship was of a strictly constitutional character, almost devoid of personal power, and old as Weizmann was, and failing, his still fiery spirit was restive under the unfamiliar limitations of this new and kingly office. He held it till his death in 1952. So ended his long and unique, illustrious political career.

Israel after the war became a land exalted by a just pride in achievement. Even its enemies could not doubt the immensity of what the nationalist party had accomplished. Within three and a half years of sufferings such as few other people had undergone in the whole course of recorded history, after the loss of a third of their whole population in the world, the Jews had formed a Jewish state, only fifty-one years after Theodor Herzl had called the first Zionist Congress.

14   SEEN AT A DISTANCE

At the time of writing it is nearly seventeen years since David Ben-Gurion proclaimed the State of Israel. The country has gone through several phases since then, moving from the bleakest austerity to a life that is still hard but normal by Western standards. There has been an important change in the character of the population. The most extraordinary single fact about the new state at the time of its proclamation was that more than three-quarters of its population were immigrants and far less than half spoke its language with instinctive facility. The growth of generations born within Eretz Israel has already diminished this anomaly. The Polish-Russian-German community of Jewish Palestine which many people will remember with affection from the 1930's had already changed in character by the midwar years and is now changed even more radically. Slowly, and in spite of continuing immigrations, the Israel-born are taking over. This new national type is often described as "the Sabra," meaning "the of the time they should have devoted to strengthening his position in jealously and successfully intriguing against him. As a result the main direction of Arab Palestine policy fell once more into the hands of that utterly inadequate man the Mufti. When incompetence is practiced on the scale maintained by the Arab leaders, even the best case is apt to go by default in the judgment of the harsh world, but the price had to be paid as usual by the innocent and the simple.

The existence of hundreds of thousands of homeless refugees from Israel on all the frontiers of the State has brought about an intense condition of hostility of which there is no sign of abatement so far. Many of the political leaders of the Arab states surrounding Israel would as individuals be glad to reach an accommodation with the Jews, but as with the hopes of peace within the Arab League in 1948, any initiative is not only dangerous but foredoomed to failure by patriotic mob-enthusiasm and mob-anger. The most sagacious realist among the Arab leaders and princes, Abdullah ibn Hussein, was murdered in 1951 by an agent of the Mufti, his offense being common sense.

If the forces of Zion in 1948 and 1949 had retained something of the spirit if not the policy of Havlegah, then the exodus of 1948 and 1949 would, in all probability have been about half the size it was, and Israel would have been left with a difficult Arab minority problem with which she might have found it hard to deal on the relatively (if imperfectly) liberal terms of the present. But it is conceivable, perhaps one might say it is certain, that some door to negotiation would have remained open where they are now all closed. They cannot be opened now till the worst memories of Zionism are remote. Seen from a distance, Irgun Zvai Leumi and the followers of Abraham Stern count to the Jewish national cause as pure loss.

The insoluble problem devised by Arthur Balfour has taken on a new form, aggravated in some respects by the suffering caused by the foundation of the State, diminished only in the sense that there are now Jewish and Arab frontiers so that some of the ambiguity of Zionism, the cause of many of the troubles of the mandate before the war, is removed. It is optimistic to suppose that the problem will be solved within a century. The notion of an "unchanging East" is a myth built on a half truth as the manifold changes in the Arabic-speaking world of Islam during thirty years can testify alone. The familiar, narrow, uncompromising, boycotting Arab nationalist attitude has already caused opportunities for a settlement of the appalling refugee problem to be missed: if politicians acting in unison had preferred to use the wretchedness of these people as a means to force the United Nations Organization to make generous provision for resettlement, instead (speaking very generally) of maintaining their wretchedness as a bargaining counter to ask for an impossible reversion to the *status quo ante,* then they might have achieved much at some sacrifice of national pride. But there is no reason to suppose that new generations may not come to react against present preoccupations.

To hug woes is the natural propensity of any man who has suffered injustice within his own experience, but that does not necessarily mean that it will figure as the natural choice of a career to his son or grandson. It may do so, as the history of nationalism in many parts of the world makes plain, but the very extremism of Arab character, its mixture of tenacity and levity, may come to its rescue and allow Arabs to see satisfaction away from a barren pursuit of ancient loyalties. The recent past gives a slight pointer that this may happen. In the early 1920's Arab nationalism was fixed on the dream of a Greater Syria. When this came within Arab grasp in the next decade, they had forgotten it. If there is hope, it is that the dynamism of the new state may provoke Israel's neighbors into other pursuits than that of claiming an irrecoverable loss. This may strike a reader as a somewhat feeble hope, but it is worth remembering that the greatest changes have usually had puny and improbable beginnings. No one foresaw the establishment of the United States fifty years before it occurred. There was no reason why anyone should.

It may be apposite to recall a saying of Dr. Weizmann's on the subject of change. The occasion was a private interview with the Peel commissioners in Jerusalem. This was before the proposal of partition and Dr. Weizmann was still thinking in terms of the establishment of a National Home, not a state, in a unitary Palestine. Sir Horace Rumbold asked him if he could tell the commissioners how he envisaged the Jewish National Home in its final development. To the surprise, one may suppose, of those present Weizmann answered: "Never." Sir Horace Rumbold returned to the question. "You could *never* do it?" he asked. Weizmann replied that he could never do so because such work as his for the National Home in Palestine was never seen as "finished." Characteristically he changed his ground. He asked the commissioners to consider the case of England. It had been "built up," he said, over many years by many generations, but was it possible, he asked, to say that a time had ever occurred, or would occur, when it could be said that England, or any other country or state, had been finally built and that the task was at an end.

APPENDIX

JEWISH REFUGEES IN BRITAIN
AND AMERICA 1943

What the authentic figures are for Jewish victims of Nazism who were given asylum in Britain and America has been the subject of much dispute.

The original American statement was made at Ottawa in March 1943 by the Hon. Breckinridge Long on behalf of the United States government. He asserted that 547,775 refugees from Nazism had been admitted into the U.S. since 1933. In a further statement before the Foreign Affairs Committee of the House of Representatives in November 1943 Mr. Long said: "We have taken into this country, since the beginning of the Hitler régime and the persecution of the Jews until today, approximately 580,-000 refugees." When making both statements Mr. Long gave an impression that he was referring exclusively to Jewish refugees, since on both occasions the subject under discussion was the Final Solution. In fact the enormous figures mentioned could only have been applied to refugees in general. This point was raised in committee but Mr. Long's replies did not clarify it.

Researches by the Commission on Rescue of the American Jewish Conference, and by the Yiddish Scientific Institute, in December, 1943, reduced the figures quoted by Mr. Long. The Commission on Rescue calculated the correct figure at 166,843, the Institute at 138,000, both referring only to Jewish refugees. A further analysis by Mr. Victor H. Bernstein gave a figure of 182,956 Jewish refugees. The differences between these three sets of figures are mainly accounted for by different interpretations of the term "refugee."

A fourth analysis was conducted by the Hebrew Sheltering and Immigrant Aid Society (HIAS) of New York which gave figures of 165,756 Jewish immigrants and 42,182 Jewish nonimmigrants (i.e. persons not applying for U.S. citizenship and residence) who arrived in the U.S. between July 1933 and July 1943. This total (207,938) was found by HIAS to include 21,611 nonimmigrants who were obliged by American law to leave the U.S. after the expiration of their temporary visas. Those who had been obliged to leave and wished to return had to apply at a U.S. consulate in a nearby country for an immigrant visa. The result of the consequent movement of population was that a certain number remained on the records as Jewish persons enjoying asylum in the U.S. after they had left, and a certain number were counted twice as new arrivals. After research on this HIAS deducted 21,611 from the total.

The original HIAS figure also included 3,886 Jewish immigrants from Palestine. As they could not be classified as refugees, this figure was also deducted. HIAS made a further deduction of 24,514 which they calculated as the normal Jewish number who in normal times would have entered the U.S. as immigrants in the course of ten years (1933–43). This deduction appears to the writer to be quite inadmissible, if only because in common parlance the idea of the reception of distressed aliens into the U.S.A., or elsewhere, does not assume that this is in excess of a normal immigration quota, unless such a provision is expressly stated. If the third HIAS deduction is not accepted, but the other two are, then the total of Jewish immigrants (165,756) and nonimmigrants (42,182) is reduced from 207,938 to 182,441, a figure near to that calculated by Mr. Bernstein. If all the HIAS deductions are accepted the figure is reduced to 157,927. In the writer's opinion the figure should be accepted as 182,441.

According to a HIAS communication with the writer, the results of their statistical inquiry, which they published in their bulletin *Rescue* in

February, 1944, were not effectively challenged, so far as is remembered today, by any American official authority.

The British figure is far more difficult to check, since, following the British practice, no official record was made of Jewish origin among immigrants. Palestine was the only country under British administration at any time where immigrants were classified into Jewish and non-Jewish. The British announcement at Ottawa that approximately 100,000 (presumably Jewish) refugees had been given asylum in Great Britain was received skeptically and Wischnitzer states that the figure was reduced by American statisticians to 42,000. This figure may be compared with other British ones.

According to a written answer to a Parliamentary question on the 4th of July, 1940, there were 82,630 refugees of all kinds in Great Britain at that time. Of these, 55,750 were Germans and Austrians who had come to Great Britain before the war, and of whom the large majority were known to be Jews. According to a communication with the writer from the Colonial Office, these figures excluded Hungarian and Polish refugees (of whom the great majority were Jews) who came to England before the war. For political reasons they were not classified as refugees. The overall Hungarian figure was approximately 4,000 in late 1939, an increase of some 3,400 since 1935. The latter figure undoubtedly represented an almost entirely Jewish immigration.

The Colonial Office do not regard the figures given in Parliament in 1940 as definitive. Research shows them to be at considerable variance with others which can be obtained elsewhere. The Jewish Refugee Committee of London has furnished the writer with statistics which show that between 1933 and 1943 they registered over 67,000 Jewish immigrants from Germany and Austria alone, an advance of over 10,000 from the Home Office 1940 figure of 55,750, which was not given as an exclusively Jewish figure. The Committee point out that there was no obligation to register with them and that their figures account only for immigrants who needed, or felt they might need, the J.R.C.'s help. The figures should not be taken as accounting for the full total.

The contradiction between the statistics of the J.R.C., those given to the House of Commons in 1940, and those given by the British government at Ottawa, may be open to a simple explanation. In 1940 there was general anxiety about rationing and when addressing the British public through Parliament it was to the interest of the British government to minimize the number of aliens being maintained in the country. It is conceivable (though not so far evidenced) that the Home Secretary, Sir John Anderson, heavily reduced his refugee figures by subtracting those seeking naturalization, in addition to those who had been naturalized, and whom he would have been fully justified in subtracting. In 1943 the interest of the British government at Ottawa was the contrary of what it had been in 1940 in the U.K., and it became their endeavor to stress the fact that Great Britain had given refuge to large numbers of Jews. If the figure of 100,000 referred to refugees received in England from 1933 to 1943 regardless of origin, the claim was very modest, but, as with Mr. Long's statements, confused drafting (notably in a M.O.I. hand-out in Washington of March 4th, 1943) often resulted in a misleading impression that Jewish refugees were being referred to when in fact general refugee figures were being quoted. In the writer's opinion the misleading impression was caused intentionally.

It would seem that the accusation against Britain and the U.S. that there was conscious exaggeration of Jewish refugee statistics at Ottawa is fully proved in the case of the U.S. and that in the case of the U.K. the charge has an uncomfortable measure of substance. But the statistics known to the Jewish Refugee Committee strongly suggest that in the case of the U.K. any such exaggeration was far less than was suspected by British and American critics at the time, and may, in fact, have been relatively trivial.

BIBLIOGRAPHY

Abrahams, Gerald, *The Jewish Mind.* Boston: The Beacon Press; London: Constable and Company, Ltd., 1962.

Agar, Herbert, *The Saving Remnant: an Account of Jewish Survival.* New York: The Viking Press, Inc.; London: Rupert Hart-Davis, Ltd., 1960.

Antonius, George, *The Arab Awakening,* 2nd ed. London: Hamish Hamilton, Ltd., 1946.

Attlee, Clement R., *As It Happened* (autobiography). New York: The Viking Press, Inc.; London: William Heinemann, Ltd., 1954.

Barbour, Nevill, *Nisi Dominus. A Survey of the Palestine Controversy.* London: George G. Harrap & Company, Ltd., 1946. Under title *Palestine: Star or Crescent?* New York: The Odyssey Press, Inc., 1947.

Bauer, Yehuda, *Scripta Hierosolymitana,* Vol. VII. Jerusalem: Publications of the Hebrew University of Jerusalem, 1961.

Begin, Menachem Wolfovitch, *The Revolt.* Translated from the Hebrew by

Samuel Katz. New York: Henry Schuman, Inc.; London: W. H. Allen and Company, Ltd., 1951.

Bentwich, Norman, *A Wanderer Between Two Worlds* (autobiography). London: Routledge & Kegan Paul, 1941.

————, *For Zion's Sake.* Philadelphia: Jewish Publication Society of America, 1954. Under the title *Judah L. Magnes;* London: Horovitz Publishing Company, 1955.

Bullock, Alan, *Hitler: a Study in Tyranny.* London: Odhams Press, Ltd., 1952; New York: Harper and Brothers, 1953 (rev. ed., 1960).

Casper, Bernard, *With the Jewish Brigade.* London: E. Edward Goldston, Ltd., 1947.

Chesterton, G. K., *The New Jerusalem.* London: Hodder & Stoughton, Ltd., 1920.

Churchill, Winston, *The Second World War,* Vol. III, *The Grand Alliance.* New York: Houghton Mifflin Company; London: Cassell and Company, 1951.

Cohen, Israel, *The Zionist Movement.* London: Frederick Muller, Ltd., 1945; New York: (rev. ed.) Zionist Organization of America, 1946.

Crossman, Richard H. S., *Palestine Mission.* London: Hamish Hamilton, Ltd., 1950.

————, *A Nation Reborn.* New York: Atheneum Publishers; London: Hamish Hamilton, Ltd., 1960.

Crum, Bartley, C., *Behind the Silken Curtain.* New York: Simon and Schuster, Inc.; London: Victor Gollancz, Ltd., 1947.

Daniels, Jonathan, *Man of Independence: a Biography of Harry S. Truman.* Philadelphia: J. B. Lippincott Company, 1950; London: Victor Gollancz, Ltd., 1951.

Duff, Douglas V., *A Sword for Hire.* London: John Murray, Ltd., 1934.

————, *Galilee Galloper.* London: John Murray, Ltd., 1935.

————, *May the Winds Blow!* (autobiography). London: Hollis and Carter, Ltd., 1948.

Frank, Gerold, *The Deed.* New York: Simon and Schuster, Inc., 1963.

Gabbay, Rony E., *A Political Study of the Arab-Jewish Conflict.* (*Etudes d'Histoire Economique, Politique et Sociale.*) Paris: Libraire Minard; New York: Gregory Lounz, 1959.

Glubb, John, *A Soldier with the Arabs.* New York: Harper and Brothers; London: Hodder & Stoughton, Ltd., 1957.

————, *Britain and the Arabs.* London: Hodder & Stoughton, Ltd. 1959.

Graves, Richard M., *Experiment in Anarchy.* London: Victor Gollancz, Ltd., 1949.

Harington, Charles, *Plumer of Messines.* London: John Murray, Ltd., 1935.

Hurewitz, J. C. *The Struggle for Palestine.* New York: W. W. Norton and Company, 1950.

Hyamson, Albert, *Palestine Under the Mandate.* London: Methuen and Co., Ltd., 1950; New York: British Book Centre, 1951.

Ionides, Michael, *Divide and Lose.* London: Geoffrey Bles, 1960; New York: International Publishing Service, 1961.

Jeffries, J. M. N., *Palestine the Reality.* London: Longmans, Green and Co., Ltd., 1939.

Joseph, Dov, *The Faithful City.* New York: Simon and Schuster, Inc.; Tel Aviv: Schocken, 1960.

Kimche, Jon, *Seven Fallen Pillars.* London: Secker and Warburg, Ltd., 1950; New York: British Book Centre, 1951.

————, Jon and David, *Clash of Destinies.* New York: Frederick A. Praeger, Inc., 1960. Under the title *Both Sides of the Hill.* London: Secker and Warburg, Ltd., 1960.

Kirk, George, *Survey of International Affairs: 1939-46: The Middle East in the War.* Oxford: Oxford University Press, 1952.

————, *Survey of International Affairs: The Middle East 1945-50.* New York, London: Oxford University Press, 1954.

————, *A Short History of the Middle East.* London: Methuen & Co., Ltd., 1948; New York: (5th rev. ed.) Frederick A. Praeger, Inc., 1959.

Kirkbride, Alec, *A Crackle of Thorns.* London: John Murray, Ltd., 1956.

Koestler, Arthur, *Promise and Fulfilment.* London and New York: Macmillan and Co., Ltd., 1949.

Lawrence, A. W., ed., *T. E. Lawrence by His Friends.* New York: Doubleday and Company, Inc.; London: Jonathan Cape, Ltd., 1937.

Lowdermilk, Walter C., *Palestine, Land of Promise.* New York and London: Harper and Brothers, 1944.

————, *The Untried Approach to the Palestine Problem.* New York: American Christian Palestine Committee Publications, 1948.

Manuel, Frank E., *The Realities of American-Palestine Relations.* Washington: Public Affairs Press, 1949.

Marlowe, John, *Rebellion in Palestine.* London: Cresset Press, Ltd., 1946.

————, *The Seat of Pilate.* London: Cresset Press, Ltd., 1959.

Meinertzhagen, Richard, *Middle East Diary: 1917-1956.* London: Cresset Press, Ltd., 1959; New York: Thomas Yoseloff, Inc., 1960.

Meltzer, Julian L., *Chaim Weizmann.* London: Weidenfeld and Nicholson, Ltd., 1962.

Millis, Walter, ed., *The Forrestal Diaries.* New York: The Viking Press, Inc., 1951; London: Cassell and Company, Ltd., 1952.

Monroe, Elizabeth, *Britain's Moment in the Middle East: 1914-1956.* Baltimore: Johns Hopkins Press; London: Chatto & Windus, Ltd., 1963.

Newton, Frances Emily, *Fifty Years in Palestine.* Wrotham: Coldharbour Press, 1948.

Parkes, J. W., *A History of Palestine from 135 A.D. to Modern Times.* New

York: Oxford University Press; London: Victor Gollancz, Ltd., 1949.

Philby, Harry St. John Bridger, *Arabian Jubilee*. London: Robert Hale, Ltd., 1952; New York: The John Day Company, Inc., 1953.

Reynier, Jacques de, *A Jérusalem un drapeau flottait sur la ligne de feu*. Neuchâtel: La Baconnière, 1950.

Sacher, Harry, *Israel, the Establishment of a State*. New York: British Book Centre; London: Weidenfeld and Nicholson, Ltd., 1952.

Samuel, Herbert Louis, *Memoirs*. London: Cresset Press, Ltd., 1945. Under the title *Grooves of Change*. New York: Bobbs-Merrill Company, 1946.

Samuel, Horace, *Unholy Memories of the Holy Land*. London: Hogarth Press, 1930.

Schwarz, Walter, *The Arabs in Israel*. London: Faber & Faber, Ltd., 1959.

Sharef, Zeev, *Three Days*. Translated from the Hebrew by Julian Louis Meltzer. New York: Doubleday & Company, Inc.; London: W. H. Allen and Company, Ltd., 1962.

Simpson, John Hope, *The Refugee Problem*. London: Oxford University Press, 1939.

Slutzki, Yehuda, *History of Haganah*. Jerusalem, 1954.

Stark, Freya, *Dust in the Lion's Paw* (autobiography). London: John Murray, Ltd., 1961; New York: Harcourt, Brace & World, Inc., 1962.

Stein, Leonard, *The Balfour Declaration*. London: Vallentine, Mitchell & Co., Ltd.; New York: Simon and Schuster, Inc., 1961.

Storrs, Ronald, *Memoirs*. New York: G. P. Putnam's Sons, 1937. Under the title *Orientations*. London: Ivor Nicholson & Watson, Ltd., 1937.

Sykes, Christopher, *Two Studies in Virtue*. New York: Alfred A. Knopf, Inc., London: William Collins Sons & Co., Ltd., 1953.

————, *Orde Wingate*. New York: The World Publishing Company; London: William Collins Sons & Co., Ltd., 1959.

Trevor, Daphne, *Under the White Paper*. Jerusalem: The Jerusalem Press, 1948.

Truman, Harry S., *Memoirs,* Vol. II, *Years of Trial and Hope*. New York: Doubleday, 1958.

Vester, Bertha Hedges, *Our Jerusalem*. New York: Doubleday & Company, Inc., 1950; London: Evans Brothers, Ltd., 1951.

Watt, D. C., *History Today* (London), March, 1963.

Webster, Charles, *The Art and Practice of Diplomacy*. London: Chatto & Windus, Ltd., 1961; New York: Barnes & Noble, Inc., 1962.

Weisgal, Meyer, and Carmichael, Joel, *Chaim Weizmann: a Biography by Several Hands*. London: Weidenfeld and Nicholson, Ltd., 1962; New York: Atheneum Publishers, 1963.

Weizmann, Chaim, *Trial and Error*. New York: Harper and Brothers; London: Hamish Hamilton, Ltd., 1949.

Williams, Francis, *Ernest Bevin: Portrait of a Great Englishman*. London:

Hutchinson & Co., Ltd., 1952; New York: British Book Centre, 1953.
———, ed., *Twilight of Empire*. New York: A. S. Barnes & Co., 1962. Under the title *A Prime Minister Remembers* (Memoirs of the Rt. Hon. Earl Attlee). London: William Heinemann, Ltd., 1962.

Wilson, R. D. *Cordon and Search*. Aldershot: Gale and Polden, 1949; New York: British Book Centre, 1952.

Wischnitzer, Mark, *To Dwell in Safety*. Philadelphia: Jewish Publication Society of America, 1948.

Zeine, Zeine N., *The Struggle for Arab Independence*. Beirut: Khayats, 1960.

INDEX

Sinclair, Sir Archibald (Lord Thurso), 146, 170, 174
Singleton, Sir John, 283n
Slutzki, Dr. Yehuda, 155n
Smart, Sir Walter, 73n, 255n
Smuts, Field-Marshal Jan, 112
Sneh, Moshe, 250, 280, 282
Snell, Henry (later Lord), 114
Sofar, Conference of, 325
Sokolov, Nahum, 11, 12, 44n, 104, 268
South Africa, 166, 188
South America, 117
Spain, 242
Special Night Squads, 183, 207
Spectator, The, 354n, 355n
Stanley, Oliver, 302; Colonial Secretary, 252, 253, 262
Stark, Freya, 271n
Stein, Leonard, 4, 65n, 160
Stern, Abraham, 243, 245
Stern Group, 243, 245, 246, 248-9, 256, 257, 270, 280, 283, 295-6, 307, 319, 320, 351, 352, 367, 375
Stettinius, Edward R., 274
Stimson, Henry L., 272, 286
Storrs, Sir Ronald, 14n, 24n, 42n, 73, 100, 126, 146n; Zionist campaign against, 25-6, 122
Strabolgi, Lord, 212
Struma (refugee ship), 225-7, 228, 229
Sudan, 307, 361
Suez Canal, 9, 58, 125, 273
Supreme Moslem Council: Arab leadership, 101-2, 142; and Wailing Wall riots, 102, 108-9, 113, 124; boycotts Administration, 142
Sursok family, 89-90, 93
Sweden, 185n, 318
Switzerland, 185n, 242, 289
Sydenham, Lord, 68-9
Sykes, Christopher, 182n, 208n
Sykes, Sir Mark, 11, 12, 18, 28, 31, 102n, 191n, 268
Sykes-Picot Agreement, 28, 29, 33, 102n
Syria, 4, 5, 27, 80, 150n, 162, 240, 293; France and, 5, 8, 9, 18, 28, 29, 33, 35, 36, 95, 140, 267, 282, 321; MacMahon letter, 27-8, 63-4; French Mandate, 28, 33; Sykes-Picot Agreement, 28; Feisal's idea of Greater Syria, 32, 35, 47, 123, 376; Feisal proclaimed King of, 35-6; and Turkey, 36; collapse of Feisal's Kingdom in, 36-7, 43, 44, 47; effect on British mandated territory, 43-4;

Abdullah's threat to, 44-5; rebellion (1927), 95, 140; partial independence, 140; and Arab federation, 172; protests against partition, 176; United Syria plan, 192-3; German attempt to seize, 198-9; British invade, 218, 267; independence secured, 267, 270, 282, 328; and Zionism, 327, 328; pro-British sentiment after 1946, 328-9; and Arab-Israel war, 337-8, 340, 366, 367, 368
Szold, Henrietta, 239

Taylor, Myron, C., 185
Tel Aviv, 51, 83, 190, 249; riots (1933), 136, 142; (1936) 148; (1945) 285; Stern atrocities (1946), 295; Irgun kidnapping, 307-8; in Arab-Israel war, 332, 338, 366, 367; State of Israel proclaimed in, 365
Tel Hai, 21
Temperley, H. V., 47
Terrorist Organizations:
Arab, see Al Najjadah, Ikhwana e Muslamin, and Al Futuwwah
Zionist, see Irgun Tsva'i Leumi (Etzel) and Stern Group (F.F.I.)
see also Counter-Terrorism
Tewfik Pasha Abu Al Huda, Prime Minister of Transjordan, 342-3
Tewfik Saleh el Husseini, 266
Thomas, J. H., 146, 147, 150
Thompson, Major, 253
Tiberias, 159, 169, 350
Tiger Hill (refugee ship), 222
Times, The, 71, 112
Tirat Zvi, 343, 349
Tobruk, 230
Toynbee, Philip, 237n
Transfer of Land Ordinance: (1920) 90, 92; (1932) 90; (1940) 90
Transjordan, 94, 151, 164-5, 191, 251, 317; British Mandate, 33, 47, 139; abortive plan to resettle Arabs in, 44, 48; Abdullah established as Emir, 45, 46-7, 123; British support, 47-8, 57; Zionism and, 47-9; exempted from National Home Clauses in Mandate, 48, 49; treaty with Britain (1928), 139; Peel Commission, 168-9; and Arab federation, 172; and United Syria, 192; independence, 290; aims in Palestine, 327-31, 361-2; Arab Legion, 338, 342-343, 361; arms supplied to, 339, 367,

reconstituted as the Kingdom of Jordan, 368

Trevelyan, G. M., 150

Trevor, Daphne, 210n, 227n, 247n

Tripoli, 218, 285

Trotsky, Lev, 51

Truman, President Harry S., 274-5, 299, 319, 358; policy of, 274, 278, 286-7, 348-9, 356, 357, 359-60, 362-6; and displaced persons, 277-8, 279-81, 286-287, 294, 296, 297, 298, 302, 303-4, 349; curious relations with Weizmann, 345-9, 358, 360, 362, 363-4; secret agreement with, 360, 364-5; recognizes Israel, 365-6

Trumpledor, Captain Joseph, 21, 36

Tubas, 359

Tul Karm, 366

Turkey, 11, 12, 13, 17, 91, 159, 162; Arab revolt against, 17, 25, 26-7, 30; nationalism, 19, 27, 125; Sykes-Picot Agreement, 28; Allied powers and, 27, 29, 37, 45, 154; and Syria, 36; San Remo Conference, 37, 45; Greeks evicted from, 125, 169, 171, 353; and Jewish refugees, 225-6, 228, 242; anti-Semitism, 227, 235; Russian pressure, 268

Umm Rash Rash (Elath), 368

United Nations Organization: and administration of Palestine, 280, 310, 317-318, 329, 344-5, 356; General Assembly, 290, 324, 325, 332, 345, 348, 356, 357, 366; Special Committee on Palestine—see Unscop; British refusal to cooperate, 325, 332, 339; withdrawal announced to, 329; votes for Unscop, 332, 336; Security Council, 345, 356, 357, 360, 367; trusteeship proposal, 348, 356, 357, 358, 363; truce proposal, 356; last scenes at, 357, 362-3; and announcement of Israel, 366; Bernadotte as mediator, 367

United Nations Relief and Rehabilitation Administration (UNRRA), 242, 281, 289

Unscop: membership of, 318; in Palestine, 319; report, 323-5; partition scheme, 323, 325, 341, 353; Federal State Plan, 324; opposed by Britain, 332, 334; accepted by U.N.O., 332, 336, 339; requests U.N.O. mission for Palestine,

341; American commitment, 332, 345, 346; America drops, 348

Uruguay, 185n, 318

Ussishkin, Menachem, 173

Va'ad Leumi (Jewish National Council), 97, 319, 348; and Jewish Agency, 105; opposes partition, 260; and terrorism, 309; and proclamation of Israel, 365

Vatican, The, 88, 103

Vester, Mrs., 351

Vienna: 14th Zionist Congress (1925), 95; Hitler in, 131, 132; Anglo-American Committee (1946), 288-9

Vilna, 78

"Voice of Israel" (Radio Station), 281

War Office, 207; and Jewish army, 206, 208, 212

Warburg, Felix, 104, 118, 175

Warsaw, 78

Washington, 230, 287, 346-8, 364-5

Waterfield, Percival, 184

Watt, D. C., 133n

Wauchope, Major-Gen. Sir Arthur, High Commissioner, 133, 141-9, 150-1, 166, 170; and idea of Legislative Council, 141, 142, 144, 145; and Arab Rebellion, 149; and Peel Report, 170, 173, 176; resigns, 177

Wavell, Sir Archibald (later F.-M. Lord), 182-3, 206; and idea of Jewish army, 208, 209

Webb, Beatrice, 111, 112

Webb, Sidney—see Passfield, Lord

Webster, Sir Charles, 157n

Wedgwood, Josiah, 57, 58, 112, 147n, 221

Weisgal, Meyer W., 160n, 364

Weizmann, Dr. Chaim, 7, 10, 24, 48n, 88n, 117n, 127, 133, 140, 143, 191, 250, 252n, 268n, 278; and Lloyd George, 7, 13; gradualist approach to Jewish State, 12, 33, 39, 67, 238; heads Zionist Commission, 22; agreement with Feisal, 31-2, 33-4, 36, 37, 67, 160; interview with leading Ministers (1921), 58-61; complex character, 67-8, 157; accepts 1922 White Paper, 69-70; Anglo-Zionist cooperation, 70; political moderation, 94-5, 106, 156, 238, 260; seeks Jewish-Arab